The Road to Prosperity

The Road to Prosperity

An Economic History of Finland

Edited by Jari Ojala, Jari Eloranta and Jukka Jalava

Suomalaisen Kirjallisuuden Seura • Helsinki

Suomalaisen Kirjallisuuden Seuran Toimituksia 1076

Editor-in-Chief: Jari Ojala
Co-editors: Jari Eloranta and Jukka Jalava
Language editor: Gerard MacAlester
Picture editor: Jukka Kukkonen
Layout: Timo Jaakola
Graphs: Kauko Kyöstiö
Printed: Gummerus Oy, Jyväskylä 2006

ISBN 951-746-818-0
ISSN 0355-1768

www.finlit.fi

Contents

Foreword

This book on Finnish economic history would not have been possible without the help of a number of people. The editors wish to thank, first of all, the authors, who succeeded in completing their articles within a strict timetable. We are also grateful to numerous scholars and colleagues who have commented on earlier versions of some of the articles in conferences, including the Summer Seminar of the School of Business and Economics at the University of Jyväskylä, meetings organized by the Finnish Economic History Association, and the Annual Meeting of the Finnish Society for Economic Research. The Finnish Economic History Association has also provided us with organisational help.

We have received financial support from the Academy of Finland, the Alfred Kordelin Foundation and the Emil Aaltonen Foundation, for which we are deeply grateful. Furthermore, without the cooperation of the Finnish Ministry for Foreign Affairs, this book would not have been possible in its current format; moreover, the commitment of the Director of Publishing of the Ministry, Juha Parikka, to our project has been outstanding.

We are grateful to the Finnish Literature Society (Suomalaisen Kirjallisuuden Seura) for taking our book into their publishing program – the managing editor, Rauno Endén, and the publishing director, Päivi Vallisaari, have been highly supportive throughout the process. The language editor, Gerard McAlester, has done magnificent work with the manuscripts, as has the picture editor, Jukka Kukkonen, in compiling the illustrations. Joseph Brady of the Finnish Ministry for Foreign Affairs has also provided efficient help with language editing.

We sincerely hope that this volume will serve as an illuminating description of the long transformation of the Finnish welfare society, revealing the changes that have occurred over time.

Jyväskylä – Boone – Kerava, February 2006

Jari Ojala, Jari Eloranta, and Jukka Jalava

Preface:
Successful Small Open Economies
and the Importance of Good Institutions

Joel Mokyr

For students of Economic History in the Anglo-Saxon world, the economic history of Europe seems almost inevitably to concentrate on the big countries: the U.K., France, Germany, and Russia seem to occupy practically the entire curriculum, leaving a little room only for Italy and perhaps Iberia. The smaller countries make only episodic appearances: the Dutch have a Golden Age but seemingly little after that, Belgium and Switzerland (perhaps also the Czech lands) are mentioned as "early industrialisers" and Denmark makes an appearance as a free-trade country that stuck with agriculture. A systematic and detailed analysis of the small economies is rarely found in textbooks.[1]

There is much to be learned from the small economies. For one thing, a substantial number of people live in them. In 2004, the combined population of the five Scandinavian countries, the three Benelux, Switzerland, Ireland, and Austria, was 69.4 millions, exceeding that of France or the United Kingdom by about 10 millions. For another, on the whole their economic history in the twentieth century has been the most successful of the European continent and perhaps the most heart-warming tale of economic and social success: these are societies that became rich while still preserving human rights, guarding the environment and maintaining a balance between equality and efficiency that is the envy of the rest of the world. This would not have been easy to predict ex ante: in 1914, the three powers to watch were the U.K., Germany and Russia. These three represented, at least symbolically, the economic success of the past, the present and the future. Yet these three large economies – for very different reasons – had disappointing growth rates in the twentieth century.[2] On the other hand, the small western countries did quite well. Even Ireland, always the glaring exception to economic success in the Western world, eventually joined the club of economically successful small European economies. In economic growth, apparently, size did not matter.

Should it have mattered? Some theorists obviously think so. Economies of scale and the "extent of the market" are central to the argument made a decade ago by the pioneer of the new growth theory, Paul Romer.[3] There are some obvious advantages of being a large country. The three most obvious ones are market size and the concomitant economies of scale, greater internal diversity, and larger political bargaining power. In the more remote past, the third factor seems to have been decisive. Successful small economies and city states were in the long run unviable because they could not defend themselves against larger predatory neighbours. The Italian and Flemish cities and city states learned that lesson, as did the Dutch, the Irish and the Czechs. To be sure, a few small city states managed to survive for centuries (one thinks of eighteenth-century Venice or Hamburg), but their economies were constrained in an age in which national boundaries were a real impediment to the movement of goods.

In the twentieth century, however, there seem to have been fewer advantages to being big. Small countries were still invaded by large ones, but the economic effects seem to have been more fleeting once the war was over. Norway, Denmark, the Netherlands, Belgium, and Finland were all dragged willy-nilly into the 1939–45 conflict by nasty neighbours, but despite high costs and disruption this seems to have affected their long-term economic development only to a limited degree. Moreover, after 1945 the custom of powerful countries to bully small neighbours ran into the indignant righteousness of the United States (as long as they were on the right side of the iron curtain). In the table below I contrast the experience of the small countries with the big ones over the period 1913–98.

Table A.1.   Annual average Rates of Growth of Real GDP

	1913–1950	1950–1973	1973–1998	1913–1998
Small countries	1.47a	3.57c	2.08c	2.10a
Large Countries	0.81b	4.12d	1.70d	1.98b

a = Austria, Belgium, Denmark, Finland, Netherlands, Norway, Sweden, Switzerland
b = Germany, France, UK, Italy, Spain, USA
c = Also includes Ireland and Portugal
d = Also includes Poland

Clearly, on average the small countries could hold up against the big ones and their experience is somewhat less erratic (though this is in part because they were somewhat better at not being involved in major wars).

Finland's twentieth century economic miracle, documented in the following pages, was thus far from unique: though the details differ from country to country, there is a pattern of the "Small Successful European economy" (SSEE) that is shared by these countries. They are all small but open, thus offsetting the disadvantages of scale. The ratio of foreign trade to GDP tends to be very large. This is of course natural in that very large and diverse countries can secure many of the gains from trade through interregional commerce. But there is nothing automatic about it. Many small countries have failed to fully understand this and are mired in poverty precisely because of a deadly combination of small size and lack of openness. Thus, the ratio of international trade to GDP in Finland is 39.2 percent and in Ireland 61.1 percent, whereas in Albania it is 8.8 percent, in Syria 9 per cent, and in Myanmar 3.1 percent.[4] The advantage of openness in these economies goes far beyond the static gains from trade. In small economies the danger that well-organised special interests will be able to control political institutions for the purpose of rent-seeking (at a colossal cost in terms of efficiency and long-run development), as has happened in Latin America, always looms large. Openness is the best defence against such institutional ossification. But openness is a two-way street. It was hard to be a small open economy in a world of large states following mercantilist-protectionist policies, as the United Provinces learned in the eighteenth century and the Czechs in the difficult 1930s.

The other characteristic of the SSEE's was their ability to find "niches" in advanced technology, in which a small economy could establish leadership while still retaining its ability to adopt and utilise other techniques the development of which they conceded to others. The specialisation of the Swiss in food processing and pharmaceutics, the Israelis in software, and the Dutch in electrical and electronic products come to mind. The need to operate near the technological frontier means, of course, that the cost of R&D is high and the payoff highly uncertain. This placed small countries at a disadvantage, since the cost of betting on wrong horses was higher in proportion. Moreover, smallness in the presence of specialisation created serious coordination problems with the institutions that produced the high-skilled labour needed for these industries. Highly specialised human capital requires complementarities and a critical mass of scientists, chemists, engineers and other experts, yet with rapidly changing technology and quickly-saturated markets in the cutting-edge industries, this process required constant coordination and collaboration between the public sector (which is in charge of accumulating human capital) and the private sector, which carried out much of the R&D and the actual production. Yet the search for such "niches" is itself a skill that has to be learned and constantly updated. The net result is that SSEE's have a high ratio of patents per capita though they tend to be disproportionately concentrated in certain areas.

Above all, the economic success of SSEE's is due to their firm commitment to free markets and fairly well-operating political institutions. The unweighted average of the "economic freedom" index (the lower the freer) for 11 SSEE's was 1.877, whereas for 6 larger countries it was 2.147, a difference which is statistically significant.[5] Not all small countries – in Europe or elsewhere – opted for economic freedom. Those that did, however, were able to overcome

10

whatever putative disadvantages are associated with small scale, and outperform larger countries. Of course, without a more precise economic model it is hard to know for sure whether economic freedom leads to economic success, or whether reverse causality was at work here. The gap is even more striking in the well-known "Transparency-international" index of perceived corruption, based on surveys of businessmen. Of the top twelve ("least corrupt"), no fewer than nine were SSEE's, the others being the UK and its Pacific offshoots. The mean index of economic honesty (lack of corruption, the higher the better, top score = 10) for the eleven SSEE's was 8.78, while for the six larger countries it was 7.32. Including Portugal in the former group and Poland in the latter, the respective scores change to 8.59 and 6.76 respectively.[6] SSEE's have somewhat more equal income distributions, which, together with greater ethnic homogeneity – or well-honed institutions that resolved ethnic and language differences (as in Belgium or Switzerland) – minimised social conflict. The mean Gini coefficient for ten small countries including Portugal is 0.288 whereas for six large countries it is 0.333.[7] Finally, SSEE's have a tendency to invest somewhat more in human capital. The proportion population that has "tertiary education" in nine SSEE's is 60.2 percent as opposed to 57 in large countries.[8] The percentage of GDP spent on education in SSEE's was 6.16 percent, as opposed to 4.82 for the six large countries. In short, in the twentieth century, small countries with a strong institutional tradition were able to take advantage of the opportunities that technological progress and globalisation provided them and achieve unprecedented success in economic performance.

Underneath these differences lie two very separate phenomena. One is being a member of the European Enlightenment Club. As I have argued elsewhere, the key historical phenomenon that drew the line between economic success and failure was the penetration, through one mechanism or another, of the ideology associated with the European Enlightenment in the operation of the economy.[9] Enlightenment values meant both an acceptance of the idea that science and technology, or "useful knowledge," were the keys to long-run economic growth, and the willingness to curb rent-seeking and rely on the competitive market, free entry, factor mobility, and a reasonably constrained government.[10] That still leaves a fair amount of variability, but it precludes Iran, Belarus, Myanmar and most of Africa and Latin America. The other factor is size itself. Small countries had slightly different problems from large ones, and therefore had to engage in somewhat different economic strategies in terms of their specialisation, their relationships with larger and more powerful neighbours, and their need to control distributional coalitions and forge internal alliances within. The SSEE's did substantially better than small countries almost anywhere else, but they also outperformed the larger European economies, which were obviously as much influenced by the Enlightenment (or more so) than the small countries, but which were drawn into global conflicts and were less able to maintain the institutional agility that was so essential in adapting to an ever-changing technological environment.

The amazing phenomenon of the SSEE's is that, despite rather striking historical differences in backgrounds, religious and cultural foundations, and economic endowments, they seemed to have converged to become more and more like one another. In that sense, their development mirrors the famous opening line in *Anna Karenina:* all rich and successful economies are alike, every economic failure fails in its own way. It is easy to point to differences between Finland, Austria, Switzerland and their economies, but what they share is a similar formula for success, applied to slightly different parameters but yielding much the same outcome of prosperity and harmony. This is not to say that this success is sustainable and that there is room for complacency. History is full of examples of highly successful institutional structures that gradually turned sour, mostly because entrenched interests deliberately rigidified technology and set up barriers to entry.[11] More seriously, all SSEE's, much like the rest of Europe, are facing grave problems brought about by their own success. Above all they are concerned with the threats to the physical environment (resources with poorly specified property rights) and the growing inclination of European societies – successful or not – to reduce family size to the point of nearing absolute demographic decline.

Part of the Finnish miracle, then, is due to its being a paradigmatic member of this club. Its membership in it, like all cases of economic success, was by no means historically inevitable. Good fortune counts for a lot in economic development. Finland might well have remained part of the Russian Empire if events in 1917 or in 1939 had played themselves out slightly differently. In that case, its history might have been more like its sister countries across the Gulf of Finland. GDP per capita in Estonia is about half of what it is Finland, and virtually every other socio-economic indicator is substantially worse. In a similar fashion, one could compare Hungary and Austria, or Romania and Italy (to say nothing of North and South Korea). In that sense at least, Finland, and other countries like it, had to be both smart and lucky. In the pages that follow, this mixture of good judgment and industriousness with historical and geographical contingency is described in full detail with a scholarly depth and care that will hopefully serve as a model for scholars in other countries to follow.

12

Midnight Sun – Terra Ultima.

The Finlandia Hall.

On the Road to Prosperity: An Introduction

Jari Eloranta, Concepción García-Iglesias, Jari Ojala and Jukka Jalava

Over the past 100 years Finland has experienced rapid transformation from an agrarian economy to the age of information technology. In the process the country has also developed an advanced welfare state, adapted to globalisation, and become part of the European Union. How was this economic miracle achieved? This introductory chapter summarizes the answers in the book, placing a great deal of importance on institutional legacies, natural resources, structural change, human capital creation, and a persistent focus on egalitarianism.

An Economic Success Story

Today, Finland is known for its efficient economy (Table 1.1), its welfare policies, advanced educational system (Table 1.2), the competitiveness of its economy (Table 1.3), low corruption rate (Table 1.4), and companies of worldwide repute (like Nokia, Kone, and UPM). Up to the period after the Second World War, Finland was an agrarian country, and the forest industry was the dominant sector in industry. By the turn of the millennium, rapid economic growth together with diversification of the economy and the building of a welfare state had made the country one of the wealthiest Western economies in the world. During recent decades, the Finnish economy has been characterised by membership in the European Union (1995), adaptation to globalisation and an enormous growth of high tech industries. At the same time, welfare policies have faced challenges from rising government expenditure, unemployment and regional inequality. Finland is still, nevertheless, a small country with only 1.1 per cent of the total population of the EU (25) nations and 0.5 per cent of the total population of the OECD countries in 2005. Finland produced approx. 1.4 per cent of total EU and 0.5 per cent of total OECD gross domestic product in 2004 (see Table 1.1).

Historically, factors of production have been scarce in Finland. The population roughly doubled every fifty years from the 1750s to the 1950s, but thereafter the growth has become slower (Figure 1.1). The development can be explained largely by the ratio of births to deaths, since immigration has not played a significant role in Finland. The rapid growth of the population has been caused mainly by the rather high (from a European perspective) birth rates and the decline of infant mortality since the early 18th century. The age structure of the population has also changed: in the early 20th century, children below fourteen years of age constituted 35 per cent and persons over 65 years six per cent of the population. In 2004, these figures were 17.5 per cent and 15.9 per cent respectively. With a total land area of 304,473 km^2, Finland is the seventh largest country in Europe. Thus, population density has been rather low throughout Finnish history: in the mid-18th century, it was below two persons per square kilometre, while in 2004 the figure was around fifteen.

Of its natural resources, the forests – Finland's "green gold" – have been the most important for the economy during the last 500 years. Forests still cover three quarters of the country's surface area, constituting 23 million hectares of forest cover. However, other resources do exist, although Finland does not have its own sources of oil and coal, for example. In fact, between 1530 and 2001, altogether 1,032 different mines and metal works operated in Finland, producing and refining ores such as iron (accounting for 10 per cent of total production during the above-mentioned period), various other metals (40 per cent), sulphide (26 per cent), and phosphate (21 per cent)[2].

16

Gross Domestic Product	149.7 € billion
GDP per capita	28,643 €/inhabitant
State budget	36,320 € million
EMU debt of general government	45.1 per cent of GDP
Total labour force	2.4 million
Unemployment rate	8.8 per cent
Surface area	338,145 km2

Table 1.1 Finland's economy in brief in 2004

Source: Statistics Finland. **Note:** partly preliminary data. GDP at current prices.

Finnish GDP per capita is above OECD and EU averages (108 and 104 per cent respectively) and was around 75 per cent of that of the United States in 2004 (based on purchasing power parities). With a population of 5.2 million, Finland is numerically among the small countries in the European Union but the size of its national territory places Finland physically among the large members of the EU.

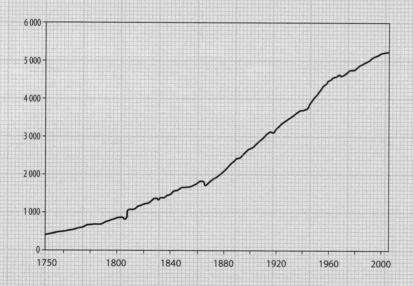

Figure 1.1 The population of Finland 1750–2004, in thousands

Source: Statistical Yearbook of Finland 2005, Statistics Finland. Appendix Table 3.

The total population in Finland in the late 16th century was about 300,000, and grew to 450,000 by the end of the following century. However, Finland lost around one third of its population during a catastrophic famine in the late 17th century, and the pre-famine population level was reached again only in the mid-18th century. The Finnish population roughly doubled every fifty years from 1750 to 1950. There are only a few troughs in the curve: first, in 1808 as a result of the annexation of Finland into the Russian Empire; second, in the late 1860s owing to a famine; third, in 1918 as a consequence of the Civil War; fourth, in the 1940s because of the Second World War; and last, at the turn of the 1970s as a result of emigration. The emigration to Sweden affected up to 7.2 per mil of the total population between 1966 and 1970. The previous mass emigration occurred in the years 1901–1905 when a total of 6.0 per mil of the population emigrated, mostly to North America.[*]

[*] See especially Koskinen, Martelin, Notkola, Notkola and Pitkänen 1994.

The Finnish economy in retrospect

Finland gained independence in 1917, after being a part of imperial Russia since 1809, and before that a part of Sweden. The institutional structure of Finland, including judicial, religious and local government authorities, was largely established during the Swedish period. Thus, in its institutions, Finland has a lot in common with Sweden. The central government structure was, by and large, established during the Russian period, as Finland enjoyed a large degree of autonomy in terms of its domestic policies. A unicameral parliament and general suffrage were instituted in 1906 – at the time it was the most democratically elected parliament in Europe since all citizens aged 24 years or over, both men and women, had the right to vote. Overshadowed by a grim civil war in 1918, the first years of independence were a time of building up the institutions. For example, Finland was now able to exercise its own foreign trade policies, and especially the Leaseholder's Act of 1922 changed the structure of the economy since a huge number of crofters received estates of their own.

In the Second World War, Finland fought against the Soviet Union: first in the Winter War (1939–1940), and thereafter in the Continuation War alongside Germany (1941–1944). The hostilities ended in a short war – the War in Lapland (1944–1945) – against the country's former ally Germany. In the Paris

Enormous structural change in the economy and accelerating growth have been witnessed over the past 150 years. Examples of change can be seen in infrastructure and housing.

Reading score		Science score	
Finland	**543**	**Finland**	**548**
Korea	534	Japan	548
Canada	528	Korea	538
Australia	525	Australia	525
New Zealand	522	Netherlands	524
OECD average	494	OECD average	500

Mathematics score	
Finland	**544**
Korea	542
Netherlands	538
Japan	534
Canada	532
OECD average	500

Table 1.2 The top five countries in reading, science and mathematics in the OECD's Programme for International Student Assessment (PISA), 2003

Source: OECD 2004, Kupari and Välijärvi 2005.

PISA (the OECD's Programme for International Student Assessment, 2003) assesses student's knowledge and skills in mathematics, science, and reading at the age of fifteen. Finland outperformed other OECD countries in all these three categories. According to an analysis of the PISA tests, the Finnish performance is mostly based on the egalitarian nature of the comprehensive school system – an outcome of Finnish welfare policies. The standard deviation in the case of Finland was fairly low in all categories, which bears witness to the equality of the education.

(WEF)		(IMD)	
Finland	**1**	United States	1
United States	2	Hong Kong SAR	2
Sweden	3	Singapore	3
Denmark	4	Iceland	4
Taiwan	5	Canada	5
Singapore	6	**Finland**	**6**

Table 1.3 The top six countries in Growth Competitiveness (WEF) and Business Competitiveness (IMD) Rankings 2005

Sources: World Economic Forum (WEF), The International Institute for Management Development (IMD).

The World Economic Forum (WEF) ranked Finland as number one in terms of growth competitiveness in 2003. Finland maintained this position in 2004 and 2005. The Institute for Management Development (IMD), for its part, ranked Finland as number six in terms of business competitiveness in 2005. The WEF Growth Competitiveness Index comprises three components, namely technology (based on innovations and technology transfers, e.g. the number of patents and the role played by ICT – measured for example by the number of cellular phones or personal computers per inhabitant), public institutions (including such components as corruption and the law) and the macroeconomic environment (including stability and government waste). The list of criteria for IMD consists of four competitiveness factors: economic performance, government efficiency, business efficiency, and infrastructure.

Anders Chydenius (1729–1803) was a clergyman, writer, and enlightened thinker in late 18th-century Finland. Sometimes he is compared with Adam Smith, since he wrote a number of pamphlets questioning contemporary "mercantilistic" rules before Smith's Wealth of Nations (1776). His image was placed on the last thousand *markka* banknote before the *markka* was replaced by the euro in 2002.

Peace Treaty (1947), Finland lost approximately ten per cent of her land area to the Soviet Union and was forced to pay heavy reparations. During the Cold War period, Finland had to perform a balancing feat both politically and economically between East and West. Along with the war reparations, exports to the Soviet Union rose in significance, although at the same time Western Europe was still Finland's principal trading partner. Thus, Finland made a number of agreements both with EC and SEV countries to secure trade relations. After the collapse of the Soviet block in the early 1990s, it was a quite natural step for Finland to apply for EU membership, which it obtained in 1995.

The Finnish economy has experienced remarkable growth in the last 150 years, the period for which we have accurate statistical data. However, evidence suggests that the growth had already begun during the era of Swedish rule and continued during the first part of the 19th century. At the beginning of the 19th century, Finland was still an agrarian economy that was heavily regulated and reliant on foreign trade. Indeed, by the close of the century it was still in a very similar situation, since the budding industrialisation had only had a limited impact. Even as late as the outbreak of the Second World War, the majority of the Finnish population was still employed in agriculture. Finland became independent in 1917, experienced strong growth in the interwar period (even recovering from the Great Depression relatively quickly) and, despite being on the losing side, emerged from the Second World War as a sovereign nation. The latter part

Table 1.4 The top ten least corrupt countries in the Transparency International 2005 Corruption Perception Index (CPI)

Source: Transparency International 2005. (http://www.transparency.org/policy_and_research/surveys_indices/cpi/2005)

Country rank	Country	2005 CPI score
1	Iceland	9.7
2	**Finland**	**9.6**
	New Zealand	9.6
4	Denmark	9.5
5	Singapore	9.4
6	Sweden	9.2
7	Switzerland	9.1
8	Norway	8.9
9	Australia	8.8
10	Austria	8.7

Finland was classified among the least corrupt countries in the Transparency International 2005 Corruption Perception Index (CPI). The CPI score is based on perceptions of the degree of corruption as seen by business people and country analysts, and it ranges between 10 (highly clean) and 0 (highly corrupt).

Table 1.5 Industrial statistics of Finland, 2003

Source: Statistics Finland.

Branch of industry	Establishments	Personnel	Value added in production € million	%
Electrical and optical equipment	1,815	60,909	7,511	23.6
Pulp, paper, paper products	276	35,966	3,640	11.5
Machinery and equipment	3,609	58,679	3,206	10.1
Chemicals, chemical products	1,152	37,523	2,974	9.4
Food, beverages, etc.	2,012	39,344	2,094	6.6
Fabricated metal products	4,580	41,206	2,035	6.4
Publishing and printing	2,799	29,047	1,610	5.1
Wood and wood products	2,860	26,933	1,274	4.0
Basic metals	178	15,530	1,202	3.8
Transport equipment	912	22,131	1,124	3.5
Non-metallic mineral products	1,066	14,914	905	2.9
Textiles, etc.	2,542	12,488	521	1.6
Furniture	1,591	10,722	409	1.3
Other manufacturing	1,076	3,757	201	0.6
Mining and quarrying	1,184	4,386	348	1.1
Electricity, gas and water supply	1,269	14,914	2,732	8.6
Total industry	28,921	428,451	31,786	100.0

Today, electronics and the IT sector represent the most important branch of industry both as an employer and in terms of its share of value added in production. The forest industry as a whole, including both paper and wood products, is still important, though its share has diminished especially as an employer. At the beginning of industrialisation in the mid-19th century, textile manufacturing played an important role, but it has since lost its position, especially from the 1970s on.

of the 20th century saw Finland becoming a highly versatile economy with both industries and services blossoming simultaneously, developing an extensive welfare state with a highly educated population, and experiencing an extensive population shift from the countryside to the growing cities of southern Finland.

As seen in Table 1.7, the Finnish economy was significantly behind most Western economies in 1820, mainly because it had not yet experienced the First Industrial Revolution. On the cusp of the Second Industrial Revolution, in 1870, Finland was falling further behind the industrializing West. Then, in the interwar period, independent Finland started to catch up to these economic leaders, and this catch-up process (embodying diversification of the economy in all three sectors: primary, secondary, and tertiary production) accelerated in the postwar period. The creation of comprehensive government services and a stronger regulatory role of the government apparently did not slow this process down in the latter part of the 20th century. Of course, Finland has had to adapt to various institutional and economic changes from the 1980s onwards, such as the decline of the Soviet Union (its powerful neighbour), deregulation of the financial markets, the rise of ICT and globalisation. Since Finland is a small country with limited natural resources (mainly forests) and has always been dependent on its foreign trade, the Finns have had to adapt to changes in the international economic and political markets.

To meet the needs of adaptation and change in the last 30 years, Finland has invested heavily in the creation of human capital, especially via an efficient elementary and secondary education system, deregulated its financial markets, encouraged mergers of forestry companies into bigger, more competitive units and joined the European Union to protect its economic and political interests. These measures exhibit both the country's ability to adapt to changing external conditions and its initiative in overcoming some of the limitations posed by external markets, the small size of the country, and its peripheral geographic location.

At the beginning of the 21st century, Finland has caught up with, or even overtaken, most of the Western states. How? Is there a particular "Finnish model" of economic success? In the long run, the "Finnish model" has included certain key ingredients: 1) solid institutional legacies, including a centuries-long continuity in government structures and policies, ethnic homogeneity, and a strong government role in regulating the economy; 2) the long-term utilisation of the key natural resource, namely the abundant forests, as a source of energy and raw material in industrialisation; 3) the ability to adapt quickly to structural changes (from an agricultural orientation to an industrial and services-oriented one) and external crises (such as political changes and economic recessions); 4) the strong emphasis on the creation of human capital, going back in fact to the educational reforms of the 19th century, which has aided economic growth; 5) the development of an egalitarian society with an extensive welfare state, created to alleviate some of the social discontent of the industrialisation era, which has included pro-growth policies, highly regressive taxation and gender

22

equality; 6) innovation, manifested especially in its ability to ride the crest of the recent ICT revolution and to create many key inventions ranging from GSM technologies to the Linux operating system. Even though it could be argued that the Finnish government has at times had too extensive of a role in regulating the economy and that taxation has become too high in recent decades, the strengths embodied by the "Finnish model" seem to outweigh the negative impacts.

The prism of economic history can provide insights into the long-term development of economies, at least in broad terms. Yet, can the analysis of economic history answer the biggest question of all: How can we explain economic growth? International research on economic history no longer has a monopoly in offering incisive new insights into several key economic events in history as it did in the 1960s and 1970s, when the so-called New Economic History (or Cliometrics as it is sometimes called) made its entry into the field. While traditional economic history focused more on the analysis of history using qualitative

About two thirds of the Finnish population now live in towns, while in 1800 the figure was only six per cent. The picture shows a motorway junction in 1991, with Jakomäki, a suburb of Helsinki, in the background.

methods and fairly simple quantitative techniques, the new wave of economic historians, most of them of Anglo-American origin, applied economic theory and econometric methods in their analyses. Nowadays these techniques and methods have become an integral part of economic history research generally. Moreover, historians working in the humanities and dealing with economic history have come closer both methodologically and theoretically to the social sciences and economics. However, the uneasy relationship between economics and history continues to exist – and this book for its part tries to lower the barrier between them.[3]

What separates economic history from mainstream economics or from historiography generally? Economic historians have tended to be more open to approaches originating outside mainstream economics, such as institutional economics (focusing on the creation and impact of institutions and organisations) and game theory (a quantitative way of modelling human interactions like negotiations). Economic historians, moreover, are more interested in the long- term dynamics of economic growth. In historical research, the recent decades have seen a resurgence of social and especially cultural history, which have been strongly influenced by post-modern theories and committed to the use of qualitative methods. In contrast, economic historians are interested in the use of quantitative methods to assess economic development, usually in a comparative fashion.[4]

What could a long-term perspective of Finnish economic history offer to increase our understanding of, first, Finnish economic development, and second, economic development generally? The influence of the New Economic History has been relatively small in Finland, as in most of Europe, with the exception of a handful of researchers and research projects. The extension of historical growth studies (which got underway during and after the Second World War and were based on the efforts of the Nobel-Prize-winning economist Simon Kutzets to construct growth statistics, for example in the form of GDP figures), in order to produce long-term series depicting the performance of the Finnish economy has been one of the key contributions of quantitative economic history in Finland. The Finnish growth studies project got started back in the 1950s, and it has since produced extensive sectoral and aggregate statistics on the development of the Finnish economy from 1860 until today.[5]

In the Nordic countries, as well as in Finland, growth studies have featured strongly in the last few decades, at least on the pages of the Scandinavian Economic History Review (SEHR).[6] Nonetheless, growth studies are no longer the focal point of economic history in Finland or elsewhere. However, according to Riitta Hjerppe, "growth studies will never be completed", since for example in Sweden the first growth studies were constructed in the 1930s, and now the fifth round of this project is ongoing.[7] The biggest future challenges, at least as far as growth studies are concerned, relate to the extension of the statistical series backwards in time and the actual use of these data in the historical analysis. In the Finnish case, there is a particularly pressing need to utilize these

24

rich data in order to understand the evolution of the Finnish economy over the long run. No effort, at least one based on these quantitative data and possessing the methodological rigor of typical quantitative economic history, has been compiled so far.

Likewise, quantitative economic history has focused more and more on the economic phenomena of the pre-industrial era, as is indicated by the contributions in the main journal in the field, the Journal of Economic History (JEH).[8] Previously, economic historians both in Finland and abroad studied primarily the industrial era and the massive economic growth that followed it from the 19th century onwards. In current research, the interests of the scholars have become broader and now include both the pre- and post-industrial societies, transitions from one to the other, structural change and economic growth, and various kinds of comparisons between national and supranational economic units.[9] The authors in this book have, in fact, adopted this approach, with some of the contributions looking at short-run phenomena, and others evaluating the long-run evolution of various sectors of the Finnish economy. The analysis of continuities and discontinuities between the pre- and the post-industrial economy will give us a more complete picture of Finnish economic development.

The contributions in this book

This book features analyses of the evolution of the Finnish economy during the past 500 years. The main objective is to explain the "Finnish model" of development – if such a path can indeed be detected. The authors of the book include prominent economists and historians who are experts on the various facets of Finnish economic history. Generally, this book is meant to provide a variety of perspectives on the Finnish economy, mostly based on analyses of particular sectors, which will be both accessible to the general public and useful for the more specialised audience.

Chapter 2 focuses on Finland's general long-term economic growth during the 19th and 20th centuries. The authors, Riitta Hjerppe and Jukka Jalava present an analysis of Finland's development from being a late industrialized country to its recent impressive economic growth. They start with a detailed description of the merits and problems involved in GDP calculations as well as calculations of labour inputs and private consumption. They also study changes in labour productivity as this is considered to be the most important contributory factor to improved living standards in Finland. The article compares these indicators with GDP per capita and explains why they differ. A comparison with Sweden and the EU 15 is also presented in the chapter, which is a good way of bringing out, in comparative terms, the rapid economic growth in Finland. Moreover, in the 20th century there was a clear transformation from primary production into a modern welfare state with a large service sector. The important role played by labour productivity (with secondary production predominant) was tied to rapid technological progress. Hjerppe and Jalava conclude that structural change was more an effect than a cause of the long-term Finnish economic growth.

The economic growth and development experience of the Finnish economy in moving from one based on the primary sector to a more modern industrialized welfare state requires a deep analysis of the different sectors of the economy. This subject is, therefore, addressed by Jari Ojala and Ilkka Nummela, who emphasize the importance of agriculture during the first phases of development. During the 19th century, the Finnish primary sector employed 90 per cent of the labour force, indicating that, in comparison with other countries, a high percentage of the population was working in agriculture. One of the main characteristics of Finnish agricultural production was the fact that the farms were operated and owned mostly by farmers themselves as estate farming was never widespread in Finland. There was no real commercial expansion in this period, due mainly to the cold climate. During the 20th century, however, agriculture experienced an important change, moving from labour-intensive to capital-intensive production methods. Commercialisation finally began, and the production adjusted to a market economy. Finnish farming changed from diversified production to a more concentrated type of production. By the end of the 20th century, overproduction was ubiquitous, and EU membership required the imposition of structural changes on this sector of the economy. The authors present a very detailed exposition of the evolution of farms (farm ownership) as well as the importance of the government, which used its rights to control land ownership at several times in Finnish history. The role played by cooperatives – organisations jointly owned by the rural populace to ensure the satisfaction of people's needs – was fundamental in transforming, modernizing, and reorganizing Finnish agriculture throughout the 20th century. The authors conclude the chapter by explaining how agriculture has changed from a nature-based to a science-based activity with an increase in productivity and also a shift to more capital-intensive production.

The next chapter focuses on Finnish business and the Finnish way of doing business. Jari Ojala and Petri Karonen point out that Finland is characterised by not having many multinational corporations, and that this has always been the case. Markets in Finland have been modest, and therefore there was a need to look for new markets elsewhere. During the last century, big Finnish companies and business in general have been able to open up and integrate into the global, or at least, European business world. The authors advance two main factors to explain the development of business in Finland, although they recognize that these are not the only ones. First, there seems to have been a close relationship and long-term co-operation within and between companies in different industrial sectors. Second, one can detect a close, co-evolutionary development in business and Finnish society as a whole. In addition, Ojala and Karonen introduce us to the driving forces of Finnish business: the competi-

26

	Per cent
Oil	25
Wood fuel	21
Nuclear energy	16
Coal	15
Natural gas	11
Peat	6
Hydro power	4
Net imports of electricity	1
Other energy sources	2
Total	100
Renewable energy sources	25.0

Table 1.6 Total energy consumption in Finland, 2004 (per cent shares)

Source: Statistics Finland. Note: preliminary data, calculated from petajoule consumption.

Oil still plays a crucial role in total energy consumption. This is due not only to the needs of transport, but is also based on the needs of industry and space heating. Nuclear energy has increased in importance since 1977, when the first nuclear plant started to operate in Finland. The building of a fifth nuclear power plant in Finland started in 2002.

Table 1.7 Finnish economic growth (GDP per capita, in 1990 Geary-Khamis Dollars) compared with selected western countries, 1820–2005

Year	Finland	UK	USA	France	Sweden	Belgium	Netherlands
1820	759	1,756	1,287	1,218	1,198	1,291	1,561
1870	1,107	3,263	2,457	1,858	1,664	2,641	2,640
1900	1,621	4,593	4,096	2,849	2,561	3,652	3,533
1938	3,486	5,983	6,134	4,424	4,725	4,730	5,122
1970	9,577	10,767	15,030	11,664	12,716	10,611	11,923
2004	21,305	21,847	30,243	21,777	22,325	21,773	21,594

Sources: Maddison 2001; Groningen Growth and Development Centre, Total Economy database. Available from: http://www.ggdc.net/dseries/totecon.html. See also Appendix Table 1.

tive and institutional forces accompanying the four different phases of Finnish business evolution. These phases were: merchant (from the late 17th to the end of the 19th century), industrial (from the mid-19th to the early 20th century), financial (from the early 20th century to the mid-1980s), and global capitalism (the mid-1980s onwards). Overall, co-operation was the key factor explaining the evolution of Finnish business. As an example, the authors refer to the best-known Finnish company in the world, Nokia, and present its development from a paper company (established in 1865) that diversified into the forest and rubber industries as well as cable production, and from there into a high-technology company.

Yrjö Kaukiainen concludes that from the early 17th century up to the mid-20th century Finland was primarily a supplier of raw-materials and semi-finished products in the international trade flows. Thus, Finland was a supplier of forest and other primary products such as furs, fish, tar and timber. These were replaced by manufactured wood products, sawn goods, pulp and paper. Only in the last two decades of the 20th century was there a transition to high-value-added, high-technology exports. According to Kaukiainen, the process of Finland's integration into the world economy already started during the early modern period, although the trade was for a long time quite modest in scale. He also stresses the role played by the maritime sector in Finnish development; in fact, by the 1870s Finland merchant tonnage was the fifth largest in the world when compared to the country's population.

The article by Matti Hannikainen and Sakari Heikkinen analyse the labour market in Finland from 1850 to 2000. Up to the mid-19th century, there was no labour market as such, and it was only during the latter half of that century that the labour market started to evolve. The number of wage-labourers increased, and economic legislation was modernized. This was a very slow process, but as the economy became more industrialized, so did the labour market. The Finnish labour market evolved over the long run with changes in the structure of labour, institutional settings, the nature of unemployment, and public policies. There was a transformation from rural "multi-employment" to modern full-time wage work. This was possible due to a wage development that took place over the years as employment contracts changed from contracts of service to bilateral agreements between the employers and the employees. There was also a fundamental change in the institutional status of labour, which moved from a master-servant relationship to one in which the labourer was a free wage-worker. The introduction of workers' associations and trade unions started in the 1880s. However, the structural change experienced in Finland was "belated", as the authors put it, compared to other industrialized countries. The development of the welfare state with new opportunities for women, strong trade unions, centralized collective bargaining, high real wages, and extensive wage flexibility occurred after the Second World War. Therefore, even though the Finnish development of institutions resembled the patterns evident in many Western countries, there were certain unique features in this process as well.

28

The later development of the welfare state system and the differences found in the labour market with respect to other developed countries lead us into the next topic of this book: the monetary aspects of the Finnish economy. In this chapter, Concepción García-Iglesias and Juha Kilponen claim that the Finnish case was different from that of other countries, as the strong involvement of the government and the central bank in regulating the financial markets after the Second World War delayed the start of the development of modern financial markets. This is apparent in their analysis of the income velocity of money. Finland joined all the international monetary systems from the nineteenth century onwards. Being a small, relatively open economy, this was a natural choice, although recurrent and sometimes large devaluations were needed to restore the external balance. Overall, the devaluations accomplished their objectives in the short run but worsened the long-term economic prospects of the country because the monetary policy lacked credibility.

Jari Eloranta and Jari Kauppila study the development of the welfare state in Finland through an analysis of the long-term demand for Finnish central government spending. Eloranta and Kauppila maintain that, while growth in Finnish central government spending was primarily a matter of institutional expansion, other factors also need to be considered. This process included the incremental expansion of the welfare state, especially in the postwar period, while at the same time there were significant limitations imposed on Finnish military spending in the Paris Peace Treaty (1947). It is a case of the changes in domestic and foreign policy influencing the spending behaviour of the Finnish central government (the so-called "guns versus butter" trade-off). Hence the building of the Finnish welfare state was inextricably tied to the strong economic growth and diversification of the economy during this period. A multiple regression analysis confirms that a large amount of the variation can be explained by the military and social spending trade-off effect (or the lack of it), although institutions are also found to be a relevant explanatory variable. As a result, Finland was able to develop an extensive welfare state without experiencing slower economic growth. The challenges imposed by the depression of the 1990s have, by and large, been met with the impressive economic performance (and limited welfare reforms) of the last ten years.

Markus Jäntti presents results on the distribution of income in Finland from 1920 onwards. The evidence is drawn from tax records, and the data strongly suggest that inequality varied to some extent in the inter-war period, increased substantially in the years 1950–1970, and declined quite rapidly after 1970. While inequality has increased substantially during the past ten years, this increase appears not to be very unusual, given the historical record. Jäntti furthermore shows that the notion that Finland is a country with small income differences is of a quite recent origin. These findings are particularly interesting in the light of the other contributions on the history and current status of the Finnish welfare state.

The idea that output grows when the proportion of more productive workers increases at the expense of less productive workers comes out in Rita Asplund's and Mika Maliranta's paper. Education and human capital contribute substantially to sustained economic growth by enhancing the innovative capabilities of workers. In Finland, high investment in education and training has been an instrumental part of its economic success. The article goes on to explain the role played by education and technology policies in the productivity performance of the Finnish economy. Technology policy is important in stimulating innovations (a skilled workforce, on-the-job training). The focus on R&D and ICT investment has been fundamental in Finland. The economy moved from being an investment-driven to an innovative-driven. The joint efforts of the private sector and the government to increase R&D and ICT have been a key determinant in the Finnish success story, a story that can be defined as business-driven. Overall, the authors remark that all this development has been a result of the state's strong investment in its higher education policy.

The last chapter of the book, titled "The Tension between the social and the economic – a perspective on the history of a welfare state" by Pauli Kettunen offers a nice conclusion to this volume. Finland was a late-comer among the Nordic countries in terms of the development of the welfare state. The industrial take-off occurred late, and the social structure remained for a long time predominantly agrarian and rural. The egalitarian nature of Finnish society can be characterized as having led to a welfare society, similar to those of the other Nordic countries. However, the Finnish version has absorbed only certain features from its Nordic neighbours, and generally it has preserved a unique aspect of its own. The "Finnish model" has in fact been characterised by egalitarianism, a strong government role, innovativeness, and the country's geographic position between the East and the West.

31

"Compound interest"

by Laila Pullinen

(1968, bronze, 350 x 500 cm).

Economic Growth and Structural Change
A Century and a Half of Catching-up

Riitta Hjerppe and Jukka Jalava

Finland has experienced fast economic growth since the second half of the 19th century, catching-up with the standard of living of the 15 member countries of the European Union (members before 1 May 2004). The significant periods for catching-up with Western Europe were the interwar period and particularly the 1980s. The income gap with Sweden was narrowed gradually in the post-Second World War period and especially in the 1980s. It discusses the pattern of the late structural change into industrialisation and the importance of labour productivity in this development. It shows the complex relationship involving investments, labour productivity, and the substitution of labour with capital because of their real price developments. Finally, it briefly mentions other aspects of economic development, the significance of which is not as easily assessed with quantification.

Introduction

Finland in the early 2000s is an industrialised country with a standard of living among the top fifteen to twenty countries in the world. The World Economic Forum (2005) even ranked it first in competitiveness. Finland has been a member of the European Union since 1995 and has belonged to the European Economic and Monetary Union since 1999 with the Euro as its currency. One hundred years ago it was a poor agrarian country, where as late as 1867–8 a significant part of the population suffered a serious famine when the crops failed. At that time the Finnish Gross Domestic Product (GDP) per capita was less than half of that of the world leaders, the United Kingdom and the United States. By 2001 Finnish GDP per capita had reached parity with the UK and was three quarters of that of the US[1].

Finland was part of Sweden until 1809 and a Grand Duchy of Russia from 1809 to 1917, with a relatively wide autonomy in economic affairs and even a customs border between Russia and the Finnish Grand Duchy. Finland became an independent republic in 1917. Not directly involved in fighting in the First World War, Finland experienced a Civil War immediately after independence in 1918 and fought against the Soviet Union during the Second World War. It is one of the larger countries in Europe in area, but it is sparsely populated with 15 persons per square km and a total population of 5.2 million people. The population is very homogeneous. It has a small number of people of foreign origin,

The foods consumed by an average Finnish family of four (the "index family") in 1952.

about two percent, but two language groups, a Finnish-speaking majority and a Swedish-speaking minority. The population is growing by 0.3 per cent[2] per annum in the early 2000s.

Finland has large forest areas of coniferous trees, and forests have been and still are an important factor in its economic development. Two thirds of Finland's total area consists of forests and other wooded land. Other natural resources are scarce; there is no coal or oil and relatively few minerals. Outokumpu, in its time the biggest copper mine in Europe, was exhausted in the 1980s. Though not blessed with abundant natural resources Finland embarked on the road of industrialisation utilizing its forest sector, its hydropower potential and the rural labour reserve. The role of electrification and other technical innovations in enabling an increase in productivity was important.

Finland in the pre-industrial period was an agrarian country, with a few small towns mostly in the coastal area. Money came to the countryside from tar burning and some water-powered sawmills, while the towns flourished by exporting the products of these activities; Finland was among the most important tar-producing areas in the world in the 18th century (see also Kaukiainen in this volume). Sailing ships built in the coastal area exported these items to the Baltic Sea area and western and southern European ports. The ships brought back necessities like salt and iron as well as a few luxuries like cloth, wines and spices. A few iron works processed Swedish iron ore in south-western Finland, artisans and some pre-industrial workshops produced items such as household utensils, tools, clothing, shoes and tobacco in the towns (see also Ojala and Karonen in this volume).

We know Finland's GDP growth from 1860 on from the historical national accounts research project, which ended in the late 1980s.[3] The lengthy research was done by researchers of Statistics Finland, the Bank of Finland and the Department of Economic and Social History at the University of Helsinki. We thus have fairly detailed annual series for the balance of total supply and demand in current and constant prices since 1860, production and employment for the different industries, the structure of foreign trade according to commodities and countries, and so forth. It was characteristic of the Finnish long run economic transformation that industrialisation started late and that for a long time both secondary production and services increased directly at the expense of primary production. The share of secondary production in GDP did not decrease until the 1970s. The classical view of structural change is that the main contributor to economic growth first shifts from primary production to secondary production during the process of industrialisation, and subsequently from secondary production to tertiary production as the post-industrial stage is entered.[4] What happens to growth when the gains from industrialisation are depleted or the labour-saving nature of productivity growth in secondary production shifts the focus of the economy to services? In 2001 the Finnish share of services in GDP was only two thirds while the respective U.S. ratio was close to three quarters.[5]

The distance to the technology frontier, that is to the most advanced producers, plays an important role.[6] It is not possible to adapt technology developed elsewhere if one is on or close to the frontier. In 2005 Finnish research and development expenditures were at the internationally high level of 3.5 per cent in relation to GDP. This signifies that Finland has had to abandon the previously successful strategy of growth through investment and adopt a new strategy of growth through innovation (see also Asplund and Maliranta in this volume). Our presentation aims at giving a description of Finland's general long run economic growth in the 19th and 20th centuries and then discusses the basic factors of economic growth in the light of the Finnish economic historical literature. In this way, it gives an account of what we can say about the factors of growth. The evolution of the present industrial structure will be described and the impact of structural change on growth and productivity quantified.

A modern
forest harvester.

GDP per capita

A nation's economic standard of living is usually measured by Gross Domestic Product per capita. GDP is a flow measure that denotes the value of the goods and services produced during one year. GDP includes goods and services that have markets (or which could have markets) and products which are produced by general government and non-profit institutions. GDP is the best known and most widely used indicator of national accounts. The system of national accounts, the current version of which is SNA93, comprehensively connects flow accounts that capture various economic transactions taking place during the accounting period. Such activities as production, generation of income and the distribution or use of income are all accounted for. These flows are linked to the balance sheets (stocks) of assets and liabilities. The flow accounts are also linked to each other so that the balancing item of each account, which is defined as the difference between total uses and resources, is carried forward to the following account. In that way, the transactions of each institutional sector are enumerated beginning with production and going all the way to the financial status of the sector. This shows whether the sector is a net lender or net borrower with regard to other sectors.

Unfortunately, national accounts do not measure positive factors relating to the quality of life such as life expectancy, health and a clean environment. Nor do national accounts measure the ill effects on nature and human well-being caused by negative side effects of production such as the pollution of the environment caused by spills or leaks from production plants. Furthermore, the production of "ills" like tobacco and pesticides are recorded as increases in output. An additional drawback with national accounts is that they are not designed to quantify income and wealth inequalities between social and economic classes.

36

Finland is a land of forest owners. The total area of forest land in 2003 was 26,319,000 hectares. Of this, 52 per cent was owned privately, 35 per cent by the state, 8 per cent by companies, and 5 per cent by others. During the 1960s, over 50 per cent of forest land was owned by farmers. This decreased to around 34 per cent in the years 1986–1994. In 2001 only 18 per cent of forest owners were farmers. The volume of growing stock was 2,091 million cubic metres in the period 1996–2003, of which 48 per cent consisted of pine, 33 per cent spruce, and 19 per cent deciduous trees.

Notwithstanding the aforementioned caveats, GDP per person is the most valuable and the most widely used tool for measuring the economic well-being of a nation.[7] For an inter-temporal comparison of how a nation's living standards have evolved over time, the impact of inflation needs to be subtracted; i.e., the GDPs per person in consecutive years must be expressed in the prices of some base year. The standard of living can be expressed as the product of its two components: labour productivity and labour input per capita. Labour productivity (GDP per labour input) is the more important of the two as it can grow without bounds, while there is an upper limit to the amount of work that can be done per person. Therefore, economic growth can in the long run perspective only be sustained by a change in labour productivity. Equation 1 shows GDP per person and its components:

$$(1) \quad \frac{GDP}{population} = \frac{GDP}{labour\ input} \times \frac{labour\ input}{population}.$$

Labour input can be quantified either by using the number of persons employed or by the hours actually worked. The latter is preferable as changes in the hours worked by employees due to longer vacations or shifts to atypical employment patterns can distort the results. Hence the basic unit for labour productivity is GDP per hour worked. GDP per person is the higher the greater labour productivity is, the larger the proportion of the population in employment is and the more each employee works. Economies can settle for a lower living standard by choosing to work less. This choice depends on how much society values leisure above material well-being. A point in case can be discerned from the numbers compiled by the Groningen Growth and Development Centre (Groningen University, the Netherlands). Their purchasing power corrected GDP per capita figures for 2004 reveal that the United States had one of the highest living standards in the world,[8] a result that is hardly surprising. Yet countries such as Belgium, France, Ireland, the Netherlands, and Norway all simultaneously exhibited a higher level of labour productivity and a lower level of GDP per capita than the USA. Looking at Equation 1 it is easy to figure out that the work done per average person was less in these countries than in the USA.

Figure 2.1 shows the levels of Finnish GDP per capita and its components for the years 1860–2004. GDP at market prices is expressed in the constant prices of the year 2000. The variables are in natural logarithms so that the logarithm of the material living standard is the sum of the logarithms of labour productivity and labour input per person:

$$(2)\ \ln(GDP\,/\,population) = \ln(GDP\,/\,labour\ input) + \ln(labour\ input\,/\,population)\,.$$

Two lessons can be learned from Figure 2.1. First, it is obvious that the main contribution to the standard of living came from labour input. In 2004 each Finn worked on average 778 hours per year, and the GDP per hour worked

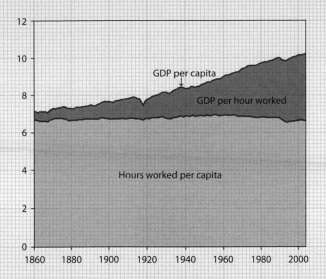

Figure 2.1 GDP per capita and its components in Finland, 1860–2004, GDP at year 2000 prices in natural logarithms

Source: Own calculations; data from Hjerppe (1996) and Statistics Finland.

The number of hours worked per person is the main contributor to economic growth. However, as the proportion of the population in employment and the labour input per person can be increased only up to a point, it is the change in labour productivity that is the more important contributor to an increased living standard.

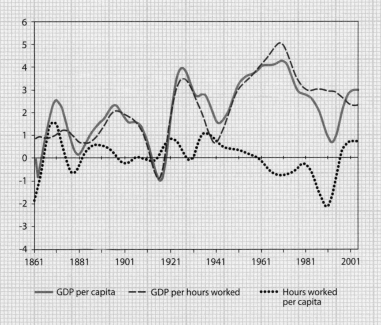

GDP per capita   GDP per hours worked   Hours worked per capita

Figure 2.2 Growth rates in the Finnish standard of living, labour productivity and labour input, 1860–2004, expressed as percentages

Source: Own calculations; data from Hjerppe (1996) and Statistics Finland. **Note.** The observed yearly changes were smoothed with the Hodrick-Prescott (1997) filter with the smoothing parameter λ=100.

With the exception of periods of warfares, the average growth rate of GDP per capita increased until the 1970s. More recently , GDP per capita growth slowed down as a result of a disquieting slump in labour productivity. Now that Finland has reached a Western European standard of living, it is difficult to sustain rapid growth. On the other hand, there is still room for improvement since Finland's GDP per capita is only three quarters of that of the USA.

was 35.3 euros. This means that GDP per capita was 27,400 euros. Second, the graph shows that the increase in material well-being stemmed from labour productivity growth. In 1860 each Finn worked approximately 794 hours, while labour productivity was only 1.5 euros per hour. This amounted to 1,225 euros per person in the prices of the year 2000. The standard of living grew 22-fold in less than a century and a half, even though fewer hours were worked per capita in 2004 than in 1860. The explanation for this is that labour productivity increased 23-fold.

The labour input increased to approximately 1,000 hours per person in the 1940s. This level was maintained until the late 1960s, when the hours worked started to decline because of shorter working weeks or the greater numbers of people in education or retirement. The recession of the early 1990s brought the hours down to 700 per person from which level they rebounded to somewhat less than 800 hours. Interestingly, Finns are presently working less than ever before since Finland became an independent country in 1917.

Figure 2.2 shows the growth rates of the three level variables in Figure 2.1 for the years 1860–2004. Since the annual observations often fluctuate quite appreciably from year to year, we show the average growth rates. The solid black line in Figure 2.2 depicts GDP per capita growth. The standard of living gradually increased its growth rate from the 1920s – with the exception of times of war – peaking in the 1960s at 4 per cent. This growth stemmed in the early years from both labour productivity and hours worked. During the latest decades, growth relied solely on labour productivity. This changed once again after the recession of the early 1990s, when labour input also contributed to GDP per capita growth. The most recent average observations of GDP per capita change show a slower growth – around 3 per cent per annum – due to a decline in labour productivity. The decline in hours worked that began in the late 1960s stands out as negative growth from then on. It did not turn positive until the mid-1990s. Labour productivity growth has also halved from the 1960s peak of 4–5 per cent growth to slightly over 2 per cent per annum recently.

It is easy to show that the slowdown in labour productivity growth – and not a decrease in labour input – poses a threat to the future growth of the Finnish standard of living. From Equation 1 and Figure 2.1, it can be seen that an increase in labour input has a level effect on GDP per capita. Productivity growth, on the other hand, acts through the interest-on-interest principle. Even a slight change in growth rates has significant long-term implications.

Private consumption

Gross Domestic Product per capita is the most commonly used indicator of standard of living. Another suitable indicator is private consumption or household consumption, since GDP also consists of investments and exports which are not available for household use. It has even been suggested that in order

40

Finland has the highest proportion of protected land and wilderness reserves in Europe, some 2.8 million hectares, equivalent to about 11 per cent of the total land area. Strictly protected forests comprised over 1.5 million hectares, i.e. 6.6 per cent of the total land area. Protected old-growth forests, such as the one pictured, total approximately 10,000 hectares.

to ascertain the welfare of households we should add elements of public consumption, i.e. individual consumption expenditures like educational, social, health, and recreational services to private consumption.[9] Private consumption is and has been an important factor in total demand, and accordingly in economic growth. In the late 19th century, private consumption accounted for 70 per cent of total demand, but by the early 2000s the share had gradually fallen to 40 per cent.

Here we look at private consumption, its volume per capita and its changing content over time. In Figure 2.3, we see the volume index of private consumption together with the curve of GDP per capita from 1860 to 2004. The overall private consumption per capita has grown 21-fold, which means a very fast improvement of the standard of living. However, compared with GDP per capita, it can be noted that private consumption has often fallen more sharply and for a longer time than GDP. This is due to the fact that Finnish economic policy measures often have been geared towards fostering exports or investments more than household consumption. The difference is very clear during the 1930s depression and the Second World War. During the 1930s depression, exports recovered because of devaluation and decreasing wages, which improved the competitive capacity of export products but lowered private consumption for many years. During the Second World War, the nation's resources were directed to warfare, i.e. public consumption (see also Eloranta and Kauppila in this volume), and the home front had to be satisfied with small rationed amounts of consumption goods. The same phenomenon also continued in times of recession in the post-war periods when devaluations moved resources from wage earners to export industry profits. In contrast to these, during the deep depression of the early 1990s, social security measures kept private consumption afloat, and the losses in private consumption were not quite as big as the fall in GDP per capita.

In Figure 2.4 we see a typical private consumption pattern when the standard of living is rising, and gradually rising incomes move consumption patterns from mere necessities to the comforts of life. In the late 19th century households used two thirds of their incomes on necessities like food and, beverages. The fact that the share of food and beverages did not start falling until around the turn of the 20th century implies that accepted levels of food consumption had not been attained, and that extra incomes were spent on more and better quality food. Some studies of average calorie intake also indicate rising food consumption in the last decades of the 19th century.[10] The share of another necessity, housing, was also relatively big. The low share of clothing is partly explained by the fact that home production is not included here. One sixth of private consumption was used on transport, education, social services, health, recreation and other consumption. In the first part of the 20th century, rising incomes led to a gradually declining share of food and beverages and to a higher share of clothing and other consumption. Rent rationing kept housing consumption at a relatively low level after the two world wars for several years.

42

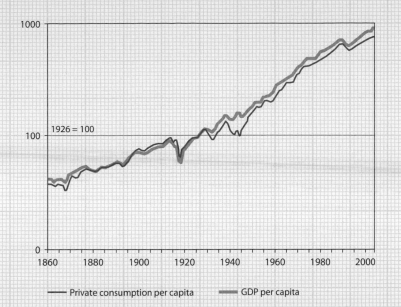

Figure 2.3   Volume indices of private consumption per capita and GDP per capita, 1860–2004.
1926 = 100

Source: Own calculations; data from Hjerppe (1989) and Statistics Finland.

Overall private consumption per capita has grown 21-fold, which means a very fast improvement in the standard of living. However, compared with GDP per capita, it can be noted that private consumption has often fallen more sharply and for a longer time than GDP. This is due to the fact that economic policy measures often have been geared towards fostering exports or investments more than household consumption.

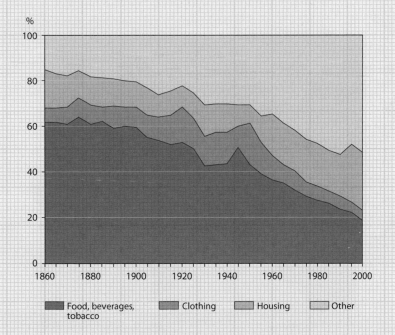

Figure 2.4   Distribution of private consumption at five-yearly intervals, 1860–2000, expressed as percentages.

Source: Own calculations; data from Hjerppe (1989) and Statistics Finland.

Above is a typical private consumption pattern when the standard of living is rising; gradually rising incomes move consumption patterns from mere necessities to the comforts of life. In the late 19th century, households used two thirds of their incomes on necessities such as food and beverages. Nowadays households spend up to half of their disposable incomes on non-necessities.

In the post-Second World War period, food and beverages consumption finally decreased in line with other industrialised countries. The share of clothing decreased because of lower relative prices, and the share of housing increased because of clearly rising housing standards. Nowadays households spend up to half of their disposable incomes on non-necessities.

In 2005 the World Bank ranked Finland twelfth wealthiest nation in the world, with total wealth of USD 419,346 per capita. Of this sum, over 80 per cent was intangible capital, i.e. intellectual and social capital such as education and administration. Natural resources accounted for just under three per cent of national wealth while generated capital, mainly from secondary production, amounted to fifteen per cent.

Catching-up

In the middle of the 19th century, Finnish GDP per capita was growing and the growth was slightly accelerating. The growth continued to accelerate, war periods excepted, until the 1970s. Acceleration is a known feature of other countries, too.[11] In early stage of modern economic growth, the traditional, mainly agriculturally oriented, sector of the economy is still very large and continues to develop slowly as the modern sector starts to emerge. Gradually the modern sector overtakes and surpasses the traditional sector in size, but that takes a long time. This initially slow but accelerating growth was a new, unexpected result established in the historical national accounts of Finland, where the take-off period of industrialisation has been the subject of discussion. Industrialisation in Finland has been dated to various decades ranging from the 1840s to the 1920s and 1930s.[12] Contrary to some arguments, Finland's GDP per capita figures since 1860 do not reveal any jump or sudden burst of industrialisation. The first modern industrial establishments started appearing during the first half of the 19th century, but their impact on the whole economy remained modest for a long time.

Speaking about the catching-up of income levels implies comparison with other countries or areas. Here we compare Finnish economic development with that of fifteen European Union countries (the member states before 1 May 2004) and with Sweden, a neighbouring country with many similar features in the economy, but initially with a higher living standard.

The Finnish GDP per person – quite astonishingly – grew 21-fold from 1860 to 2000. That means a growth of 2.2 percent per annum, while that of the 15 European Union countries grew 11-fold or 1.7 percent per annum in 1860–2000. Both experienced incredibly fast growth compared to any previous period in known history. As a result of this growth, Finland moved from poverty to become one of the richest countries in the world. In the second half of the 1800s, Finland was behind all other Western European countries except perhaps Ireland; GDP per capita was only 40 percent of that of the UK and 70–80 percent of that of Sweden. Only Japan and some South-East Asian countries and Ireland have experienced higher growth rates during the 20th century. In Figures 2.5 and 2.6, one can see the convergence of Finland's Gross Domestic Product per capita with the European Union (EU15) and Swedish levels. Figure 2.6 shows that the long-term economic growth has been an almost continuous process of societal change, albeit with severe disruptions to the growth during the World Wars and the 1930s depression especially in Finland and in EU15. Some acceleration of growth can be seen from the 1860s to the 1970s, but all the curves flatten down to clearly slower growth rates in the 1970s, after the so-called "Years of Golden Economic Growth" in the post-Second World War period. In the early 1990s, the Finnish economy quite unexpectedly fell into a serious depression for several years, and the GDP fell by 10 per cent. The depression was deeper than any other peace-time depression since 1860. The European Union countries also experienced recessions or depressions then, but not nearly as bad as that in Finland.

Finland started from a level of about a half of the Western European GDP per capita (Figure 2.6) in the 1860s. There was slow but indisputable convergence until the First World War, especially in the 1890s, which narrowed the gap to 40 per cent. The drop in the Finnish GDP per capita during the First World War and the Finnish Civil War increased the gap again to the 60 per cent level. The recovery of the economy was quite fast in Finland compared with Western Europe, and during the interwar period the Finnish economy did much better than the Western world; according to Krantz (2001) this was the period of the Finnish take-off. The GDP per capita gap narrowed to about 20 per cent and even less before the outbreak of the Second World War.

The development of the Finnish economy after the Second World War compared with EU15 was more uneven than in the other peacetime periods under consideration. First there was a brisk catching-up immediately after the war, the Finnish GDP per capita actually surpassing the EU15 level in the years 1946–48. Obviously, the reconstruction of Finland, the re-settlement of the Karelian evacuees and de-mobilised soldiers as well as the payments of the war reparations to the Soviet Union galvanised the Finnish economy into brisker and more rapid development than those of the other countries that had suffered in the Second World War. The physical civil destruction was also less extensive than it was in many of the other belligerent countries. The gap, however, widened again in the 1950s, the reasons for which are unclear and would need economic historical research. Why was Finland left behind? The Korean boom in 1950–51 increased the demand for Finnish wood-based exports and raised export prices. Did the government efforts to curb inflation then lead to slower growth? And what was the role of labour disputes? Or did strict government rationing of imports and prioritising imports of investment goods over other imports slow down economic growth? The rationale behind import rationing was to avoid deficits in the balance of trade, because the financing of imbalances was difficult in a situation where international loans were virtually impossible to obtain. The gap continued to widen until the end of the 1950s, and only after the easing of foreign trade regulations in 1957 was followed by a virtual lack of change in the gap until the end of the 1960s. The tide turned after Finland's devaluation of 1967. The Finnish economy closed the gap with EU15 over the 1970s despite the difficulties caused by the oil crises, to exceed the EU15 level in 1980. The early 1990s depression again changed the situation and caused a 15 percent collapse. This was followed by a fast recovery during the second half of the 1990s.

Compared with Sweden, the Finnish economy did less well during the half century before the First World War (Figure 2.6). Sweden experienced very rapid growth, and the gap in GDP per capita with it widened from 20 percent to 30 percent, due to Sweden's earlier industrialisation. The hardships of the First World War and Finland's Civil War in 1918 increased the difference further.

46

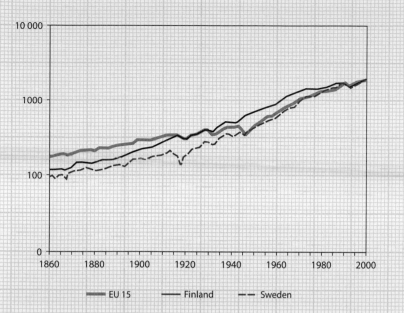

Figure 2.5 GDP per capita in EU15, Finland, and Sweden, 1860–2000, logarithmic scale

Sources: Own calculations; data from Hjerppe (1996) and Statistics Finland; Carreras and Tafunell (2004); Krantz (2000); Maddison (2001).

Finnish GDP per person grew 21-fold from 1860 to 2000, while that of EU15 (the 15 members states of the EU before 1 May 2004) grew 11-fold in the same period. Both experienced incredibly fast growth compared with any previous period. This growth brought Finland from poverty to being one of the richest countries in the world.

Figure 2.6 Finland's GDP per capita compared with EU15 and Sweden, 1860–2000, expressed as percentages

Sources: Own calculations; data from Hjerppe (1996) and Statistics Finland; Carreras and Tafunell (2004); Krantz (2001).

Compared with EU15, in the 1860s Finland started from a level that represented one half of the Western European GDP per capita. The Finnish economy closed the gap to EU15 over the 1970s to exceed the EU15 level in 1980. The depression of the early 1990s again changed the situation and caused a 15 percent collapse. This was followed by a fast recovery during the second half of the 1990s. Compared with Sweden, the Finnish economy did less well during the half century before the First World War and the gap widened. In the late 1940s, Finland's finally started to catch up steadily, albeit slowly at the beginning. The speed of catching-up accelerated and was very rapid in the 1970s and 1980s. The gap was almost closed before the devastating 1990s depression set in and widened it again for several years, although there was recovery after 1997.

Nokia's head office at Keilaniemi in 2004.

48

Finland's fast recovery in the early 1920s reduced the difference back to 30 per cent. This gap prevailed in the interwar period on average: Finland's deeper 1930s depression widened the gap, but fast growth after the depression corrected the situation. The Second World War again expanded the deficit but not to the same extent as the late 1910s. Finland's GDP fell less during the Second World War, i.e. during continuous active hostilities, than in the First World War and the short Civil War for all the hardships they brought. In the late 1940s, Finland's more continuous catching-up process finally started, slowly at the beginning. Some set-back occurred in the middle of the 1960s, but then the speed of catching-up accelerated and was very rapid in the 1970s and 1980s. The gap was almost closed, until the devastating 1990s depression set in and widened it again for many years, with some recovery after 1997. The reasons for this rapid catching-up by more than 20 percentage points from the late 1960s to the late 1980s are not at all clear. It would require a careful study of the differences in development in these countries during those years. What was the significance of the large-scale emigration from Finland to Sweden around 1970? Were the productivity developments different in these countries? How did the differences in the structures of these economies affect economic growth?

Structural change

Economic activity takes place in three major sectors: in primary production, which encompasses agriculture, forestry, hunting and fishing; in secondary production, which includes mining and quarrying, manufacturing, electricity and water services as well as construction, and in services, which includes the rest. Kuznets (1966) stressed four factors which cause a decline in the share of primary production in total output. Firstly, as incomes per capita grow, there might be a proportionately larger demand for non-agricultural products. Secondly, as an increasing agricultural output volume goes hand in hand with increased population and incomes, the widening domestic markets provide more opportunities for import competing industries. Thirdly, Kuznets noted declining primary production shares in developed countries especially after they began trading with less developed countries, and fourthly he observed that technological change was an important factor; he actually stated that the more rapid the technological change, the faster was the change in the structure of the economy. In Kuznets' (1966) own words:

"One may conclude that a substantial rise in productivity of resources in the domestic agriculture sector is a condition of the large increase in overall productivity in modern economic growth. It is such a rise in productivity, combined with the low income elasticity of demand for products of the agriculture sector, that accounts for the marked decline in the share of that sector in the total of labor and capital used."

49

Hartwell (1973), on the other hand, defined successive stages of economic development according to the share employed in services. First, agricultural countries with a small industrial sector exhibit slow growth rates in services. Second, industrialising nations display declining agricultural employment and industry and services that grow at similar rates. The third stage is industrial nations with minimum agricultural and maximum industrial employment. The final stage is a service economy where services grow at the expense of secondary production. Hartwell (1973) found phase one to have ended in Western Europe between 1800 and 1850. Stage two took place between 1840 and 1910 and stage three between 1920 and 1970. Writing in the early 1970s, he concluded that stage four was just beginning. Hjerppe (1990) estimated that stage one lasted in Finland until the mid-1880s. She found stage two to have continued until the 1950s. No similar development to that portrayed in Hartwell's stage three was found by Hjerppe (1990) for Finland at all. She concluded that the employment share of primary production was still high in the 1950s, and that it subsequently diminished directly in favour of services. At the time of writing (1990), she found the employment share in secondary production to have decreased only slightly. It is easy to concur with Hjerppe that Hartwell's stage three as such did not take place in Finland. Industrial employment did not peak simultaneously with a trough in primary production employment. Secondary production employment is at present in a post-peak declining phase, and employment in agriculture and forestry obviously have not yet reached a nadir.

In 1860 four out of five persons were employed in primary production (Figure 2.8). As productivity was low, they managed to generate only 60 per cent of value added (Figure 2.7). Less than 15 per cent were working in secondary production, and their value added shares and employment ratios were approximately commensurable. The labour share of services was low: just 7 per cent. Yet their share of GDP was one fifth. This high productivity is to a significant extent explained by the large share of ownership of dwellings in services: two fifths of services' value added with no labour input in 1860 (Hjerppe, 1996). Also many affluent persons were occupied in services: entrepreneurs in trade and transport, civil servants, clergy, teachers, doctors, lawyers, artists, etc.

What was the role of the three sectors in overall growth? It was characteristic of the Finnish long run economic transformation that industrialisation started late and that services increased directly at the expense of primary production, since the share of secondary production in GDP did not decrease until the 1970s (Figure 2.7). In 1950 the share of agricultural population was still almost a half, and one quarter of production was in primary industries. Part of the explanation, but not the whole explanation, for the persistently high share of the primary sector is the role of forestry as a supplier of raw material to the forest industry. Forestry was very labour intensive until long after the Second World War. Another explanatory factor may be the low productivity of grain growing in Finland. This is due to the northern climatic conditions as well as the late modernisation of agriculture (see also Nummela and Ojala in this volume).

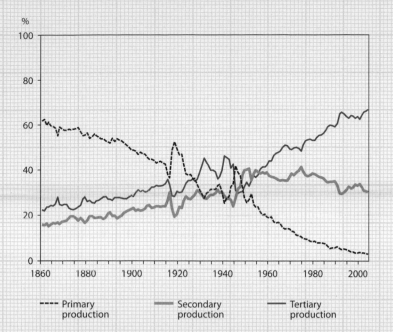

%

Figure 2.7 Shares of primary production, secondary production and tertiary production in Finnish GDP, 1860–2004, expressed as percentages

Source: Own calculations; data from Hjerppe (1996) and Statistics Finland.

---- Primary production   Secondary production   Tertiary production

In the 1800s agriculture and forestry were the dominant activities in the economy. The shares of secondary production and services increased simultaneously. It was characteristic of the long-run economic transformation that industrialisation started late and that services increased directly at the expense of primary production, since the share of secondary production in GDP did not decrease until the 1970s.

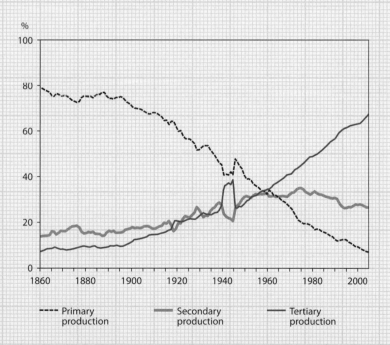

%

Figure 2.8 Shares of primary production, secondary production and tertiary production in Finnish labour input, 1860–2004, expressed as percentages

Source: Own calculations; data from Hjerppe (1996) and Statistics Finland.

---- Primary production   Secondary production   Tertiary production

In 1860 four out of five persons were employed in primary production. As productivity was low, they managed to generate only 60 per cent of value added. Finland embarked on the road of industrialisation by exploiting its forest sector, its hydropower potential and its rural labour reserve as well as the Russian market for consumption goods. The role of electrification in enabling productivity and boosting technical innovation was critical, and in the interwar years manufacturing became fully electrified.

Table 2.1 Growth rates of value added for the period 1860–2004 at year 2000 prices, expressed as percentages

	1860–1890	1890–1913	1920–1938	1950–1973	1973–1990	1995–2004	1860–2004
Primary production	1.5	1.7	1.9	1.1	−0.1	1.3	0.9
Secondary production	3.8	4.3	7.3	5.7	2.7	4.3	4.0
Tertiary production	2.6	3.7	4.4	5.1	3.5	3.5	3.3
Total	2.2	2.9	4.6	4.8	2.9	3.5	2.9

Source: Own calculations, data from Hjerppe (1996) and Statistics Finland.

Table 2.2 Growth rates of labour input for the period 1860–2004, expressed as percentages

	1860–1890	1890–1913	1920–1938	1950–1973	1973–1990	1995–2004	1860–2004
Primary production	1.0	0.6	0.0	−2.6	−3.6	−5.2	−1.0
Secondary production	1.8	1.7	3.6	1.3	−1.1	0.6	1.3
Tertiary production	2.1	3.3	2.7	2.4	1.5	2.1	2.3
Total	1.2	1.2	1.5	0.5	−0.1	1.2	0.7

Source: Own calculations, data from Hjerppe (1996) and Statistics Finland.

Table 2.3 Growth rates of labour productivity for the period 1860–2004, expressed as percentages

	1860–1890	1890–1913	1920–1938	1950–1973	1973–1990	1995–2004	1860–2004
Primary production	0.5	1.1	1.9	3.8	3.5	6.5	1.9
Secondary production	2.0	2.5	3.7	4.4	3.8	3.7	2.7
Tertiary production	0.4	0.5	1.7	2.7	2.0	1.4	1.0
Total	1.0	1.8	3.1	4.3	3.0	2.4	2.2

Source: Own calculations, data from Hjerppe (1996) and Statistics Finland.

Table 2.4 The impact of structural change on labour productivity growth for the period 1860–2004, expressed as percentages

	1860–1890	1890–1913	1920–1938	1950–1973	1973–1990	1860–2004
Within	68.2 %	52.6 %	75.6 %	77.3 %	83.8 %	88.2 %
Static	34.1 %	48.0 %	23.5 %	22.1 %	16.3 %	12.3 %
Dynamic	−2.3 %	−0.6 %	0.8 %	0.6 %	−0.2 %	−0.5 %
Total	100.0 %	100.0 %	100.0 %	100.0 %	100.0 %	100.0 %

Source: Own calculations, data from Hjerppe (1996) and Statistics Finland.

52

Finland embarked on the road of industrialisation by exploiting its forest sector, its hydropower potential and its rural labour reserve as well as the Russian market for consumption goods. The role of electrification in enabling productivity and boosting technical innovation was critical, and in the interwar years Finnish manufacturing became fully electrified.[13] In the 1860s, only a fraction of the Finnish populace was employed in industry or industrial handicrafts. Fifty years later, a tenth of the workforce was employed in industry, achieving a share in total output of one fifth by 1913. On the eve of the Second World War, the share of industry in GDP amounted to nearly one fourth. In the early 21st century the share of the former major sector – sawmilling – has shrunk to just a few percentage points, but the paper industry has maintained its position quite well. Finland's paper industry is the largest producer of writing paper and among the few largest newsprint producers in the world. The Finnish firm Nokia is the largest mobile phone producer in the world, but because Nokia is a multinational company, many of the phones are manufactured outside Finland (see also Ojala and Karonen in this volume). The metal and mechanical engineering industries hold the largest share in the manufacturing sector.

The labour share of tertiary production caught up with that of secondary production during and after the Civil War of 1918, during the turbulent early 1930s and during the Second World War. Employment in industry and construction rebounded each time.[14] From 1955 on, services permanently employed more persons than secondary production, and three years later even more than primary production. The share of secondary production in GDP peaked at more than 40 per cent in 1974, after which it started to decline. At the beginning of the 21st century, the share of industry and construction of GDP was 30 per cent and that of primary production only three per cent. The rest originated from services.

Secondary production: the engine of growth?

During the whole 1860–2004 period, GDP grew on average by almost three per cent, the value added of primary production by one per cent, secondary production by four per cent and services by three (Table 2.1). Value added growth can be broken up into the contributions of a change in labour input and a change in labour productivity. Tables 2.2 and 2.3 show the average yearly growth rates of labour input and labour productivity. Tables 2.1–2.3 can be interpreted in the following way: of the average yearly 1.5 per cent GDP growth in primary production in 1860–1890, 1.0 percent stemmed from increases in labour input and 0.5 percent from increases in labour productivity. Of the overall average GDP growth of 2.9 per cent in the period 1860–2004, only 0.7 percent was the result of increased labour input while 2.2 percent came from labour productivity improvement.

The growth of labour input in primary production was consistently slower than in the other sectors. Growth turned negative after the Second World War. The decline accelerated from period to period until it was more than 5 per cent annually in the period 1995–2004. The improvement in labour productivity in agriculture and forestry was above average in the periods 1973–1990 and 1995–2004 thanks to extensive labour shedding – and not as result of a rapid growth in value added. Labour input in secondary production grew faster than the national average until the first oil crisis. The labour input in services increased at a pace above average in every period. The supply of labour was never really a problem. Rather, unemployment has plagued the economy from time to time and persistently since 1990 (see Hannikainen and Heikkinen in this volume).

All through the 20th century, labour productivity has grown faster than labour input, while the decades in the end of the 19th century can be characterised as a period of extensive growth, where production rises because of higher labour and capital inputs and productivity growth is insignificant. Labour productivity reached the highest average growth rates in the 1950s and 1960s, but slowed down from the 1970s (the decade of the oil crises) on, as in other Western economies.

A study of labour productivity in the manufacturing industries of Denmark, Finland and Sweden in the early 20th century shows that in 1900 Finnish manufacturing was clearly behind the other two in almost all branches of industry. The gap was narrowed considerably in most industries by the 1930s.

The development was, however, fastest in the paper industry, where Finland's paper sector reached, and in some factories, surpassed the Swedish level (Hjerppe, 2001). The causes of the backwardness in 1900 could have been the very low wages, which did not push companies into the rationalisation of production. Particularly in the manufacturing industry, labour productivity has narrowed the gap with other advanced countries, and in 1996–2000 Finland had labour productivity levels comparable to those of the Netherlands, Belgium and the USA.[15]

One way in which labour productivity rises is by shifting from low productivity industries to high productivity industries. A shift-share analysis was performed in order to find out what the impact of structural change, that is of labour shifting to industries with either a higher level or higher growth rate of labour productivity, was on labour productivity growth.[16] It can be seen from table 2.4 that one half to nine tenths of labour productivity growth emanated from an increase in internal productivity. The rest was due to structural change. The effect of structural change was greatest in the late 1800s and early 1900s, when labour shifted from primary production to industry and construction. The impact of static shift diminished when there was a step-up in labour productivity growth across all sectors in the post-Second World War period (Table 2.3). The dynamic shift slowed productivity growth in the first observation period, whereas it was negligible in the latter period. All in all, the impact of the dynamic effect has been minor. Table 2.4 shows us that internal productivity growth is more important than structural change, and that productivity change was more concentrated than ever before in the latest period. Jalava (2006) showed that productivity growth in the manufacturing industry was broad-based in the 1970s and 1980s, with contributions from the paper and metal industries dominating. In the 1990s productivity growth was much more concentrated in the electronics industry.

The proximate sources of growth

Above we saw the important contribution of increasing labour productivity to economic growth. The most important reason for labour productivity growth is new and better technology and production methods. New technology is usually adopted in an economy through fixed capital formation, mainly through new machinery and equipment. Growing investment ratios have secured an increasing amount of machinery and equipment and a relatively short life-span for much of it. Finland is not known for major or pioneering inventions, but clearly Finnish entrepreneurs have been effective borrowers of technology, thus actually saving themselves the development costs of the pioneers. In the 19th century, the legislation was very slow in allowing new technology like steam-powered sawmills to be adopted. The 20th century has been different in this respect. We have seen a very early introduction of electricity and telephones, for example. Typically, the introduction was in the hands of a few enthusiastic pioneers, and it normally took a long time for the new technologies to become a standard procedure. Comparisons show that Finnish industry has clearly been behind the other Nordic countries in adopting new technologies (Myllyntaus, Michelsen and Herranen, 1986).

Since the early 19th century, the government has taken a favourable stand towards investments, and the support has been considerable. This can also be seen in Figure 2.9, where the investment ratio is shown. During early industrialisation, the government granted loans for the establishment of factories; these were sometimes commuted into grants when the factories were finished and working. There were also grants for experimenting with new techniques and developing mining sites. For a long time the only industry without governmental support was sawmilling. In general, the government aided manufacturing companies by guaranteeing them foreign loans, by rescuing large companies and/or by becoming a co-owner or the sole owner of them when they were in financial difficulties. In the post-Second World War period, governmental support for investments was mainly in the form of tax support and even direct regional support.

In the early 20th century, the investment ratio was over a tenth, rising to an average of 15 per cent in the interwar period but with big fluctuations between boom and depression periods. After the end of the Second Wold War, the investment ratio took another leap to an average level of 25 per cent or more, where it stayed from the 1950s to the 1980s. Pohjola (1996) has shown that, although the massive investments contributed to growth, capital inefficiency eventually ensued. The early 1990s depression saw a halving of investments and, after the depression, somewhat lower investment ratios until the present day.

In production, labour is combined with capital and technology. These inputs into economic growth, i.e. labour, capital and productivity, are called the proximate sources of growth.[17] Both labour and capital have their prices, developments which influence their use and possible substitution with some other factor of production. These complex relations are studied in Figure 2.10, where we compare the productivity of labour and capital and the prices of labour and capital. We see two major developments: the productivity of capital (Y/K) is almost zero in the long run, while the productivity of labour (Y/L) grows.

Figure 2.10 shows that in the Finnish non-residential market sector, the curve for capital productivity (Y/K) is virtually horizontal. This means that change in capital productivity has been zero over the long run. Thus the property of the neoclassical growth theory that postulates that the capital stock and real economic growth of the economy expand at the same rate and thus keep the capital-output ratio constant is satisfied. The growth of labour productivity (Y/L), on the other hand, has not been zero; indeed, quite the opposite. The ratio of capital to labour (K/L) closely followed labour productivity since capital input per unit of labour increased steadily. Growth can be said to have been labour-saving.

56

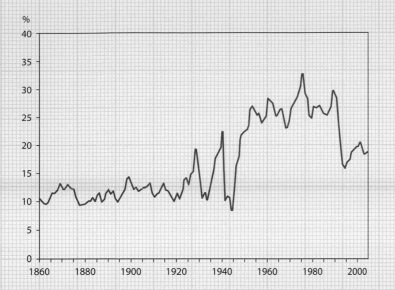

Figure 2.9 The investment ratio (nominal investments per nominal GDP) for the period 1860–2004, expressed as percentages

Source: Hjerppe (1996) and Statistics Finland.

Since the early 19th century, the government has taken a very favourable stand towards investments, and the support has been considerable. During early industrialisation, the government granted loans for the establishment of factories; these were sometimes commuted into grants when the factories were built and working. There were also grants for experimenting with new techniques and developing mining sites. For a long time the only industry without governmental support was sawmilling. In the early 20th century, the investment ratio was over a tenth, rising to an average of 15 per cent in the interwar period but with big fluctuations between boom and depression periods. After the end of the Second Wold War, the investment ratio took another leap to an average level of 25 per cent or more, where it stayed from the 1950s to the 1980s.

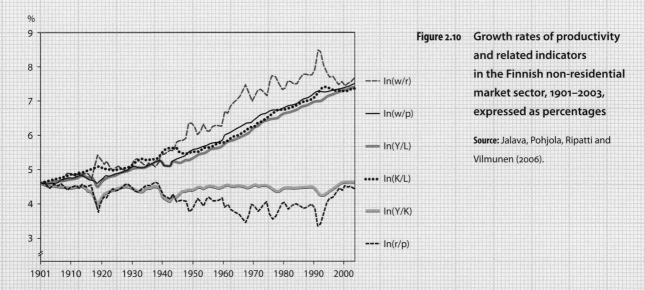

Figure 2.10 Growth rates of productivity and related indicators in the Finnish non-residential market sector, 1901–2003, expressed as percentages

Source: Jalava, Pohjola, Ripatti and Vilmunen (2006).

The curve for capital productivity (Y/K) is virtually horizontal. This means that capital productivity change has been zero over the long run. Thus the property of the neoclassical growth theory that postulates that the economy's capital stock and real economic growth expand at the same rate is satisfied. The growth of labour productivity (Y/L), on the other hand, has not been zero, quite the opposite. Growth can be said to have been labour-saving.

Labour and capital cannot be used free of charge in production. The rental prices, the costs of using one unit of labour or capital, are denoted by (w) and (r), respectively. The real wage (w/p) series increased steadily following the change in labour productivity and the capital-labour (K/L) ratio closely. It is understandable that, given the steadily increasing real wage, growth is labour-saving. Conversely, given the fact that growth is labour-saving, it is possible to continuously increase the real wage. The rental price of capital was cheaper than the price of using labour, as is shown by the rising (w/r) curve. The ratio of the price of using one unit of labour to the price of using one unit of capital (w/r) increased until the 1990s. The real rental price of capital (the rental price deflated with the GDP deflator, (r/p)) more or less declined until the 1990s. Thus substituting labour with capital has been relatively cheap especially after the Second World War. After the early 1990s depression, the share of capital in GDP increased, and there was a clear change in some of these relationships. The real rental price of capital (r/p) rose, capital intensity (K/L) stopped growing and capital productivity (Y/K) improved. This could be related to the rise in the real interest rate, when after decades of zero and sometimes even negative real interest rates there started to be a positive interest on capital in the 1990s.

Neoclassical growth accounting basically divides output growth into the contributions of input growth, i.e. labour and capital, with multi-factor productivity growth (MFP) constituting the residual.[18] As in other countries, growth accounting analyses of Finland's data also show an increasing share of multi-factor productivity over the whole 20th century, pointing to a growing share of growth left unexplained by capital and labour input. The coefficient of multi-factor productivity was about one third for the early 20th century and about two thirds of total growth for the last decades of the 20th century. Since MFP catches all unmeasured factors such as disembodied technical change (a shift of the production function), organisational improvements, economies of scale and measurement errors, Abramovitz (1956) quite rightly called the residual a "measure of our ignorance".[19]

The lower investment rate of the late 1990s has not led to lower economic growth. It may be partly due to lower relative prices of investment goods. Another possible explanation is the new use of knowledge in production, and the increased importance of information and communications technology.[20] Recently Jalava and Pohjola (2005) have taken stock of the impacts of information and communications technology on GDP and labour productivity growth in Finland in the years 1995–2002. They found that nearly one-third of GDP growth stemmed from ICT production. This is remarkable as the nominal share of ICT production was only 6 per cent. On the input side, they found that ICT capital services contributed more than one-half of the capital contribution. Of the overall multi-factor productivity increase, ICT production accounted for a quarter. The overall impact of ICT on GDP growth was less than a third of the observed growth rate and 40 per cent of the labour productivity growth.

58

Other aspects of economic growth

We now shortly turn to some aspects of economic growth the significance of which are not easily measured. During recent decades, a lot of attention has been paid to research and development efforts. An early Finnish pioneer in research and development was the Central Laboratory, set up in 1916 by paper companies to do research and development for the paper industry. Other pioneering measures were regular evaluations of forest reserves since the early 1920s carried out by the government's Finnish Forest Research Institute and demands made on the forest owners for reforestation. Thanks to these activities, Finland's large forest industry can count on obtaining most of its raw material from domestic sources. In the late 1980s, however, Finland was still slightly behind the average Western European R&D level. This has been corrected now, and Finland is among the top investors in R&D in the world, with 3.5 per cent of outlays in relation to GDP (see also Asplund and Maliranta in this volume).

One way for new technology to be introduced is by foreign entrepreneurs. Several early modern industrial production establishments in textiles, iron and consumer goods in the 19th century were set up by foreigners, and a number of the early steam sawmills were started by foreigners, mainly Norwegians or Swedes in the 1870s. Hjerppe (2004) shows that considerable numbers of multinationals founded sales offices with installation and service activities and even industrial plants in the interwar years. Foreigners were active, though not alone, in setting up electricity works, tramways, telephone lines, factories in the chemical and metal industries and construction companies. The foreign share of production was never very high, however; Finland was a small market, and only a few foreigners came to engage in production for the Finnish market

59

or for export. Normally selling and installation and maintenance were enough. What is surprising is that the paper industry, where Finland was to have a clear comparative advantage, had no foreign pioneers and even later on very few foreign owners; the Scandinavians in the interwar period were kept away by means of Nordic cartel agreements, and almost no others came either.

The recent developments since the 1980s have seen a rapid internationalisation of the economy in Finland too and there is a lot of foreign ownership, both portfolio and direct, in almost all sectors of the economy at the same time as Finnish enterprises have been even more active in establishing production in foreign countries. For example, all big Finnish paper, metal and chemical companies are multinationals nowadays (see Ojala and Karonen in this volume).

A feature typical of Finland has been the high share of foreign trade. In principle, it does not matter which sector, domestic or export, demands goods and services. In a small economy, openness is to be expected; participation in international exchange is of great importance. Exports have made possible specialisation and economies of scale in production. Because of the openness, the economy has been exposed to business cycles, brought to the country through fluctuations in international demand. On the other hand, access to export markets has been of crucial importance to the Finnish economy.

The continuous high share of exports and imports from the 1860s and 1870s onwards was one of the new results emerging from the historical national accounts research. It is well-known that Finland was a tar and timber exporting country for a long time (see Kaukiainen in this volume), but how much did these products contribute to the Finnish economy? Another surprise was the continued high share of exports even in the interwar period, when nations experiencing difficulties generally resorted to import restrictions and high tariffs.

The Finnish economy was clearly more open than the EU15 average until the Second World War (Figure 2.11). Foreign trade was very limited during the World Wars. The recovery of trade after the Second World War took a long time, due to the strict trade limitations that were in force until 1957. The recent development has followed the general European path of growing trade shares with, however, a deep fall in the early 1990s both in Finland and the EU15.

The historical national accounts also showed one explanation for the favourable developments of foreign trade and the whole economy: the terms of trade, i.e. the relationship between the price of exports and price of imports, improved almost one hundred percent during the last decades of the 19th century (Figure 2.12). While agricultural and industrial prices declined in world trade, the relative price of timber and pulp did not fall. In the interwar period, the rising demand for paper, a relatively new product, kept Finland's exports afloat. The rationalisation of the paper industry made price decreases possible, and the export volumes of paper did not fall during the 1930s depression. Another boom in the terms of trade occurred in the last years of the 1940s and early 1950s. The reasons for this are still unclear, and there is ongoing research on this subject.

60

%

Figure 2.11 Openness of the economies (imports + exports per GDP) in EU15, 1860–2000, and Finland, 1860–2002, expressed as percentages

Sources: Carreras and Tafunell (2004); Hjerppe (1996) and Statistics Finland.

━━━ EU 15   ━━━ Finland

In a small economy, openness is to be expected; participation in international exchange is of great importance. Exports have made possible specialisation and economies of scale in production. The Finnish economy was more open than the EU15 average until the Second World War. Foreign trade was very limited during the World Wars. The recovery of trade after the Second World War took a long time, as a result of the strict trade limitations that were in force until 1957. The recent development has followed the general European path of growing trade shares.

1926=100

Figure 2.12 The terms of trade, 1865–2002, 1926=100

Source: Hjerppe (1996) and Statistics Finland. The terms of trade of a country are calculated by dividing the price of its exports by the price of its imports.

One explanation to the favourable developments of foreign trade and the whole economy is the fact that the terms of trade improved almost one hundred percent during the late 19th century. While agricultural and industrial prices declined in world trade, the relative price of timber and pulp did not fall. In the interwar period the rising demand for paper, a relatively new product, kept exports afloat. The rationalisation of the paper industry made price decreases possible, and the export volumes of paper did not fall during the 1930s depression.

In principle, exports force production into harsh competition on the export markets. The Finnish economy until the new era of globalisation, the 1980s, was able to limit competition in several ways. The paper and pulp companies formed strong domestic cartels in order to find joint export markets, and they were also active in international cartels. They received support from the government for their investments. The big banks, also in a cartel from the 1930s to the 1980s and under the strict surveillance of the central bank, used to direct their extra profits to their big client companies (see also Ojala and Karonen in this volume). Finnish ownership of the forests, mineral resources and water power was safeguarded by legislation limiting direct foreign investments from early independence to the early 1990s. One important component of exports, those to the Soviet Union, from the late 1940s until the collapse of the Soviet Union in 1991 were always negotiated by high-level government officials.

Finally, the government economic policy has favoured economic development in several ways, some of which have been mentioned above. The Finnish economy used to be prone to inflation, which was often faster than in countries competing with Finnish exports. This problem used to be solved by devaluations of the Finnish *markka* agreed upon by the government, the central bank and the forest companies (see García-Iglesias and Kilponen in this volume). This helped export industries, but in the short run it meant higher import prices for the domestic household sector and a change in income distribution in favour of capital. On the home market, competition has also been limited by cartels or sheltered by high tariffs on consumption goods. Agriculture was subsidised and carefully protected by high tariffs from the beginning of Finnish independence to membership in the European Union in 1995, and it now receives the subsidies of the Common Agricultural Policy. On the home market, large agricultural producers' cooperatives may have also diminished competition.

Conclusions

In this chapter we have outlined some of the stylized facts behind the Finnish "from rags to riches story". The fast economic growth, 2.2 per cent per annum and per capita from 1860 to the present day, has not been surpassed by many other countries in the world. This has meant the rise of per capita incomes to Western European levels and to three quarters of the US level. This development has been extraordinary because in Europe there are countries with ample natural resources that could not match the Finnish experience. Finland was a late industrialised country that managed to transform itself from a predominantly primary production based economy to a modern welfare state with a large service sector. In this development, the role of labour productivity has been cardinal. In labour productivity improvement, secondary production was the leading sector as a result of rapid technical progress. Until the first oil crisis, the labour input in secondary production grew faster than the national average, whereas the labour

62

input in services increased at a pace that was above average in every period. In the late 19th and early 20th centuries, labour shifting out of primary production contributed at most half of the overall labour productivity growth.

Productivity growth was labour-saving with especially high investment ratios after the Second World War. Capital productivity change was zero over the long run, thus satisfying the property of the neoclassical growth theory that the economy's capital stock and real economic growth expand at the same rate. Recently productivity growth has been more concentrated than before as the rural surplus labour has long since shifted to secondary production and services. Growth has become innovation-driven with the ratio of R&D expenditure to GDP at 3.5 per cent. Also relatively large foreign trade has been of significance in the growth process. Finland has been also fortunate in that the terms of trade have shown a positive development; i.e. export prices have risen more than import prices.

In conclusion, we can say that our analysis confirmed Hartwell's basic idea of economic growth taking place in different phases. Finland's industrialisation changed its economic structure irrevocably. Structural change in itself was an effect of Finnish economic growth rather than the cause of it. It does not take a crystal ball to see that the Finnish economic structure will continue evolving, since Finland's share of secondary production in GDP still exceeded its US equivalent by approximately ten percentage points at the turn of the millennium.

The importance of timber floating has lessened over the years as more and more raw wood is transported to manufacturing units by road.

"Log Drivers"

by Unto Pusa

64   oil on canvas, 165 x 210 cm, 1964

Feeding Economic Growth: Agriculture

Jari Ojala and Ilkka Nummela

Developed agriculture is a basic requirement for a developed economy: economic growth, industrialisation and urbanisation are only possible after there is enough food available at reasonable prices. Finland offers an example of rather late but rapid development in agriculture. Despite the constraints of a cold climate and short growing season, Finnish agriculture has witnessed an enormous growth in productivity especially during the last two decades of the 20th century.

Economic growth in every country is dependent on the capacity of the agriculture to feed its people. The development of agriculture leads to a fall in the price of food and to the reduction of poverty. Economic historians have debated when, why and how the second agricultural revolution occurred, that is, the increase in productivity that enabled an escape from the "Malthusian trap" – referring to an assumption made by Thomas Malthus (1766–1834) that, because in the long term population growth is more rapid than the increase in agricultural production, this will ultimately lead to crises. Productivity growth, i.e. the decrease in the aggregate inputs of land and labour to produce agricultural products, occurred in developed countries from the turn of the nineteenth century on. However, even in many of these countries, this change did not take place until the latter part of the twentieth century. For some countries, the change has not even begun yet.[1]

Finland offers an example of a country with a rather late but rapid development of productivity growth in agriculture. Between the world wars, a growth in production was still mainly achieved by increasing the cultivated area, and even after the Second World War, a huge number of new farms were established. Finnish agriculture is also an example of a model in which rather small family farms, supported by cooperatives, have been the dominant form up to the end of the 20th century. Furthermore, the role played by the state in constraining, promoting and enabling agricultural production has played a vital role throughout Finland's history.

At the beginning of the 19th century, almost 90 per cent of employment in Finland came from the primary sector (Table 3.1). A characteristic phenomenon during the following decades until the end of the century, when urbanisation and industrialisation really began, was a downward social spiral owing to the high population growth rate in the later part of the 18th century (1.3% p.a.) and also in the period 1815–1865 (1.0% p.a.). The economy was not able to cope with the rapid population growth. Primary production in 1860 accounted for about 60 per cent of gross domestic production (GDP) and around 80 per cent of the labour force, while in 2000 its share had declined to 1.5 per cent of GDP and four per cent of the labour force. In the fifteen European countries studied by van Zanden (1991), 55 per cent of the population were working in the primary sector in the 1870s. In Finland, the corresponding figure for the 1880s was 75 per cent. Similarly, by 1910 the European percentage had decreased to 46, while in Finland it was still around 70.[2]

Even after the Second World War, Finland was still highly dependent on the agricultural sector, in terms of both its role as employer and its share of the GDP. By the end of the century, the situation had changed dramatically: the status of agriculture in Finland declined in terms of both its contribution to the national economy and its role as an employer. The rise in production and productivity made it possible to lower the prices of foodstuffs; together with the growth of wealth people spent less on food and drink. As Hjerppe and Jalava note in this volume, in the late 19th century over 50 per cent of the private con-

66

sumption expenditure still went on food, but this share had decreased to one third by the early 1950s, to a quarter by the early 1980s, and to approx. 14 percent by the early 21st century. Thus, as in other Western economies as well, there has been a decline in the aggregate input to produce farm products.[3] Though the importance of agriculture in Finnish GDP has declined during the postwar era, it still plays a fairly important role in large areas of the country – and also in government policies, as can be seen especially from the important role played by agriculture in Finnish-EU negotiations in the mid-1990s. Even in the early 21st century, "farmer" was among the most common occupations in Finland; for example, in 2002 there were almost 80,000 farmers in Finland.

The history of Finnish agriculture followed the general trends of development in Swedish agriculture during the era when Finland was under Swedish rule. However, when Finland was annexed to imperial Russia in 1809, Russian agriculture was not taken as a model; for example, serfdom was never introduced into Finland – with the exception of the area called "Old Finland", which was already part of Russia in the 18th century. Feudalism in the continental

Pictured here is a scene typical of the 1980s; a Finnish family, living and working in a Finnish or Swedish urban setting, spent their summer holidays in the countryside where they were born and brought up.

67

Table 3.1 Finnish agricultural population and labour force, 1754–2000.

Sources: Kilpi 1913, Tilastollisia 1979; Official statistics of Finland.

Note: agricultural population and labour force refer here to the whole primary sector. Agriculture constituted about 90 per cent of the labour force in the total primary sector during the late 19th century. The data is not available for all years due to the differences in statistics.

Year	Total population, 1000	Total labour force, 1000	Total agricultural population, 1000	Total agricultural labour force, 1000	Proportion of agricultural population in total population (%)	Proportion of agricultural labour force in total labour force (%)
1754	450	180	350	..	77	..
1805	898	359	702	..	78	..
1820	1178	521	..	448	..	86
1850	1637	694	..	589	..	85
1880	2061	639	1545	502	75	73
1900	2656	832	1845	566	69	68
1920	3148	1499	2057	1051	65	70
1950	4030	1984	1674	912	42	46
1980	4788	2214	..	279	..	13
2000	5181	2589	..	142	..	4

The proportions of the agricultural population and labour force in the total population and labour force can be used as indirect estimates of the productivity growth in agriculture, although the calculation takes into account neither changes in consumption patterns nor the role played by imports of foodstuffs[*]. However, the aggregate labour input in agriculture of the total population has diminished at an increasing rate, especially from the early 20th century on. Urbanisation occurred rather late: even in the early 19th century only around five per cent of Finns lived in towns, and by the start of the 20th century this figure was still only around 13 per cent. In the mid-20th century, around one third of the population lived in urban municipalities, while by the end of the millennium the figure was two thirds.

* See especially Allen 2000, Zanden 1991.

Table 3.2 Self-sufficiency in foodstuffs: production as a percentage of consumption

Sources: Official Statistics of Finland and Ministry of Agriculture and Forestry.

Product group	1970	1980	1990	2000
Cereals	114	70	175	103
Dairy products – liquids	..	129	122	112
Dairy products – fats	126	128	143	132
Beef	110	102	109	93
Pork	110	119	114	101
Eggs	136	151	137	114
Sugar	27	60	91	71

Early in the 21st century, Finland produces certain products way over its needs; this is the case especially with dairy products and eggs. The situation was different at the start of the 20th century: self sufficiency in cereals was then only around 44 per cent owing to imports from Russia. In the mid-19th century, the country was vulnerable in the imports of foodstuffs: thus, when crops failed in the late 1860s and ships loaded with grain were unable to sail to Finland owing to the early freezing over of the Baltic, the country faced a severe famine. However, as the country was sparsely populated it was possible to use supplementary sources of food such as game and fish.

sense never played a significant role in Finland, and large manors with tenant farmers never occurred in large scale. One of the main characteristics of Finnish agricultural production has been the fact that the farms have been owned and operated mostly by the farmers themselves. The societal importance of agriculture and rural areas as whole can be seen from the importance of the agrarian parties in Finnish politics throughout the 20th century – a phenomenon that has some similarity with the situation in eastern central Europe between the world wars. The development of agriculture during the 20th century was closely related to the building of the welfare society, since even the socialist parties had strong rural roots in the early part of the 20th century. The Finnish story – especially from the late 1980s on, when Finnish agriculture had to be adjusted not only to the standards and restrictions of the European Union but also to GATT and WTO agreements, to a great extent reflects international structural changes in agriculture, the food industries, consumption patterns, politics and the trade in agricultural products.[5]

In the following, we will first describe the development of Finnish agriculture during the last 500 years and follow with an analysis of how state policies, ownership structure and cooperatives have affected this development especially during the 20th century. In the third section of the article, a productivity analysis over the long term is presented, followed by some concluding remarks. The basic argument in this article is that the increase in agricultural production was a result of extensions of the cultivated area and an increase in labour intensity up to the late 19th century. Thereafter productivity growth, both in terms of land and labour, has been of increasing significance. Relatively small family farms have played an important role in the development up to the late 20th century; they have been supported by state legislation and joint marketing through cooperatives. Finally, we argue that the development of agriculture during the 20th century was closely related to the building of the welfare society

From famine to overproduction

On the one hand, a large, sparsely populated land area with a cold climate has constrained the possibilities for the commercial expansion of Finnish agriculture (owing to logistic problems, for example). On the other hand, the large land area has enabled the expansion of agriculture, unlike in many European countries, where a scarcity of land has been an important constraint. That was not, however, the case in Finland. On the contrary, forests and marshland were still being cleared for cultivation even in the late 20th century.

As Finland is one of the northernmost agricultural countries in the world, the short growing season and disadvantageous weather conditions are the basic constraints on its agricultural production – although the effect of the Gulf Stream enables cultivation even in Lapland. The growing season in the southernmost parts of Finland is around 180 days, while in the north it is only 120 days. However, there are also a number of advantages accruing from Finnish weather conditions. During the summer, the amount of daylight is greater than for example in central Europe, and in the winter the cold weather has provided a resistance to some diseases both in animal husbandry and in plant cultivation. The winter is favourable especially for fur-farming. Owing to an adequate amount of rain there has not been any need for expensive irrigation systems.

The traditional slash-and-burn technique was the dominant form of agriculture from medieval times on, especially in the eastern parts of the country; during the 17th century, over half of the grain was produced by the slash-and-burn method in these areas. In the western parts of the country, however, field husbandry already flourished during the Middle Ages, and in the 17th century only one-fifth or less of the grain was produced by slash-and-burn cultivation in western Finland. Dairy farming became the dominant form in the late 19th century, though field husbandry grew in importance especially in the southernmost parts of the country. Cattle raising has been closely connected not only with meat and dairy products, but also with the demand for manure. Particularly in Ostrobothnia (the north-western coastal area of Finland), cattle raising grew in importance at a quite early period, and butter even began to be exported quite early on.

It is not possible to point to a "typical" Finnish farm because of the variation in types of production (for example, from grain growing in the southernmost parts of the country to reindeer husbandry in the north) and because geographic and climatic conditions are so different in different parts of the country. For example, the modernisation of rural Finland spread from the south-west to the north-east. Thus it was not until the last decades of the 20th century that the structural change in society occurred on a large scale in the eastern and northernmost parts of the country.[6]

The settlement of Finland was dictated by the habitats of game animals, and in the early modern period also the areas where it was possible to cultivate rye.[7] The settlement extended rapidly during the 16th century and thereafter – the reason being the population growth and the general rise in grain prices in Europe. It was the above-mentioned slash-and-burn technique in rye cultivation that was responsible for in the spreading of settlement to the eastern and northern parts of country. In fact, the slash-and-burn technique was developed in the Savo region in eastern Finland so as to use the conifer forests as a source of good yields. Indeed, the Swedish Crown actually encouraged these cultivators to move to Sweden with their (high) technology – and from there, some of them even emigrated in the early 17th century to North America (the Delaware area), thus, providing an excellent example of an early modern technology transfer.

During the early 19th century, the Finnish economy came to be even more dominated by agriculture after the area called "Old Finland" was attached to the autonomous Grand Duchy of Finland. These areas in the south-east were part of Russia during the 18th century and were important areas of agricultural

70

Slash-and-burn cultivation was practised in eastern Finland to utilise old conifer forests as resources. Crop yields increased significantly. Yield-to-seed ratios could rise to 40:1 or even higher. The method was highly resource-dependent as the same area could be sown only once or twice after burning. Thereafter, it took 80 to 100 years before the area could be re-burned. As this picture from 1893 shows, slash-and-burn agriculture was also labour-intensive. This meant that land productivity in slash-and-burn agriculture was high, but labour productivity was low.

In western parts of the country, field husbandry flourished from the Middle Ages. This picture shows the oat fields of the vicarage of Kiikoinen in southwest Finland in the 1920s. Vicarages usually had large areas of farmland and they were often pioneers in the scientific development of agriculture.

production, even exporting agricultural products to Russia, especially to nearby St. Petersburg. Before the 19th century, agricultural exports had not played a significant role in the economy. For example, during the 17th century, the share of agricultural production in exports was around one per cent. The exports to Russia expanded from the early 19th century on, and by the 1890s agricultural products accounted for around one third of the value of Finnish exports. Agricultural exports, however, collapsed after the Russian Revolution and the independence of Finland: in the 1920s the share of agriculture was only around two per cent of the total exports, and it remained at a low level throughout the 20th century (see also Yrjö Kaukiainen in this volume). The commercialisation of agriculture occurred in conjunction with the expansion of exports, and a monetary economy spread to the rural areas. At the same time, the liability to pay taxes was also extended, and this in turn increased the need for people to have money incomes.

During the 20th century, agricultural production changed from labour-intensive working methods to capital-intensive production as the "agribusiness" emerged in Finland. This commercialisation of production led to specialisation in production and to an overall adjustment of production to the market economy. During the 20th century, Finnish agriculture faced a number of changes, including the afore mentioned collapse of export markets in the east. Exports to other areas were not possible owing to the general rise of protectionism in Europe.

72

Between the world wars, the arable area of the country increased by around a quarter. This was due to the technological development and agricultural reforms carried out during the period. Although technology developed, and fertilizers became more general, in the central areas of the country malnutrition was still widespread in the 1920s owing to the low productivity in subsistence agriculture and lack of complementary incomes. Cultivation of hay in open fields became general, which increased the nitrogen gain of the land and thus, land productivity. At the same time, agriculture was further commercialized, cooperatives became more general, and "entrepreneurship" in farming emerged. The expansion of agriculture after the Second World War through land acquisition acts was followed by mass emigration from rural areas from the 1960s on, when overproduction also emerged as a problem. Finally, readjustment to EU legislation has characterised the change from the 1990s on.

Finnish farming has over the course of time changed from diversified production to a more concentrated type of production. This meant that farms specialised in different types of production. For example, in the early 1960s, almost all Finnish farms produced dairy products (milk), while in the early 1980s only one third of Finnish farms still had cows. The proportion of dairy production in Finnish agriculture has further decreased during the 1990s and early 21st century: in 1995 one third of farms produced dairy products, while in 2002 the share was a little over a quarter. At the same time, the proportion of crop farms increased from 42 to 55 per cent. Certain farm animals such as sheep almost disappeared from rural areas.[8]

By the end of the 20th century, agriculture in Finland, as in the other industrialised countries, was facing a severe problem of overproduction. Even in the early 20th century, there were still a few famines, and in the late 1860s Finland experienced the last known major peacetime famine, losing one tenth of its population through starvation. The worst known famine, however, occurred in the years 1695–1697, when around one third of the population died. The period 1870–1913 was characterized by a commercialisation of agriculture and a shift from crop production to animal husbandry with exports of butter and imports of cereals especially from Russia, as stated by Yrjö Kaukiainen in this volume. As a result of this shift, the degree of self-sufficiency in cereals decreased to 44 per cent, while self-sufficiency in animal products was over 90 per cent. Therefore, during the First World War, there were huge problems in feeding the people. This was also partly due to the collapse of the logistics system in Russia. In 1917 the deficiency in foodstuffs lead to civil disorder, and this was one cause of the outbreak of civil war in Finland in January 1918. In the very early years of Finnish independence, the "ideal" of self sufficiency in foodstuffs was adopted as one of the primary objectives of the government, and legislative changes and land reforms were carried out in order to achieve it. By the end of the 1930s, self sufficiency in cereals was already around 70 per cent, and in animal products 83 percent – thus implying a declining trend in animal products compared to the situation two decades earlier (see Table 3.2).[9]

Overproduction became a subject of public discussion in the late 1950s (see Table 3.2). The overproduction of dairy products and eggs in particular caused problems. Overproduction, the above-mentioned ideal of self-sufficiency and the objective to provide food at reasonable prices all led to the subsidisation of agriculture. In Finland the subsidies to agriculture were controversial. The restrictive methods and subsidies formed a complex system, in which most of the export subsidies were paid by the farmers themselves. More drastic measures to cut the overproduction were introduced during the 1960s and 1970s. Among the most innovative institutional restrictions was the set-aside system, where compensation was paid for fields that were allowed to lie fallow. Around ten per cent of the total area of cultivated land was withdrawn from active cultivation. The set-aside system was widely criticised, on the one hand on emotional grounds: it was seen as the embodiment of the stagnation of rural areas, where land previously cleared for farming land with hard work was now abandoned or reforested. On the other hand, the set-aside system also proved to be an inadequate measure for dealing with the problems of overproduction. At the same time, the market situation became easier owing to sales to the Soviet Union, weak crops and the oil crises of the 1970s, which all increased world market prices for agricultural products. Furthermore, the massive emigration from almost all the rural areas of the country decreased the number of active farms, especially small ones. There was an emigration not only of people but also of capital from rural to urban areas, and the patterns of forest ownership in particular changed drastically. The effects of migration were profound throughout Finnish society: in 1950 around one third of the population lived in urban municipalities, while by the end of the millennium the proportion was two thirds; by comparison, in Britain in 1850, about 50 per cent of the population already lived in towns, and in 1950 about 80 per cent.[10]

During the 1990s, Finnish agriculture again faced a period of change. The main cause was Finnish membership in the European Union. Finnish agriculture had to adjust itself to EU agricultural policies, diminishing farming subsidies, production quotas and other restrictions. Though Finland got a number of advantages for its agriculture in the Treaty of Accession to the EU, membership has caused the most profound structural changes in production since the resettlement of demobilised soldiers and evacuees from the territories lost to the Soviet Union after the Second World War. The number of active farms was decreasing rapidly, people were again moving from the countryside to urban centres, and the population in rural areas was growing old. The number of milk suppliers decreased to over half in the period 1990–2002, from about 43,500 to 20,000 farms. Furthermore, about 74,000 farms applied for the basic forms of agricultural support in 2002, while the number in 1994 was about 105,600 farms.[11] Thus almost one third of active farms had disappeared in less than ten years. More emphasis in political discussion was placed on the viability of the rural areas and on the need to keep the countryside inhabited. The cultural values of rural areas and the countryside were stressed in public discussion.

74

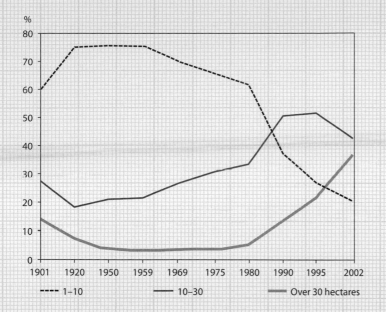

Figure 3.1 **Farms by size of arable land area (hectares) 1901–2000, in percentages**

Sources: Peltonen 2004, 516; Niemelä 1996, 351, 420; Kuhmonen 1996, 16–18; Finnish Official Statistics; Information Centre of the Ministry of Agriculture and Forestry.

Note: owing to the slight differences in statistics, the middlemost category includes farms of 10 to 25 hectares in the years 1901–1969 and 10 to 30 hectares in the years 1975–2002.

A number of structural changes, most of them related to legislative reforms, affected the size of farms during the 20th century. In the early 20th century the proportion of small farms increased notably after the Leaseholders' Act. The share of the largest farms diminished respectively. Again, after the Second World War the share of the largest farms diminished notably as a result of the Land Acquisition Act. It was not until the 1990s that the proportion of farms in the largest size category (over 30 hectares) reached the same level as in 1901. During the 1990s and the early 21st century, there has been a rapid change as the share of the largest size category has increased.

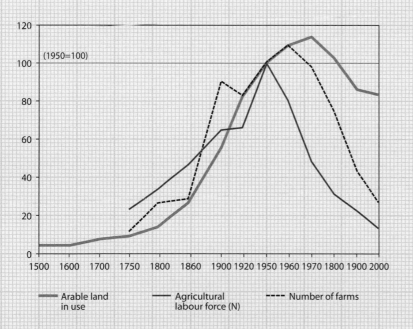

Figure 3.2 **Input indices in Finnish agriculture, 1500 –2000 (1950=100)***

Sources: Niemelä 1996, Viita 1965; STV, Suomen tilastollinen vuosikirja (Statistical yearbook of Finland); SVT, Suomen Virallinen Tilasto III, Maatalous; Maatalouslaskenta 1992, Maataloustilastollinen 2002; Siltanen and Ala-Mantila 1989, 6–7; Hjerppe 1988, Kilpi 1913, Koskinen, Martelin, Notkola, Notkola and Pitkänen 1994.

* The figure is based on the area of arable land in hectares and the number of farms (including crofts). Since there are differences in the sources used, Figures 2 and 3 should be understood as only estimates. The arable land in use in 1500 is based on extrapolation; the other years are partly interpolated. Further details available from the authors by request.

Scarcity of land was a significant constraint on the expansion of agriculture in many European countries. That was not, however, the case in Finland. On the contrary, forests and marshland were still being cleared for cultivation even in the late 20th century. The area of arable land in use increased especially from the beginning of the 19th century up to the 1970s, although the growth diminished between the World Wars. The size of the agricultural labour force has decreased from the mid-20th century on owing to the reduction in the use of outside labour after the Second World War. The number of farms, however, decreased only from the 1960s on, when there was migration from rural to urban areas.

Adaptation to conditions:
the state, family farms, and cooperatives

The Finnish model of agricultural policy was created in the very early years of independence in order to boost the production of foodstuffs and improve the status of crofters. This was inspired by the fact that inadequate sources of foodstuffs and the crofters' unfavourable position were among the major reasons for the Civil War that broke out in 1918. Domestic production was therefore subsidised in the 1920s and 1930s, and the subsidisation was further increased in conjunction with the above-mentioned resettlement programme after the Second World War. The government has used its authority to control land ownership at several times in Finnish history, starting with the settlement regulated by the state from the 16th century on, the general parcelling out of land in the 18th and 19th centuries (the change from open-field villages to unified farms, somewhat similar to the British enclosures); and the land acquisition acts in the early 20th century and immediately after the Second World War. All these changes were only possible by infringing private ownership, and they all laid the basis for the further development not only of agricultural production but for the countryside in Finland as a whole.

The development of Finnish agriculture during the post-war period was highly dependent – at least at the political level – on a nexus of contracts and interplay between a numbers of actors. Overall, the principal aims of Finnish agricultural policy since the first years of independence have been efficiency, self-sufficiency in farm products, an adequate income level for the farming population, ensuring the availability of foodstuffs at reasonable prices, and the need to maintain habitation over the whole country. In the corporatist system, the role played by the farmers' interest group, The Central Union of Agricultural Producers and Forest Owners (MTK), was paramount, and through it the farmers succeeded in influencing national (agricultural) policy. The corporate decision-making process enabled MTK to obtain a more powerful position in negotiations even during the last decades of the 20th century than it should have had in proportion to the share of agriculture in GDP and the number of members in the interest group.[12]

Private ownership of land is a key factor in understanding the development of Finnish agriculture. For example, in 2002 private persons owned 88 per cent of farms, heirs and family companies eleven, corporations, foundations and cooperatives 0.7, and the state, municipalities and parishes 0.1 per cent. The family ownership of farms was not questioned in public debate, and it seems evident that other modes of ownership were simply not regarded as possible in Finland because of the strong traditions of private ownership of farms.[13]

Small family farms rose in importance in Finland, as in many other European countries as well, from the late 19th century on, and large-scale farming based on wage work disappeared almost totally by the mid-20th century. Estate farming, on the other hand, was never widespread in Finland, and therefore

76

Market gardening emerged as a viable business during the late 20th century. The cultivation of produce such as tomatoes and cucumbers was made possible during the winter by the use of heated greenhouses. The long hours of daylight in summer also proved beneficial for this type of agriculture.

throughout its history the farm sizes have were relatively small. The small size of the farms is partly related to the climate: it has been argued that it takes more time to take care of twenty cows in Finland than fifty cows in France or 150 cows in New Zealand. Thus, for example in 1995, the average number of cows per dairy farm in Finland was only 11, while in Germany it was 23, in Sweden 26, in Denmark 40, and in Great Britain 64.

From the mid-19th century on, the land area of farms increased through the parcelling out of the forests, which before had been state-owned with the peasants having only usufructure of them. However, that did not increase the area of arable land. Furthermore, from the mid-19th century on, the average size of farms decreased owing to settlement and the partition of farms. The rural settlement measures favouring small farms that were implemented in the early years of independence and after the Second World War resulted in the fact that during the 1950s the typical farm was small, around 5 to 10 hectares (Figure 3.1). In the early 20th century, owing to the Land Acquisitions Acts and the Leaseholders' Act, the number of small farms increased rapidly as the crofters now got to own the land they had previously rented. Similarly, these laws increased the number of active farms. During the 1920s, over six million hectares of land changed owners, and over 130,000 new farms were created. In 1950, around 13 per cent of all active farms had been created right after independence by the Leaseholders' Act and 19 per cent by the land acquisition laws

after the war. Thus the "old" farms constituted below 70 per cent of all farms, although the area of arable land and the number of animals on the "old" farms was higher than on the "new" farms.[14]

Land acquisition by the state after the Second World War has been criticised for slowing down urbanisation, making agriculture unproductive, causing overproduction, and creating the need to subsidise farming in the postwar era. However, since the towns in Finland did not provide enough opportunities and the country did not have anything else to offer, resettlement in the countryside was an act of necessity in the post-war situation. Even in the 1930s it was realised that land acquisition was not necessarily rational in economic terms; however, it was necessary in order to keep peace in society after the Civil War. The land acquisition acts had long-term consequences. First, the average size of Finnish farms decreased owing to the fact that the new farms were small, practically all below 15 hectares. Second, the resettlement partly delayed the urbanisation process in Finland, which began only during the 1960s, when

78

Reindeer herding has
been an important
source of livelihood for
the Saami, the indige-
nous people of Lapland,
the northernmost part
of Finland.
The nomadic way of life
of the Saami is disap-
pearing, as modern
technology, notably in
the form of the snowmo-
bile, has made reindeeer
herding easier.

people from the rural areas started to move *en masse* to the urban areas. Third, again partly owing to the resettlement, agriculture remained one of the most important sources of livelihood for the majority of the people. Fourth, resettlement was one of the major reasons for the problems related to the overproduction of agricultural produce during the 1960s and 1970s.[15]

The problems related to the small size of farms were also recognized in government measures: from the early 1960s on, the focus of Finnish agricultural policy was to rationalise by increasing the size of farms. The total number of farms decreased rapidly – partly owing to the policies adopted, partly to "natural" development; from 1972 to 1992, approximately 5,500 farms were closed down every year, and the number of dairy farms halved in each decade. The average size of a farm in the late 1960s was still under ten hectares, while in the late 1980s it was around 12.5 hectares, in 1990 about 17 hectares, and in 2002 it was already 30 hectares.[16]

The role played by the cooperatives is central in Finnish agriculture and its status within the Finnish economy during the 20th century. For example, the cooperatives contributed to the maintenance of small family farms. Especially in dairy farming, the introduction of the centrifugal cream separator made it possible for farmers to sell better quality butter and cream through these cooperatives. As far as cooperatives were concerned, Finland was not an exceptional case: a similar development can be found in all the other Nordic countries and in a number of central European countries as well. All in all, the cooperatives played an important role in transforming, modernizing and reorganising Finnish agriculture throughout the 20th century.[17]

During the early 20th century, a number of local and national cooperatives were created to buy the farmers' products, to process them and market them to customers. Cooperatives were seen, at least at the time when they were established, as institutions that satisfied people's needs better than purely business-oriented organisations as they were jointly owned by the rural people themselves. Thus there was a pronounced ideological emphasis attached to the creation of the cooperatives. There were usually local cooperatives for different products, but they united to form powerful and influential national cooperatives. These national cooperatives, such as *Valio* and *Enigheten* in dairy products, *Atria, LSO,* and *Portti* (and their predecessors) in meat, and *Metsäliitto* in forestry, were farmer-controlled marketing organisations. They also had an important impact on industrialisation in the country, especially in the food industry. Other specialised cooperatives were established to sell machines and equipments to farmers (*Hankkija* and *Labor*), and there were even retail and credit cooperatives in rural areas (*SOK* in retail trade, and *Osuuspankki* in banking). In addition to the cooperatives, naturally there were also a number of privatively owned companies operating in the same lines of business.

Common to all these cooperatives was the fact that, although they were "companies", they did not act according to the "rules" of the market economy; the aim of the cooperatives was not to create value-added but to take care of the

80

Immediately after the Second World War, the key issue in domestic politics was the resettlement of soldiers and evacuees from the ceded Karelia region. The process was accelerated by a land acquisition act. Altogether 100,000 new homesteads were founded and by 1950 constituted around nineteen per cent of all active farms. New land for cultivation was cleared intensively, as in the Häme region pictured here. In the background, a typical house of the late 1940s and 1950s.

interests of the owners, namely the rural population generally. Thus, for example, the aim of *Metsäliitto* (a forest cooperative) was not only to sell forest products (pulp, paper, timber) profitably, but also to buy raw wood at a reasonable price from the forest owners. Rather than produce "market value", *Valio*'s major aim was to keep producer prices of milk at a reasonable level, just as was it was the objective of *Atria* and other meat cooperatives to achieve the same with the price of meat. A major change occurred in cooperative structures during the 1980s and 1990s: in practice all national cooperatives were reformed to be more market-oriented. This had a huge impact on the commercialisation of the whole "agribusiness" in Finland. For example, *Valio* was no longer (necessarily) the most "reliable" buyer of milk-products; neither was *Atria* of meat, nor *Metsäliitto* of raw wood. Furthermore, some cooperatives, like *Hankkija*, went bankrupt. In many parts of the country, however, (small) local cooperatives held their ground – and some of them even broke away from the national cooperatives.[18]

Throughout history, agriculture has been associated with a number of related activities, such as fishing, hunting and forestry, as agriculture itself has provided only a basic livelihood for the people. Farmers have therefore sought auxiliary incomes, for example, in industry and services, either as wage-earners or as private entrepreneurs. The employment of extra labour in agriculture, on the other hand, has been rare, except on the largest farms. Statistics show that in 1951 and 1952, 55.6 per cent of the average income of Finnish farmers came from agriculture, 28.3 per cent from forestry, and 15.3 per cent from secondary sources. The proportion of additional income was larger in small farms. In 2002, over a quarter of Finnish farmers practised other forms of entrepreneurship besides traditional farming; almost 70 per cent of them were engaged in various services such as contracting and tourism. In many parts of the country, one can argue, forestry is actually a more important source of income for farmers than agriculture. In general, the arable land area is larger and correspondingly, the forest area is smaller in the south than in the north.[19]

Productivity in agriculture over the long term

The development of Western economies can be characterised by a decline in the aggregate input in producing farm products. This includes both the use of arable land and the number of livestock, as well as a decrease in the input of labour. Land-saving and labour-saving technologies that benefited the growth of productivity must be dealt with separately. Land-saving technologies include all the means used to increase the output per hectare, whether it is new crop rotations, the introduction of clover and other plants to increase the nitrogen fertilisation of cereal crops, the more efficient use of manure, or the chemical fertilizers that became general in Finland during the latter part of the 20th century. Labour-saving technologies include all kinds of machinery introduced into agriculture especially from the late 19th century on, when first iron and steel tools, and then motive power revolutionised agricultural technology. A third catgory, livestock-saving technologies, made it possible for example to produce more dairy products with the same amount of cows, or to rise beef cattle with better animal feed (e.g. cattle cakes). Advisory organisations and developed agricultural training have played an important role in the use of land-, labour- and animal- saving technologies. The productivity of plant and cattle breeding has increased significantly. Thus agriculture has generally changed from being a "natural" activity to a scientific one, with a resulting increase in productivity. At the same time, there has been a shift to more capital-intensive production.[20]

In Finland, too, the growth in productivity was a result of technological development, and from the late 19th century on it enabled the feeding of the Finnish people with lower labour and land inputs into agricultural production. At the end of the 18th century, growth in agricultural production in Finland was primarily not based on a rise in labour productivity, but rather on an increased use of resources. Firstly, it was based on the growth of the arable land area as a result of clearing land for cultivation. Secondly, it was based on an increase in labour intensity, especially after new rotations gave way to more labour-intensive modes of agricultural production. Thirdly, it was based on an increase in

82

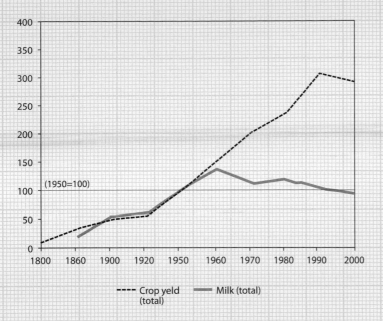

Figure 3.3 Production indices of total crop yield and milk production in Finland, 1800–2000 (1950=100)[*]

Sources: See figure 3.2.

[*] The figure is based on the combined crop yield of wheat, rye, barley, and oats in kilograms, and the production of milk in litres. The milk production for the years 1860–1960 has been taken from Viita (1965), and from official statistics thereafter. The crop yield of slash-and-burn cultivation is not included as it does not show up in the statistics. Further details available from the authors by request.

The production of milk and crop yield have increased significantly from the beginning of the 19th century. While total milk production peaked in the 1960s, crop yields continued to grow up to the early 1990s.

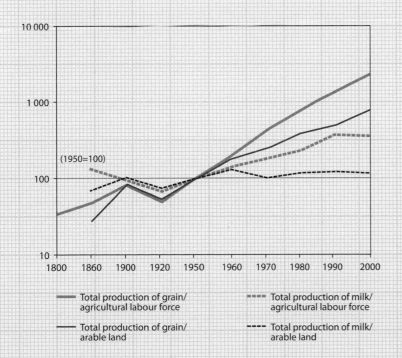

Figure 3.4 Estimated productivity indices in Finnish agriculture 1800–2000 (1950 = 100)

Sources: See figure 3.2.

Up to the mid-20th century, the growth in production in agriculture mainly resulted from increases in inputs (especially the area of arable land and the labour force), while the impressive productivity increase after the Second World War was a result of the more intensive use of resources, in terms of both labour and land productivity. On the whole, as a result of the decreasing size of the labour force and increased yields, the growth in productivity, especially during the latter part of the 20th century, has been enormous.

the number of livestock. This resulted not in a growth in the average size of the farms but in the number of production units. According to Arvo M. Soininen (1975), there is no evidence that there was a significant shift in productivity in crop production in the period 1720–1870. From the point of view of standard of living, it is interesting to note that there was in the same period no significant shift in arable land per capita. There was, however, a slight increase in yield-to-seed ratios of rye and barley between the middle of the 16th century and the beginning of the 19th century. This was caused by new methods in agriculture (rotations) and the increased use of manure. A short-sighted policy to increase the food supply caused by high population growth rates resulted in uneconomical farming in the long run. Crop fields were expanded at the expense of pastures, which resulted in a lack of manure, and yields per acre began to decline.[21] In the southern part of the country, the relation of arable field to pasture in the end of the 18th century was 1:2.8 and in the 1870s 1:1.7.

The area of arable land, the size of the agricultural labour force and the number of farms increased from the 16th century up to the 1970s (Figure 3.2). New farms were established, and new land was cleared for agricultural use especially from the mid-19th century up to the first decades of the 20th century. The arable land area decreased during the post-war era by about one fifth, the number of farms to a quarter and the agricultural labour force to one eighth. However, at the same time the production of the crop yield (the combined production of wheat, rye, barley and oats) increased almost threefold, and total milk production decreased by about one third. Thus productivity in the agricultural sector grew. (Figures 3.3 and 3.4)

During the 20th century the mean size of farms began to grow (Figure 3.5). To put it simply, one can argue that productivity corresponds with the size of a farm; the average size of farms (arable land in use) increased threefold after the Second World War. On the other hand, it has been emphasized that small farms actually operate quite efficiently.[23] The growth in the number of average-size farms during the 1980s was approximately at the same level as in EC countries at the time. During the 1990s, the productivity of agriculture increased more rapidly, for instance, in Sweden and in Denmark than in Finland. In OECD countries, the productivity growth rate of agriculture was higher than the growth of productivity in manufacturing or services, or the growth of productivity per capita GDP during the post-war era. However, the agricultural labour force decreased more rapidly in Finland than in Western European countries on average. The productivity of Finnish agriculture had already increased significantly before the Second World War, but right after the war it diminished: productivity in 1947 and 1948 was a quarter lower than it had been before the war. From the early 1950s on, however, agricultural productivity increased again, but not as much as in Finnish industry (see also Hjerppe and Jalava in this volume).[24]

The growth in productivity during the post-war period in the Finnish agricultural production was due to the modernisation and commercialisation of

84

Wintertime in the countryside: silage bales and the tracks of a hare.

agriculture. Commercialisation and specialisation made it possible for farmers to increase their production and concentrate on farming, when previously it had been essential for them to obtain income from other sources. A number of factors contributed to the modernisation of agriculture; these included the biological and natural conditions for agricultural production; urbanisation and industrialisation, which lay behind the demand for agricultural products, and also supplied tools and machinery for agricultural production; and the professional activities of farmers, including training, education and the services provided by a number of advisory organisations. In the end, modernisation is highly dependent on the possibilities of the individual farm to adapt to innovations, whether in terms of the farmer's attitudinal readiness for change or his financial prospects.[26]

Technological innovations that had an affect to the productivity growth include not only the mechanisation of agricultural production, but also plant and cattle breeding, the education of farmers, farm advisory organisations, and so. Human capital formation in terms of better education of farmers can be characterised on three levels. First, the required knowledge was acquired through "on-job-training", as father and mother introduced their youngsters to agriculture. This was supplemented with organised agricultural consultation from the 19th century on, and lastly, with formal training, which from the mid-20th century also included secondary, and even tertiary (university) level education. This was tied up with spreading of the new comprehensive school system and upper secondary schools to rural areas during the postwar period.

During the early modern period, new rotations decreased the area of fallow land, although they increased the use of labour. Even hay was introduced into the rotation (the so-called *koppeli* cultivation system), which intensified land use even more. The "green revolution" in agriculture, which started in the 16th century, brought along better, industrially produced ploughs that allowed the cultivation even of clay soil. The use of artificial fertilizers and pesticides became general in Finland fairly late. Irrigation as such was not needed, as there is usually enough rain water during the summer time. The second mechanisation period occurred from the 1950s to the 1970s, when tractors replaced horses, and combine harvesters became general.[28]

The coming of tractors to farming is usually taken as an indicator of the mechanisation of agriculture. Tractors not only enabled the use of more productive methods in cultivating and harvesting arable land, but also increased the area of production as land was not needed anymore to feed the horses that were previously used on farms. The number of tractors surpassed the number of horses during the 1960s. In the 1930s, there was approximately one tractor to every 200 farms, while by the late 1970s practically every farm had at least one tractor (see Table 3.3). In cereal cultivation, the single most important technological innovation that was taken into common use was the self-propelled combine harvester.[29] In forest work, the chainsaw also made a huge impact since, especially for small farms, wood felling by traditional methods had provided important ex-

86

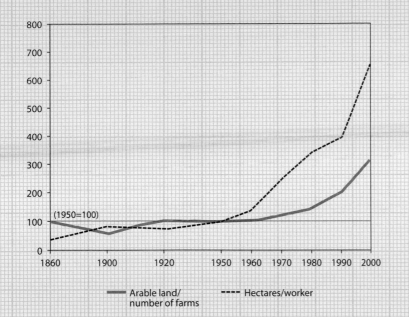

Figure 3.5. Average size and hectarage of Finnish farms, 1860–2000 (1950 = 100)

Sources: See figure 3.2.

Productivity corresponds to the size of a farm. The average size of farms (arable land in use) increased threefold after the Second World War. Hectarage (arable land in proportion to the agricultural labour force) increased even more significantly, thus reflecting the technological development in agricultural production.

tra incomc. Consequently, technological development generally led to structural change and even to internal emigration from the countryside to the towns.

Cattle breeding, better feeding, improvements in dairy barns and milking machinery, as well as farming advice and the overall professionalisation of agriculture were all reflected in the growth of productivity, particularly in dairy production. During the early modern period, on average one cow produced around 300–400 kg milk in a year, by the mid-19th century around 500– 600 kg/year, and at the beginning of the 20th century already 1,000 kg/year. Thereafter, the growth in productivity has been rapid, since in 1950 on average one cow produced approx. 3,300 kg milk in a year, while in the late 1960s the production was already around 4,000, and in 2002 the average yield was 7,100 kg of milk a year.[30] Mechanisation alone cannot explain the growth in productivity in milk production, although mechanical milking machines and highly equipped dairy barns made it possible to increase the number of cows on farms: thus, the number of cows per farm rose. The growth of milk production per cow was mainly related to the cattle control system, which included all kinds of counselling on matters ranging from animal feeding to best-practice working methods.

In work in the fields, mechanisation was by no means the most important factor in the productivity growth; mechanisation in field crops resulted in greatly increased hectarage[31]. The use of fertilizers significantly increased the crop yield. Environmental considerations such as the pollutant impact of agriculture aroused increased debate in the latter part of the 20th century as the massive use of fertilizers began. However, their use decreased during the 1990s, owing to growing interest in organic production, on the one hand, and because of a decrease in production on the other. Moreover, fertilizers have been developed in a way that has made it possible to reduce the amounts used. During the 1980s, the use of fertilizers increased from approx. 1,000 million kilos to 1,200 million kilos, but during the 1990s it decreased to approx. 750 million kilos (in 2002). Comparing the amount of fertilizers used to the area in production shows that the decrease in their use was over 35 per cent in the period 1990–2002.[32] The organic production of dairy products started in the 1960s. With state-subsidized organic production, the number of organic farms grew to 671 in 1990 and to 5,000 in 2001. Finnish organic farms comprised 6.5 per cent of all Finnish farms in 2001 and occupied 5.5 per cent of the country's arable area; in other words, 150,000 hectares was under organic cultivation.[33]

Although the growth of productivity during the postwar period enabled more production with less human input, it required more capital input. Therefore, agricultural production changed from being labour-intensive to capital-intensive. The productivity of capital, and with it, the total factor productivity has not necessarily developed as favourably as labour and land productivity. This also resulted in the fact that despite the relative increase in productivity, agricultural production was not profitable during the 1990s. This caused financial difficulties for some individual farms that had invested in more efficient machines and better facilities.[34]

The general attitude in rural areas towards modernisation has been favourable. Efficient farm production, modern production machines and facilities, commercialisation, and progressiveness are regarded by the farmers as positive values. They were also supported by governmental agricultural policy; for example, the taxation system supported (even to excess) investments in modern production technology, such as tractors, from the late 1960s on. The positive attitude towards investments can be seen in the fact that in the period 1995–2002 around one fifth of the production costs in Finnish agriculture came from machinery and equipment. Together with building costs (10 per cent), investments constituted almost one third of all production costs. The high relative share of investments can be partly explained by the fact that the proportion of hired labour in production costs was below 10 per cent as "outside" labour was not common in Finnish agriculture.[35]

Conclusions

The history of Finnish agriculture has been a continuous readjustment to climatic and geographical constraints as well as to political, economic and technological changes (Table 3.4). The agricultural sector also contributed vitally to the creation and development of the welfare society as whole. The role of

88

Year	Tractors	Horses	Tractors/1000 hectares	Horses/1000 hectares
1920	147	391,000	0.07	193.66
1938	5,916	350,000	2.35	139.17
1950	17,000	409,000	6.99	168.24
1960	87,000	225,000	33.03	85.42
1970	155,000	90,000	56.30	32.69
1980	220,000	21,000	87.82	8.38
1990	235,000	44,000	112.55	21.07
2000	332,584	58,000	165.79	28.91

Table 3.3 The number of tractors and horses on Finnish farms

Sources: Aarnio 1987, 99; Jussila 1987, 53; Tilastokatsaus 2003, 35; Maataloustilastollinen 2002; STV, Suomen tilastollinen vuosikirja (Statistical Yearbook of Finland); SVT, Suomen Virallinen Tilasto III, Maatalouslaskenta 1992, 262.

The number of tractors has grown from the 1950s on, while the number of horses has diminished during the same period of time. While there was hardly one tractor to every 10,000 hectares in 1920, by 2000 there was a tractor for every 10 hectares under cultivation. Moreover, the average power of tractors has increased significantly, and other new tools have been employed. For an individual farm, the purchase of a tractor was a huge investment. In 2000, for example, tractors alone constituted about 50 per cent of the value of sales of all farm machinery. In addition, various kinds of accessories and equipment for tractors (ploughs, harrows, fertilizers, and trailers) together constituted over 25 per cent of all investments.*

* http://www.finfood.fi/ (cited 28th January 2004).

Time period	Main features
From the Middle Ages to mid-18th century	Natural economy, spread of settlement, famines (especially in the late 17th century), population growth from the 18th century on, slash-and-burn cultivation predominant in eastern parts of Finland
From the mid-18th century to the late 19th century	Accelerating population growth, general parcelling out of land, demise of slash-and-burn cultivation, early commercialisation (exports of dairy products, imports of grain), the last known peacetime famine in western Europe (late 1860s)
From the beginning to the middle of the 20th century	Land Acquisition and Leaseholder Acts, cooperatives, emphasis on small family farms
From the 1960s to the 1990s	Overproduction, depopulation of the countryside, urbanisation, growth of productivity in agriculture
From the 1990s to the third millennium	Adaptation to European Union legislation, decrease of the number of farms, rapid productivity growth

Table 3.4 The development of Finnish agriculture from the late Middle Ages to the third millennium

The history of Finnish agriculture has been a continuous readjustment to climatic and geographical constraints, as well as to political, economic and technological changes. Family farms have remained the dominant form of ownership throughout history. There were major periods of change: the first was during the 16th century, when settlement spread to new areas using the slash-and-burn technique; the second happened from the mid-18th century on, when the accelerating population growth was sustained by increased agricultural production; the third period began in the early years of independence, when agricultural policies emphasized small family farms; the fourth started in the early 1960s, when overproduction became a problem and urbanisation really began; the final period was from the mid-1990s on, when agriculture was forced to adapt to European Union legislation.

The northern frontier of agriculture: dairy farming at Utsjoki in northern Lapland.

the state was important in manoeuvring, controlling, constraining, restricting, subsidising, and enabling agricultural production.

In the case of Finland, the increase in agricultural production was a result of an increase in the cultivated area and labour up to the turn of the 20th century. Self-sufficiency in dairy products was already achieved in the late 19th century, but it was not until the mid-20th century that self-sufficiency in cereals was gained. Thereafter overproduction has shadowed the development of Finnish agriculture. For ages, agriculture was associated with other sources of livelihood that were available in the rural areas. Particularly forestry played an important role here.

The primary sector contributed substantially to the development of society. The reforms in land ownership carried out in the first years of independence can be seen as the first steps towards the welfare society. This was continued after the Second World War, when agricultural land was distributed to the demobilised men and evacuees from the eastern parts of Finland that were lost to Soviet Union. Throughout the 20th century, the agrarian parties together with the farmers' interest group played an active role in getting the reforms enacted.

The whole development of Finnish agriculture can easily be seen deterministically, as if it was a matter of necessity, as if the actors, whether politicians, technology developers or individual farmers, did not really have any other choice than to pursue the measures that they took. Change and modernisa

90

tion are usually seen as matters of necessity, although at the same time the "nature" of agricultural production as history-dependent and slow to change and of agriculture itself as a conservative and homogeneous activity is also underlined. Sometimes agriculture is regarded more as a way of life than as a source of livelihood. Not able to cope with the rapid structural changes and growth of the economy, agriculture opted for modernisation, which meant among other things the growth of the average size of farms in Western countries and the mechanisation of production.[36] In this modernisation process, the actors actively sought opportunities for more efficient production.

As an outcome of the technological development, farming took on the characteristics of factory-like production – "an industrial logic or ideal in agriculture" emerged, as Deborah Fitzgerald has pointed out in the case of the United States – and the primary sector was commercialized towards the "agribusiness".[37] Although the commercialisation or industrialisation of agriculture in the Finnish case did not reach the level of the United States or some other major agricultural producers, the progress made in Finland has nevertheless been significant – especially taking into consideration its climatic, geographical, population and capital constraints.

The landscape at Kauhava, western Finland. The two high buildings are crop dryers, which are necessary owing to the short growing season.

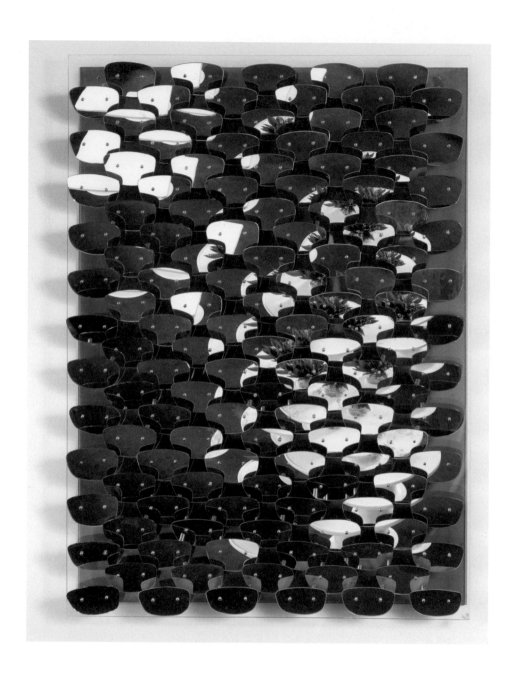

"Rush Hour"

by Eero Hiironen

(1971, plexiglass and mirror, 125 x 90 cm)

Business: Rooted in Social Capital over the Centuries

Jari Ojala and Petri Karonen

During the past two decades, Finnish companies have grown and are now among the world leaders in certain business sectors. Companies such as Nokia, Stora-Enso, UPM-Kymmene, Amer, Vaisala, and Kone are known worldwide. We argue that co-operation among the companies, together with the co-evolution of business and society, can at least partly explain the long-term evolution of Finnish business.

Introduction

Finnish business, at least big business, has to a large extent become integrated into the global, or at least the European, economy during the last five hundred years. In certain sectors of industry, most notably telecommunications and the forest industry, Finnish companies have caught up with the traditional market leaders in terms of sales, volume of production, profitability, and productivity.[1] The domestic markets have been relatively modest, and thus business has sought markets abroad (see Kaukianen in this volume). Up to the 1940s, the competitive advantages of Finnish business were cheap, mainly forestry-based, raw materials and inexpensive labour costs (see also Hjerppe and Jalava in this volume). Thereafter, factors such as human capital (see Asplund and Maliranta in this volume) and cheap energy have usually been cited as Finnish advantages.

Thus Finnish business has throughout history been constrained by external pressures (see Figure 4.1). Nevertheless the entrepreneurs, managers, and companies have been able to make independent decisions, and Finnish business has grown and has witnessed major structural changes.

We argue that certain Finnish modes of doing business can be found – and that these modes have remained fairly similar over the centuries. The first, to use a term introduced by Alfred Chandler (1990), is cooperative capitalism. In other words, close relationships and long term co-operation within and between companies in different industrial sectors. A second characteristic with regard to co-operation is the close, co-evolutionary development of business and Finnish society as whole. These vertical links between the state and the corporations have played an important role ever since the birth of the strong national state of Sweden (c. 1520), which at that time included Finland as well.

We are, however, fully aware that neither the co-operation between the firms, nor the co-evolution of business and society can fully explain the development of Finnish business over the centuries. Thus this article should be understood as view of this development which omits a number of other explanatory factors such as the longevity of business enterprises, structural change in business and in industry in particular, and the overwhelming constraints created by a small population (and thus, small domestic markets), thin capital markets, inadequate raw material resources, and an autarchic economy that lasted up to the beginning of the 20th century. Nor can we here deal in adequate detail with factors like ownership structure. Furthermore, in analysing factors such as social capital and co-evolution, we cannot undertake any straightforward accounting exercises as these factors do not show up in total productivity in growth accounting exercises. Rather, we are forced to settle for a narrative analysis and indicate their importance through illustrative cases.

Business enterprises make decisions under the pressures created by competitive and institutional forces; in order to survive and be successful, a firm has to adjust its strategy to these forces. Figure 4.1 illustrates the competitive and institutional forces that have affected Finnish business over the centuries.

Water power provided by rapids was a key element in industrialisation in Finland. The first ironworks and industrial communities were situated beside rapids, as in this picture of Kyröskoski Paper Mill in the late 19th century.

By competitive forces we refer to supply and demand side factors, like international market fluctuations and competition, the supply and quality of raw materials and labour, the adoption of new technologies, and general entry and exit barriers. By institutional forces we refer to the formal and informal constraints pointed out by the new institutional economists, for example.[2] As regards demand, export markets are vital for a small country such as Finland (as noted by Yrjö Kaukiainen in this volume), and in these markets Finnish business has faced international competition. As forest industry products were for a long time the most important export items, the competition has come from countries and areas producing similar products. With tar exports, for example, the American colonies hindered the possibilities for Finnish tar on the vital British markets up to the independence of United States, but from the 1770s on tar exports to Britain expanded. Similarly with timber exports: again on the vital Brit-

Among the first paper manufacturers were J. C. Frenckell & Son in Tampere, whose paper mill, pictured here, was established in the late 18th century. The company acquired the first paper machine in Finland in 1841. The machine used rags as the raw material for paper. Paper production expanded in the late 19th century and in the 1860s the first paper mills using conifer fibre were built. The town of Tampere is often regarded as the cradle of industrialisation in the country.

ish market, timber imports from the colonies (most notably Canada) provided obstructive competition up to the 1830s. In the paper and pulp industry, Finnish business has faced competition from Scandinavian producers (most notably Sweden and Norway), and also from domestic production in central Europe and Britain, where the markets have been located from the 1920s onwards.

On the supply side, factors of production have affected potential. For a long time, cheap labour costs and low-priced raw materials were advantages for Finnish business (as pointed out by Hjerppe and Jalava and Hannikainen and Heikkinen in this volume), however, during the 20th century, know-how and research and development (i.e. human capital generally) have taken on greater importance (as noted by Asplund and Maliranta in this volume). Technological development has also played a role, Finnish business being for a long time rather an exploiter of existing technology than an innovative creator of new methods and appliances.[3]

Institutions, or "rules of the game", as Douglass C. North (1990) calls them, include not only formal, usually governmentally enforced, structures but also informal codes of conduct and business culture generally. Within the formal rules especially governmental regulation and the close relationship between business and society from the mercantilist era onwards should be noted.

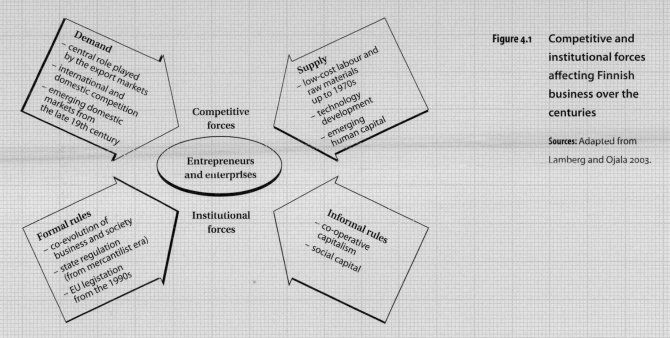

Figure 4.1 Competitive and institutional forces affecting Finnish business over the centuries

Sources: Adapted from Lamberg and Ojala 2003.

The decisions made by entrepreneurs and enterprises over the centuries have been constrained by changing competitive and institutional forces. By competitive forces we refer to factors of demand and supply, like the important role played by export markets and the low production costs that were typical of Finland for a long time – and still are to some extent even today. This article focuses on the institutional forces, which change more slowly, including both formal (mainly governmentally) enforced "rules of the game" and more informal codes of conduct. Of the former, the co-evolution of business and society, and, of the latter, co-operative capitalism should be stressed in the case of Finnish business.

Within the informal constraints, the co-operation among businessmen and companies (i.e. the social capital) is stressed.

This article attempts to link the evolution of Finnish business over the past five hundred years to general trends in capitalist development, that is to the partly overlapping phases of merchant, industrial, financial, and global capitalism.[4] The timing and forms of these periods differ in the case of Finland from those of some other Western European countries. Thus merchant capitalism in the Finnish case can be dated from the late 17th to the end of the 19th century, whilst in Britain, for example, it is usually placed to bit earlier. Similarly, the last period, global capitalism, started in Finland only in the mid-1980s after the opening-up and internationalising of the financial markets (see García-Iglesias and Kilponen in this volume), while in other Western economies the change is usually dated to the end of the Second World War.

This analysis focuses on "big business", though the concept of big business is relative and shifting as a result of the long time period and different types of dynamics in the afore-mentioned eras analysed in this article. In the article, we have tried to trace the development of the largest enterprises or most important entrepreneurs in different periods by using various kinds of measures (Tables 4.1 – 4.4). For the earliest period (1800), we only have data available for the property of the entrepreneurs; for the second one the value of production of the largest industrial enterprises (for 1913) has been found, and for the last two intersecting years the value of sales of the largest companies in Finland is presented. Therefore, these figures are not strictly commensurable, but they still reveal at least the basic patterns of growth and change within Finnish business over the centuries.

In the following, a short introduction to the basic concepts (co-operation and co-evolution) is first given; then the development of Finnish business in four different periods is described briefly, followed by some concluding remarks.

Co-operative capitalism and the co-evolution of business and society

An efficient business organisation is commonly assumed to rely on the notion that firms only seek co-operation for short term returns. Furthermore, it is usually stated that this co-operation is limited by formal institutional regulations, like the anti-cartel laws of the USA and similar legislation in the EU. Of especial interest are the links between corporations and financial institutions. Alfred D. Chandler (1990) and others have noted that in certain countries co-operative capitalism has been a typical feature for a long time. In these countries, the co-operative groups are usually relatively stable and long-term in nature.[5] Whereas in the US "big business" competed aggressively for market shares and profits, in Germany many companies preferred to co-operate, states Chandler. We argue that a similar co-operative mode of doing business was typical throughout the 20th century in Finland, and indeed even before that. And that it is still to some extent the case even today.

Co-operative capitalism can be easily misunderstood as a counterpart to the American type of competitive capitalism or the British type of personal capitalism – as if no competition existed in cooperative capitalism. However, there is a lot of competition in co-operative capitalism as well, though it is perhaps not as visible as in the other two types. The competition within the co-operating groups was sometimes tight and tough, as a number of detailed analyses of the Finnish co-operative structures in different periods of time reveals.[6]

The co-operation between (industrial) companies is usually explained through the notions of competitive constraints. Theories of resource dependence and transaction costs, for example, are used to explain the co-operation as arising from the need for vital resources. The need for resources leads to vertical integration within the industry or cluster level and to horizontal integration within the industry in order to obtain scale advantages. Horizontal co-operation *between* the industrial sectors is far more complicated. Authors like Glete (1994), Orru & al. (1992), and others have concluded that co-operation is related not only to the competitive environment but also to the institutional environ-

98

ment of the organisations (see also Figure 4.1). Organisations such as business companies are in evolving interaction with these institutions. Therefore, the institutions must be seen as dynamic rather than static, though slowly changing, structures that constrain the organisations' activities. This co-evolution of institutions and organisations is in this article understood as one of the basic explanatory characteristics of Finnish business over the long term.[7] Therefore, the evolution of Finnish business is tightly coupled to the national, or rather societal, context – keeping in mind the fact that Finland was part of Sweden up to 1809, and thereafter up to its independence in 1917 a part of imperial Russia.

In the Finnish case, the co-operation among businessmen and companies was more or less a matter of necessity over the centuries. This was due to the fact that they lacked vital resources – especially physical and human capital. The terms "high entry costs" and "lack of physical capital" are here understood as a lack of capital to be invested in business – whether it was, for example, for ships in the late eighteenth century merchant house, or for new and expensive machinery for the forest industry in the latter part of the twentieth century. Therefore, at least in capital-intensive lines of business, capital for investments was collected from a large base. The lack of human capital, for its part, is here understood basically as a lack of certain skills needed for efficient business activities – language skills being among the most notable. Therefore, a person who had the required skills acted as an agent for a number of Finnish businessmen – this was a fairly typical feature in the era of merchant capitalism, but even during the 1970s the strong role played by the export cartels can be at least partly be explained by the specialised skills they possessed.

We argue that co-operation was used to overcome the lack of this physical and human capital. Co-operation can thus be understood as social capital, namely as "the resources available though the reciprocal social relations".[8] It can be understood as "generalised trust" between the actors. This means that co-operation on a large scale is only possible in societies that enforce trust between the transacting parties. However, in the Finnish case, the co-operation was for a long time a matter of necessity, and the co-operation between the actors itself created a vital resource that enabled Finnish business to emerge and evolve. Furthermore, as far as more contemporary times are concerned, social capital, understood as the ability to co-operate within and between organisations, is proposed as a major competitive advantage for Finnish firms and the national economy.[9] The co-operative mode of activity can be seen in the fact that the Finnish companies have acted and evolved in a quite similar way over the centuries.

We base our argument not only on co-operation among business organisations and entrepreneurs but also on the links between business and society as whole. This co-evolution of business and society is here understood in a limited sense only as the interaction between business and governmental actors, although other interactive levels can of course also be found. In order to make such an analysis, the vital starting point is that both parties should have an effect on each other's evolutionary development. In this case, we are primarily interested in how formal (governmental) institutions have enabled and constrained the possibilities for businesses to emerge and grow. On the other hand, we are also interested in how the business actors have actively sought possibilities to influence this (political) decision-making. Especially from the early 20th century on, but even during the early modern era, the corporatist political culture made it necessary for companies and businessmen to co-operate in order to seek benefits in the political markets.[10]

Among the oldest metalworking companies is Fiskars, founded in 1649 and still operating. With annual net sales of approx. 600 million euros (2004), the company today is best known for its consumer products, notably scissors and garden tools. The old foundry site "Fiskars Village" still produces some metallic items, although it is now primarily a centre for crafts, design, art, and tourists.

Merchant capitalism

"That foreign trade enriched the country, experience demonstrated to the nobles and country gentlemen, as well as to the merchants; but how, or in what manner, none of them well knew. The merchants knew perfectly in what manner it enriched themselves. It was their business to know it. But to know in what manner it enriched the country, was no part of their business. This subject never came into their consideration, but when they had occasion to apply to their country for some change in the laws relating to foreign trade. It then became necessary to say something about the beneficial effects of foreign trade, and the manner in which those effects were obstructed by the laws as they then stood." (Adam Smith, Wealth of Nations 1776, vol. I, 434)

The citation from Smith's Wealth of Nations (1776) demonstrates a quite clearly the strong role played by the mercantile elite during the era of merchant capitalism – or mercantilism, as Smith described the era. Though Smith, of course, was describing situation in his home country, the same can be said of late-18th-century Sweden and Finland, where the Diet held a strong position, and the Estate of Burghers played an active role in daily politics.[11]

The era of merchant capitalism can be dated in the Finnish case as existing approximately from the turn of the seventeenth century up to the 1870s. Institutionally, business was constrained first and foremost by Swedish mercantile legislation. Secondly, business was constrained by informal institutional structures, which can be summarised as consisting of certain (honest) trade practices, networks and trust. Thirdly, business was concentrated in patriarchally led (family) enterprises such as trading houses and ironworks.

During this era, Finnish big business was mainly conducted by individual merchants, members of the aristocracy and other entrepreneurs. This kind of big business was closely connected with foreign trade in general (export-import, shipping, etc.), but it usually had components of domestic trade and other economic activities as well (see also Kaukiainen in this volume). At least from the mid-18th century on, big business consisted of a variety of different activities as firms expanded through the widespread practice of diversification. Trading houses, ironworks and factories played an important role in this era. The iron ore was mostly transported from Sweden to ironworks that were located near rapids, which provided them with water power. Factories, producing mainly textiles, operated in the larger towns, especially in Turku (Swedish name: Åbo), which was the capital of Finland up to the 1820s.

As joint stock companies were not allowed before the 1860s, the businesses were privatively owned and in the personal possession of the owners. Thus, property records can be used as an indirect measure of the big business of the time, as is done in Table 4.1. Property was concentrated in the hands of wealthy entrepreneurs like Bengt Magnus Björkman (1745–1824), who lived

Jacob Forsell: rent seeker in the age of merchant capitalism

Jakob Forsell (af Forselles after he was promoted to the nobility), a merchant and Mayor of Loviisa, who lived in towns of Hamina and Loviisa in the 18th century, was a particularly successful rent seeker. He was able to acquire almost all available privileges for himself and his home town from the state. He exerted an important background influence when the town of Loviisa was granted a long period of exemption from taxes and special privileges to engage in the trade of certain goods. Forsell himself managed to obtain various kinds of special rights in order to pursue his projects. His work in the Diet in the Age of Liberty (1719–72) showed all the features of an efficient modern business manager. In Hamina Forsell had focused on "traditional" business activities, but by the mid-century his business ventures changed and grew to be very large by Finnish standards. He amassed a huge fortune during the 1740s–1760s. The focus in his business activities shifted from the tar trade to more modern and productive businesses, and soon his shipbuilding and shipping interests were also pushed aside and replaced by iron and sawn goods. At the end of the 1750s, he owned the largest sawmills in Finland and was at that time the only "Finnish" ironworks owner in the eastern part of the realm. He was also a significant landowner. In practice, there was hardly an economic venture of any significance affecting the eastern parts of the country in which Forsell was not involved.

A statue of Jacob Forsell.

in Stockholm but owned large possessions in Finland as well – including six ironworks and a copper mine. Among his possessions was Fiskars Ironworks, a company that was established in the 17th century and is even today among the largest enterprises in Finland. While Björkman is a representative of an ironworks entrepreneur, Anders Roos and Abraham Falander are examples of owners of trading houses, which mainly operated in the western coastal areas of Finland. These trading houses grew in wealth and importance through tar and timber exports and shipping activities, as noted by Yrjö Kaukiainen in this volume. The important role played by social networks is clearly indicated by the fact that the merchant houses of Roos, Falander, Lindskog and Lang mentioned in the Table 1 were all closely related to each others through marriage.

The Swedish state secured the property rights of those few who actually had the privileges to engage in mercantile activities with supportive regulations and protectionist trade barriers. These included, for example, a British type of Navigation Act that restricted foreign trade to domestic vessels (see also Kaukiainen in this volume). Furthermore, the staple town system, created in the 17th century, ranked towns in accordance with their rights to engage in foreign

102

Name	Home town or district	Line of business	Property value in millions of euros (2004)[12]		
Björkman, Bengt	Stockholm (Sweden), and Fiskars (Finland)	Ironworks, trading house	4.5	**Table 4.1**	The ten wealthiest entrepreneurs in Finland in 1800, according to property tax
Roos, Anders	Kokkola	Trading house	2.2		
Bremer, Josef	Turku	Ironworks, factories	1.4		
Falander, Abraham	Vaasa	Trading house, ironworks	1.4		**Source:** Jutikkala 1953.
Augustin, Matts	Turku	Ironworks, trading house	1.1		
Hisinger, Mikael	Fagervik	Ironworks	1.1		
Lindskog, Adolf	Pietarsaari	Trading house	1.0		
Petersén, J. A. (heirs)	Taalintehdas	Ironworks	0.7		
Lang, Johan	Raahe	Trading house	0.7		
af Forselles, Virginia	Strömfors	Ironworks	0.5		

At the start of the 19th century, wealth was concentrated in the merchant houses and owners of the ironworks. While the rich merchant houses were mostly located in the western coastal area (Ostrobothnia), the ironworks were located in the south-western area. All the merchant houses were engaged in a number of activities, including shipping, wholesale and retail trade, tar and timber exports, and they also usually owned some sawmills and even ironworks. The comparisons in the table are made in a quite straightforward manner though there were a number of problems related to the estimation of the value of property: Björkman, for example, also owned property elsewhere, in this case in his home town of Stockholm. Though the deflated property measure can only give a rough indication of the actual wealth of the entrepreneurs at the start of the 19th century, and comparisons with more recent times are not justified, at least some comparisons can nevertheless be made. For example, in 2004 the value of the largest property in Finland according to the taxation records was almost 200 million euros, owned by Aatos Erkko, the owner of the Sanoma-WSOY printing house and newspaper company.

trade. The mercantile elite were able to affect legislation during the Swedish era, especially during the so- called "Age of Liberty" (1719–72), when the Diet held power and convened regularly. Though the Diet did not meet in the early 19th century, some actors were still able to affect political decision-making through the Finnish Senate, which was created when Finland gained autonomous status as a part of imperial Russia. The Finnish Diet assembled from the 1860s onwards, and there the business elite constituted an active player, promoting the interests of trade and industry. Their influence was notable in many economic matters, but it was mainly information and knowledge that individual businessmen gained from these meetings rather than direct benefits as such. Along with the Diet Reform of 1906, the almost self-evident right of business leaders to participate in the Diet as members of the Estate of Burghers came to an end. Thereafter, more corporative organs such as political parties and industry-specific pressure groups were created.

During this period, several institutional changes occurred that had an affect on business. The first major change happened during the first decades of the 17th century, when the position of the central government of Sweden be-

At the dawn of the 20th century, bobbin factories formed an important segment in the forest industry cluster. Later, when plastic bobbins conquered the market, the production of wooden bobbins totally disappeared and numerous companies started to make other wood-based products such as pulp and paper. Pictured here is the wife of the owner of Saastamoinen Bobbin Factory in an advertisement from the late 19th century.

came much stronger. As a result of this, control over the merchants and trading houses was tightened up, and the Crown encouraged the leading businessmen to reorganise their businesses, for example by establishing trade companies for different sectors of trade, as was the practice in several other European countries at the time.[13] Another major institutional change can be dated to the 1720s, when the structure of the Swedish constitution was reformed after Sweden lost its position as a major power in Europe. Legislative measures and subsidies were then aimed specifically at helping Swedish (and hence also Finnish) business. Initially, Finland's annexation into the Russian Empire in 1809 was not as dramatic as might have been expected, as the laws enacted by the Swedes remained in force. Even Swedish currency was still used in retail trade up to the mid-19th century, and the old commerce with Sweden continued for a long time to be regarded as domestic trade (see also García-Iglesias and Kilponen in this volume). The Swedish body of law was partly replaced from the 1860s on by a more liberal one.

The era of merchant capitalism can also be characterised as an era of emerging co-operative capitalism in Finland. Collaboration, trust and reputation were typical attributes of business practices, in both the local and the international arena. As Douglass C. North (1990) has stated, early modes of trade were characterised by personal relationships and locality. In a way, this can be seen as a starting point for explaining Finnish business too in the early modern period. The early bankers and investors of Finnish business consisted actually almost without exception of a small number of men – and sometimes even women – who managed their wealthy trading houses in a patriarchal style. These men financed their own and their relatives' new ventures, but they also participated in undertakings conducted by their close business associates. At the same time, it was not unusual for them to become involved in new and innovative, but also quite risky, business ventures. They can be found for example behind the first industrial enterprises (sawmills, textile mills, engineering works, paper mills and steamboat companies), which started in the early 1860s.[14]

Co-operation among the businessmen was extensive; it was also necessary, above all in order to ensure sufficient capital for investments (such as ships, factories or sawmills) and to obtain relevant information about overseas markets (in most cases the markets for their products were abroad). They also strove to establish long-term business contacts and networks in foreign trade. In these long-term business relationships, the generation and regeneration of respect and credibility was of the utmost importance for both of the transacting parties. In this, however, there was no particular difference between Finnish businessmen and their counterparts in other countries during the same period.

Co-operation was also vital during the era of merchant capitalism owing to the lack of certain skills. Language skills are usually emphasised in the relevant studies. Tapani Mauranen (1981) suggests that approx. 64 per cent of the "highest ranking" Finnish tradesmen during the late 1840s were able to use foreign languages (languages other than Swedish and Finnish), one fifth under-

104

Gösta Serlachius was among the early industrial capitalists in the country. The forest industry company created by him is now part of the M-Real Corporation.

Akseli Gallen-Kallela: Portait of Gustaf Adolf Serlachius, 1887.

stood one foreign language, one fourth two, 11 per cent three, and 8 per cent four. Managerial training was introduced in Finland during the 19th century; before that the skills were mainly obtained by practical training as an apprentice or by getting formal schooling abroad. However, by the early 20th century, the formal education of managers became more common. Owing to their lack of skills in general, businessmen were forced to co-operate, and in fact, "correspondence managers", who took care of the foreign business correspondence for their Finnish principals, were a typical feature of the era.[15]

Industrial capitalism

In Finland industrial capitalism can be regarded as lasting from the mid-nineteenth century up to the mid-twentieth century. Typical features of this period were rapid industrialisation, economic growth and industrial communities dominated by patriarchal ownership, with the forest industry as the leading business sector. Cooperatives also emerged as an important player both in trade and in industry in Finland, as they did in the other Nordic countries. Furthermore, public ownership became more common in big business after limited liability companies were legalised in 1864, although even in the mid-twentieth century a number of large corporations were still family-owned. After the country's independence in 1917, the Finnish state emerged as a major owner of businesses, mainly those engaged in producing intermediate products, such as chemicals or energy for industry. During the first years of independence, certain foreign-owned companies were bought by the state – including Enso-Gutzeit, today part of Stora-Enso, the second largest paper producer in the world. Vertical integration first, and after that the new opportunities provided by technological innovations, most notably the introduction of the steam engine into such a vital lines of businesses as sawmilling and shipping, were characteristic of the changes that took place in big business in the 19th century.

The era of industrial capitalism started with a major institutional change in the 1860s, when the autonomous Grand Duchy of Finland gained a number of concessionary reforms – including more liberal economic regulations, its own currency and the restoration of active parliamentary activity. New markets were found, especially in Russia, but as the total volume of industrial production grew, exports to the west increased as well (see also Kaukiainen in this volume), not to mention the domestic consumption, which for the first time made an important impact on the development of businesses. This development was threatened in 1917 when Finland gained independence. When the Russian Revolution totally closed the vital markets in the east, Finnish business was reformed in order to find new markets in the west. As a consequence of independence, completely new institutions were developed, including new trade policies, as a result of which a number of factors affecting business changed; for example, new legislation on foreign trade and cartels was introduced. Dur-

106

Company	Headquarter	Line of business	Value of production in millions of euros (2004)[17]	Size of work force
Kymmene	Kuusankoski	Forest industry (paper production)	73.0	1956
W. Gutzeit	Kotka	Forest industry (Sawmills)	54.0	1881
Finlayson	Tampere	Textile industry	34.9	2223
A. Ahlström	Noormarkku	Forest industry (Sawmills)	34.9	2129
Ph. U. Strengberg	Pietarsaari	Tobacco industry	28.6	1384
Halla	Kymi	Forest industry	28.6	1341
John Barker	Turku	Textile industry	28.6	1139
Walkiakoski	Sääksmäki	Forest industry (paper production)	28.6	644
Tampella	Tampere	Textile and metal industry	22.2	1494
Tornator	Ruokolahti	Forest industry (sawmills)	22.2	1022

Table 4.2 The ten largest industrial enterprises in Finland in 1912/1913, according to the value of production

Source: Hjerppe 1979

Even the largest industrial enterprises at the start of the 20th century were still relatively small in terms of value of production and the size of their work force. The forest industry was dominant, as six out of the ten largest companies were engaged in this line of business. All of the companies mentioned in the list above were established in the mid-19th century or later. However, there still exist certain links with the situation at the start of the 19th century (Table 4.1): of the companies above, Tampella was founded by the Falander (Wasastjerna) family, and Strengberg's tobacco company was owned at the start of the 19th century by the Lindskog family. It is also possible to trace the roots of certain companies existing today in the table: for example, Kymmene and Walkiakoski are today integral parts of UPM-Kymmene, W. Gutzeit and Tornator in turn are parts of Stora-Enso. Ahlström and Finlayson still exist and the former remains one of the largest enterprises in the country early in the 21st century.

ing the early decades of independence, the Finnish form of corporatism was created, first as an outcome of the central role played by the industrial elite in developing the institutional structure of the young state, and secondly by enabling the labour unions and leftwing parties a more active role in the decision-making process from the 1930s on. The institutional structure created at turn of the 1920s remained more or less in force up to 1995, when Finland joined European Union. (see also Kettunen in this volume)[16]

In 1918, when the country fell into civil war, the business elite was recruited to manage the organisation of the victorious rightist White army. Consequently, they had the opportunity to restructure the institutional environment that remained in place after the war. As they were recruited mostly from the forest industry, the structure adopted was for a long time highly favourable to this particular sector. Three principles crucial for the forestry industry were adopted: 1) a positive attitude towards cartelisation; 2) a trade agreement policy that favoured the export industry; 3) regulations regarding forest ownership.[18]

During the 20th century, (export) cartels were a central element of cooperative capitalism in Finland, although other forms of co-operation also existed. The first cartels in Finland were formed as sales associations during the late 19th century to compete on the Russian markets. After independence, the reformed sales associations (in fact, cartels) were especially important in finding new markets in the west to replace the lost Russian ones. Of particular importance were the associations formed within the forest industry, since that sector constituted the most important export industry. The model for the associations came mainly from Germany, though sales associations were widely known and used throughout the world in the 20th century. As Auquier and Caves (1979) stress, these cartels were part of national trade policies. They were primarily established to secure monopoly profits abroad, but at the same time they also aimed to control competition at home. Thus groups of companies were permitted to organize cartels to exploit the foreign markets. Cartelisation led to a situation where there was no need for industry-wide mergers in the most important sectors such as the forest industry, as there was no "real" competition between the companies. These organisations not only generated concrete benefits in terms of technology and production: companies obtained market information through these organisations, and because of the co-operation they had excellent knowledge of their domestic competitors. There were also a number of international cartels in which Finnish companies actively participated. For example, during the 1930s there were attempts to create a Nordic cartel in the paper industry, and in the latter part of the 20th century Nokia was a member of a European cable cartel for a long time.[19]

The associations caused numerous problems as well. First of all, the individual companies had to adjust their production to the export quotas decided upon jointly within the association. Secondly, in certain cases the associations impeded technological development because their member companies were passive and satisfied with the current situation rather than seeking new innovative ideas. The cartels remained active up to the turn of the 1990s. They ceased to exist first of all as a result of the growth of companies after the consolidation process: the multinational companies no longer needed outsourced marketing organisations. Secondly, new competition regulations in Finland in the early 1990s and the anti-cartel legislation of the European Union made their existence illegal.

Especially after independence, the domestic decision-making system evolved towards the corporatist ideal. It was not only the cartels that influenced the administration, but also other industry-specific or inter-industry interest groups emerged. At the same time, the trade unions, too, gained more influence in decision-making processes. This led to the development of organisational capitalism, as Jürgen Kocka (1999) has described it in the case of Germany. This form of activity included negotiations between industry associations, labour unions and state agencies. Although this structure was created in order to serve the needs of the industrialising society in the middle of industrial capitalism, it has remained stable up to present times. Moreover, during the era of financial capitalism, the interests of financial organisations were also implicated in the system, and the role of the Bank of Finland became pronounced as the major state actor (as also noted in the article by García-Iglesias and Kilponen in this volume).

108

A workshop of the engineering firm, Kone ja Silta Oy, in the early 20th century.

The company is today known as Kone, and it is one of the largest elevator constructors in the world.

In practice, there was no real outward internationalisation of Finnish industrial production during the era (with a few exceptions), although the markets for the products were mostly abroad since the domestic markets were still a quite thin (as described in more detail by Kaukiainen in this volume). However, there was a movement towards inward internationalisation by companies from abroad investing in Finland. In fact, one of the first "real" industrial enterprises was the Finlayson textile company, founded in Tampere in 1820 by a Scotsman called James Finlayson. In the following decades, a number of important companies were established with capital from abroad, including (Enso)-Gutzeit and Tornator. Likewise, a number of ironworks established at the 1860s and 1870s in the eastern parts of Finland were financed by the Russians.[20]

Another factor explaining the industrialisation process in Finland was technological development. Steam power made a breakthrough in the 1860s, after certain legislative changes legalised its use in sawmilling. For example, even in the 1860s below 10 per cent of all industrial power was produced by steam, but by the mid-1870 this share was already around one third and remained at that level up to the turn of the century. Thanks to steam power, the volume and value of timber exports grew rapidly: the value of exports grew sixfold in only 15 years from the beginning of the 1860s. Hydro power gained more importance, especially in the paper industry, thanks to the introduction of the water turbine in the late 19th century. In 1913, 40 per cent of the energy used in industry was generated by hydro power, 35 per cent by steam, and 23 per cent by electricity.[21]

Apart from the steam engine and other new power sources, there were other technological developments that enabled the beginning of Finnish industrialisation. The role played by innovations in the paper industry was especially important. Though the first Fournier paper machines had already been developed at the beginning of the 19th century, it was only in the mid-19th century that the process of using conifer fibre as raw material for paper was developed. The first paper mills of the new type were established at the beginning of the 1860s, and they included a number of companies and production units that still exist today, like Nokia, and the most important units of United Paper Mills.

As early as the 16th century, the Swedish historian Olaus Magnus praised the shipbuilding skills of the Finns. In more recent times, shipbuilding concentrated on icebreakers and luxury cruise ships at shipyards in Helsinki, Turku, and Rauma. In 2006, Norwegian-based Aker Yards employed approx. 3,600 persons at production units in Finland. In the picture is an Azipod propeller system that has revolutionised the manoeuvring of big ships in confined spaces.

Financial capitalism

The era of financial capitalism in Finland can be dated approximately to the period from the early or mid-20th century up to the mid-1990s. A typical feature of financial capitalism was the dominating and co-ordinating role played by financial institutions. Private financial institutions (commercial banks) together with the state-owned Bank of Finland more or less dictated the development of business in this period. The financial institutions might have either direct or indirect control over the major industries through ownership and (credit) client relationships. The emergence of financial capitalism was only made possible by the rise of financial institutions, especially banks. The positive impacts of financial capitalism were the rise of joint stock companies, managerial capitalism, and the professionalisation of business practises generally.

During the 20th century, the most notable characteristics of Finnish big business were vertical integration, followed by related and unrelated diversification. Up to the 1980s, the conglomerate form was dominant, as the largest enterprises diversified into various industrial sectors. For example, at one point in the late 1980s, Nokia had a number different businesses within its organisation, including paper production, computers, televisions, tyres, rubber boots, cables – and mobile phones.[22] These diversified structures were rapidly dismantled from the late 1970s onwards, especially unrelated ones. Companies now began to concentrate on their "core competences" in the global economy thus following the international businesses trends of the time. During the 1980s, there was also horizontal integration and concentration of the companies; the number of companies diminished rapidly through mergers and acquisitions.

The Second Word War affected Finnish business strongly, as after the war a number of industrial units were lost when large areas of eastern Finland were ceded to Russia. Furthermore, the Finns were forced to pay war reparations to the Soviet Union. These reparations included a number of industrial products that had not been manufactured in Finland in large numbers up to that time. (see also Kaukiainen in this volume). The war reparations had several implications for Finnish business. First, the metal industry in particular developed as products like ships and machinery were included in the reparations. Secondly,

the Russian markets were now regained: after the reparations were paid off, bilateral trade with the Soviet Union grew significantly. This had a direct affect on the structure of business and industry. In the long term, the Soviet Union offered a buffer market for the Finns as exports to the East increased in periods when the demand in the West was falling, as was the case after the oil crisis in the 1970s. Finland imported gas and crude oil from the Soviet Union: from the early 1950s to the turn of the 1990s, around 50 to 70 per cent of the imported crude oil came from the Soviet Union, and gas imports started in the mid-1970s. Together with Italy, Sweden and West Germany, Finland was the most important importer of Soviet oil among the Western European countries.[23] The Soviet markets were vital for a long time for some special sectors of industry like textiles, and for certain companies like Nokia.

During the era of financial capitalism, the so-called financial spheres dominated industry in Finland. The industrial spheres were either direct or indirect ownership and control groups, usually associated with the large financial institutions – although state-owned companies also created their own sphere, as did certain cooperative-linked industry. The spheres could dominate and coordinate the actions of several (large) industrial enterprises, for example through interlocking directorates. Industrial spheres provided stability, financial backing, and collaborative inside knowledge within the industry[24]. Thus they provided competitive advantages for corporations operating on the competitive international markets and enabled companies to make investment decisions that might have been impossible for them to implement independently. The control of the industrial spheres was usually limited to the "top" strategy level, that is to major investments, mergers, acquisitions and the appointment of top management.

Especially from the early 1980s on, competition between the dominant bank spheres (the Kansallis Bank, KOP and the Union Bank of Finland, SYP) tightened. Direct ownership of industrial enterprises by the banks, however, had already been restricted in the mid-20th century so that they were allowed to own directly only a ten per cent share in companies. The cross-ownership of companies within the sphere as well as the investment companies of the financial institutions were used to evade this regulation. In practice, power lay in the hands of the financial institutions.[25]

Within the practical organisation of the spheres, the role played by interlocking directorates and the mixture of social and economic relationships between the actors are often stressed. An illustrative case of interlocking directorates is the Kansallis Bank (KOP) sphere during the 1980s. According to Ruostetsaari (1989) and Kuisma (2000, 2004), during the 1980s, the CEO of the Bank, Jaakko Lassila, was a member of the board of directors of almost twenty large Finnish companies, and in six of them he was the chairman of the board.[26]

Generally, then, the sphere system led to a formalised co-operative structure within the firms in each sphere. However, inter-sphere also links existed, especially at the corporate level in industrial unions. Furthermore, not all companies were totally attached to the sphere system. Although in the 1970s, for example, the financial spheres frequently made calculations in which they regarded certain companies as belonging to their own sphere, some companies remained outsiders, or at least their position was ambiguous. One of these "outsiders" was Nokia, in which both major spheres had stakes, but which was able to get rid off sphere pressures in the 1980s. It might be argued that in this "tightrope-walker" situation the company was able to make its decisions more independently than other large corporations.[27]

The spheres were not the only arenas for co-operation between the companies. Different sectors had their own associations, and especially within the field of research and development co-operation was close, as was the case with the forest industry's central laboratory (KCL), which was jointly owned by all the major companies, and also with the electronics industry in the late 20th century. The co-operation between the companies was not, however limited to specific lines of businesses or to bank spheres. Companies co-operated within

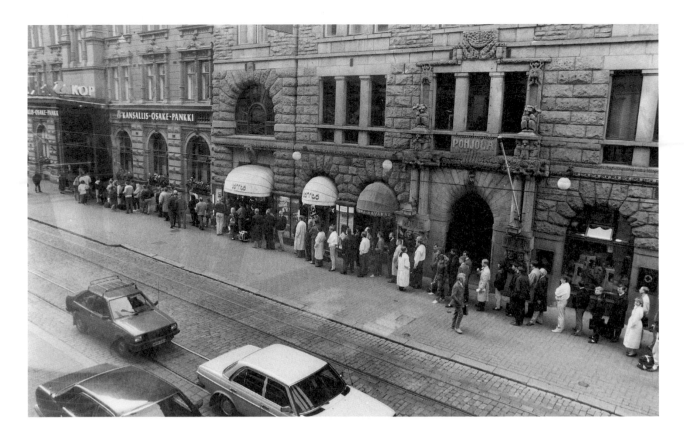

In the early 1990s, rises in stock prices enticed ordinary people to invest in securities for the first time in large numbers. People queued outside banks to buy shares.

the energy sector, first in order to gain more hydro energy right after the war, and secondly when they formed an alliance to build a nuclear power industry. Furthermore, companies co-operated within the Confederation of Finnish Industry, above all in negotiations with the state and the trade unions. The relationship between the companies and the state was close, especially during the era of financial capitalism, but not always warm. That was due to their fear that companies would be nationalised as left wing parties gained more political power. Furthermore, private companies were afraid of the competition from the state-owned companies, which were in a better position to influence political decision-making. In their political activities, the corporations used arguments based on employment and social welfare in order to gain benefits.[28]

The regulative economic policy affected business, especially during the latter part of the twentieth century (as García-Iglesias and Kilponen also point out in this volume). The main purpose of regulation was to support employment, investments and exports. Financial markets were tightly regulated and repeated devaluations gave competitive advantages to export businesses: altogether fourteen devaluations were carried out in the years 1949–1991 (see also García-Iglesias and Kilponen in this volume). The Bank of Finland played a decisive role in the regulative policies; for example, loans from abroad to finance large investments were regulated by the Bank of Finland. Furthermore, as the financial institutions had overwhelming control over industry, the most important decisions were to large extent made in negotiations between the Bank of Finland and private financial institutions. The bilateral trade with the Soviet Union and other Eastern Block countries was of especial importance – and here too the Bank of Finland played a decisive role.

Especially after the Second World War, Finnish business experienced a period of enormous growth, which took place primarily in the industrial sector. However, other business sectors, including retail trade and a wide variety of small and medium-sized businesses, also flourished. Even so, up to the 1980s, the Finnish business and industrial policies were still directed by the smoke-stack industry. The forest industry was the leader in exports, but the metal industry and engineering grew in significance in the course of time, as Kaukiainen states in his article in this volume. Technological development first brought larger industrial units, and then automation, computerisation and rationalisation – all of which affected the growth of productivity during the era. In the early 1950s, new hydro-electric power plants were built, and in the following decades the first nuclear plants, providing the cheap energy that was one of the major competitive advantages of Finnish heavy industry. By the early 1980s, nuclear power plants accounted for around 17 per cent of the total energy production.

Business also underwent a number of structural changes in the postwar period. The forest industry, for example, integrated forwards in the production chain. Sawmilling had lost its century-long role as the most important line of business by the end of the 1950s, pulp exports ceased at the beginning of the 1970s as the paper industry rose to be the leading sector of Finnish business and exports. The paper industry also changed as the companies started to make higher value added products, such as coated magazine papers and fine papers. In the mid-1980s, investments in new production facilities grew enormously owing to more advanced and expensive machinery. This led to a wave of mergers within industry, as small and usually family-owned companies could no longer make such investments. The merger wave occurred first within the spheres – in other words, sphere-ruled companies were the first to merge. Only after the era of financial capitalism came to an end in the mid-1980s, did intra-sphere mergers also become possible. Especially during the 1990s, this concentration spread to the international arena as Finnish companies bought, acquired and merged with a number of foreign companies – and Finland faced a new era: the age of global capitalism

Global Capitalism

The rise of multinational corporations marked the end of financial capitalism in the late 20th century. Finnish business had been connected to the global,

114

Company	Line of business	Employees	Turnover in 2004 million euros	Sphere	Ownership
Neste	Chemical industry	3,206	2,629	State (KOP)	State
Enso-Gutzeit	Forest industry	16,349	1,240	State (KOP)	State
Rauma-Repola	Diversified metal and forest industries	16,043	1,161	KOP	Listed
Wärtsilä	Metal industry	15,975	1,123	SYP	Listed
Nokia	Diversified metal, engineering, forest, and rubber industries	13,233	1,120	SYP (KOP)	Listed
Kemira	Chemical industry	8,190	1,072	State (KOP, SYP)	State
Ahlström	Diversified forest and metal industries	11,692	837	SYP	Family
Valmet	Metal industry	13,689	745	State (SYP & KOP)	State
Yhtyneet Paperi-tehtaat	Forest industry	8,075	741	KOP	Listed
Kymi (Kymmene)	Forest industry	8,116	704	SYP	Listed

Table 4.3 The ten largest industrial enterprises in Finland in 1975, according to turnover

Sources: Annual Reports; Hjerppe 1979.

State-owned companies played an important role in business during the postwar era. During the last decade of the 20th century these companies were mainly privatised, though even at the beginning of the third millennium the state still owned a stake in them. Of the top ten companies at the start of the 20th century (Table 4.2), only four were still among the ten largest in the mid-1970s.

or at least the European, economy for centuries owing to the important role played by the export industry. Early steps towards outward internationalisation had already been taken from the 1930s on, but it was not until the late 1980s that the internationalisation of production really expanded in the most important sectors. The companies at first expanded to nearby areas (like Scandinavia, Germany and Britain), but especially since the beginning of the third millennium, the Far-East has been one of the main focal areas for the globalisation of Finnish firms.[29] The markets for Finnish companies did not globalise that much – at least not for the traditional sectors of industry (as Yrjö Kaukiainen states in this volume) – although the production units of Finnish companies around the world did create new markets for known Finnish "brands".

Global capitalism emerged in Finland in the mid-1980s, when the capital markets were liberalized as controls on exchange rates and interest rates were lifted (for a more detailed discussion, see García-Iglesias and Kilponen in this volume). Companies could now get loans from abroad without the intervention of the Bank of Finland. This liberalisation was widely welcomed by the business elite, and even by the banks, although it demolished the power of the latter within a single decade. By 1987 most of the tight regulations over the financial markets had been dissolved.[30] The government's possibilities to influ-

A view of globalisation by Finnish performance artist Roi Vaara. "Weight of the World" was performed at the Venice Biennale in 2001.

ence business directly were limited after the financial markets were opened to global competition in the 1980s. However, it was not until the mid-1990s that the era of global capitalism really took place, as the two dominant banks (SYP and KOP) were merged and the almost century-long era of sphere domination in Finnish business came to an end. Another reason why the domination of the spheres was broken down was that the multinational companies were in many cases already larger than the domestic financial institutions.

The collapse of the Soviet Union in 1991 and Finland's membership of the European Union in 1995 affected Finnish industry profoundly. At the same time, a number of legislative measures to deregulate businesses were passed – so that by the early third millennium Finland had one of the most laissez-faire economies in the world in terms of the overall degree of regulation. The most notable measures was a new law on competition (1992) that basically made the

116

The metal industries grew in importance especially after the Second World War. For example, Avesta-Polarit Avesta-Polarit, a joint venture owned by Finland's Outokumpu Steel and British-Swedish Avesta Sheffield, opened the largest stainless steel production unit in the world in Tornio, northern Finland, at the start of the 21st century. The picture shows the engineering plant of Kalajoen Konepaja.

old cartel agreements illegal. The other change was the liberalisation of foreign ownership in 1992, which made it easier for foreigners to own shares in Finnish companies. The third change that had an impact on business was the privatisation of government-owned firms. Generally speaking, government involvement had already shifted during the 1980s from industrial policies to technology policies designed in order to create a favourable environment for businesses to emerge. From the early 1990s on, these policies included a national innovation system and cluster approaches, as noted by Asplund and Maliranta in this volume. This led, as Asplund and Maliranta suggest, to a transformation from an investment-driven to an innovation-driven economy.

Inward foreign direct investments (FDI) in Finland were made legally difficult at the beginning of the 20th century, and this legislation constrained the possibilities up to the 1990s. It was not until the late 1990s that inward FDI really took off (see also Hjerppe and Jalava in this volume). This profoundly changed the ownership structures of Finnish firms. It also reduced the cross ownership of companies that became established during the era of financial capitalism and reduced the central role played by the commercial banks. In the case of Nokia, for example, by 1997 foreign ownership already exceeded 70 per cent, when it had been around 40 per cent only three years earlier. While in the early 1990s below 10 per cent of the ownership of the Finnish companies listed on the Helsinki Stock Exchange were owned by foreigners, ten years later the figure was almost 80 per cent.[31] Within "big business", only family firms such as Kone, Sanoma-WSOY, Myllykoski, and Ahlstrom have remained predominantly in domestic ownership.

In addition to the deep economic crises which the country faced at the turn of the 1990s, all these changes in the competitive and institutional environment had a huge impact on the structure of Finnish businesses. As noted

Nokia: from a diversified conglomerate to the world's leading telecommunications business[35]

Nokia is the best-known Finnish company in the world. For the Finnish people, Nokia is a national institution – and, in fact, has been one for a number of decades. For a long time Nokia was known in Finland for products such as rubber boots, car tyres, cables, televisions, computers, and tissue paper. Only from the late 1980s on did the company become associated with telecommunications. During the following decade, it divested itself of its diversified structures, and its global success story began. Before that the company was already a domestic success story: it had for a long time been one of the largest privately owned industrial enterprises in the country. By the late 1980s, it had become the largest producer of televisions, computer monitors, rubber boots, and fifth largest producer of cables in Europe. In Scandinavia it was the largest producer of computers. Furthermore, it was involved in an alliance of tissue paper producers that had the largest capacity in Europe. As a curiosity, Nokia in the late 1980s

Soviet President Mikhail Gorbachev made a famous call with a Nokia mobile phone in Finland in 1987. The picture of the Soviet leader sampling modern technology was seen widely in the world press. The retail price of the phone, a Mobira City-man, was then a staggering 6,000 euros and it weighed nearly a kilogram. Also in the picture are then Finnish President Mauno Koivisto, left, and Prime Minister Harri Holkeri, centre.

was also already the largest mobile phone manufacturer in the world, though this line of business was then among the smallest ones in the company as mass markets for this product had yet to emerge. After shedding other lines of business, the role played by telecommunications grew rapidly within the company: in 1988 mobile phones accounted for only five per cent of Nokia's sales, but in 2000 72 per cent. At the same time, the share of mobile networks rose from 5 to 25 per cent of the total turnover.

The history of Nokia can be traced back to the mid-19th century and to the emergence of Finnish industry. The paper company Nokia was established in 1865 to produce wood pulp for paper production. In time Nokia diversified into three unrelated sectors: the forest industry (basically the manufacture of tissue), the rubber industry (boots and car tyres), and cables. During the 1960s, electronics gained in importance as the company started to integrate cable manufacturing forwards in the production chain, into machinery. Even in the 1960s, research and development played an important role in the company. Cables were undoubtedly the company's most important line of business especially in the 1970s, and its markets were mainly in the Soviet Union. Along with the cables, the sales of electronic equipment to the Soviet Union were also significant.

Nokia grew rapidly during the 1980s and diversified into new lines of business. By the end of the decade, the company was, however, in deep trouble. Huge investments in the production of televisions turned out to be disastrous, the cable exports ceased when the Soviet Union collapsed, and the company was lagging behind in the forest industry. The crisis was deepened further through managerial failure after the CEO of the company, Kari Kairamo, committed suicide in 1988.

Against this background, it is quite amazing how the company succeeded in getting back on its feet in only a couple of years in the early 1990s. In the years 1991 to 2001, the number of employees doubled, turnover grew over tenfold, profits grew a hundredfold, and the market value grew 312-fold, although at the same time all other lines of business except telecommunications were shed by the company. The growth in the value of the company meant that a number of Finnish shareholders became millionaires, as Nokia was widely owned by private citizens at the time. The importance of Nokia in the Finnish economy can be seen, for example, from the fact that by 1997 the value of Nokia on the Helsinki Stock Exchange exceeded the combined value of listed Finnish forest and metal industry firms, banks and insurance companies. When the rules constraining the foreign ownership of Finnish industry were loosened in the 1990s, the majority of the ownership of the company fell into the hands of US-based institutional investors.

The growth of Nokia was, of course, related to the rise of mass-markets for mobile phones in the 1990s. According to the author of the history of Nokia, Martti Häikiö, the reasons for the Nokia's success story in the 1990s and early third millennium have been the deregulation and digitalisation of international telecommunications and the breakthrough of GSM-technology. Nokia was able to exploit these changes in terms of both technology and business, and it also exerted its own influence on coming changes. The share of research and development in the company has been extensive, as is pointed out by Asplund and Maliranta in this volume. Moreover, the company

Jorma Ollila was CEO of Nokia during the company's period of rapid growth from 1992 to 2006. It may come as a surprise that the company shares the name "Nokia" with the town of Nokia, in central Finland, where its roots lie. As a place name, Nokia initially referred only to Nokia Manor and the Nokia River, on the banks of which the first production units of the company were established in the 1860s. Long before that, in the Middle Ages, the village of Nokia was an important trading centre. The name Nokia is said to derive from the old Finnish word nois or nokia meaning a black furred sable.

introduced modern leadership during and after the reformation of the company in the early 1990s under the direction of CEO Jorma Ollila, who is undoubtedly the best-known Finnish business leader in the world. Ollila started in 2006 as the Chairman of the Board of Directors of Royal Dutch Shell, but he will continue in Nokia as non-executive chairman.

Nokia is also a case of corporate political activity in Finland. It was among the major players in domestic industrial policies from the 1960s to the 1980s. It also had an impact on education and technology policies, especially in the 1990s. It is also an example of a company that actively sought co-operation, for instance in international cable cartels, in standardisation processes, and from the 1990s onwards in the industrial policies of the European Union. From the 1980s on, the CEO of the company has also been a major figure in domestic politics. Therefore, it was no wonder that in autumn 2005, when the presidential campaign in Finland began, it was the CEO of Nokia and the chairman of the Finnish Business and Policy Forum EVA, Jorma Ollila, who interviewed the candidates in the first television presidential debate.

120

Name	Headquarters	Line of business	Turnover in millions of euros	Employees	Operational area
Nokia	Espoo	Electronics	29,267	53,511	Global
Stora Enso	Helsinki	Forest industry	12,396	43,779	Global
Fortum	Espoo	Energy	11,665	12,859	Mainly domestic
UPM-Kymmene	Helsinki	Forest industry	9,820	34,815	Global
Metsäliitto	Helsinki	Forest industry	8,554	29,515	Global
Kesko	Helsinki	Retail and wholesale trade	7,517	17,528	Mainly domestic
Outokumpu	Espoo	Metal industry	7,136	19,761	Global
Sampo	Turku	Finance	6,017	11,972	Mainly domestic
Kone	Helsinki	Metal industry	5,562	30,976	Global
Tamro	Vantaa	Wholesale trade	4,857	3,909	Mainly domestic

Table 4.4 The ten largest enterprises in Finland in 2004, according to turnover

Source: Talouselämä magazine.

If we compare the situation of the early third millennium with the list of 30 years before (Table 4.3), we can note that only a couple of companies still exist with the same names. This is due to the wave of mergers that occurred in industry in the 1980s and 1990s. During this period, Nokia emerged to be the largest company in Finland. The growth of Nokia has been considerable: the turnover of the company in 2004 was 26 times greater than in 1975. The number of personnel, however, has grown only four-fold in the same period, thus implying an enormous growth in productivity. Other companies also grew: Stora-Enso's (known as Enso-Gutzeit in 1975) sales were tenfold and the number of personnel threefold in 2004 compared with 1975. In the case of UPM-Kymmene (if compared only with United Paper Mills in 1975), sales were 13-fold and the number of personnel fourfold in 2004 compared with 1975. There is, however, a fundamental difference in how this growth was attained: the forest industry companies such as Enso and UPM grew mainly through mergers and acquisitions, while Nokia experienced organic growth after the company divested itself of its diversified businesses and concentrated on telecommunications from the early 1990s.

in a number of articles in this volume, the change was fast and profound. The number of companies diminished rapidly owing to the mergers and acquisitions and bankruptcies of the early 1990s. In practice, the whole of Finnish "big business" was restructured in just a couple of years. Diversification came to an end as companies concentrated on core competences, horizontal integration through mergers and acquisitions was emphasised and diversified structures were either sold, or new companies were established to carry on the former businesses. Many of the old and long-standing companies simply ceased to exist, as was the case with Tampella, which had been among the largest industrial enterprises in Finland since the mid-19th century. The electro-technical industry grew in around fifteen years to become one of the leading sectors in the economy, and by the early third millennium its share of the value added was already one third, as stated by Asplund and Maliranta in this volume. There were also profound changes in other sectors. Retail trade, for example, was concentrated and Wall Mart-style stores became more general. Among the institutional changes during the era of global capitalism, one should also note the privatisation of state-owned companies, and the demise of large cooperatives, especially those connected with the agricultural sector (see Ojala and Nummela in this volume).

Finland's joining the European Union in 1995 can be regarded from the business point of view as a "natural" step forward, following the Finn-Efta agreement of 1961 and the free trade agreement with the EEC of 1973. As EU legislation now started to have an affect on Finnish companies, corporate political activity was also reoriented: domestic policy remained an important arena, but now European policies also began to be emphasised. Nokia, for example, employed a high-ranking officer from the Ministry for Foreign Affairs to obtain more influence for the company in the European Union.[32]

Technological development is another factor behind the change in Finnish business during the era of global capitalism. Most notably, the development of the telecommunications sector affected Finnish industry from the late 1980s on (for a more detailed discussion, see Asplund and Maliranta in this volume). Finnish companies, most notably Nokia, succeeded well in international competition. This was brought about by a number of factors. First, the companies had invested in research and development for a long time, and also the government had favoured this type of business from the late 1960s on, as pointed out by Asplund and Maliranta in this volume. Secondly, Finnish companies played an active part in creating the standards for mobile phones (Nordic NMT and global GSM) at the turn of the 1990s. Thirdly, the deregulation of state-owned telecommunication networks opened up the markets to private operators and increased the competition.[33]

The era of global capitalism meant the decline and stagnation of co-operative capitalism. However, the co-operation within and between the business companies and industrial clusters did not cease to exist, as can be seen from the strong role played by the Confederation of Finnish Industry (EK) in Finnish policies – and number of cartel accusations that have been made against Finnish companies by the European Union authorities. For example, companies continued to co-operate in innovation, and the government also played an increasingly important role in research and development after the National Technology Agency (Tekes) was established in 1983. In the period 1985–1998, almost 70 per cent of the innovations developed in Finland had received public funding.[34]

Conclusions

Can co-operation between companies and the co-evolution of business and society really explain the long-term evolution of Finnish business? The past five centuries have witnessed a growth in the number and size of companies, diversification and new lines of businesses, vertical and horizontal integration, productivity growth, and the internationalisation of companies. During the whole period, state regulation and deregulation have played an important role, whether it was the Swedish mercantilist state that constrained the possibilities

122

Tourism is an important branch of the economy. Lapland is a popular place for foreign visitors. Pictured here is the Suomu Hotel beside the ski slopes of Suomutunturi Fell in Lapland.

for private entrepreneurship, or Finland´s own legislation during the Russian period (1809–1917) and years of independence since 1917. In all these periods, businessmen and companies have actively sought possibilities for rent-seeking in political markets, in many cases quite successfully. The relationship between business leaders and the state was warm throughout the whole period in question, though there were some disagreements, especially in relation to the role played by state-owned companies in the 1960s and 1970s. During major economic and societal crises and the processes of change, the state invited top managers to lead important organs and conduct transactions crucial to the survival of society. This was the case, for example, when Finland gained independence and was plunged into civil war. Similarly, during and after the Second World War, the state and the business corporations co-operated actively.[36] Therefore, we argue that corporate political activity really played an important role in Finnish business.

With regard to co-operation between the companies, we pointed to the need to co-operate owing to limited resources, be it a lack of physical or of hu-

Table 4.5
The evolution of capitalist systems and Finnish big business, c. 1600–2000

Sources: Cantwell 1989, Ojala, Lamberg, Ahola and Melander 2006

Era	Time period	Typical features	Dominant lines of business	Ownership
Merchant capitalism	From the turn of the 17th to the late 19th century	Mercantilism	Trade, tar and timber exports, ironworks, shipping	Individual entrepreneurs, trading houses
Industrial capitalism	From the mid-19th century to the mid-20th century	Industrialisation, liberalisation of legislation, vertical integration	Forest and textile industry	Family ownership, emerging limited liability companies
Financial capitalism	From the early 20th century up to the 1980s	Spheres, state regulation, diversification, horizontal integration	Forest industry, emerging metal industry	Limited liability companies
Global capitalism	From the turn of the 1990s on	Internationalisation, deregulation, concentration on core competences	Telecommunications, metal and forest industries	Global ownership

man capital. Naturally, the situation was very similar in other countries. Nevertheless, we argue that Finland is a very illustrative case of the power of social capital, which was used extensively over the centuries to overcome a number of problems. In a remote, sparsely populated country that was dependent on certain export-oriented sectors, co-operation was the key to survival and growth.

The growth of Finnish business has been extensive throughout the period, as can be seen from Tables 4.1–4.4. Though the value of business is not comparable between the different periods, some conclusions can still be drawn. For the year 1800, we only have the estimated value of the assets of the most important businessmen, for the year 1913 the value of production of industrial enterprises, and for the last two intersecting years the turnover of the ten largest enterprises. With these rough measures we can note that the growth of business has been considerable: in 1800 the average wealth of the ten richest businessmen was around 1.5 million euros, the average value of production of the ten largest industrial enterprises in 1913 was around 36 million euros, the turnover of the ten largest companies in 1975 was already about 1,140 million euros, and finally the average turnover of the ten largest corporations in 2004 over 10,000 million euros.[37] At the same time, the size of the labour force has also grown rapidly – as is noted also by Hannikainen and Heikkinen in this

124

volume. We can estimate that the businessmen in 1800 employed on average some 50 to 300 people annually, while in 1913 the average number of employees in the ten largest industrial enterprises was around 1,500, in 1975 over 11,000, and in 2004 almost 26,000. Thus, productivity has risen enormously as the number of workers has not grown as fast as the turnover.

Another conclusion that can be drawn by comparing Tables 4.1–4.4 is the fact that the centre of gravity in Finnish business has moved southwards. In 2004 nine out of the ten largest companies had their headquarters in the Helsinki area (either in Helsinki, Vantaa or Espoo), while at the turn of the 20th century the companies were still located all over the country. On the other hand, the production units are still fairly widely dispersed over the country.

The eras of merchant, industrial, financial, and global capitalism are partly overlapping in the development of Finnish industry, as can be seen in Table 4.5. The same periods can be found in a number of other countries as well; likewise the types of activity, such as the emphasis on networks during the era of merchant capitalism, or the recent globalisation process, are often similar. Nevertheless, "typical" Finnish characteristics can also be found, like the dominant position of the forest industry or the unique growth of telecommunications in the 1990s.

Certain common features can be found in the all periods in Table 4.5. These include the important role played by the state. Business and even corporate political activity have evolved from personal relationships into more impersonal activities. This does not mean that individuals do not matter any more, but business associations have assumed a more pronounced role as modern industrial enterprise emerged in Finland.

The central role played by the forest industry in big business for a long time highlights the exploitation of abundant raw material resources, and partly also inexpensive manpower. This state of affairs was threatened, especially from the 1970s on, when innovations, research and development, and new lines of business took on more importance. Furthermore, even in the case of the forest industry, technological know-how has replaced the former importance of raw materials.[38]

The companies and their focus areas were shaped by a number of changes in both the competitive and the institutional environment. Particularly the changes in major export areas played a vital role, as can be seen above all in the case of the Russian markets over the last two hundred years. Social capital has played an important role over the centuries – co-operation, mutual trust, and reputation still play a significant role in Finnish business. Thus, we can say that Finnish business is still rooted in social capital.

A 20th century advertisements inviting foreign tourists to Finland.

"Ship in the Harbour"

by Gösta Diehl

(1952, oil on canvas, 70x90 cm)

Foreign Trade and Transport

Yrjö Kaukiainen

A remote and sparsely populated northern corner of Europe, Finland was for centuries a supplier of forest products and other primary merchandise, such as furs, fish, tar, and timber. Gradually these were replaced by manufactured wood products, such as sawn goods, pulp, and paper. However, it was only after the Second World War and, in particular, the last two decades of the 20th century, that a definite transition to high-value-added, high-tech exports took place.

Skirted by the gulfs of the Baltic Sea, Finland is much like an island. Therefore, the country was more easily accessible from Western Europe than most continental areas at an equal distance, and this undoubtedly accounted for the fact that the economic influence of the more densely inhabited and wealthy "core" was felt fairly early. This also made shipping an integral element in the country's international economic relations, in particular during times when freight costs were much higher than nowadays. Therefore, maritime transport has been given a prominent role in the following description, while the development of land transport has only been discussed insofar as it affected the commodity flows to and from Finnish ports.

Early commodity flows

The first Finnish exports seem to have been furs. Probably this kind of trade already existed in prehistoric times – at least it was important during the Middle Ages, when the provinces of present-day Finland were gradually incorporated into Sweden. Yet, it seems that Low German mercantile influence was more dominant in the beginning than Swedish: the leading burghers in the few medieval towns were of German origin. Gradually the Swedish capital, Stockholm, gained stronger control over western Finland, in particular the Ostrobothnian coast, but the south coast remained in the sphere of the Hansa merchants and, in particular, Tallinn, until the late 16th century. By comparison, Finnish trade with Russia was very modest. Another important medieval export commodity was fish, which mainly found markets in Estonia and around Stockholm, typically in exchange for grain. This trade also created the import of salt which, at least quantitatively, was to remain the major import commodity until the 19th century. It was, indeed, the first real bulk commodity in Finnish foreign trade, which meant that until the late 16th century imports required much more cargo space than exports. The salt trade also was connected with the development of transport technology: the introduction of Hanseatic cogs, which were able to carry much more cargo than earlier Nordic vessels.[1]

The Age of Discovery did not directly affect the Baltic world, which remained the storehouse of raw materials for the urbanized and economically

In the present century, Russia has re-emerged as one of Finland's most important trading partners. Trucks queueing at the Finnish-Russian border in May, 2000.

128

Ladoga Fishing Boats.

Commodities within the Baltic region were sometimes carried by small peasant vessels, though this trade was limited by mercantile legislation. Finnish peasants shipped firewood, foodstuffs and other goods to towns such as Tallinn, Stockholm, and, from the early 19th century, St Petersburg.

developed areas. However, the 16th century brought a major change in its maritime trade: the decline of the Hanseatic League, the hegemony of which was taken over by the rapidly developing northern Netherlands. This, however, was not a sudden break but rather a long-term development which had already begun in the late 15th century.[2] At the beginning of the 17th century, Dutch supremacy in Baltic trade was almost as complete as the previous Hanseatic domination: no less than 60% of all ships passing the Sound were Dutch. This change also brought about an increase in commodity flows from the Baltic to western Europe. The resultant growth in shipping, again, increased the demand for one special timber by-product, tar, which for centuries was the principal substance for impregnating wooden hulls and hemp ropes. Increasing demand gradually also spread to Finland, which then had practically virgin forest resources. During the early 16th century, the country was still too far away from the centres of consumption; tar and timber were mainly transported to the Low Countries from Prussia, timber also from Norway. Since tar, compared with the cargo space it required, was more valuable than raw or sawn timber, it could be shipped economically from farther afield, and from a country with a very primitive infrastructure of overland transport. In the 1610s, about half of all tar carried through the Sound still originated from Prussia, but two decades later the proportion was only 10 percent. At the same time, Finland's share rose to about 35 percent, and this only concerned the tar which was exported directly abroad. Substantial amounts were also shipped from Osthrobothnia to Stockholm and reloaded there for western Europe. This means that Finland (or rather the area which was later called Finland) had ascended to the leading position among tar-producers in Europe.[3]

In ancient times Finnish sailors were sometimes accused of witchcraft because of their alleged ability to raise storms, as illustrated in this 16th century drawing by Olaus Magnus.

The era of Stockholm tar

Thus began the era of tar – which also could be called the age of "Stockholm tar" because a large proportion of Finnish tar was exported via the Swedish capital. It lasted for more than two centuries and earmarked the Finnish economy more than ever before as a supplier of forestry produce for the "core" areas of Europe. Although the 17th century was by no means a period of economic growth – quite on the contrary – the naval arms race kept the demand for tar fairly high irrespective of population or income development. Since tar production was a typical backwoods cottage industry – only transport problems in the interior limited its spread – it deeply affected both the economy and society. Moreover, the trade had a strong impact on maritime transport. Being a real bulk commodity, at least compared with furs or fish, tar required lots of cargo space, and as soon as exports gained momentum, the physical volume of Finnish exports vastly exceeded that of imports. In a period when maritime transport was expensive, such an imbalance greatly affected the total transport economy. In fact, the excess of export cargo became a lasting feature of Finnish foreign trade: it was only during the 1960s that oil imports reversed the scales.

It is obvious that these early commercial flows exerted some influence upon the Finnish economy. By affecting not only the few coastal towns but also creating new production in the backwoods, they started to connect the country with Germany, the Netherlands and other "core" areas of Europe. However, this was a rather passive mode of connection, which could well be described in terms of the Wallersteinian core – periphery metaphor. The economic relations were dominated by foreign (first Hanseatic and then Dutch) traders. Their supremacy depended on both skills and capital, and their superiority was not only manifested in cash and credit but also in maritime transportation: typically, the bulk of Finnish exports was carried in foreign keels.[4]

During the late Hanseatic times, there was some Finnish shipping to Danzig (today: Gdansk) and to some destinations beyond the Baltic Sea. However, the beginning of the tar era did not – in spite of the increasing demand for tonnage – result in any growth of local shipping, rather the contrary: during the 17th century very few Finnish ships ever sailed beyond the Danish Sounds. Such a lack of interest obviously depended on a couple of factors: local burghers knew very little of the world beyond the Baltic, and above all they had little capital to build the bigger ships which were necessary for conducting an active trade with western European customers. Moreover, what capital the Finnish burghers did have was bound up in stocks of tar, the turnover of which was fairly slow. Because of a high demand for capital and skills, maritime transport was the bottleneck in this commodity flow. Not only was it expensive but inadequate transport potential was also a major factor limiting the actual volume of trade. Therefore, whoever controlled the transport controlled the whole flow. On the other side of the coin, of course, active and efficient shipping could produce substantial, direct and indirect profits.

The merchant ship King Gustaf III, built in 1772 in Loviisa. Like other similar ships at the time, she carried exports such as pine tar and timber to the Netherlands, Britain, the Iberian peninsula and the western Mediterranean. They brought back salt from Portugal and Spain, earning themselves the nickname "Spain traders".

What the Dutch had been able to gain with their skills, capital and, above all, the efficient use of both was, however, challenged by the Crowns of Sweden and Great Britain. While the British resorted to restrictive Navigation Acts, Sweden created a system of domestic monopolies which controlled trade in the principal export and import commodities. This system also involved tar, which was the third biggest Swedish export item after copper and iron. The first tar company was created in 1648, and from that date until 1715 – with the exception of the years 1682–89 – practically all the tar that was exported from Finland and northern Sweden was sold abroad by this company or its successors.

It is obvious that the new monopolistic system resulted in a redistribution of profit between Swedish and Dutch merchants. However, while in principle the former gained, the gains were not evenly distributed. The tar company was, in practice, a cartel controlled by wealthy Stockholm burghers whose interests by no means aimed at redistributing profits to tar traders in Finnish coastal towns, or producers in the backwoods; rather the company was a tool for exploiting the resources of what was regarded the capital's natural hinterland. Finnish merchants gained hardly anything: in fact their loud and repeated protests give the impression that they were worse off than when doing business directly with the Dutch, and it is also quite clear that the income of peasant producers did not increase during the monopoly period. On the Gulf of Bothnia, however, the new system did not change as much. Since local merchants were not allowed to sail abroad, nor foreigners to enter the area – and this closure of the Gulf was renewed at the beginning of the 17th century – it was in effect a private hinterland of the capital, and the Bothnian tar trade was, right from the beginning, in the hands of Stockholm.

Thus, Finnish tar was carried to western Europe on either Dutch or Stockholm ships. There was only one limited area in which domestic shipping was able to participate: transports from the Ostrobothnian production areas to the capital took place in local vessels. Coastal traffic between the Finnish or Estonian coasts and Stockholm, providing the capital with grain, fish and firewood, also employed a large fleet of small ships, mainly owned by the coastal peasants. This division of labour is also reflected in the shipping statistics of the late 17th century: around 1680 the few Finnish foreign-trading towns only owned a dozen ships with a total carrying capacity of about two thousand tons, while Ostrobothnian towns employed a fleet of almost 5000 tons, and the southern coastal districts owned something like 400 small ships (8000–9000 tons).[5]

The beginnings of the saw-mill industry and active foreign shipping

Although in terms of quantity Finnish tar exports continued to grow up to the late 1860s, in value they were surpassed before that by sawn goods (see below). In the late 17th century, the prices of sawn timber in western Europe rose enough to offset transport costs from the far end of the Baltic. The first big water-powered sawmills were erected around Narva and Nyen (at the mouth of the River Neva) by Dutch merchants and agents from c. 1660 onwards, and around the turn of the century they were also to be found in the vicinity of Wiborg (today: Vyborg). Although south-eastern Finland was conquered by Russia in the 1710s and 1740s, the sawmill industry grew rapidly in this fairly small area, which was known as "Old Finland". At the end of the 18th century, Old Finland was one of the major sawmilling centres in the Baltic area – and indeed in the whole of Europe. Around 1780, the two seaports of the province, Wiborg

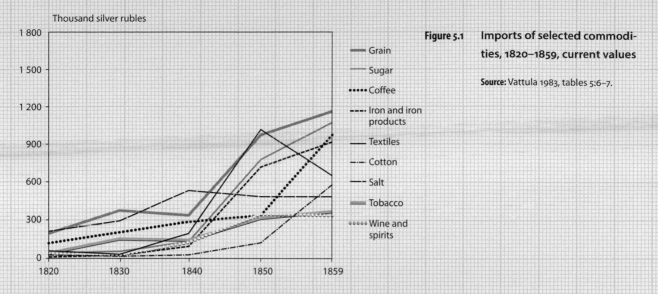

Thousand silver rubles

Legend:
- Grain
- Sugar
- Coffee
- Iron and iron products
- Textiles
- Cotton
- Salt
- Tobacco
- Wine and spirits

Figure 5.1 Imports of selected commodities, 1820–1859, current values

Source: Vattula 1983, tables 5:6–7.

Comprehensive statistics of Finnish exports and imports in the 18th century cannot be collected because a substantial proportion of both were shipped via Stockholm. Even after Finland was ceded to Russia in the Peace of Hamina (1809), trade with Sweden remained free of customs duties until 1818. This naturally means that data on imports from the former capital are necessarily unreliable. As commodities like sugar, coffee, tobacco and spirits were commonly smuggled even after that date, until dues were reduced at the beginning of the 1840s, the growth in the imports of these commodities probably was not as steep as the official figures suggest. In any case, it is noteworthy that after 1840 the value of sugar and coffee vastly exceeded that of the former "staple" import commodity, salt.

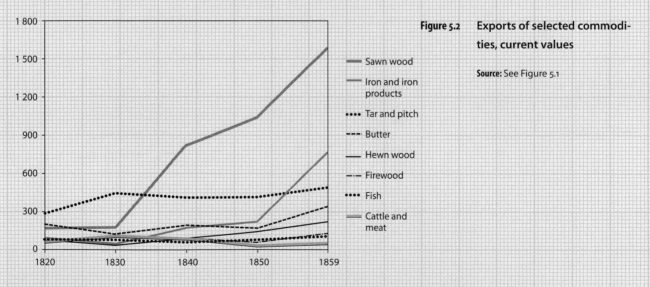

Legend:
- Sawn wood
- Iron and iron products
- Tar and pitch
- Butter
- Hewn wood
- Firewood
- Fish
- Cattle and meat

Figure 5.2 Exports of selected commodities, current values

Source: See Figure 5.1

After Finland was ceded to Russia, exports transported overland or on coastal vessels to St. Petersburg were inadequately registered until the 1850s. Accordingly, the exports of agricultural produce and firewood show volumes that are much too low. The most important point revealed by these figures is the rapid growth in the export of sawn wood, which overtook tar and pitch in value during the 1830s.

and Hamina, exported more sawn goods than the whole Swedish realm. On the other hand, they no longer sold any substantial quantities of tar.

Sawmills were also built in Swedish Finland, mainly on the southern coast but occasionally even on the Bothnian coast. On average, however, they were quite small and their exports were much smaller than those from the Russian side. It must, of course, be remembered, that these early sawmills were not able to exploit forests beyond the vicinity of coasts. It was only after exports of sawn wood were strongly limited by the Russian government that substantial production was started in the interior of Swedish Finland around the Saimaa waterway system (this production was the shipped abroad via Wiborg).

Overall, the tar era still continued in Swedish Finland, and exports grew at a steady pace. This difference between Swedish Finland and Old Finland was at least partly due to the tight Swedish restrictions regarding both the use of forest resources and forestry-based production, which in particular affected sawmills.[6] However, there was also another factor which limited the growth of this industry in Swedish Finland. Shipping became a more attractive opportunity after Sweden followed the British example and decreed its own navigation act (produktplacat) in 1724. Like the earlier models, it prohibited foreign ships from unloading in Swedish ports other than their own products, or goods from their colonies, thus reserving a substantial proportion of imports for domestic vessels. This partial monopoly was later further widened by special customs tariffs which increased the export dues of foreign ships, insofar as they were loading iron or sawn wood, making them much higher than those levied on Swedish ones. Thus, Finnish shipowners, too, were materially favoured in both the export and the import trade. It is obvious that freight rates were accordingly higher than they had been in a competitive market. Thus the system did not favour the export industries, such as ironworks or sawmills, which were bur-

Barrels of Finnish tar in Copenhagen harbour in 1918.

134

Pine tar was the most important export commodity until the 19th century. The production of tar was time-consuming and labour-intensive. This picture from the 1930s shows a tar pit being constructed.

dened by higher transport costs, and it may be said that the net result was a transfer of profits from manufacturing to transport.

At first, the lack of capital and previous expertise in shipbuilding and navigation obviously hindered the growth of Finnish shipping (indeed, both Dutch and Stockholm capital and know-how were initially invaluable to Finnish merchants). Before the 1750s, the number of Finnish vessels sailing westwards through the Sound only exceptionally amounted to more than ten per year. It was only in the 1770s that the annual average exceeded thirty, but after 1780 (with the exception of times of war) the figure already approached sixty. The modest scale of Finnish exports, of course, limited the growth, but by around 1760 foreign ships were only exceptionally loaded in Finnish ports, and at the end of the century more Finnish ships were sailing west of the Sound than were needed to take care of the respective exports. Thus some of them were now also carrying export products from other regions, for example timber

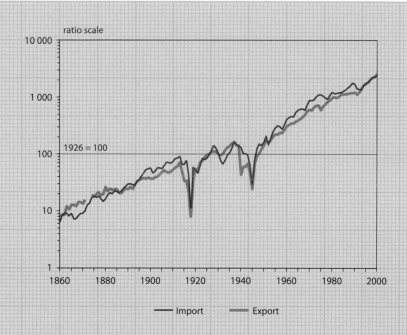

Figure 5.3 Volume indices of imports and exports 1860–2000, ratio scale, 1926 = 100

Source: Hjerppe 1989, 155; *Statistical Yearbook of Finland.*

According to statistical conventions, the values of imports and exports are gauged by their respective prices at the border: thus, imports refer to cif prices (cost, insurance, freight), which include all international transport costs, while exports refer to fob prices (free on board), which only include domestic transport to the port (plus eventual export dues). In practice, transport costs often affect both sellers and buyers, depending on the market situation and the actual goods (or rather their price elasticities,) but in trade balance calculations they are only taken into account on the debit (import) side. This means that changes in international transport costs also affect terms of trade (see: Hjerppe and Jalava, fig. 2.12, in this volume): if they sink substantially – as happened in the late 19th century – the cif value of imports (other things being equal) will decrease while the fob value of exports remains unchanged. On the other hand, changes in customs dues do not affect terms of trade because the most important of these, import dues, are not included in the value of imports.

from Riga. They also carried salt to Russian Baltic ports, and during the winter, when the Baltic was ice-bound, they carried freight in the Mediterranean.[7]

These new opportunities not only gave Finnish merchants additional profit from shipping, they also seem to have improved their terms of trade. A dominant feature in the development was that exports were increasingly directed to Spain, Portugal and western Mediterranean ports, which not only demanded both sawn wood and tar but also were exporters of high-class sea-salt. By excluding the (mainly) Dutch middlemen, Finnish merchants both obtained better prices for their exports and were able to purchase salt at a lower cost than before. To some degree, tar exporters were also released from the control of Stockholm, although a substantial share was still marketed through the capital. The Mediterranean market also proved valuable when Britain started to favour its American colonies in its forest-produce imports. Moreover, the transportation of cargoes in wintertime, not only in the Mediterranean but someti-

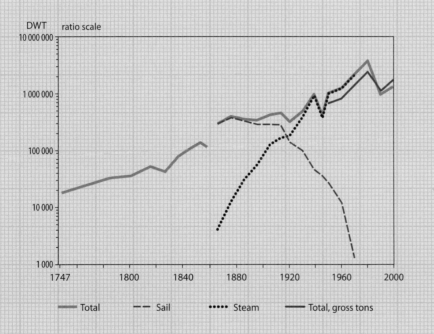

Figure 5.4 Finnish merchant tonnage 1747–2000, estimated in deadweight tons, ratio scale.

Source: Kaukiainen 1993, 46, 69, 78–79, 87, 102, 137, 161; Finnish Official Shipping Statistics, 1980–2004 (www.fma.fi/palvelut/tilastot).

The figure aims to represent the merchant tonnage which actually sailed in foreign trade. Thus, it does not include coastal vessels and those sailing on lakes, nor so-called peasant ships insofar as they were not allowed to sail abroad. From 1865 onwards, the original tonnage statistics have been systematically controlled for faults and inconsistencies, which means that earlier figures may not be fully comparable.

For consistency, tonnage has been expressed as deadweight tons (the weight of cargo and stores of fuel, etc. that the ship is able to carry). Lasts (Sw. läst), which were used before the 1870s, have been converted to tons according to the ratio: 1 last = 2,448 tons. Register tons, again, have been converted to dw tons by multipliers computed (separately for steam and sail) from a number of chron. samples (or examples) of vessels for which both figures are known. After the last ship measurement reform, which became effective in 1982–1994, earlier register tons were replaced by new gross and net tonnages, which, compared with dw-tons, are for certain types of vessel such as container and ro-ro ships ("volume ships"), much greater than the earlier ones. Therefore, gross "tons" have also been recorded for the most recent times.

mes also in actual ocean trade, brought the northern shipowners into contact with the opportunities offered by international freight markets.

Although the upswing started because of political measures which excluded competitors with more capital and know-how, it was also based on some very real comparative advantages. Both labour and timber were abundant and cheap in the periphery, which meant that Swedes and Finns were able to build and man ships at much lower costs than the British and other western Europeans. Moreover, shipbuilding skills also accumulated in Finnish towns, particularly in Ostrobothnia, which even in the late 17th century was already building ships for Stockholm merchants. In the following century, shipbuilding expanded further and developed into a fairly important industry producing hundreds of vessels both for local and Swedish owners. This know-how also became an important asset for local shipping after the 1760s, when Ostrobothnian coastal towns were allowed to send their ships and exports directly abroad.

The comparative advantages described above also sufficed to prolong the "golden" era of blue-water shipping decades beyond the end of the mercantilist era proper: at least in Finland, it lasted until the 1870s, while many of the restrictions stipulated in the old Swedish navigation act became obsolete in the 1840s. The Swedish productplacat thus presents us with an excellent example of a policy which, by protecting an infant industry, allowed it to develop its natural strong points.

The other side of the coin was that profitable shipping attracted investments away from other ventures. Even allowing for the Swedish restrictions on the use of timber, this may well have retarded the growth of the sawmill industry. Quite the contrary situation was experienced in those south-eastern Finnish provinces which belonged to Russia. As Russia had no effective navigation act, exports and imports were almost exclusively carried on Dutch and British ships. These circumstances promoted the development of sawmills in two different ways. First, competition kept freight levels moderate and lowered the price of sawn wood at destination. Secondly, there were no other equivalent opportunities for local merchants to attract their capital away from the sawmill industry.

The heyday of Finnish merchant capitalism

The development described above can be taken as an example of exports following the flag, that is, the export market expanding as a consequence of expanding shipping. The same formula remained valid in the following century, in spite of the fact that Sweden had to cede Finland to Russia after a war in 1808–09. However, the country – with the addition of the provinces which had belonged to Russia in the 18th century – was made an autonomous Grand Duchy and, most importantly, the political and economic system that had been in force in the time of Swedish rule remained intact. This meant that, for example, the Swedish navigation act was still valid. On the other hand, it also meant that the restric-

138

UTSIGT AF EN SÅG-QVARN,
emellan Allerøllet och Helsingborpe i Finland

VUE D'UN MOULIN À PLANCHES,
entre, Allerøllet et Helsingborpe en Finlande.

Voyage Pittoresque de la Suede Petri .... par A.Kühøøp et Næst par J.A. Cypher.

Sawn timber surpassed tar as the most important export commodity in the early 19th century, and held this position until the mid-20th century. Raala, founded in 1709, is one of the oldest water-powered sawmills in the country.

tions on sawmills were continued. Onc major change, however, did take place: exports of tar were now totally freed from the interference of Stockholm.

The first decade after the Napoleonic Wars was a period of economic depression in Europe. This was also seen in Finnish foreign trade, the volume of which remained at roughly the same level as in the 1790s. Exports to the Mediterranean in particular were badly hit because Russia had no agreements with the so-called Barbary states, which used to attack the ships of all nations that did not pay tribute to them. It was only in the late 1830s that a new growth started, one which then persisted with few interruptions until the Crimean War and was resumed again with the coming of peace in 1856. For all the Nordic countries, the most important impact was that the demand for sawn goods in western Europe grew; accordingly, new water-powered mills were built, and the total production capacity of the industry rose steadily. From the 1810s to the early 1850s, Finnish exports of sawn wood grew almost fourfold. Although tar exports, too, still slowly increased, the total value of sawn goods surpassed that of tar in the middle of the 1830s, and by around 1850 they were already almost three times higher.

In Sweden, the great breakthrough of the sawmill industry already took place in the 1840s; in Finland this happened two decades later, between 1860 and 1875. Then all the earlier restrictions were removed, and in addition steam was allowed as the motive power for sawmills. These changes coincided with the ending of the British preferences for colonial imports, which lowered the

Production of mechanical and chemical pulp as raw material for making paper expanded in the late 19th century. By the mid-20th century, pulp had replaced sawn timber as the most important export commodity. But from the early 1970s most of the pulp was processed into paper, and exports of pulp fell rapidly. A sulphite pulp mill in Enso in 1934.

customs dues of Finnish sawn wood to a fraction of their previous levels – and accordingly improved their competitiveness on the British market. In a single decade, production and export volumes more than trebled. This expansion, in fact, can be regarded the first phase of the Finnish industrial revolution. Around 1875, the exports of sawn wood, in value, were no less than ten times higher than those of tar. By then butter and iron had also surpassed the former principal export item.

However, during the second quarter of the 19th century, new impacts started to change the traditional simple pattern of Finnish foreign trade. As was stated above, the country's annexation into the Russian empire did not result in any sudden rupture in the destinations of its foreign trade. However, gradually economic connections with north-western Russia increased. South-eastern Finland had already sold firewood, butter and other agricultural products to St. Petersburg in the 18th century, and these exports increased – the precise amounts, however, are difficult to estimate because the trade across the border was not very carefully recorded. From the 1830s on, cheap Russian grain started to be imported into Finland, and at roughly the same time certain Finnish industries, above all ironworks and the new cotton mills, found markets in Estonia and the province of St. Petersburg. Thus, Finland was following the British example on a small scale: food imports made it easier to supply the populations of growing industrial centres.[8]

These developments were also aided by the development of transport. Regular steamship connections between Helsinki and St. Petersburg (as well as with Stockholm and Tallinn) were established in the 1830s, and in 1870 the railway between the Finnish and Russian capitals was opened. Communications between coasts and the interior were also improved: in the 1850s a new canal connected sawmills in the Lake Saimaa area with the port of Wiborg. Even more important was the domestic railway network which was built between 1860 and 1913, making it possible to establish industry far away from the coasts and navigable waterways. In any case, the rapid development of Russian trade, plus the fact that exports to southern Europe practically stopped in the 1810s and 1820s, increased its share of the total to more than 40 percent.

From the 1830s onwards, growing exports of sawn wood involved a corresponding increase in the demand for shipping: it can be estimated that, compared with the levels of the late 1810s, the physical volume of Finnish sea-born exports grew sevenfold until the early 1870s – and then doubled again during a single decade. Since these shiploads were in practice reserved for Finnish ships, the growth of exports guaranteed – indeed, required – a corresponding growth of tonnage. Therefore, it is no wonder that the merchant fleets of Finnish seaports increased at a good pace: from about 40,000 deadweight tons in 1825 to over 130,000 dw tons in 1853 and – in spite of the Crimean War, during which the British and French navies caused them heavy losses – to more than 350,000 dw tons (or over 230,000 net register tons) in 1875. Of course, in actual number the Finnish merchant navy was fairly small; however, compared with the country's population it seems to have grown into the fifth largest in the world.[9]

It can be seen that the growth of tonnage correlated closely with that of exports. Thus it made a substantial contribution to the country's balance of payments. During the period 1815–1860, the average (cif) value of Finnish imports exceeded the (fob) value[10] of exports by a large margin. As the general level of freights was still high, this difference was mainly bridged with shipping income, both from exports and imports. However, this is not the whole story: the Finnish merchant navy was not solely employed in transporting the country's foreign trade, far from it. The 18th-century tradition of "cross-trade" (freight between foreign countries) continued in the following century – indeed, it became even more important than before. Contemporary shipping statistics show that in good times, when international freights were high, two-thirds or three-quarters of urban tonnage passed the winter on southern waters and even in not so good years this proportion was close to a half. During the fairly typical years of the 1860s and 1870s, no less than about 55–60 percent of all Finnish shipping income was generated in international cross-trade. Since such trade frequently involved long voyages over the Atlantic, to South America, the Far East and even Australia, that is, much longer hauls than were typical of the carriage of Finnish exports and imports, it is obvious that Finnish shipowners controlled a much bigger tonnage than would have been needed to take care of the country's foreign trade. This heavy reliance on foreign freight markets was undoubtedly quite unusual – it is probable that only Norway and Greece could present a higher proportion of cross-trading tonnage at that time.[11]

Although shipping took on a fairly independent role, the traditional ties with foreign trade were not yet severed. The majority of shipowners were still urban burghers who also engaged in the export and import trade as well as in manufacturing in that they owned and ran sawmills or ironworks, and later also paper mills. In this sense, the expansion of the sawmill industry also took place in the spirit of merchant capitalism. It is also obvious that, for many merchants, foreign shipping seemed a more lucrative opportunity than domestic industries. One indication of this is the fact that, at least in the 1860s and 1870s, it was not uncommon that local ships were not available to carry wood products abroad, and foreign vessels had to be chartered instead. It is, indeed, possible that the flourishing shipping business continued to hinder the development of the forest industries. However, before any far-reaching conclusions are drawn, it must be remembered that – until the 1850s and 1860s – the levels of import dues and duties in many western and southern European countries were still so high that they substantially affected the prices and – accordingly – the demand for northern bulk goods. Thus it can only be concluded that the positive contribution of shipping to the growth of foreign trade does not seem to have been high. If trade was still following the flag, it did so after an appreciable time lag.

Industrial growth and foreign trade

In the late 1870s, 50 per cent or even more of all industrial products which Finland exported consisted of timber products, and they went exclusively to the west. Of the remainder, again, practically all were sold to Russia – thus, there was a very clear division of markets. Of course, there also were the home markets, but as far as industrial production was concerned the same branches that exported to Russia, above all the metal and textile industries, were also the most important in domestic trade.

In the late 1870s, international economic trends deteriorated with the onset of a depression – often dubbed the "Long Depression" – which was to last up to the first decade of the 20th century. As might be expected, it first hit the exports of sawn wood but, at the same time, financial problems in Russia also dulled the prospects of the metal and textile industries. Their exports sank even more after the late 1880s, when Russia increased the customs dues of many Finnish products, or limited the volume of such imports. The net result was an even sharper division between export and home market industries, with forest-based products dominating the former. Just before the First World War, non-forest exports amounted to only a quarter of the total.

In the 1880s, the international demand for sawn wood grew slowly, and the competition between major producers was intensified when Russia joined the ranks of Sweden, Norway and Finland. Finnish exports, which exceeded

142

Paper machine number 4 at UPM's paper mills in Rauma started to operate in 1998. The machine produces lightweight coated paper at world record speed. In January 2006 it achieved a rate of 1,912 metres of paper over 10 metres wide per minute. It annually produces over 400,000 tons of paper.

one million cubic metres in the late 1870s, increased only marginally during the following decade. A new rise started in the 1890s, and the exports reached a record of some 3.4 million cubic metres in 1913. This volume brought Finland into the number three position among European producers.

This period also saw the export take-off of forestry products with even lower value-added than tar or sawn wood. This was because railways and timber-floating along the interior waterways made it possible to transport raw wood to seaports; the declining maritime transport costs also contributed substantially to this development. Thus from the 1890s onwards, pit-props, pulpwood, beams and other timber were loaded from Finland for Western Europe in rapidly growing volumes. Just before the First World War, the cubic volume of such exports exceeded that of sawn wood – in value, however, they only amounted to a quarter of the latter.

This trend towards low-value exports was, however, balanced by the beginning of the pulp and paper industries in the 1860s and 1870s. True, there was already in the early 19th century a couple of mills producing paper from textile rags, but a real expansion was experienced only after wood pulp began to be used as raw material for paper. After the 1870s, the value of these exports – which already exceeded that of pit-props and other raw wood – grew to substantial volumes, reaching to about 45 percent of the corresponding figure for sawn wood just before the First World War. However, while other wood products were sold to central and western Europe, Russia became the most important buyer of Finnish paper. Between 1860 and 1913, the total value of forestry exports increased about 25-fold – thus it was no wonder that their share rose to three-quarters of all exports. At that time, tar comprised a mere 0.15 percent of this total.[12]

The trends described above also meant that Russia's share of Finland's foreign trade slowly decreased. In addition to the products of the metal and textile industries, the exports of butter also decreased (or, rather, the exports were redirected to western Europe). At the same time, goods from Germany, grain included, started to compete with Russian imports and rose to the number one position around the turn of the century. As for exports, Great Britain rose from the second to the first place in the 1890s. Overall, the share of Russia sank from about a half in the 1860s to 30 percent after 1905, and the proportion were virtually the same in both exports and imports.

Between 1870 and 1913, the overall volume of exports grew almost ninefold and that of imports fifteenfold – on average 50 and 65 percent respectively per decade, which was somewhat faster than the estimated growth for world trade in the same period. As previously mentioned, the actual value of imports regularly exceeded that of exports, typically by a third or so. The most important factor compensating for the deficit, however, was no longer income from shipping but the favourable development of the country's terms of trade. From the 1860s to 1911–13, the index of export prices increased 50 per cent more than that of import prices.[13] Thus, the actual volume of imports was able to grow at a faster rate than that of exports. Another positive feature was that raw materials, fuel and investment goods always accounted for more than half of the total imports and their share rose to three-quarters towards the end of the period.

With the rapid increase of bulky forest exports the demand for cargo-space in Finnish foreign trade grew in this period even faster than during the preceding half century. In spite of that, the previous rapid expansion of tonnage came to a halt in the late 1870s and was followed by a distinct decline. Although a moderate recovery started in the 1890s, the overall tonnage of the Finnish seaworthy (excluding coastal and lake tonnage) merchant navy was ten percent smaller in 1913 than around 1875. At the same time, the total world tonnage had doubled. Even more dramatic was the decline of domestic tonnage in export and import shipping: around 1910, if coastal and short-sea shipping to Russia and Sweden is excluded, over 70 percent of all departures and entrances with cargo at Finnish ports were recorded by foreign vessels (paradoxically, this proportion seems to have been highest, almost 90 percent, in timber exporting ports).[14] Accordingly, a substantial deficit developed in the balance of payments for Finnish export and import shipping.

The dramatic change was not really connected with Finnish foreign trade; rather it can explained as a result of certain external factors, economic as well as technological. First, the general level of international freights started to

144

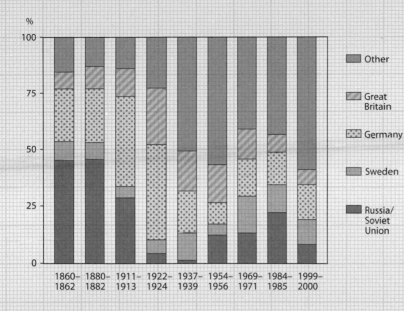

Figure 5.5a. Distribution of imports by country, selected years

Source: Pihkala 1969; Oksanen and Pihkala 1975; Pihkala 1988; *Finnish Statistical Yearbook.*

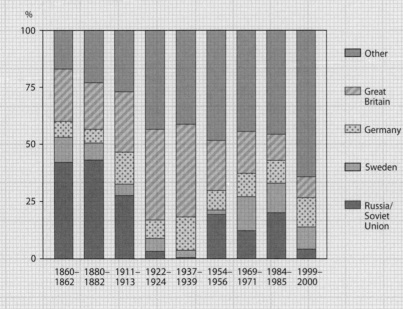

Figure 5.5b. Distribution of exports by country, selected years

Source: Pihkala 1969; Oksanen and Pihkala 1975; Pihkala 1988; *Finnish Statistical Yearbook.*

sink rapidly in the late 1870s, and the decline continued – with only a couple brief reverses – until the first decade of the 20th century. Since the demand for shipping is basically derived demand, this decline was inevitably connected with the slow growth of international trade during the "Long Depression". However, markets were also affected by the ongoing transition from sail to steam, which was producing tonnage with a much higher transport output than traditional sailing vessels. It was precisely in the 1870s that steam was taking over the cargo markets in the Baltic and the Mediterranean.

At that time, there were a small number of steamers in Finland, almost exclusively built of wood. Most of them were intended for passenger transportation, and very few were able to carry any large amounts of cargo. It became more difficult to finance changing over from sail to steam after the decline of freights, particularly since the transition to iron-hulled steamers meant the loss of the earlier comparative advantage of cheap home-built wooden ships. In this situation, most owners only had two choices: to continue sailing on long, and more peripheral, ocean routes where sail was still competitive, or to abandon shipping altogether. Many of the biggest shipowners chose the latter, sold their ships and invested more heavily in sawmills or the paper industry or other forms of manufacturing, while the option to continue sailing was mainly taken up by owners in those provinces, such as the Åland Islands, which did not experience any real industrial take-off.

With a substantial drain of capital from shipping, it was perhaps no wonder that the transition from sail to steam was slower in Finland than practically anywhere else in Europe. As late as 1895, steamships comprised only about eleven percent of Finland's total merchant (net register) tonnage, while in the vanguard maritime nations the proportion was well over 50 and rates below 20 percent were only found – in addition to Finland – in the USA, Canada and Norway. In 1913, the Finnish rate had improved to 24 percent but by then all other maritime nations with the exception of the USA (approx. 40%) had already exceeded the 50 percent mark, and proportions over 80 percent were common. Overall, in view of the fact that steamers were able to transport some three times as much cargo as sailing-vessels in a given time, the actual carrying capacity of global tonnage had grown as much as four- or fivefold between 1875 and 1913; the corresponding Finnish ratio was only about 1.5.

On the other hand, gross income from shipping (in real terms) also had increased about 1.5-fold, and in the early 1910s two-thirds of this was generated by steamers in spite of the fact that they represented only a quarter of overall tonnage. Moreover, the lion's share, about 85 percent,[15] of their income originated in regular lines of trade that served Finnish exports and imports (at the same time, the bulk of sailing tonnage consisted of big "windjammers" that were totally engaged in long-haul ocean trade) – which means that around 1875 they were earning roughly as much as all Finnish shipping together. About 40 percent of this amount, however, was income from Finnish and north Russian emigrants travelling to North America via Sweden or Britain, which had very

146

The icebreaker "Sampo" in the Gulf of Bothnia in 1996.

little to do with the country's foreign trade. The net result still seems to be that, at least measured by income, more imports and exports – maybe some 70 percent more – were carried by Finnish tonnage just before the First World War than in the 1870s. However, compared with the value of the trade, it represented a decidedly smaller fraction than before.[16]

There was only one bright spot in this bleak picture: winter traffic through the coastal ice-barriers started during this period. A small, strongly-built steamer, supported by subventions from the state, started in 1878 to ply between Stockholm and Finland's southernmost port, Hanko (Hangö) in wintertime. The next step was taken in March 1890, when the Finnish state commissioned its first real icebreaker. Three more icebreakers were built during the next two decades, and they made it possible to carry on traffic to Hanko and Turku throughout the winter months and also to substantially lengthen the season of navigation in Helsinki and a few other ports.[17]

Independent Finland: the primacy of the forestry industries continues

Statue of Paavo Nurmi being completed by sculptor Wäinö Aaltonen.

The First World War caused a sudden break in the Finnish economy by cutting its western trade to a fraction of the earlier levels. After the return of peace, the pendulum swung to the other extreme: Bolshevik Russia closed its borders, and its trade with the new republic of Finland sank almost to nil. The rapid growth of western trade, however, compensated for this, and the pre-war volume of foreign trade was re-attained by 1923–24.

During the 1920s and 1930s, the volume of Finnish exports continued to grow in spite of the fact that this was no golden age for the industrialized world. In this respect, however, developments in Finland were similar to those in the Scandinavian countries. This success resulted largely from Russia's withdrawal from the world timber market, as a result of which both Finland and Sweden were able to increase their production of sawn wood and became the undisputed market leaders. Finland was also successful in finding new western markets for its pulp and paper and, since the demand for these products continued to grow fairly quickly, exports increased at a similar rate. The sawmill boom, however, ended abruptly in 1928, when Russia re-entered the world timber market. Not surprisingly, supply exceeded demand, and soon the "Great Depression" increased the imbalance still further. In the sawmill business, prospects remained gloomy until the Second World War.

Developments in the inter-war period, however, did not result in any dramatic change from resource-intensive to high-value-added products. Although the proportion of what is generally called the "paper industry" increased, it was mainly because the export of pulp grew. As customs barriers for finished products were generally higher than those for semi-finished goods, Finnish pulp was more competitive on the world market than Finnish paper. Moreover, exports of timber, pit props and other raw timber continued to have an important role in forestry exports. Thus Finland still remained a producer of rather simple bulk products. This was, in fact, still the case some time after the Second World War.[18]

At least in one respect, by aiming at improved self-sufficiency, the economy of Finland took a step back from the trend of increasing the international division of labour. In agriculture, butter exports in the late 19th century reflected a specialisation in dairy produce which was compensated for by considerable imports of grain. After the war, butter exports revived, but subsequently their volume grew more slowly than total exports. Accordingly, the shares of agricultural produce never regained their previous, Russian-time levels. The import of grain, on the other hand, never again reached

148

the pre-war volumes and was gradually, mainly during the 1930s, reduced by more than a third.

Between 1919 and 1939, the volume of exports grew fourfold and that of imports almost threefold; compared with the level of 1913, both had doubled. This was an impressive rate during a period when protectionism was rising and international trade typically increased one percent a year, or 20 percent in two decades; it also was much faster than during the latter half of the 19th century. An important difference from the earlier trends was that exports regularly reached higher values in the 1920s and 1930s than imports; this feature was particularly conspicuous during the "Great Depression". Terms of trade, on the other hand, improved only marginally, but raw materials, fuels and investment goods dominated imports even more than they previously had: during both decades their share exceeded 80 percent.[19]

The First World War caused heavy losses to the Finnish merchant marine. At the end of 1918, the total seaworthy tonnage (excluding vessels sailing on the lakes) amounted to only about half of the tonnage in 1913. Although the proportion of steamers now was somewhat higher than before this, the fleet had lost most of its largest modern ships.

The rapid growth of foreign trade guaranteed a plentiful demand for shipping, particularly since the demise of Russian trade greatly decreased the proportion that was not seaborne. On the other hand, the dwindling of emigration and disappearance of Russian westbound passengers meant a big drop in the income of liner companies and, accordingly, decreased their possibilities of obtaining new tonnage. It is true that the net tonnage of steamships had exceeded that of sailing vessels even before 1925, but in 1930 the merchant marine's overall figure was still clearly below the pre-war level. Thus it was no wonder that the share of domestic vessels in export and import transports in the 1920s sank still lower than before the war: in the period 1922–27, the overall proportions fluctuated around 21–22 percent, while in exports they amounted to only 16 or 17 percent.

An up-turn started at the end of the decade, and, interestingly, the most rapid rise coincided with the worst years of the "Great Depression". In 1931, 1932 and 1933, Finnish steamship tonnage grew by as much as a half. As these were the very years when freights were at their lowest levels and large fleets of tramp ships were laid up, this was a good example of buying when everyone else was selling. Such behaviour was quite logical because Finnish shipowners were short of capital but had access to abundant low-wage labour. Accordingly, they bought cheap, elderly steamers which required larger crews than new ships, but they could man the vessels for less than their more modern competitors in high-wage countries.

Later, when freights and ship prices rose, tonnage growth continued at a much more moderate pace. In any case, total tonnage amounted in 1939 to 630,000 gross register tons (approx. 940,000 tons deadweight), some 60 percent more than before the war and, in view of the fact that steamships now

Marimekko clothes for men, women and children alike, designed by Annikki Rimala in the 1960s.

amounted to over 90 percent, its actual carrying capacity can be estimated as four times higher than in 1913. Thus Finland too had now completed the transition from sail to steam. However, the proportion of very old steamers was so high that this can be called a poor man's transition – moreover, the registers still contained a substantial number of sailing vessels, both large iron and steel ocean-going ships and small wooden coastal sailing vessels.

In any case, the growth of tonnage exceeded the growth of foreign trade in the 1930s. Accordingly, the share of domestic tonnage started to rise. At the end of the 1930s, it reached about 40 percent of Finland's export and import transports. Finnish ships also increased their participation in international cross-trades: around 1939, some 35 percent of total shipping income was generated by voyages between foreign countries.

Finland's comparative advantages in international competition were still related to abundant forest resources and cheap labour. The size of the latter advantage is tangibly shown by the fact that sailors' wages were lower than in Greece, and almost as low as in Estonia and Latvia. Indeed, in the 1930s, the Finnish flag was gaining favour as a "flag of convenience" as some British and Swedish owners adopted it in order to gain access to cheaper labour.[20]

Fiskars scissors and shell by Tapio Wirkkala (1960).

Increasingly free trade with east and west

The Second World War once again severed normal trading relations for half a decade. It also resulted in an important change: Finland's trade with the Soviet Union grew much more significant than before the war, thus reviving the former traditions of Russian times. This development started with the war reparations which Finland, according to the peace agreement, was obliged to pay to the Soviet Union. These were mainly in the form of machines, cables and ships, not in forestry products or paper. After the reparations had been paid off, there was still a demand for similar products beyond the Iron Curtain and, later, textiles and other consumption goods were also exported. In return, Finland imported oil and heavy industrial products. By the 1950s, the Soviet Union had become one of Finland's most important trading partners. However, its share shrank in the 1960s, when Western trade expanded: typically, its share of both exports and imports fluctuated between 12 and 15 percent. After the oil crises of the 1970s, it rose to a good 20, but declined with sinking oil prices after 1983, dropping to around ten percent during the last years of the Soviet era.

In the 1950s, Western trade remained much as it had been before the war: sawn wood, pulp and paper dominated exports, and Britain remained the most important partner; in imports West Germany regained the leading position during the latter half of the 1950s. In the following decade, the development of European free-trade blocks introduced some interesting new trends. After Finland joined EFTA in 1960, its trade with the relevant Scandinavian and Western European countries started to increase. Equally predictable was the fact that, after

150

the conclusion of an agreement with the expanding EEC – and the demise of EFTA – Finland's trade with the former grew. These free trade arrangements did not, however, directly affect Finnish-Soviet trade because in both cases Finland granted similar tariff reductions to the Soviet Union and other Eastern block countries. Neither did they result in any sudden changes because the reductions in customs duties were gradual.

In principle, the most interesting new trend was the growth of trade with Sweden, which started right from the beginning of the 1960s. Previously, it had been quite modest, which was really no wonder in view of the fact that that both countries enjoyed similar comparative advantages, particularly as far as forest products were concerned. The growth was systematic until the oil crises, and at the beginning of the 1970s, Sweden was already one of Finland's most important trading partners.

Flying Finns:
Janne Ahonen and
Mika Häkkinen.

This change was parallel with a substantial structural change in Finland's exports. In the 1950s, about 75–80 percent of them still consisted of wood and paper products. From the mid-1960s on, this proportion sank steadily down to 35 percent around 1985. At the same time, the share of the metal industry increased from a few percent to about 35, that of other industrial products, such as textiles and chemicals, to about 20 percent and the export of raw wood ceased. The growth in percentages indicates that these products also found markets outside the Eastern block, at first in Sweden and subsequently in Western Europe. Accordingly, the share of the Eastern block in the exports of these commodities sank from 80 percent to about 20 until the early 1970s, while that of Sweden rose to about 30 and the share of other Efta countries to 20 percent.

As the forest industries also moved from timber to paper products, and from pulp to increasingly high-quality paper, there was a substantial overall improvement in the average value-added of exports. On the other hand, really high-technology products still comprised a very modest share of the total, some 2.5 percent in the early 1970s and about six percent after 1985. Moreover, even at the latter date, the imports of such products still amounted to double the corresponding exports. On the other hand, it is quite clear that Finland was not a low-wage country anymore: the general level of labour costs increased so much after the Second World War that the competitive edge of the country's products increasingly depended on other factors of production.

The growing importance of machines, textiles and other non-forest products also meant that Finland's exports became increasingly similar to its imports – and the products of many other industrialized countries, such as Sweden. Similar developments, the exchange of increasingly similar products, suggesting a weakening of the former division of labour, have been observed all over the industrial world. It seems that the comparative advantages, at least those that depend on resources and other natural endowments, have lost in importance compared with capital and know-how.[21]

As far as imports are concerned, the share of consumer goods increased slightly until high oil prices changed the situation. In any case, raw-materials and capital goods systematically fluctuated around 80 percent, which can be regarded as a very healthy proportion.

The volume of exports and imports reached pre-war levels by 1950, and by 1985 they had grown about eightfold. This implies an average rate of six percent a year, which was clearly faster than in the 1920s and 1930s. The balance of trade, however, was negative more often than otherwise. Before 1960, the deficit was partly compensated for by a marked improvement in the terms of trade, but after that there was no such trend any more.[22]

Finland's merchant marine suffered heavy losses during the war, and after it many ships had to be handed over to the Soviet Union as war reparations. Accordingly, until the early 1950s, there was a continuous deficit of tonnage, which actually may have hampered the growth of exports.

On the other hand, the rapid growth of foreign trade – not only in Finland but all over the industrialized world – heralded brighter prospects for shipping. The increasing proportion of trade with the Soviet Union and Sweden, of course, meant that shorter transports became more common than before. Another interesting feature was the fact that the earlier imbalance in the physical volume of exports and imports diminished with the growth of oil imports and was already reversed in the mid-1960s. However, because crude oil is transported in special tankers which seldom carry any other cargo, this did not decrease the frequency of ballasted voyages.

The 1950s and 1960s were not bad times for European shipping, and the Finnish merchant marine also grew at a good pace. From a low point of about 270,000 gross tons in 1945, it increased to approx. 650,000 in 1950, which already exceeded the tonnage of 1939. One million gross tons were recorded in 1966, two million in 1975 and the development culminated at the beginning of the 1980s with a total capacity slightly exceeding 2.5 million tons gross (3.8 mill. tons deadweight). This brought shipping back to an international status similar to the one it had enjoyed in the third quarter of the 19th century: gauged by the tonnage per population ratio – and excluding flag-of-convenience fleets – Finland occupied the sixth rank in the world in 1975; at this time, however, all the Scandinavian countries ranked higher.

It was not only a matter of quantitative growth but also of a qualitative transition. Old steamers were replaced with new motorships, and sailing vessels disappeared altogether. Steamers also became so rare that their tonnage amounted to only five percent in 1970. An important background factor in the technical transition was the development of the country's own shipbuilding industry, which in certain areas such as icebreakers, ro-ro (roll-on – roll-off) ships and passenger-cargo ferries ranked among the best in the world in the 1970s.

Linked to this rapid modernisation was an increase in labour costs. An the end of the 1940s, working conditions similar to those in Sweden were adopted in Finland – including a three-watch system instead of the traditional two-watch one and increased time-off for sailors. Wages also rose to the same level as those of industrial workers. Thus, in the span of a single decade, the

152

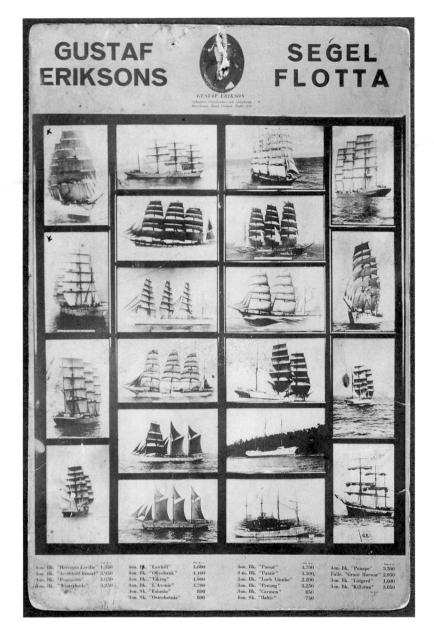

The barque *Herzogin Cecilie*, pictured here, is probably the best-known of Gustaf Erikson's tall ships. A number of books have been written about its voyages. The loss of the vessel, after it ran aground off the British coast, in 1936, was world news. The remains of the *Herzogin Cecilie* can still be found in Starhole Bay, in Devon, England.

Gustaf Eriksons's fleet. Gustaf Erikson was a Finnish shipowner from the Åland Islands who bought up second-hand, iron-hulled sailing ships after the First World War and, thanks to low labour and capital costs, was able to run a fleet of them efficiently and profitably despite competition from modern vessels. Erikson's ships were mainly used to carry grain from Australia to Europe, as steamers could not make sufficient profit in this low-value business. Erikson's fleet was the largest and the last of its kind in the world. After the Second World War, the grain trade declined although Erikson's windjammers did not make their last voyages on the grain run until 1949. The picture shows Erikson's fleet. Some of the vessels have been preserved as museum ships: The *Pommern* in Marienhamn (Åland), the *Viking* in Gothenburg (Sweden), the *Passat* in Travemünde (Germany), and the *Moshulu* in Philadelphia (USA).

Finnish flag ceased to be one of the cheapest and moved into the high-cost group. The loss of the former comparative advantage created a strong impetus for owners to modernize in order to compensate for the increasing wage-bill with technical efficiency. Another impetus factor was port costs, which led to the adoption of container and ro-ro systems in liner traffic. The transition was made easier in the 1960s and 1970s, when most European states started to subsidize their shipbuilding, and this inevitably kept the prices for newly built vessels quite attractive. Good profitability is clearly indicated by the fact that many manufacturing companies invested heavily in ships in the 1960s. In this respect, too, the 19th-century competition between shipping and exporting industries was repeated.

The expansion of tonnage was clearly seen in export and import shipping. Around 1950, the proportion of domestic tonnage was at roughly the same level as just before the war, about 35 percent in exports and 50 percent in imports; at the beginning of the 1980s, the respective ratios ranged between 60 and 65 percent. At the same time, Finnish ships increased their participation in foreign cross-trade. Even so, around 1980 some 70 percent of shipping income was still earned in carrying the country's own foreign trade.[23] Overall, shipping was also the most important element in balancing the deficits of foreign trade.

Another important contribution to foreign trade transportation was the expansion of winter traffic that took place in the 1960s and 1970s. In the 1930s the volume of shipping during the winter (December–April) season still amounted to only about 20 percent of the annual total; this, compared with the share in the 1910s, was not a huge improvement. The modernisation and expansion of the state's icebreaker fleet raised this proportion to 30 percent by 1960 and to 38–40 percent in the 1980s. The latter percentage in fact indicates that most of the seasonal variations in shipping had disappeared. This was also reflected in the fact that the number of winter harbours expanded. By the late 1950s they included all ports between Kotka and Pori, and in the early 1970s, the northern Finnish ports also remained open during normal winters. Finally, in 1975, a decision was made that all ports catering for foreign shipping should be kept open even during the coldest winters. Such a program was, of course, a heavy blow to the railways, which had earned well carrying northern export products to southern ports in wintertime.[24]

The growth of the Finnish merchant marine culminated in the early 1980s, when portents of a great transformation in international shipping were becoming increasingly obvious. Cheap tonnage prices and national subventions had created a massive over-production of shipping, and the growth of tonnage sailing under so-called flags of convenience, and other cheap flags, increased competition. When ocean freights plunged at the end of the 1970s, many more shipowners in high-cost countries started to "outflag" their vessels to cheaper registers. In less than a decade, this led to the demise of traditional national merchant navies in the West. This also happened in Finland. From 2.5 millions in 1981, the country's overall tonnage dropped to 0.84 million tons gross in 1987.

154

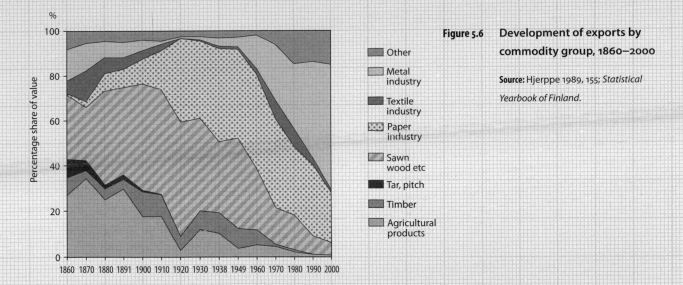

Figure 5.6 **Development of exports by commodity group, 1860–2000**

Source: Hjerppe 1989, 155; *Statistical Yearbook of Finland.*

Legend: Other; Metal industry; Textile industry; Paper industry; Sawn wood etc; Tar, pitch; Timber; Agricultural products

Compared with earlier data, the volume of agricultural exports seems much larger. Over half of these went to Russia (St. Petersburg), but they were not adequately recorded before the 1850s. The graph clearly demonstrates the growth of forest-based exports from the 1870s on and their dominance between 1920 and 1950. With regard to the rapid growth of the exports of the metal and engineering industries after 1980, it must be remembered that this sector included those industries which developed into the strong telecommunications sector in the 1990s. In 2000, the share of this sector was about 30% of all exports, which means that the "traditional" engineering industries only accounted for some 25%.

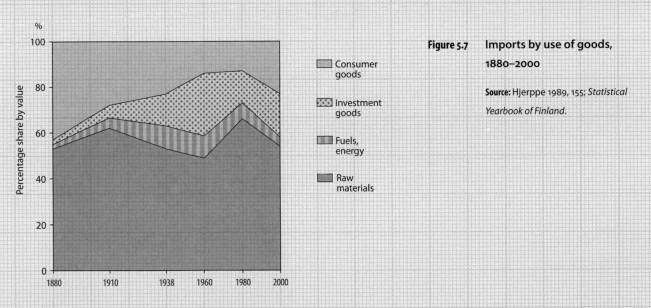

Figure 5.7 **Imports by use of goods, 1880–2000**

Source: Hjerppe 1989, 155; *Statistical Yearbook of Finland.*

Legend: Consumer goods; Investment goods; Fuels, energy; Raw materials

Before 1880, the way fuels were classified in import statistics was inadequate; therefore the series cannot be extended to earlier times. Raw materials include unground grain.

Basically, this "great shipping crisis" was the first powerful example of the new forces in the international economy that we now call globalisation. Because of its nature as an extremely international activity, shipping was the first to be affected. Manufacturing and other industries as well as foreign trade were to feel the effects of globalisation in due course.

Towards a global world

The last fifteen years of the 20th century were a period of unusually dramatic fluctuations in the Finnish economy. The boom period at the end of the 1980s ended abruptly, and the following depression was deepened by a serious banking crisis. At the same time, the collapse of the Soviet system and the following economic disorder shrank Russia's imports from Finland to a fraction of their former levels, thus making the economic recession even worse. The great depression also started substantial structural changes in both the private and the public sectors, which seem to have improved the country's international competitiveness. The resulting upswing was just as impressive as the previous decline, with new, technologically advanced industries – such as telecommunications – emerging as the engines of growth.

The structural change can clearly be seen in exports. The forest and traditional metal industries, which shared the top positions in the mid-1980s, have continued roughly on equal terms up to the first years of the 21st century (the forest industries having a slight edge before 2000 and the metal industry thereafter), but their shares of the total have declined from the earlier level of 35 percent to 25–30 percent. The rapid expansion of the electro-technical industry (telecommunications – earlier it was classified among the metal industries), which really started in the 1990s, brought this new branch right to the top in 2000 with a share of approx. 30 percent (of which Nokia alone accounted for 24 percent),[25] but since then they have experienced a slight relative decline. At present, these three sectors are pretty well on a par with each other – and they are the undisputed leaders with a combined share of some 80 percent of the country's exports. Not surprisingly, this development also resulted in a prominent rise of the value-added of exports, and the proportion of so-called high-tech products grew from well below ten percent in 1990 to a level around 20 percent at the turn of the millennium. This also meant that the exports of such products exceeded the corresponding imports.

The structure of imports, on the other hand, has changed relatively little. Around 2000, raw-materials (energy included) amounted to a half, and capital goods increased the share of producer goods to 70–75 percent. The relative weight of consumer goods undoubtedly increased but still remains at a fairly sound level.

Over these fifteen years, the growth of foreign trade fluctuated strongly. The modest boom at the end of the 1980s was followed by stagnation after the

156

turn of the decade. Exports started to expand rapidly already in 1993, and imports followed them after a time lag of one year; the boom culminated in 2000 and was then followed by a slowdown. Overall, the volume of trade doubled during the period, which was slower than during the previous three decades (about 5 percent a year). Exports grew faster than imports, in particular between 1991 and 2000, when the average growth rate approached ten percent a year. This resulted in a substantial surplus in the balance of trade. The terms of trade, on other hand, did not change in the long term.

The distribution of Finland's trade by countries does not really indicate that globalisation is taking place everywhere. If partners are ranked according to the sums of their respective volumes of exports and imports, the top three positions are occupied by the same countries which – excluding the Soviet Union – did so around 1985: Germany (now including, of course, the former East Germany), Sweden and Great Britain. The trade with Russia has also increased from the nadir around 1992 and it now (2006) ranks at the same level as that of Great Britain – mainly because of oil imports. On about the same level as both of these is the USA, which means that its relative importance has doubled since 1985.

Although the share of Asia has increased moderately – mainly because of China – Finland's foreign trade still remains very Eurocentric, with only a quarter of the exchange of goods taking place with other continents. As the share of the European Union amounts to almost 60 percent, and those of Germany, Sweden, Russia and Estonia to about 35 percent, the geographic focus of Finland's foreign trade seems even more north European, or Baltic, than it was in the early 20th century. This may be taken as a further indication of the demise of Finland's traditional comparative advantages. But does it also mean that globalisation is just an imaginary "paper tiger"? Before such a conclusion is drawn we must note that conventional foreign trade statistics are very im-

perfect instruments for analysing the forces of globalisation. Global firms and
worldwide movements of capital have created an international, or supra-natio-
nal, "no-mans land", of which national statistics can only grasp isolated slices. A
good example is Nokia, with factories in China, India and many other countries
– only a fraction (a quarter or a fifth) of the firm's production is exported from
Finland. The same also applies to the biggest forest industry concerns.[26]

Similar signs of globalisation are also clearly to be seen in modern international shipping. Thus, it has become increasingly difficult to define what
"Finnish shipping" is: many shipping companies based in Finland fly the co-
lours of different "open" or "convenience" registers but, at the same time, several ships registered in Finland are owned by foreign companies. Shipping
between Finland and foreign countries is easier to define and, irrespective of
the nationality of the ships engaged in such traffic, it can be claimed that the
growth of Finnish foreign trade has continued to increase the demand for shipping services. On the other hand, the economic growth of the Baltic republics
as well as the recovery of Russia (with the opening of their freight market) has
benefited all shipping visiting the Baltic Sea.

In global shipping, the growth of tonnage has taken place mainly under
different flags of convenience; from about 30 percent of global tonnage in 1980,
their share rose to some 60 percent in 2000 and has now reached at least 65
percent. In comparison, the development of Finnish-flag tonnage does not fit
too well in this picture. From the lowest point in 1987 (0.84 mill. gross tons), it
recovered slowly and reached 1.7 million tons in 1999.[27] This optimistic mood
may have been caused by Finland's joining the EU, but as this did not increase
the national subventions to shipping, the rise was aborted after 2000.

The tonnage which Finnish companies owned abroad also increased at
first, reaching 1.7 million gross tons in 1994 (which means that Finnish owners

158

controlled some 3.3 million gross tons of shipping, or a third more than in 1981). Since then, this fleet has declined and was about 1.1 million tons in 2000.

There is a fairly clear-cut division of labour between the tonnages sailing under low-cost (convenience) and high-cost flags. The former consist of tankers and bulk-carriers, most of which sail on long-haul ocean routes. The latter, that is ships which remained in the Finnish register (or Finnish-owned ships in for example Swedish and German registers), were mainly container or ro-ro cargo vessels or passenger-cargo vessels engaged in regular liner services, mainly on the Baltic. Accordingly, this specialisation also means that the Finnish flag has almost disappeared from the oceans and can nowadays mainly be found in "short-sea" feeder services. This division of labour is also connected with the economics of shipping. During "the great shipping crisis", freights seem to have declined most in bulk trade (both dry and oil), in particular on long intercontinental routes, while liner traffic on short seas may have suffered less. Thus, while western crews have totally disappeared from intercontinental shipping, they can still be found in the latter type of traffic.

The tonnage still registered in Finland seems to be intimately associated with cargo and passenger traffic to and from Finnish ports. In spite of this, the proportion of Finnish ships in such traffic has systematically declined – so much so that the transport balance – which in the mid-1990s still presented a substantial surplus, turned negative around the turn of the millennium. It seems obvious that the demand for cargo space to and from Finland increased faster than Finnish-flag tonnage.[28]

Some conclusions

This overview shows clearly that, from the early 17th century to the First World War, the position of Finland in relation to the world economy, and in particular to the developed "core" areas, that is, western Europe, remained mainly unaltered: the country was a supplier of forestry produce, that is, of cheap raw materials and semi-finished products. Moreover, between World War I and the 1950s, the changes were still modest – indeed, a real transition was only experienced after the latter decade and particularly during the two last decades of the 20th century.

At least in quantitative terms, Finland's integration with the "world economy" was a process which started in the early modern period. The progress of this integration can be roughly gauged by the volume of forestry exports, both in actual terms and in relation to the local economy. Around 1630, the value of tar exports (at local selling prices) corresponded with the value of sufficient grain to feed a population of about 20,000 (or five percent of the contemporary total) for a whole year; around 1840, exports of tar and sawn and other timber already corresponded with similar provisions for 135,000–140,000 people (about ten percent), and by 1913 forestry product exports (incl. pulp and pa-

159

per) rose to a value high enough to buy their daily bread for over 7.5 million people (that is: for double the population of Finland at that time).[29]

Around 1860, the total value of Finnish exports corresponded to some ten percent of the gross domestic product; by 1910, the ratio was already around 20–25 percent. Although the country is fairly small (it is noteworthy that foreign trade ratios tend to be larger in small than big economies), the latter may be regarded a rather high proportion. This decade, however, seems to have been a turning point. Levels which were attained in the inter-war period were only marginally higher, but they sank considerably after the Second World War and rose to 20 percent only at the end of 1960s. During the following decade, mainly because of oil prices, the share of imports rose quickly, with exports following after some delay; around 1980 both ratios fluctuated between 25 and 30 percent. Since then, no dramatic changes have taken place, but most recently exports have tended to rate higher (about 30%) than imports (around 23–24%). Thus it may be concluded that exports, by growing clearly faster than domestic demand, were the primary "engine of growth" until the end of the 19th century; since then, the roles of foreign and domestic demand have been more balanced. It was only during the last two decades of the 20th century that exports amounted to higher proportions of domestic production than in the 1920s and 1930s.[30]

The progress of Finnish economic integration was also affected by maritime transport. As was seen above, it could be an important source of foreign income – and even an instrument of economic control. So long as freights were high, the distribution of foreign trade income to a large degree depended on who did the actual carrying. Thus the Dutch dominance in the 17th century meant that most of the profits in the tar trade went to the Dutch rather than to the Finnish economy. The partial success of the Swedish Crown in challenging the Dutch again mainly profited the capital, Stockholm, and in particular tho-

160

se merchants who were shareholders in the tar company. It was only the rise of local shipping in the wake of the Swedish navigation act which turned the scales and transformed Finnish merchants from passive deliverers of tar and other forest produce to active maritime traders. Interestingly, this led to a situation which was an antithesis of the former, to shipping which rather was an independent industry competing with exporting industries. If some 50–60 percent of the cross income from shipping originated in foreign cross trades in the 1860s and 1870s, and if Finnish exports and imports were burdened by freight costs of about a quarter of the total value of the trade, it can be estimated that shipping earned an income amounting to more than a half of the overall value of the country's foreign trade, that is, more than the value of exports.

While profitable blue-water shipping may have lured investments away from industry, it was at the same time an important agent of integration. Active involvement in international markets created business contacts and information networks which were of great value even when shipping was no longer the primary interest. Shipping also accumulated capital which could be transferred to the forest industries later, after the decline in international freights. Thus it seems that in Finland, too, merchant capitalism paved the way for industrial capitalism, that foreign trade and shipping should be regarded as the "twin-engines of growth" until the late 1870s.

The role of transport in the process of economic integration was also important in another sense: as long as freight rates were very high, they affected the international division of labour in a rather decisive way. In the 1790s, the freight price for transports from Wiborg to Hull amounted to about the same as the fob price in Wiborg; in other words, transport doubled the price for the consumer (or halved the price received by the exporter). At the end of the 1860s, it was still almost a third of the fob price.[31] It was only the transport revolution of the late 19th century which started a more rapid decline in freights: from the 1860s until the First World War, the overall transport costs of Finnish exports, for example, sank from about a quarter to around 10 percent – a decrease which must have contributed quite a lot to the improvement of Finland's terms of trade. In the 1990s, after "the great shipping crisis", the corresponding "freight ratios" seem to have amounted to a mere 3–3.5 percent.[32]

If the cost of transporting goods from one country to another added to the price by a third, no imported products could compete with similar domestic ones – unless the former could be manufactured at much lower costs, or could not be produced at all in the importing country. Thus, for a long time, international trade concentrated on goods for which the seller enjoyed a comparative, or absolute advantage. This "iron law" confined Finland to being an exporter of forest produce, and made it a market for Atlantic and Mediterranean salt. But it must be remembered that this depended not only on differences of natural conditions but also on transport costs. Afterwards, the big decline in both maritime and overland freights made it possible to successfully market those exports that do not depend on any classical comparative advantages, not

In Finland, the key to success has always been innovation, not cheap labour, says Professor Pekka Himanen, leading researcher of the information society. He sees Finland's future in creativity that permeates the whole economy from traditional industries like wood processing and services to the new cutting edge technologies. The picture represents internationalisation in Oulu, northern Finland, in the 21st century.

at least on those derived from special natural resources. This dramatic demise in the price of distance has been a sine qua non prerequisite of the creation of the modern global economy.[33]

In addition to transport costs, foreign trade has naturally been affected by another classical impediment, customs dues. Their overall effect, however, is difficult to estimate because they are very selective: typically, they mainly concerned imports, and in particular those of luxury goods (tobacco, coffee, sugar) or products which competed with articles produced by domestic industries, and they might even differ for different countries according to existing trade agreements. Accordingly, customs have hardly ever been a systematic burden on all kind of trade. In some cases, states have used income from them for productive investments, and they may have protected the development of nascent industries – but more often they have simply constituted an additional cost.

A rough idea of the height of customs barriers can be gained by comparing the sum of the collected revenues with the value of trade. In Finland, the ratios were quite low at the beginning of the Russian era, with import dues amounting to about five percent of the overall value of imports, and export dues to a couple of percent of the respective export value. These ratios seem to have been quite close to those existing during the last decades of Swedish rule; Thus they were, on average, small compared with transport costs.

Export dues sank during the 19th century and were abolished altogether in 1882. Import dues, on the other hand, increased up to the 1850s to an overall level of over 15 percent. After free trade agreements, they were lowered in Finland, too, by almost a half in the 1860s, but a new wave of protectionism in the 1880s raised the level back to that of the 1850s, and this was maintained to the end of the Russian period. Not surprisingly, import dues were raised further in the 1920s until the overall level was about 30 percent of imports. The ratio declined slightly in the 1930s, but even after the Second World War, until the 1960s, it remained at around 20 percent. It was only the formation of European free-trade blocks that started a big decrease. By 1965, 43 percent of Finland's imports were already duty-free and by the end of the 1990s the proportion had risen to 84 percent. At the same time, customs barriers were also lowered worldwide, and around 1990, import customs amounted to only 1.3 percent of the overall value of Finnish imports.[34]

The figures presented above tell only one half of the story; it would be of equal importance to know the size of the customs dues that Finnish exports had to pay abroad – however, collecting such data would be a rather difficult exercise. Fortunately, customs policies developed in roughly similar ways all over the developed Western world – thus we may suppose that there was at least some reciprocity between the dues collected in Finland for imports and those which Finnish exports had to pay abroad. Moreover, the general trend was that countries charged higher dues for finished, or high value-added, products than for primary or semi-finished goods. Accordingly, customs policies in general tended to reinforce the effects of transport costs in maintaining the position

162

Imports of raw wood from Russia increased early in the 21st century.

of Finland as a supplier of low-value-added products. In this respect, a fundamental change took place only during the last three or four decades of the 20th century. The removal of customs within the European free-trade areas may not have been a sufficient condition for the transition towards high-value-added exports, but it can be regarded at least as an important contributing factor.

At least as far as Finnish timber exports are concerned, a plausible conclusion seems to be that transport costs were a more common impediment than customs dues until the late 19th century. However, the huge rise in the productivity of shipping after the third quarter of that century, in addition to increases in import duties since the 1880s, seems to have reversed the situation – indeed, one may well ask whether the new wave of protectionism was a reaction to increased international competition resulting from the ongoing drop in transport costs. In any case, there is no doubt that customs dues took on a primary role as impediments to trade in the 1920s or 1930s, and this pattern prevailed until the new wave of free trade began. On the other hand, the recent demise of customs duties was almost contemporary with a big decrease in ocean freights and, since the 1980s, the majority of Finnish foreign trade has taken place in an environment which for all practical purposes functions like a home market. On a global scale, customs barriers still exist, but with the long-haul transportation of raw-materials being cheaper than ever before, natural resources have lost much of their importance as sources of comparative advantages. As the transfer of capital and know-how is also relatively easy, the most obvious competitive differences between different economic blocks or individual market economies are connected with the price of labour and social capital.

"Workday"

by Armas Mikola

(1970, oil on canvas, 75 x 147 cm)

The Labour Market, 1850–2000

Matti Hannikainen and Sakari Heikkinen

Industrialisation, the expansion of the wage-labourer class and a structural change in the labour force all took place in Finland late, compared with other Western European countries. Finland started to industrialise in the late 19th century, and its industrialisation period lasted long into the 20th. During the second half of the 20th century, the expansion of private services and the formation of the welfare state created job opportunities, especially for women. During this transformation period, the labour market changed from domination by employers to a system with strong trade unions and centralised collective bargaining. In addition to the exceptional structural change, there were two major peacetime crises in the Finnish labour market during the 20th century, namely the depressions of the 1930s and the 1990s. In the former crisis, both employment and real wages fell, whereas in the latter in practice only employment declined. At the beginning of the 21st century, the Scandinavian-style social contract between employers and employees in industrial relations and the Nordic welfare state have been threatened by an ageing workforce, European integration and globalisation.

Introduction

Finland turned into a modern wage-work society relatively late compared with other Western European countries. Rural "multi-employment" and different forms of "self-employment" characterised the Finnish economy long into the 20th century before giving way to modern full-time wage-work. While the transformation was comparatively late – taking place to a great extent after the Second World War – it was on the other hand quite rapid. The labour market too has changed fundamentally. Nowadays Finland has a regulated labour market with high female employment (especially in public services), strong trade unions, centralised collective bargaining, a high wage level, and strong wage rigidity.

In the middle of the 19th century, the industrialisation process in Finland was only beginning. We might also claim that there was no labour market in the modern sense of the word. During the latter half of the 19th century, the labour market started to evolve: the number of wage-labourers increased, and economic legislation – including labour laws – was modernised. The process was, however, rather slow, since Finland was to a great extent an agricultural economy where much of the economic activity was not directly governed by the market mechanism. However, as the economy became more industrialised, the labour market too was modernised.

In this article we examine the long-term changes in the Finnish labour market. The structure of the article is as follows. First, we outline the major changes in the structure of labour. Second, we describe the changes in the institutional setting of the Finnish labour market. Third, we analyse the changing nature of unemployment and government policy in this field. Fourth, we examine some features of wage development and what they indicate about the functioning of the labour market. Finally, we discuss the present state of the Finnish labour market in a historical perspective.

The structure of labour

The structure of labour in Finland has changed in several respects during the last 150 years. Firstly, the distribution of employment between industries has changed dramatically: the share of primary production has decreased steadily, the share of secondary production – manufacturing and construction – has first increased and then stayed constant, and the share of services has grown throughout the period (see Figure 6.1). The big picture is same as in other developed economies, but there are also some differences mainly resulting from the late start of industrialisation in Finland (on the structural change of the Finnish economy, see Hjerppe and Jalava in this volume).

During the latter half of the 19th century, Finland was predominantly an agricultural economy, and in 1900 the employment share of primary produc-

166

tion was still 70%. Industrialisation had already started, but its pace was rather slow. After the 1890s industrialisation accelerated, and during the first half of the 20th century the employment share of primary production fell to under 50% (39% in 1950), so that the majority of the labour force was in secondary production and services (32% and 29% respectively in 1950). By comparison with Western European nations, Finland was in 1950 still a very agrarian country, where manufacturing and other secondary production never achieved the same dominating position as in early industrialised countries as the share of services grew simultaneously with secondary production.[1]

Finland reached her industrialisation peak relatively late, in the 1970s, after which the employment share of manufacturing declined. The nadir was reached during the recession of the early 1990s; after that a wave of "new industrialisation"[2] kept the employment share of secondary production at a stable level – despite leaps in productivity. In 2000 the share of secondary production in employment was only few percentage points smaller than in 1950 (a decrease from 32% to 28%). During the decades after the Second-World-War, the on-going decline in the share of primary production on one hand and the increase in the share of services on the other caused big changes in the labour force.

By the start of the 21st century more than 60 per cent of working Finns were employed in service industries. The picture shows opening day at a shopping centre in Espoo in 2003.

167

The employment share of services exceeded 60% at the turn of the 21st century, whereas the share of primary production was well under 10%. A further feature to be noted in the postwar development was the rising share of employment in public services. The growth of the public sector and the formation of the welfare state were rapid in Finland, especially in the 1970s and 1980s, which is somewhat later than for instance in Sweden (see Eloranta and Kauppila on the public sector and Kettunen on the welfare state in this volume).

The structural change in Finland after the Second World War thus resembled the development in Western countries in some respects but also differed from it in others. The postwar period until the first oil crisis of the 1970s has been regarded as a "Golden Age" in Western societies, a unique episode in "modern economic growth". Compared with the previous decades and the post-1973 period, the "Golden Age" witnessed rapid economic growth, an increase in productivity, mild cyclical fluctuations, low unemployment and decreasing inequality. Many European countries experienced a rapid catching-up process with extensive welfare-enhancing policy interventions. Characteristic of this period in Finland was a "belated" structural change from a rural society into an industrialised and urbanised society: the country was industrialised, and at the same time services became the largest sector of employment. The number of salaried white-collar employees increased in all sectors of the economy: their share doubled from 15% to 30% in the period 1950–1970. Another dramatic phenomenon in the structural change of these decades was the extensive emigration from the rural and northern parts of Finland to Sweden in the late 1960s. It seems probable that this phenomenon – the emigration of potential unemployed persons – made it easier to implement structural and technological change in society. It is also a sign of the relative "backwardness" of the Finnish economy (on the migration from rural areas, see Ojala and Nummela in this volume).

Although the oil crisis also affected Finland, the break in the favourable development was not as abrupt as in many other countries, and for instance the 1980s were again a period of favourable growth. There are at least two reasons for the exceptional development in Finland: the bilateral trade with the Soviet Union continued to grow (exports increasing as the price of imported oil rose), and the public sector was expanding. The formation of the welfare state decreased resistance to structural changes in the economy and at the same time created new job opportunities especially for women. The participation rate of women also increased because of several welfare reforms from the 1970s to the1990s that provided incentives or made it easier for women to be employed.[3] The difference between male and female participation rates narrowed considerably: in 1970 the participation rate of men was 82.0% and that of women 62.1%, whereas in 2001 the rates were 76.6% and 72.4% respectively (calculated from the population aged 15–64 years). The wage gap between men and women has also narrowed. In the 20th century the ratio of female manufacturing workers' wages to male workers' wages developed as follows:[4]

168

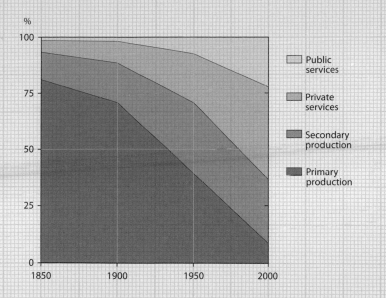

Figure 6.1 **Distribution of employment, 1850–2000 (%)**

Sources: Hjerppe 1989; National Accounts, Statistics Finland.

Industrialisation started in the late 19th century; however, manufacturing and other secondary production never achieved the same dominating position as in early industrialised countries as the share of services grew simultaneously with secondary production. The expansion of private services and the formation of the welfare state have created job opportunities especially for women. Until the Second World War, Finland was a very agrarian country.

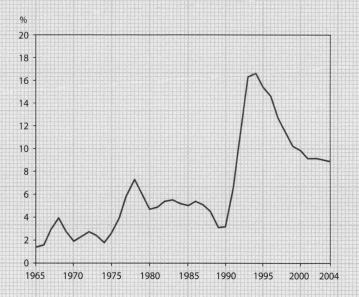

Figure 6.2 **Unemployment rate 1965–2004 (%)**

Source: Labour Force Survey, Statistics Finland.

Unemployment has peaked twice since the 1960s: first in the 1970s and then in the 1990s – both times without returning to pre-depression levels. Reliable figures on unemployment exist from the 1960s onwards. In earlier years, the lack of appropriate data complicates the construction of long-term figures on unemployment. Moreover, the concept of unemployment describes inaccurately the livelihood problems of those people who obtained their living from agriculture. It is important to note that the definition of unemployment has changed during the period covered by the Labour Force Survey. Furthermore, the Employment Service data compiled by the Ministry of Labour describe unemployment in a different way.

c. 1910	55%
1936	58%
1950	65%
1975	72%
2000	81 %

The narrowing of the wage gap to a great extent resulted from the decrease in the human-capital differences between men and women. In the early 20th century, the proportion of experienced – and thus more skilled – workers was notably higher among male than female workers. After the Second World War, and especially since the 1960s, the gender differences in education and work careers have diminished, and this – together with growing non-tolerance of wage discrimination based on sex – has helped to narrow the wage gap.[5] Centralised collective bargaining together with legislation have also decreased the gap in earnings between men and women.

Labour market institutions

Juridically speaking, we can date the birth of the "modern" free wage-worker in Finland to the 1860s and 1870s. A new liberalist view of the employment relationship as a voluntary contract between juridically equal free individuals was recorded in the Craft and Manufacture Act of 1859, the Trade Acts of 1868 and 1879, and in other related acts. Before this liberalist transformation, the wage-labour relationship was seen as a master–servant relationship. This was in accordance with the general socio-political philosophy of the "Society of the Estates", where the population was divided into different estates, i.e. social groups with different rights. According to the new liberalist ideals, the employment relationship as a relationship involving the selling and buying of labour was not fundamentally different from other business contracts because workers had ownership of their property, that is their labour, just as entrepreneurs had of their capital.[6]

The nature of the employment contract changed with the reforms of the 1850s–1870s. According to the "old" labour legislation, it was a contract of service, but in the new law, the employment contract became more clearly a bilateral legal act between employer and employee. This change in the juridical form of the employment relationship can be also characterised as "individualisation". According to "modern" liberalist legal thinking, the employment contract belonged to the realm of civil law and was a contract between individuals. The labour laws of the *ancien régime*, on the contrary, not only regulated the relationship between individual employers and their employees but also contained stipulations – on "legal protection" and "compulsory service" – concerning hired labourers, or potential ones, *en bloc*.

However, a new kind of collectivity developed after the introduction of liberalist labour legislation. This was the collectivity of trade unions and em-

170

ployer's associations. Workers' associations and trade unions started to be established in Finland in the 1880s. This relatively late start accords with the low degree of industrialisation in the Finnish economy, and with the small size of its wage-worker population. From the 1890s onwards, the labour movement grew quite rapidly and actively aimed at moulding labour relations. In 1907 both employees and employers founded their own central organisations: The Finnish Federation of Trade Unions *(Suomen Ammattijärjestö, SAJ)* and The

General Confederation of Employers in Finland (*Suomen Työnantajain Keskus-liitto*, STK).

As the trade unions gained strength, they sought collective bargaining and strikes became common. The first nation-wide collective labour agreement was concluded in the printing and publishing industry, but it remained the only one of its kind. However, local collective agreements were concluded. In 1914 there were about 200 labour agreements concerning more than 170,000 workers. Even if we omit agricultural and other rural workers, this was still only a minority of all wage labourers, as in 1910 the number of workers in manufacturing, commerce and transport, and in urban construction and "general" works was 170,000. Thus, although it gained ground, organised collective bargaining was still not the dominant mode of wage contracting.[7]

The Russian Revolution and the Finnish Civil War in 1918 also caused a rupture in the institutional development of the Finnish labour market. Trade unions had a close relationship with the political left, and they lost some of their strength when the workers' side was defeated in the Civil War. After the war the previously unified labour party SDP split into Social Democrats and Communists. Because the activities of the Communists were constrained in the political arena in the 1920s, the rivalry between them and the Social Democrats was especially intense within the trade unions. In 1929 and 1930 this contention reached an acute phase, while the Lapua Movement, an extreme right-wing association, entered the Finnish political stage. The trade unions' central organisation, the Finnish Federation of Trade Unions (SAJ) was dissolved in the political turmoil, and the new trade union central organisation – the Confederation of Finnish Trade Unions (*Suomen Ammattiyhdistysten Keskusliitto*, SAK) and its member organisations – remained weak in the first half of the 1930s.[8]

Until the Second World War, the labour market was characterised by flexibility and the domination of the employers. Especially in the manufacturing industry, employers generally refused to enter into collective labour agreements with the trade unions. Of course, at the local level and in workplaces employers and employees collaborated, and the employees were able to influence many labour market practices. As mentioned earlier, there were also collective labour agreements at the local level, especially in the construction industry and in handicrafts from the beginning of the century until the early 1930s. Unionising was common in those industries, where the need for skill and co-operation and cyclical fluctuations improved the workers' position. However, formal co-operation ended during the Great Depression of the 1930s, and the consequence was an extreme lack of trust between employers and employees and a free fall of the wage-level in many industries during the Depression.

Increasing unionism and the emergence of the collective bargaining system at the national level were important features after the Second World War. During the war, the employers, in the name of national solidarity, finally recognised the trade unions as negotiating partners, and this paved the way to collective bargaining. However, the blue-collar trade union movement suf-

172

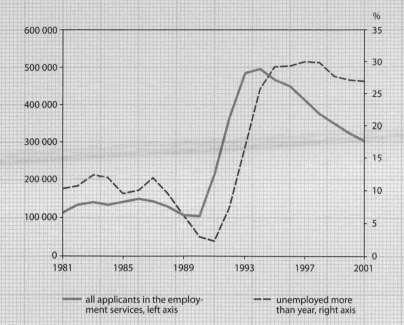

Figure 6.3 The number of applicants in the employment services and the share of long-term unemployed (%), 1981–2001

Sources: Employment Service data, Ministry of Labour.

——— all applicants in the employment services, left axis

– – unemployed more
than year, right axis

Widespread long-term unemployment became a new phenomenon on the labour market in the 1990s. Long-term unemployment in the figure above means that a person has been an applicant in the employment service uninterruptedly for more than one year. When the number of unemployed decreased in the late 1990s, the long-term unemployment figure still remained high. Elderly workers in particular had difficulty in finding new jobs outside the employment programmes organised by the authorities.

Figure 6.4 The wage share in manufacturing 1900–1999 (3 year moving average)

Sources: Hjerppe 1989; National Accounts, Statistics Finland.

Functional income distribution measures how value added has been distributed between wages on one hand and capital income on the other. The share of wages declined notably in three crisis periods: during the First World War (and Civil War) years of the late 1910s, during and after the depression of the 1930s and during the depression of the 1990s. On the other hand, it rose after the Second World War, perhaps reflecting the strengthening of the trade unions' position in wage setting.

173

fered from political rivalry within its organisations. Several affiliated unions left the Confederation of Finnish Trade Unions (SAK) in the early 1960s. Re-unification occurred in 1969. The name of SAK changed to the Central Organisation of Finnish Trade Unions (*Suomen Ammattiliittojen Keskusjärjestö*).[9]

Moreover, the old patriarchal system, in which the white-collar/salaried employees identified with the employers, eroded during the post-war years. Although employees with a college or university education had a long history of organising themselves into professional representative associations, the post-war years led to a real rise in trade unionism with the birth of new confederations:

– The white-collar Intellectual Employment Union (*Henkisen Työn Yhtymä*) 1922 → the Confederation of Intellectual Employment (*Henkisen Työn Keskusliitto – HTK*) 1944 → the Federation of Clerical Employees' and Civil Servants' Organisations (*Toimihenkilö- ja Virkamiesjärjestöjen Keskusliitto, TVK*) 1956. TVK went bankrupt in 1992 and its member-organisations joined STTK.
– The Finnish Confederation of Technical Salaried Employees (*Suomen Teknisten Toimihenkilöjärjestöjen Keskusliitto, STTK*) 1946.
– The Confederation of Unions for Academic Professionals (*Akateeminen valtuuskunta, AKAVA*) 1950.

A further "corporatist" element was introduced to the Finnish labour market in the late 1960s, when the government took an active role in wage bargaining. The term "corporatism" has often been associated with a system in which labour market parties are comprehensively organised and co-operate with the government in wage bargaining and social policy. The politicians try to integrate the labour market parties with governmental decision-making. The aim is that trade unions should moderate their wage claims.[10] In Finland, attempts to introduce an "incomes policy" aimed to halt the rise of wages had already been made in the 1950s, but only at the end of the 1960s did governmental intervention in the labour market take on established forms. In addition, many other welfare benefits were created in the 1960s, including reforms of unemployment benefits and pensions (see Kettunen in this volume).

The position of the trade unions strengthened in Finland from the 1960s onwards. In addition to its increasing bargaining power and improved status in society, there are other factors which have contributed the growth of the trade union movement: earnings-related unemployment benefits are generally tied to union membership, union dues are tax deductible and they are mainly collected by the employers. Whereas union members constituted approximately one third of the labour force in the early 1960s, the corresponding share in the early 1970s exceeded one half. Union membership continued to grow during the following decades, and the number of members in the trade unions doubled from one million in the early 1970s to over two million in the 1990s. These

174

Until the 1960s, the principal way of alleviating unemployment was emergency relief, which included food aid, and low-paid, temporary jobs created in the public sector. In the picture, a man employed through a public job creation scheme in the mid-1960s.

An ironworker taking a break, 1957.

numbers also include those members who are students and pensioners. However, according to Working Life Barometer published by the Ministry of Labour, union density reached its peak (85%) in 1993 in the middle of a deep recession.[11]

During recent years, union density has declined in Finland, a feature typical of other Western European countries as well. In 2003 union density was approximately 73%. One important reason for the decline in union density is the emergence of an independent unemployment insurance fund that provides unemployment insurance without requiring union membership. Unlike in many other countries, union density is higher among female employees than male and among those with more education and working in the public sector. From the trade union's point of view, the future challenge will be to attract especially members of the younger generation and immigrant employees to join a union.

Collective agreements in Finland nowadays cover around 95% of all employees, one of the highest rates in the OECD countries. Furthermore, the employers' organisations have also supported collective labour agreements, at least in recent decades. Formal wage-bargaining institutions have decreased uncertainty, increased predictability and helped to maintain industrial peace. Similar benefits were already argued for in the boom period of the 1920s in those industries in which there were local collective labour agreements. Moreover, the European Monetary Union has increased the demand for low inflation and thus co-ordination on the labour market. On the other hand, increasing competition and the globalisation process create the need for flexibility in wage setting and consequently present a challenge to centralised wage formation.[12]

Changing unemployment

In historical studies of the labour market, one of the most extensively debated subjects has been the measurement of unemployment: that is, who should be counted as unemployed.[13] It has been difficult to define unemployment in such a way that the definition would apply to different historical situations and institutional environments. Unemployment in the modern sense of the word is of the "open" kind: the unemployed are willing to work, searching for jobs but unable to find them, and they are counted as part of the labour force. This modern concept does not fit very well with the situation of the Finnish economy in the latter half of the 19th century. We cannot define precisely who were unemployed, and who should be counted as belonging to the labour force. This is because of a phenomenon that in the scholarly literature is known as "disguised unemployment", "underemployment" or "surplus population", terms which refer particularly to the situation of rural economies.[14]

The notion of "surplus population" was already being used in Finnish scholarly discussion at the turn of the 19th and 20th centuries, and since then the concept and explanations based on it have become part of conventional wisdom among Finnish historians. Relative surplus population has been seen as a problem of the countryside, where it is assumed there was a large excess population in proportion to the available land, to production capacity and to the technological level of agriculture, as well as to the size of sectors outside agriculture. It is obvious that the "agricultural population", as defined in the Finnish population statistics, was notably larger than the labour input necessary for agricultural production. This does not mean, however, that the "surplus population" was unemployed, since people had different kinds of employment outside agriculture proper. Because of this "multi-employment" and various forms of "self-employment", it is virtually impossible to measure the actual unemployment. Furthermore, it should be noted that in many respects the household rather than the individual should be taken as the research unit in analysing the rural labour market. The "modern" mono-occupational and individual-based way of conceptualising labour markets and defining the labour force simply does not fit the situation in nineteenth-century rural Finland.

A depression in the early 1890s can be regarded as the first manifestation of open-market-economy unemployment in contrast to the "disguised unemployment" of the agricultural society. The world wars, the Finnish Civil War and the Great Depression of the 1930s caused major ruptures in the Finnish labour

176

Seasonal climatic variations, characteristically severe at high latitudes, used to have a
significant influence on employment. Thus, temporary redundancy was a problem for many
workers in winter time. In the picture, a worker in a timber yard in summer.

market. In the late 1920s and the late 1930s, Finland experienced boom periods with good employment and raising wages throughout the country. Thus the
whole period between the start of the First World War and the end of the Second World War manifested instability in the economy and the labour market. In
addition to wars and business cycles, seasonal variation, a characteristic phenomenon of a northern climate, continued to be an integral factor in employment even in normal years, and hence a lack of work was a problem for many
workers during the winter months.

In order to understand changes in employment and unemployment, it
is important to take into account the structures of the economy and various

aspects connected to unemployment assistance and the registration and measurement of unemployment. Firstly, as mentioned above, the majority of the Finnish population lived in the countryside before the Second World War. Thus it is highly controversial to use the concept of unemployment to describe the livelihood problems of those people who obtained their living from agriculture. Unskilled labourers in particular often lived at a minimum level of subsistence, and even a fairly short period out of work combined with lowered wages placed them at the "poverty level".[15]

Secondly, until the 1960s the most important system of unemployment assistance consisted of relief work and poor relief, which included food assistance. Relief work was a low-paying and temporary job organised by local and central government. The status of relief workers raises important issues in quantifying unemployment. During the depression hidden unemployment became visible, because relief work and food assistance were connected to registration at the labour exchange. When the likelihood of finding a job in the private sector decreased and wages fell, the probability of survival without public assistance decreased. Relief work increased the incentives to register in the labour exchange, but by the same token, it diminished the number of applicants because relief work increased employment. It is legitimate to argue that relief workers should be regarded as employed although it would seem to be faulty reasoning to claim that relief measures in Finland were first and foremost planned to be counter-cyclical governmental or local projects.

Thirdly, it is difficult to construct long-term figures on unemployment in Finland; before the Second World War, benefits from the trade unions and the unemployment insurance fund did not play a significant role. The most reliable picture of unemployment can be obtained from the Great Depression of the 1930s and from the bigger cities owing to the existence of a more organised system of labour exchanges and unemployment assistance. On the other hand, in the rural areas and during the "normal" years and boom periods, there did not exist similar incentives to register at a labour exchange. It is probable that labour exchange data do not represent female unemployment as accurately as male unemployment for the reason that the motivation for women to register was smaller and the discouraged-worker effect was bigger. Most relief work was planned for male outdoor workers, although local authorities did organise sewing courses for female applicants at the labour exchange.[16]

In spite of difficulties connected to unemployment records, intensive work has been carried out in recent years in Finland in order to develop a method to measure unemployment as accurately as possible, especially for the years of the Great Depression. According to one estimate, the highest rate of unemployment was 6.2% in 1932.[17] Thus the unemployment rate was much lower in Finland than in many other countries. However, in many industries unemployment was much higher. For instance, for all construction workers in Helsinki, the unemployment rate was at its height in late 1932 approximately 45%, in spite of extensive relief work organised by local and central government authorities.[18]

178

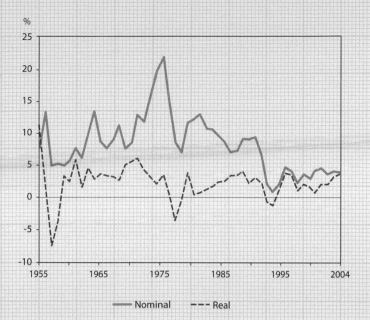

Figure 6.5   Annual changes in wage and
salary earnings, 1955–2004 (%)

Source: Statistical Yearbook of Finland.

During the last fifty years the real earnings of wage-workers and salaried employees have risen almost without interruption. Real wages and earnings declined only in the late 1950s, in the late 1970s and during the depression of the 1990s. In nominal wages, the highest growth percentages
were attained during the high inflation years of the 1970s. Since the depression of the early 1990s, the inflation rate has been notably lower than
before, so that real wages have risen in spite of the – in the historical perspective – record-low growth rates of nominal earnings.

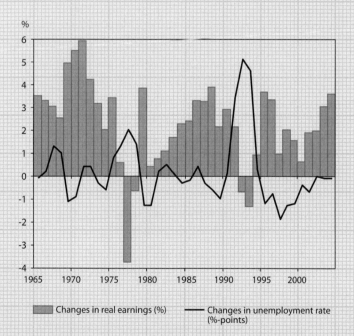

Figure 6.6   Changes in real earnings (%)
and in the unemployment rate
(%-point), 1965–2004

Source: Statistical Yearbook of Finland.

The long-term increase in the unemployment rate – meaning the rise of "structural unemployment" – is a characteristic feature of the labour
market in the last few decades. In the long-term situation there is no clear connection between the unemployment rate and real wages: that is
to say real wages have continued to rise despite the notable rise in the unemployment rate (especially during the depression of the 1990s). In the
short term, however, there has been a clear negative correlation between changes in the unemployment rate (measured here as the percentage-
point change) and changes in real earnings: increases in unemployment have coincided with declines in real earnings.

The situation was different during the recession of the 1990s. Various unemployment and social insurance systems, which had been developed during the preceding decades, alleviated the impact of unemployment. In fact, the government decided to cut down some welfare benefits during and after the turbulent years of the banking crisis. Furthermore, in the highly developed wage-work society, the methods for measuring and analysing changes in unemployment were also more exact than during the interwar years. According to the Labour Force Survey collected by Statistics Finland, the unemployment rate was on average 17%, and in the employment services the monthly average of unemployed job-seekers was almost 500,000 persons (20% of the labour force) in 1994.[19] These figures were unparalleled in Finnish history.

Fourthly, one significant aspect of unemployment during the Great Depression of the 1930s and the deep recession of the 1990s was an increase in the duration of unemployment. An essential feature of both crises was a concurrent increase in the inflow to unemployment and a decrease in the outflow from unemployment. This means that a smaller portion of the unemployed got work as the population of the unemployed increased. This consequently meant longer spells of unemployment. During the depressions, the employability of the labour force on average decreased, and many older workers in particular had low re-employment potential.

Finally, in spite of similarities there were also differences in unemployment durations. No reliable evidence of widespread long-term unemployment and the duration-dependence of unemployment during the Depression of the 1930s has been found. On the other hand, both long-term unemployment and the duration-dependence of unemployment became serious problems in the 1990s. Although unemployment decreased after the recession, the proportion of the long-term unemployed remained stable.[20] The reasons for the difference in the duration of unemployment between the two recessions are linked to the structure of the economy, the system of unemployment assistance and the flexibility of the labour market.

Wages and the dynamics of the labour market

A scrutiny of the unemployment figures above shows that there were two major peacetime crises in the Finnish labour market: the depressions of the 1930s and the 1990s. In addition to these crises, the situation in the Finnish labour market was also exceptional during both the world wars. The changes in the supply and demand for labour as well as in the institutional composition of the labour market are also reflected in the development of wages.

One way to examine the situation of the labour market in the light of wage data is to measure the functional distribution of income, that is the respective shares of wages and capital income. Figure 6.4 presents the wage share (= wage bill/value added) in manufacturing, which is the industry with

180

As a result of the Depression, the unemployment rate for construction workers in Helsinki was at its height, at approx. 45 per cent, in late 1932, in spite of extensive relief measures organised by local authorities and central government. The painting of a building site in Helsinki is by Tove Jansson (1941).

the most reliable long-term data. The depressions of the 1930s and the 1990s are also visible in this curve: in both cases, the share of wages in value added decreased notably. Furthermore, we see that the wage share dropped sharply in the late 1910s – during the First World War and the Finnish Civil War of 1918 – but recovered quite swiftly. During the Second World War the low level of the 1930s persisted.

There were two major rises in the wage share in Finnish manufacturing during the 20th century: a smaller one in the first half of the 1920s and a bigger one after the Second World War. The first is surprising in that the labour movement had been defeated in the Civil War and lost much of its former power – a

Forestry work was hard manual labour until well after the Second World War. Today it is highly mechanised and benefits from high technology.

process one would expect to decrease rather than increase the income share of labour. It is interesting that this change coincided with the introduction of the eight-hour workday, enacted in 1917 (before the Civil War) and put into effect in manufacturing mainly in 1920.[21] The rising wage share indicates that the shortening of the workday was not implemented at the expense of labour. The other – and sharper – rise in the wage share that took place after the Second World War, is less puzzling: it accords very well with the rising influence of the trade unions and the labour movement in general. The decline during the latter half of the 1950s, again, fits nicely with the general picture of these years, when postwar regulation ended and the unions lost some of their former power.

The wage share, of course, does not tell us, how wages themselves have changed, since there are also other factors influencing functional income distribution – primarily changes in productivity. An overview of the changes in nominal and real earnings in the period 1955–2004 is presented in Figure 6.5.

182

Paper mills were built by rapids and over time a community grew around the mills, as was the case in the town of Valkeakoski pictured here.

It confirms the conventional conception of favourable economic development. Average real earnings grew in almost every one of these fifty years. Real wages and earnings declined on only three occasions: in the late 1950s (1957 and 1958), during the oil crisis of the 1970s (1977 and 1978) and during the depression of the 1990s (1992 and 1993). The increase in nominal wages and salaries was much smaller in the early 1990s than before. The highest inflation peak was attained in the middle of the 1970s.

What catches one's attention in the real earnings curve above is the modest decline during the depression of the 1990s in comparison with the huge increase in unemployment (cf. Figure 6.2). Furthermore, the downturn in real earnings was very short, although unemployment has remained on high level since the depression. Thus the high-level of long-term unemployment has not kept real wages from rising. This phenomenon supports the so-called insider-outsider -argument. Trade unions (insiders) are able to improve the wage-level in spite of the large number of people out of jobs. Many of these "outsiders" lack the education and skills needed in the growing industries.[22] However, it should be remembered that, in terms of the functional income distribution, wage- and salary-earners lost out during and after the 1990s depression (cf. the wage share in manufacturing, Figure 6.4).

The decline in real earnings in the early 1990s was also small in comparison with the fall in the mid-1970s, when unemployment was on a notably lower level than in the 1990s. Thus it seems that the connection between unemployment and wages is not a simple one. Unemployment has peaked twice since the 1960s: first in the 1970s and then in the 1990s – both times without returning back to pre-depression levels. There have not been comparable dramatic changes in real wages, so that the labour market has, so to say, adjusted to a new higher unemployment rate. This is not to say that changes in real earnings have been insensitive to variation in unemployment. As can be seen in Figure 6.6, there seems to be a clear negative correlation between the changes in real earnings (measured in percentages) and changes in the unemployment rate (measured in percentage points).[23]

Thus real wages have been rather sticky in Finland since the late 1970s: they have been flexible only upwards – with the exception of the depression years 1992 and 1993. It was employment and not real wages that adapted during this exceptionally deep recession. The difference with the other big depression of the century – the 1930s – is notable. Unlike in many other countries, real wages were flexible in many industries in Finland during the Great Depression of the 1930s.[24] For instance, real hourly wages in the urban construction industry dropped by 25–35% and in piecework by 40–60%. The decline was of about the same magnitude in logging and timber floating work, an important form of wage-work in the countryside. In manufacturing real wages declined less: 20% in the sawmill industry, 12% in the pulp and paper industry and 7% in the metal industry. The main difference in the functioning of the Finnish labour market in the two major depressions of the 20th century was that in the 1930s both employment and real wages were flexible downwards, whereas in the 1990s in practice only employment declined. There are two obvious explanations for the greater flexibility in the 1930s: the lack of unemployment benefits on one hand and the weak position of the trade unions on the other.

Conclusions

Finland is a latecomer compared with the economic core of Europe: industrialisation and the structural change in the economy started later in Finland than in the advanced European economies. The relative "backwardness" is also reflected in the development of the Finnish labour market: the expansion of the wage-labourer class and the structural change in the labour force happened quite late in Finland compared with other Western European countries. Since the Second World War, however, the transformation has been quite rapid. The structure of employment has changed fundamentally as the share of agriculture and other primary production has declined swiftly, the share of services – private and public – has increased, while that of manufacturing has remained on fairly high level. At the same time, the participation rate of women has risen to a high level.

Also the institutional composition of the labour market has changed profoundly during the postwar years. Finland is – with the other Scandinavian countries – among the most unionised economies, and the coverage of collective agreements is wide.[25] A Finnish characteristic since the late 1960s has been the significant role of government in wage setting; various measures concerning social benefits and tax policy have been linked to centralised wage negotia-

184

tions. The Scandinavian-style social contract between employers and employees in industrial relations together with the coordinating role of the government has been mostly considered as beneficial to Finnish economic growth as well as to the welfare of citizens (rising real wages, increased social benefits).

During the last ten to fifteen years, the consensus on the benefits of the "Finnish model" has, however, started to crack. The globalisation process has profoundly transformed the economic environment, and it is seen to offer significant challenges to the developed Western countries. One of the key questions in Finland and in Europe is how – in this changing environment – to sustain growth and employment, and how to secure the welfare of the citizens. On one hand, it has been argued that the standardisation of labour market practices and centralised collective bargaining have created too much rigidity on the labour market. On the other hand, efficient institutions, a well-trained work force, a well-dimensioned welfare system and people's trust in society can be regarded as forming an important basis for sustaining favourable growth in the future. Besides these long-term challenges of the future the Finnish economy has still to deal with the burden of the past – the long-term unemployment caused by the deep recession of the 1990s.

In the future, Finland, like many other Western countries, must cope with the problem of an ageing work-force. This means that that the future of the Finnish labour market will be in many respects different from its past. The average annual growth rate of the Finnish population was 1.0% from 1850 to 1900, 0.8% from 1900 to 1950 and 0.5% from 1950 to 2000. The respective growth rates of the working-age population (aged 15–64 years) were somewhat different: 0.9% from 1850 to1900, 1.0% from 1900 to 1950 and 0.6% from 1950 to 2000. The proportion of the working-age population of the total population was 61.1% in 1850, 59.6% in 1900, 63.4% in 1950, and 66.9% in 2000. According to population forecasts, the future development of the Finnish population will be different. If immigration does not increase from the present level, the Finnish population around 2030 will be about the same as it is now. This means that the proportion of the working-age population will decrease to 59%, that is to the 1850-level.[26]

The ageing of the population will notably affect the supply of labour in the future, whereas globalisation will alter the demand for it. How the Finnish labour market will adjust to these conflicting pressures will be one of the key questions for the Finnish economy in the coming decades.

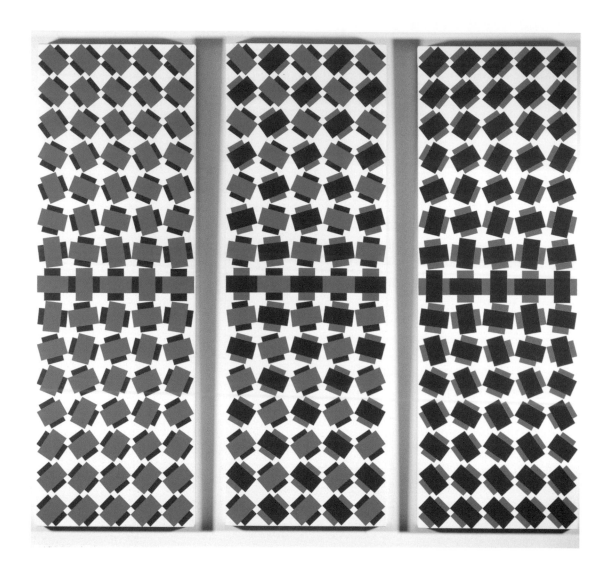

"Triptych"

by Matti Kujasalo

186

(1979, acrylic on board, 144 x 47.5 cm)

Monetary Aspects of a Changing Economy

Concepción García-Iglesias and Juha Kilponen*

Finland has joined all the international monetary systems from the nineteenth century onwards. Being a small, relatively open economy, this was a natural choice, although recurrent and sometimes large devaluations were needed to restore the external balance. The strong involvement of the government and the central bank in regulating the financial markets after the Second World War prolonged the start of the development of modern financial markets. This shows up in the pattern of income velocity of money studied in this article. The analysis reveals that, in contrast to many other Western economies, the income velocity of money has been fairly stable since the Second World War. Before that, the declining velocity pattern suggests an early monetisation that followed the general trend in other Western economies.

*   For helpful comments and suggestions on earlier drafts of this article, we are grateful to Antti Kuusterä and Juha Tarkka. We would also like to thank Vappu Ikonen and Tuula Taipale from the Bank of Finland for helping us with the data on interest rates and money. Usual disclaimer applies.

Introduction

The monetary history of any country shows how the evolution of financial markets and monetary systems plays a crucial role in its economic development, with respect both to its long-term trends and to short-term fluctuations and stability. Finnish monetary history, though relatively short, is not an exception. This article explores the development of the monetary and financial systems in Finland from historical curiosity as well as in the light of the income velocity of money – a long-term view – and the choice of the right exchange rate regime – a short-term analysis.

The income velocity of money measures the frequency at which money is exchanged among money holders. It varies directly with the opportunity cost of holding money – the interest rate – and inversely with real income, but it is also claimed that variables such as monetisation, financial sophistication and the development of the welfare state are contributory factors in explaining the long-term behaviour of the velocity of circulation. Changes in the monetary and financial systems are the underlying explanation for changes in the velocity pattern, which in many countries is characterized by a U-shape curve. The downward sloping velocity is typically explained by the monetisation process of the economy, while the upward trend is regarded as being due to the sophistication of the financial system as well as to the development of the welfare state.

The findings of this article suggest that there was a clear downward trend in the Finnish velocity of money associated with the monetisation process of the economy as predicted. However, the U-shape is not complete as there is no clear upward movement. Our analysis shows that since the Second World War the income velocity of money has been relatively stable. One of the potential explanations for this is that the financial markets were heavily regulated until the 1980s, for a somewhat longer period of time than in many other Western industrialized economies. In particular, the Bank of Finland regulated the banks' lending and discount rates, as well as capital movements and banking in general. This caused the financial system to develop late.

The analysis then continues with different exchange rate regimes and, in particular, the frequent devaluations of the Finnish currency. Finland has joined all the international monetary systems from the nineteenth century onwards. Being a small, open economy, this was a fairly natural choice, although the historical overview shows how rather frequent and sometimes massive devaluations have been needed to restore the external balance.

Figure 7.1 provides an overview of Finnish monetary history from the standpoint of different international monetary systems and the associated currency fluctuations of the Finnish *markka*. The nineteenth century saw the birth of the so-called Classical Gold Standard with fixed exchange rates. This was suspended in 1914 with advent of the First World War. In 1926 a new international monetary system with fixed exchange rates was established, the Gold-Exchange Standard. Again as a consequence of international difficulties, that monetary

188

A statue of Johan Vilhelm Snellman (1806–1881) in front of the Bank of Finland. Snellman was a philosopher, journalist, professor and senator. In 1863, he was appointed Director of Finance of the Senate. In this office he was responsible for Finland's economic policy. His key achievement was pegging the markka to the silver standard in 1865. This stabilised the country's currency. Note the scars of wartime bombing on the plinth.

regime ended in 1931. In order to rebuild the international economic system, a new framework on international monetary cooperation was laid down at a conference held at Bretton Woods in 1944. After a sufficient number of countries had signed the agreement in 1945 and the relevant institutions were in place, the Bretton Woods monetary system continued to operate until the early 1970s. During the operation of this international monetary system, there was a pegged but adjustable exchange rate which meant possible currency fluctuations if

On 4 April 1860, the Russian Emperor issued a "Gracious Announcement" concerning Finland's own monetary unit. It was to be called the markka, which was an old Finnish word for money. J. V. Snellman is portrayed on this 100 markka note. The original picture is from an advertisement of the Kansallis Bank (KOP) promoting the role of forestry in the economy.

there were disequilibria in the country's economy. Since then there have not longer been any international monetary agreements as such, although there has been a European one, now called the European Monetary Union.

We can see all these monetary systems and their corresponding exchange rate regimes for Finland in Figure 7.1. It shows how the exchange rate remained fairly stable during the Classical Gold Standard period, while the period between the collapse of the Classical Gold Standard and the Second World War with its aftermath is characterized by massive devaluations – except during the short life of the Gold-Exchange Standard. The period from the 1950s until the adoption of the Euro is also characterized by frequent, but less pronounced realignments of the Finnish *markka*.

Frequent devaluations could in general be seen as a consequence of the tendency of the economic policy to produce higher inflation than in the country's main trading partners. The analysis suggests that devaluations were typically used to restore the trade balance. Often the devaluations where preceded by excessive wage inflation, loss of competitiveness and a sharp drop in investment activity. Overall, devaluations accomplished their objectives in the short run, but worsened the long-term economic prospects of the country because the monetary policy lacked credibility.

Historical Overview

After the Napoleonic wars in 1809, Finland was annexed to Russia as an autonomous Grand Duchy of the Russian Empire. The creation of a new capital its own, Helsinki, in 1812 as a new administrative centre was a clear indication

190

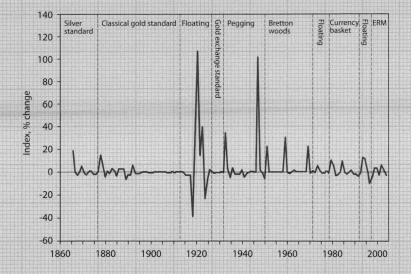

Figure 7.1. Currency systems and percentage changes in the exchange rate index

Source: Autio (1992) for the years 1864–1991. Bank of Finland Database for the years 1991–2004

The exchange rate index, and thus the external value of the markka, remained fairly stable during the time of the Classical Gold Standard and the Gold-Exchange Standard. During the periods of floating and other international monetary systems, the index experienced major realignments. In particular, frequent devaluations took place between 1945 and 1991. The exchange rate index is a weighted index of the markka's external value against a basket of international currencies. Weights are determined by the proportion of trade between Finland and each country.

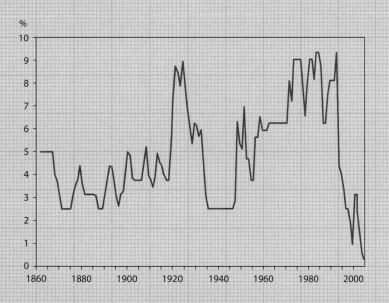

Figure 7.2 Bank of Finland discount rate, 1862–2004

Source: Autio (1996) for the years 1862–1952. Bank of Finland Database for the years 1952–2004.
Notes: For the period 1862–1952, we use the discount rate. The base rate is used thereafter.

The discount rate was used as an active monetary policy instrument until the early 1950s. During the period from the late 1950s to the early 1980s, monetary policy was primarily based on the quantity ceilings on rediscounting imposed to the commercial banks, the adjustment of related interest rates on rediscounting, and interest rate controls on loans. The base rate was effective to the extent that it directed the interest rates on loans issued by the commercial banks. After the liberalisation of the financial markets in the 1980s and the lifting of the interest rate controls on loans, the base rate gradually lost its role as inter-bank markets developed.

191

of Russia's desire to lessen the influence on Finland of its long cultural, political and economic ties with Sweden. At the same time, the first banking institution, which later on became the central bank of Finland, was created by an imperial decree in 1811.

The activities of the bank were restricted to the acceptance of deposits, lending, and the right to issue low denomination bank notes. One of the aims of the central bank at that time was to drive the Swedish currency out of circulation – it remained valid in the country after the annexation to Russia in 1809. However, until the 1830s, Swedish currency remained more common than Russian roubles in domestic trade. With both currencies, Swedish and Russian, circulating at the same time, the currency flows were guided by trade relations. All in all, there were up to five different currencies in Finland: three currencies were of Swedish denomination while the other two were Russian. With so many different currencies, fluctuations in the exchange rate caused monetary instability with obviously harmful consequences for the real economy.[1]

At the end of the 1830s and the beginning of the 1840s, Sweden and Russia returned to a metal standard based on silver. This meant that the central banks needed to have in their vaults silver reserves in proportion to the money in circulation at a fixed rate. At the same time, Finland implemented a monetary reform in which it adopted the rouble as the sole legal tender in 1840. Swedish currency was withdrawn from circulation by the Bank of Finland exchanging it for silver in Stockholm. In addition, the Bank of Finland followed a monetary reform that had already been implemented in Russia, and notes of the old denomination were taken out of circulation and exchanged for Bank of Finland notes – the denomination of which was, nevertheless, in roubles.[2] Last but not least, Finland moved to a silver standard with its own silver reserves and the ability to conduct transactions in foreign bills. With all these moves towards improvement and independence, there is no doubt that the 1840 monetary reform was an important milestone in Finnish monetary history. Monetary conditions became relatively stable, but unfortunately this state of affairs was not to last very long.

In 1854 the Crimean War started, and Russia was forced out of the silver standard, with a depreciated rouble. As a result, the money in circulation was reduced as there were outflows of silver coins to St. Petersburg, where they were sold according to their silver value. By 1855, there was 40 per cent less money in circulation in Finland than five years earlier. The situation was quite problematic as Finland would have preferred the silver standard. Then Russia decided not to go back to the metal standard but agreed to Finland having its own currency. On 4 April 1860, the Finnish *markka* was established by an imperial manifesto. The manifesto declared that the Finnish *markka* would be worth one quarter of the rouble. However, a return to silver was practically impossible as it was required by law that the depreciated paper rouble should be redeemed at its nominal value, which was equivalent to four Finnish *markka*s. If this manifesto had been put into practice, paper roubles would have been exchanged for

In the Kalevala, the national epic, the Sampo was a magic device that brought wealth, nourishment, and good fortune to the people. It was forged by the blacksmith Ilmarinen, "the first of all ironworkers", depicted in this painting by Akseli Gallen Kallela (1893). In the epic, the Sampo aroused envy between two rival tribes. Ultimately, it was smashed during a battle and lost at sea.

*markka*s and then again exchanged into silver. This would have exhausted the silver reserves of the Bank of Finland. Finally, on 1 February 1865, Tsar Alexander II issued a decree making the paper rouble obsolete. The only legal tender in Finland was silver money, in the form of either *markka*s or roubles. Half a year later, the Bank of Finland started redeeming *markka*s into silver, and so Finland returned to the silver standard.[3] Due to the depreciated paper rouble, there was a roughly 20 percent revaluation of the new Finnish coin. This caused economic difficulties as Finland was trading with Russia, and the increased real value of debt led to several bankruptcies.

The Classical Gold Standard, 1870–1914

During the 1870s, world monetary conditions were changing. There was a movement toward the new international monetary regime, the Classical Gold Standard. Countries started joining this system because a stable exchange rate and monetary conditions promoted international transactions and growth. International trade and investment were undertaken with almost no risk of exchange rate fluctuations causing capital losses. Finland was no exception. Following the French franc value at one to one, it joined the Classical Gold Standard in 1877–1878. This event further reinforced Finnish autonomy from Russia, which remained outside the gold standard. The adherence to the Classical Gold Standard had an important effect on the country's political and economic life as well as on the process of modernisation. The adoption of a new currency and the international monetary regime were both symbols of the country's monetary independence and internal self-government, which Finland managed to keep until the outbreak of the First World War, when the Classical Gold Standard was suspended.

The monetary stability provided by the international gold standard promoted the beginning of industrialisation in Finland, although there is no clear evidence of growth spurts as in many other countries. Formal statistical tests suggest that Finland experienced steady economic growth during this period without any breaks or discontinuities. Industrialisation may have begun slowly in the mid-nineteenth century and might have grown in importance at the turn of the century,[4] but there is no consensus about the existence of any major industrial breakthrough during the time of the Classical Gold Standard. The financial system remained undeveloped with only a central bank and about ten savings banks functioning. The first commercial bank was established in 1862. Despite the fact that the Bank of Finland granted the savings and commercial banks credit, it also continued itself to compete for private customers. At the end of the century, the Bank of Finland adopted regulatory tasks – acting as a bank of banks – in addition to other functions of a central bank. These included its position as the holder of foreign currency reserves, determining foreign exchange rates, note-printing at its printing works (the Security Printing House, established in 1885), and the rediscounting of bills, which started in 1890.

From 1890 to 1913, the Finnish economy seemed to be moving towards greater stability, enjoying the benefits of the world monetary regime. The stability provided by the system led to increased credibility in the international financial markets, and it was easier to access capital markets by getting loans at a lower interest rate. There were no deficits, and the prices of factors of production were fairly flexible. Finland was moving towards the industrialized world and integration into the Western markets. This period has been referred to by Finnish scholars as Finland's first phase of industrialisation.[5]

At the same time, however, Finland's economic development was still strongly influenced by fluctuations in harvests and the supply of agricultural

194

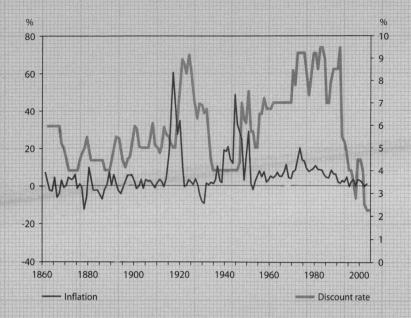

Figure 7.3 **Inflation and discount rates**

Source: Autio (1996) for the years 1862–1952 (discount rates). Bank of Finland Database for the years 1952–2004 (base rate). Hjerppe (1996) for inflation. Statistics Finland up to date.

Note: The inflation rate is based on the GDP deflator. Inflation on the left axis. Discount rate on the right axis.

In general, the fluctuations in the discount rate reflect the monetary authority's reactions to changes in economic activity, such as inflation and economic growth, and its desire for price stability. In Finland, the price stability objective of the central bank was often compromised by other objectives. The link between the base rate and inflation is less clear after the 1950s as monetary policy was focused on liquidity controls, while the interest rates were used with more caution because of their political implications and their effect on housing costs. Periods of high inflation are apparent between the collapse of the Classical Gold Standard in 1913 and the early 1990s. Since then, inflation has remained remarkably stable.

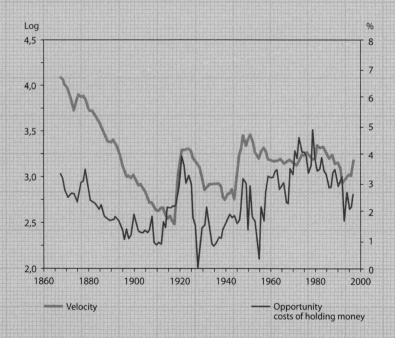

Figure 7.4 **The Finnish velocity of circulation in relation to opportunity costs of holding money, 1868–1997**

Source: Bank of Finland Database and Autio 1996 for opportunity costs and M2. Hjerppe (1996) for GDP.

Note: Own calculations. The opportunity costs of holding money have been calculated as the difference between the discount rate and the nominal return on M2.

The Finnish velocity of circulation presents a clear downward trend until 1918, a trend that cannot be explained solely by fluctuations in the opportunity costs of holding money. A sharp upward movement in velocity, clearly related to a similar sharp increase in the opportunity costs of money, occurs thereafter. The trend in velocity continues to decrease until 1944. In contrast to many other western economies, after the Second World War, the velocity is fairly stable with a downward trend at the end of the period. The upward trend in the opportunity costs does not seem to be associated with the velocity pattern until the mid-1980s. Afterwards the opportunity costs of money and the velocity pattern seem better linked, as is suggested by standard theories of money demand. When the opportunity costs of holding money cannot explain the velocity trend, institutional variables are taken into account as they influence the actual transaction costs of money and the precautionary motives for holding it.

products, as well as by developments in Russia. For instance, the 1892 and 1902 crop failures slowed down the recovery, and so did the general strike in 1905, albeit to a lesser extent. Similarly, economic development in Russia was disrupted by several crop failures, the wars against Turkey and Japan, and the increasing turmoil in society towards the end of the Classical Gold Standard period. Fluctuations in the external price of the rouble, combined with the underdeveloped domestic financial markets made the Finnish trading sector vulnerable to external shocks, as happened in connection with the events that began in 1914.[6]

The Interwar Period, 1914–1939

The outbreak of the First World War disrupted the long period of political stability, economic growth, and free trade for decades to come. Gold – together with new taxes and issues of government bonds – became of fundamental importance in order to buy from abroad all the supplies needed to finance the war. As a result, governments passed laws prohibiting gold outflows. Under these circumstances, a fixed exchange rate was impossible to maintain, and exchange rates began to float. The fluctuating rates were limited by the application of controls that forbade most transactions in foreign money.[7] Convertibility was consequently suspended.

In Finland, things were not much better. Interest rates started moving up during the summer of 1914, there were some slight signs of deposit runs, and the Bank of Finland decided to suspend convertibility in December 1914. The decision to leave the Classical Gold Standard was officially accepted and signed by the Tsar six months later, in April 1915.[8] The Bank of Finland found itself in a very difficult position. The rouble was losing its value on the capital markets, western trade was blocked, there was no access to imported goods, and the trade deficit was increasing heavily. Under these circumstances, the Bank of Finland was forced to borrow money for the government while its possibility to control prices by means of interest rate adjustments was very limited, indeed mainly non-existent. The political pressure on Finnish monetary sovereignty from Russia increased as the Bank of Finland was forced to redeem roubles at the predetermined rate. In 1915, restrictions on gold exports and more generally on foreign exchange transactions came into force. Moreover, as the value of the rouble continued its sharp decline, the Bank of Finland suffered substantial losses.

The Russian Revolution of 1917 and the disintegration of the Russian Empire were felt heavily in Finland. The two political eruptions in Russia – the February Revolution, which overturned the Tsarist monarchy and then the October Revolution, or coup d'état, which installed the Bolshevik dictatorship augmented the monetary sovereignty of Finland. The process ended with Finland's declaration of independence on 6 December 1917, but the outbreak of the Finnish Civil War was imminent, and there was a consequent halt in industrial production combined with increased money supply and inflation.

196

The inter-war period, which is conventionally regarded as beginning on Armistice Day (11 November 1918) and ending on 1 September 1939, was characterized by a postwar after-shock period in the 1920s, while the 1930s passed under the apprehension of a new global conflict.[9] Armistice Day was followed by a short boom in Europe and the United States, lasting until the middle of 1920. The upswing was especially strong in the United Kingdom and the United States, but also in some of the neutral countries. The boom was, however, followed by a worldwide economic downturn which lasted until 1921, and in some cases a year later.[10] Finland, despite its neutral position during the First World War, was struggling during the 1920s to re-stabilize its economy in the aftermath of its Civil War. Inflation had peaked at over 60 per cent during the Civil War and was followed by a sharp decline in economic activity and deflation in 1922.

The Finnish government established controls on foreign trade, and later on, in 1922, the Bank of Finland aimed at stabilizing the heavily fluctuating *markka* by intervening in the foreign exchange markets. The central bank used the discount rate actively as an instrument of monetary policy in the 1920s, in order to control rising inflation rates and to stabilize the exchange rate. In some years the discount rate went up to 9 and 10 per cent (1921 and 1924 respectively, see Figure 7.2). However, the deterioration of the government's fiscal balances forced the Bank of Finland to finance the government's activities heavily during the period 1915–1922. Similarly, commercial banks actively used the central bank's rediscounting of bills in response to the growing demand for loans.

Once the exchange rate was stabilized towards the mid-1920s, Finland was in a position to adopt the next international monetary regime, the Gold-Exchange Standard, in 1926. In order to do so, a new Currency Act was passed at the beginning of that year. In the meantime, the value of the Finnish *markka* had collapsed due to the Civil War and disturbed trade relationships with Russia. The *markka* had lost 87 per cent of its value – in terms of US dollars – since 1913. A revaluation of that magnitude to re-establish parity with the pre-war value would have been simply too costly for the economy, particularly because Finland had lost practically all of its Russian export market.

197

A bank in the 1940s.

The Russian economy was in complete chaos with a series of civil wars and conflicts between "Reds" and "Whites" that lasted until 1921. In the last part of the nineteenth century, the Russian Empire had been increasingly integrated into Western Europe. However, after the Bolshevik Revolution, the country effectively broke off most of its pre-war links with the rest of the world, and trade was reduced to a fraction of its pre-1914 level. This was felt heavily in Finland, too, as exports to Russia collapsed (see also Kaukiainen in this volume). Consequently, Finland's exporters sought other markets for their products from the West.[11]

The economic experience of the first half of the 1920s lent weight to the idea of adopting a new international monetary system that was similar to the previous one. The new regime, the Gold-Exchange Standard, was intended to be an image of the previous system. Currencies had to be convertible into gold at fixed domestic prices, and most significant restrictions on capital and gold were to be removed. With stable exchange rates and free international gold flows, the equilibrium in the balance of payments was assured. However, even though from 1924 to 1929 there was economic growth and a strong demand for money and credit worldwide, the increase in the stock of international reserves did not develop as expected. France and Germany accumulated most of the gold reserves, which put pressure on other central banks. As there were gold inflows in these two countries, other central banks were forced to increase interest rates and tighten credit to defend their insecure amounts of reserves.[12] It did not take long to figure out that the system was not working as planned. The Great Depression did not help either, and the disintegration of the Gold-Exchange Standard was doomed to collapse as soon as any country experienced a balance of payments crisis.

From the mid-1920s on, the Finnish economy coped with its membership of the new monetary regime. After 1926 investments started to boom, re-

198

flecting on the one hand rising liquidity, and on the other hand increased confidence thanks to stabilized inflation and exchange rates. At the same time, the undervalued currency supported a strong world demand for sawn wood (see Kaukiainen in this volume).[13] This together with rapid credit expansion and increasing liquidity led to a boom, which peaked in 1927 and 1928. The urban building sector was overheated, and it has been argued that the monetary policy was after all – despite the relatively high discount rate (see Figure 7.2) – not tight enough to cool down the economy.[14]

A crop failure in 1928 and an investment boom, which had caused a strong import demand for investment goods, resulted in a trade deficit and a serious balance of payments crisis. As a consequence, the Bank of Finland had to adopt a tighter monetary stance to protect its gold and foreign exchange reserves. A strong credit squeeze and increasing real interest rates caused problems for the agricultural and banking sectors, investors, and those who were heavily in debt. Several new commercial banks had been established since the First Word War. However, deficient banking regulation had allowed the banks to start up with insufficient capital. Interest rate controls by the Bank of Finland had been suspended in 1920, and the competition for customers led to a deposit interest rate hike and a decline in the banks' profit margins. Many of the small banks ran into difficulties and went out of business. The construction sector collapsed, and the boom turned into a bust. The Finnish economy slipped into a deflation in 1929.

In the meantime, the stock prices on the New York Stock Exchange collapsed on 24 October 1929, a day that has become known as "Black Thursday". Panic set in, the banks recalled their loans, and the Great Depression started to spread throughout those countries with which the USA was trading. In Europe, which was still struggling to pay its war debts, often from dwindling reserves of gold, the effects of the depression were felt with a lag of slightly over a year. In May 1931, Austria's leading bank, the Kreditanstalt of Vienna, declared itself insolvent. In June, the United States had to accept a moratorium on all debts owed by European governments, and finally in September 1931 the Bank of England was forced to suspend the convertibility of sterling.

The Great Depression, which began at the end of the 1920s and continued into the 1930s, was felt in Finland as well, both financially and politically. With its fragile economy, Finland was squeezed between Stalin's revolution in the USSR and the crisis of the Western economies. Generally, trade with the West was slowing down, while trade with Russia was already quite modest. Many banks were forced to close or to merge with larger banks. By the mid-1930s, the number of banks had halved by comparison with the early 1920s. This development continued after the Second World War, when the country's commercial bank sector was highly concentrated and most of the other banks, savings and cooperative banks, operated as small local units.[15] Unemployment increased, and falling prices of agricultural products caused bankruptcies among farmers as the real interest rate remained high. The Bank of Finland and the major banking institutions established a multilateral agreement on deposit rates in March 1931 – it lasted until 1938 – but this came too late.[16] This was to be the precursor of a long period of financial market regulation, in which Finland was not alone. In fact, from the 1930s onwards, the Finnish authorities emphasized regulatory policy measures in order to avoid any further banking crisis.

In October 1931, Finland announced the suspension of convertibility as heavy currency outflows could not be prevented. The end of the Gold-Exchange Standard had arrived, symbolized by the British suspension of convertibility in September of that same year. This undermined confidence in foreign currencies. Foreign central banks shifted away from dollar reserves into gold for fear of suffering capital losses on their dollar balances. The markets, unexpectedly, sold off reserves forcing the Federal Reserve to raise interest rates. The movement away from dollars to gold increased the pressure on the reserve base of the global monetary system. At the beginning of 1932, countries responded to this pressure by abandoning convertibility and depreciating their currencies. By then the Gold-Exchange Standard was history.[17]

The Finnish *markka* had at that time depreciated by 40 per cent against its gold parity. Finland let the currency float, but at the end of 1932, the exchange rate was stabilized. In 1933, Finland followed the Bank of England away from gold and pegged its currency to sterling roughly at the prevailing rate. The countries that behaved the same way enjoyed many of the benefits of exchange rate stability and, like Britain, reduced interest rates to stimulate recovery after the Great Depression. By the mid-1930s, stability was restored. The exchange rate supported export led growth, resulting into considerable trade surplus. Both unemployment and interest rates were decreasing.

The Winter War started when the Soviet Union attacked Finland by surprise in 30 November 1939 – three months after the Second World War broke out. The beginning of the Winter War led to five years of warfare and hardship. Inflation went up to over 50 percent but did not reach the same high level as in many other European countries that were fighting in the Second World War. This was achieved by effective price and wage restrictions. The Finnish government was also compelled to enforce significant restrictions on trade and financial transactions. By 1944, after severe losses suffered in the war, Finland's economy was in trouble. Under the terms of the 1947 peace treaty with the Soviet Union, Finland ceded about 12 percent of its territory, including valuable farmland and industrial facilities, and agreed to pay heavy war reparations.

The Bretton Woods System, 1944–1971

Once the war was over, Finland was burdened by the obligation to pay war reparation to the Soviet Union, which it finally succeeded in paying off in 1952 (for a more detailed discussion, see Eloranta and Kauppila in this volume). Resettling the Finnish evacuees (over 400,000 people) from the areas ceded to the

200

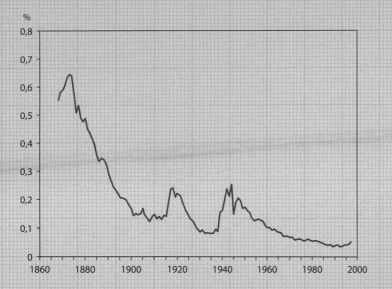

Figure 7.5 **Currency money ratio**

Source: Bank of Finland Database.
Note: Own calculations.

The currency money ratio is calculated by measuring currency as the coinage and bank notes in circulation whereas money corresponds to the money supply (M2). In the past households mainly kept their money in cash, and deposits were small. The development of the banking system helped deposits to grow in importance, thus reducing the use of currency. These two facts led to a decrease in the currency-money ratio. Up to the end of the 1930s, the ratio shows a very steep negative slope, contributing strongly to the downward sloping part of the velocity of money. As commercial banking develops, ceteris paribus, both the velocity and the currency-money ratio move in the same direction.

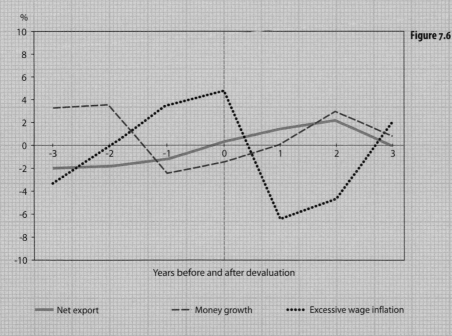

Net export ——— Money growth – – – Excessive wage inflation •••••

Figure 7.6 **Money, net exports and infla-tionary wages**

Source: Bank of Finland Database and Hjerppe (1996).
Notes: Own calculations. The data cover the years 1928–1994. All variables are expressed as deviations from their mean values over the period. Net exports are calculated as a share of GDP (X-M)/GDP. Excessive wage inflation has been calculated as the difference between the growth rate of wages and labour productivity in manufacturing industry. Money growth corresponds to M2 growth rate.

Trade balance (net exports) is upward sloping, while money supply (money growth) shows a U-shaped pattern around the devaluation. Similarly evident is a surge in excessive wage inflation prior to and during the devaluation year, with a later downward movement. The positive movement of net exports after the devaluation shows how the external balance is restored.

201

Soviet Union required another land acquisition act, subsidies for agricultural infrastructure, and support for displaced industrial workers.

Seigniorage – government revenue from a duty on the coining of money – had been an important source of funds to finance the costs of war. The government, together with the Bank of Finland, implemented a monetary reform in 1945 by which it attempted to restore monetary equilibrium. The monetary reform consisted of an exchange of notes by means of which the private citizens were forced to lend part of their cash holdings to the government. However, the whole reform turned out to be ineffective. The government's attempt to hold down price increases by cutting the money supply, according to the quantity theory of money, failed.

After the war, some of the strict government regulations were gradually lifted, and the economy started to stabilize during the 1950s. The Bank of Finland established quantity ceilings for the rediscounting of the banks. The use of the discount rate as a primary instrument of monetary policy was limited by political pressure, and the interest rates were kept low to promote growth and investment. These ceilings together with interest rate controls on loans by the central bank were effective in controlling the growth of the money supply. Inflation stabilized in the 1950s, but the price level was nine-fold that of 1938 (see Figure 7.3). Foreign exchange and trade controls were, however, enforced throughout the 1950s and beyond. In general, financial markets remained heavily regulated for the next 30 years.

Once more, the Finnish economy experienced a period of high inflation, and it seemed impossible to keep the currency fixed for long periods of time. The *markka* was devalued in 1945 as many as four times, and twice more in 1949, although officially Finland was trying to keep the currency fixed to the dollar. During the war years, trade had mainly been based on bilateral agreements, and the exchange rate itself was not an important determinant of Finland's price level. However, the country's economic tendency toward inflation and hence its decreased competitiveness continued, albeit on a smaller scale, during the following decades and caused major devaluations in 1957 and 1967 – as well as some other minor devaluations.[18]

Although, under these conditions, it was difficult for Finland to adopt the Bretton Woods system, the country did join this new international monetary regime in 1948 and, the exchange rate parity was approved in 1951. The Bretton Woods system was different from the two previous monetary regimes. Exchange rates were pegged but adjustable depending on specific conditions known as fundamental disequilibrium.[19] Capital controls were permitted to limit flows, and an international institution, the International Monetary Fund (IMF), was created to coordinate national economic policies and help countries with balance of payments disequilibria. To some extent, the success of the Bretton Woods' system was due more to the postwar golden age of growth and the expansion of international trade and investments than to its institutional set up.

202

The Kluuvi self-service bank, which opened in Helsinki in 1989, was among the first of its kind.

Member countries had fixed exchange rates pegged to the US dollar at a price of $35 per ounce of gold, exactly the same value it had since 1934. The pegged exchange rate system was confirmed in 1951 and convertibility restored in 1959. Finland considered that it was important to join the IMF as it would keep the country integrated into the Western monetary regime. However, the Finnish government refused the Marshall Plan in 1947, fearing the political reactions from Russia. Nevertheless, it received considerable loans from the United States that helped to stabilize the country's economic situation and expand the export industry. Finland also stayed out of the OEEC (Organisation for European Economic Cooperation) and the European Payments Union (EPU). Although Finland remained outside international economic institutions, it fought to implement its trading relationships by bilateral agreements. In 1958 Finland was able to sign an agreement with its major trading partners about the liberalisation of the current account, as had been done within the OEEC.[20] In this way, Finland was able to adopt a *de facto* Bretton Woods system. The focus of the Finnish government's policy was the promotion of growth, even if the trade-off was inflation and recurring devaluations of the currency. This was achieved by keeping the real interest rates low in comparison with those of other countries in order to promote investment. The financial markets benefited from this liberalisation as well. International capital markets started opening up, and foreign investment was permitted. Lifting some of the import restrictions towards the end of 1950s meant that trade now had to be balanced by demand management policy. As a result, fiscal policy became countercyclical, and labour disputes during the 1960s only amplified the business cycle fluctuations. A wage-price spiral, typical of the Nordic countries, caused frequent and sometimes massive devaluations of the *markka*, as in 1967 (see Figure 7.1).

203

García-Iglesias & Kilponen: Monetary Aspects of a Changing Economy

During the 1960s, a new Currency Act was also passed, establishing a new monetary unit, the new *markka*, in 1963. This new unit of account was worth 100 units of the old currency. Furthermore, the Bank of Finland's right to alter the exchange rate now became subject to its approval by the Council of State (the cabinet). The Council of State is made up of the prime minister and ministers of the various departments of the central government as well as an ex-officio member, the Chancellor of Justice. If the Bank of Finland's proposal was not considered appropriate, the Council of the State could refuse permission to change the external value of the *markka*. This mechanism was in force throughout the Bretton Woods period.

In summary, the monetary policy of this epoch was characterized by regulatory measures. The financial market regulations were part of a wider government market intervention scheme. The regulations covered foreign-exchange restrictions, regulation of bank lending rates, and an inter-bank agreement on deposit rates. As money markets were not in operation, the Bank of Finland provided specific quotas on credits to banks, while strict limits on the foreign-exchange market protected the banking system from international competition. Through interest rate controls, the lending rates of the banks were kept artificially low to favour investment and regulate housing costs. Interest earnings on bank deposits were tax-free, and interest charges paid by companies on loans fully deductible.

From the 1970s until the European Monetary Union

When the Bretton Woods system collapsed in 1971, the "pegged but adjustable" exchange rate regime ended, and countries looked to one of the two extreme alternatives: floating or pegging against main currencies. Finland pegged the *markka* to the US dollar, after its depreciation was allowed. However, the dollar peg was gradually abandoned in 1972 and 1973, and a period of "managed float" started. This period was characterized in 1973 by the First Oil Crisis, which had a worldwide effect, causing high inflation and slowing down growth. Finland was no exception, and by 1975 it was facing a depression. The bilateral trade with Russia, however, saved the Finnish economy from a deeper depression because, in order to pay the higher prices of oil imports from the Soviet Union, Finnish exports there of industrial products correspondingly increased (see also Kaukiainen in this volume). There was a strictly regulated money market, and interest rates remained relatively low. This is the time when several European economic agreements regarding exchange rate regimes developed. First came the European Currency Snake and later the European Monetary System (EMS). Finland preferred to remain outside both systems. In 1977, an exchange rate band was introduced in order to stabilize the external value of the *markka* against the currencies of Finland's main trading partners. Afterwards, the regu-

After a period of strong economic growth in the 1980s, in the early 1990s the economy headed into a recession comparable to the Great Depression. Debts increased, causing bankruptcies and leaving the entire banking system in a severe crisis. The SKOP savings bank fell into bankruptcy, and two other, competing, commercial banks, the Union Bank of Finland (SYP) and the Kansallis Bank (KOP), were eventually merged. Neon fascia signs were changed repeatedly during this period.

Pentti Kouri was a high-profile venture capitalist of the late 1980s. In transactions known as "the Kouri deals", he orchestrated a cornering operation to buy majority holdings in some of Finland's leading financial institutions. For a short time, Kouri was the major shareholder in two big commercial banks, the Kansallis Bank and the Union Bank of Finland. But this venture, financed by loans, never fully succeeded. The "Kouri deals" overheated the markets and caused a political outcry.

lation of the external value of the *markka* was expressed in terms of a currency basket. The idea of the currency basket was to keep the *markka*'s external value stable relative to the currencies of the country's major trading partners. The index was calculated on the basis of the 1970's exchange rates weighted by the relative trade shares.

The 1980s brought financial liberalisation to the Finnish economic situation as noted by Ojala and Karonen in this volume. Controls on both the exchange rate and interest rates were lifted. The deregulation of the financial markets required a complete reform of the credit system.[21] As its monetary policy tools, the Bank of Finland adopted open-market operations and the collection of cash reserve deposits. In June 1991, Finland switched from its own currency basket to the ECU (European Currency Unit) of the European Monetary System

206

as part of its process of integration. The collapse of Russian trade together with the lack of credibility of the Finnish economy and its policies culminated, once more, in the 1991–1992 exchange rate crises. After a strong period of economic growth in the 1980s, the Finnish economy headed into a recession that was comparable to the Great Depression. Deregulation of the money market led to increased borrowing by business, private citizens and local government authorities. Debts grew, causing bankruptcies and leaving the entire banking system in a serious crisis. The government then acted as a borrower of last resort in order to prevent a deeper crisis and complete economic chaos. In the meantime, the unemployment rate went up to nearly 20 per cent, causing difficulties for many (for a more detailed discussion, see Hannikainen and Heikkinen in this volume). Some of the reasons for the crisis can be found in the collapse of trade with the Soviet Union (see Kaukiainen in this volume for details) and the excessive debt contracted in previous years. High levels of unemployment also resulted from the high cost of labour and the technological change that led to the labour force being reduced in consequence of the introduction of high technology. The Bank of Finland tried to defend its currency over the crisis, but a devaluation of 12 per cent in November 1991 was not enough. Uncertainty increased, interest rates went up, the financial bubble burst, Russian trade collapsed as it had during the 1920s, and finally in September 1992 the *markka* was left to float.

After this deep recession in the early 1990s, Finland experienced a strong and significant recovery in 1994. Competitiveness was quickly restored when the Finnish *markka* depreciated in 1992. The floating exchange rate allowed for an independent monetary policy and lower interest rates. Improved credibility helped the stabilisation of prices, and the banking crisis came to an end. This time the crisis led to structural changes in the economy as well as to the different behaviour of the economic actors. Old associations, e.g. in the forest market, were abolished and new mergers changed the whole industry as pointed out by Ojala and Karonen in this volume. On top of that, the development of new technology together with its exports gave a new orientation to the Finnish economy (see also Asplund and Maliranta in this volume). [22]

Finland then joined the European Union in 1995, which put an end to the floating exchange rate system in October 1996. Finland was one of the early advocates of the European Monetary Union (EMU), accepting the common currency without a referendum in 1995. Looking back into history, it is interesting to note that during the Classical Gold Standard period, the Scandinavian countries, Denmark, Norway, and Sweden, established the Scandinavian Currency Union with apparently strong public support. More than 100 years later, the very same Scandinavian countries decided to stay outside of the European Monetary Union, while Finland chose a different path. In Finland, there was a strong political momentum towards deeper integration into the Western democracies, while the above-mentioned Scandinavian countries felt rather differently. There is no doubt that Finland's proximity to Russia and the historical relations between the two countries played a fundamental role in the process. Finally, after Finland joined the European Union, the charter of the Bank of Finland was changed in 1998, and it became a member of the European System of Central Banks. In 1999, Finland became a member of the European Monetary Union, adopting the euro in 2002. This was the fourth time since the 1860s that Finland entered an international monetary system.

The Finnish Velocity of Circulation

One of the key concepts in monetary theory is the income velocity of circulation, which measures the frequency at which money is exchanged between money holders. The income velocity of money is based on the traditional quantity theory of money, $MV = PT$, where M is the money stock, V the income velocity of circulation, P the price level, and T the volume of real transactions in an economy. Evidence for the quantity theory of money was provided by one of the most celebrated monetary economists, Milton Friedman, in his famous book *Studies in the Quantity Theory of Money*, published in 1956. This led him to propose that the Federal Reserve board should increase the money supply at a fixed rate in order to control inflation. Friedman's approach came to the forefront when he and Anna Schwartz co-authored *A Monetary History of the United States, 1867–1960* in 1963. In it they contend that the Great Depression was the result of misguided monetary policies by the Federal Reserve.

During the last few decades, and starting from Friedman and Schwartz's book, M2 has been used as the best representation of the money stock. For prices the best variable has been the deflator of GDP, while GDP itself has been the best approximation to T. Based on this, the velocity is defined as the ratio of the current value of total nominal transactions to the stock of money, $V = PY/M$. It thus determines how much money is required to service a particular level of nominal transactions, and it can be thought of as the inverse of the demand for money.

Money demand models in general indicate that the velocity of money varies directly with the opportunity cost of holding money (the difference between market and money interest rates) and inversely with real (permanent) income. But there are other factors. Transaction costs occur in exchanging non-money assets for money, and these costs include monetary costs, such as brokerage fees, as well as the implicit costs associated with inconvenience, sometimes called menu and shoe-leather costs. These costs can change over time, as monetary arrangements develop, and contribute to velocity patterns independently of fluctuations in the interest rate or real (permanent) income. Moreover, according to the uncertainty explanation, uncertainty about the future need for liquid funds creates incentives to hold money. The demand for money arises because wealth holders cannot anticipate their future transaction needs in the face of uncertainty. This is often referred to as the precautionary

208

motive for holding money. Like the transaction approach, it is not difficult to imagine institutional changes that will have an influence on households' precautionary motives and thus affect the velocity trend over time.

Approaches that go beyond the standard real permanent income and interest rate explanations of velocity are often referred to as institutional approaches to money demand. The institutional approach, first proposed by Knut Wicksell (1936), considered the effects of credit as a substitute for hard money on the velocity of circulation. According to this approach, phenomena like the monetisation process, the development of the commercial banking system, and financial sophistication are considered important determinants of velocity in addition to the opportunity costs of money. These are the institutional variables that influence the actual transaction costs of money and precautionary motives for holding money.

Following the institutional approach, several studies have calculated and analysed the long-term behaviour of the velocity of circulation for a series of industrialised countries.[23] The velocity of circulation seems to follow a U-shaped pattern from 1870 onwards. In almost all the countries studied, i.e. Canada, Norway, Sweden, the United Kingdom and the United States, the velocity has a high value around 1870. Afterwards, it shows a downward trend until 1913. In some cases, we can see that this fall continues during the inter-war years. However, at some moment, in most cases after the Second World War, velocity reaches a minimum level and starts moving smoothly up again. This trend continues until the end of the analysis, this being the normal behaviour of the velocity of circulation.

The interpretation of the U-shape of the velocity is two-fold, according to Bordo and Jonung. The downward trend is explained by the monetisation process and the development of the commercial banking system. As money replaces other media of exchange, the demand for it increases at a faster rate than aggregate demand, resulting in a downward trend in the velocity of circulation. The upward trend is due to the increasing sophistication of the financial system as well as improved economic security and stability, i.e. the development of the welfare state. When the first substitutes for money as a form of payment (i.e. credit cards) appear, the demand for money diminishes. The velocity of circulation starts moving upwards as the demand for money increases at a slower rate than aggregate demand. In the same way, improved economic security and stability reduce the demand for money as a precautionary reason. The precautionary motive for holding money is reduced as improved social security (e.g. unemployment benefits, pensions, government health care systems) provides insurance against uncertainty. The sooner the social security system develops, the sooner the velocity changes its pattern. Bordo and Jonung show evidence of all these phenomena by analyzing the income velocity behaviour of different countries.

Figure 7.4 shows the Finnish income velocity of money from 1868 to 1998 combined with the opportunity costs of holding money. There is a very clear decreasing trend in velocity from 1868 until 1918, but apparently the trend cannot be explained by fluctuations in the opportunity costs of holding money. A sharp upward movement in velocity occurs thereafter reaching a peak in 1921. This upward movement seems clearly associated with a similar sharp increase in opportunity costs. Then the trend continues to decrease until 1944, together with declining opportunity costs, but moves up again in 1945. The two sharp increases in the velocity of money in 1918 and later on in 1945 also coincide with the turbulent movements in inflation and output (see also Figure 7.3 and Hjerppe and Jalava in this volume) and are thus partly explained by transitory movements in the demand for money. These transitory movements notwithstanding, the whole period from 1868 until 1944 can be regarded as the downward sloping side of the velocity of circulation with an inflexion point around 1944. After the Second World War, the velocity presents a very interesting pattern compared with that of other industrialized countries and especially the other Nordic countries like Norway and Sweden, which show an upward trend after the 1940s. From the 1950s until the mid-1980s the path is rather stable but then shows a clear downward trend until the early 1990s. The upward movement in the opportunity costs of holding money does not seem to be associated with the velocity pattern until the early 1980s. In light of the regulated financial markets this is less surprising than it seems.

All in all, it is rather difficult to assert that movements in the income velocity of circulation can at all times be explained by an invariable relationship with the opportunity costs of holding money. Moreover, the velocity does not seem to follow a well-defined U-shape as suggested by Bordo and Jonung. In what follows, we attempt to interpret the velocity patterns in relation to institutional changes in the economy – in particular in relation to its monetary and financial conditions.

First of all, and in order to explain the monetisation process, we use the currency-money ratio as a proxy. We use this proxy to assess the spread of commercial banking as it is also part of the process of economic modernisation and monetisation. This ratio is calculated by measuring currency as the coinage and bank notes in circulation, while money corresponds to the money supply (M2) (Figure 7.5). In the beginning, households mainly kept their money in cash, and deposits in the banks were initially very small. Later, with the development of the banking system, deposits grew in importance, and the use of currency decreased. These two facts led to a decrease in the currency-money ratio. Up to the end of the 1930s, the ratio shows a very steep negative slope, contributing strongly to the downward sloping part of the velocity of money. As commercial banking develops, *ceteris paribus*, both the velocity and the currency-money ratio move in the same direction.

The institutional explanation behind the upward trend in velocity typically relies on increasing financial sophistication and improved economic security and stability. While economic security and stability certainly increased after the 1950s, the development of financial sophistication was hindered by

210

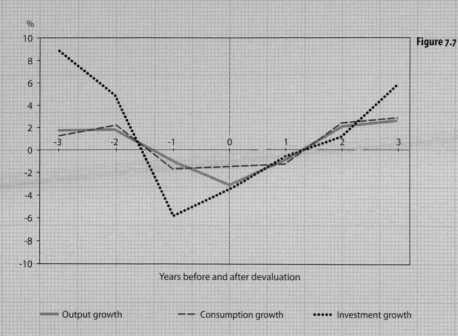

Figure 7.7 **Real economy and devaluation cycle**

Source: Hjerppe (1996). Statistics Finland to date.

Note: Own calculations. The data cover the years from 1928–1994. All the variables are expressed as deviations from their mean values over the period. Output growth is the growth rate of the Gross Domestic Product, consumption growth is the growth rate of private consumption and investment growth is the growth rate of private investments.

The output growth rate was lower than the consumption growth rate at the time of the devaluation, while investments dropped sharply prior to the devaluation. Private consumption followed a rather similar pattern although fluctuations were less pronounced than in the case of investments – as one might expect by comparing the volatility of consumption and investments.

the strict regulation of the financial markets. In particular, the banking sector remained heavily regulated until the 1980s. This jeopardized the development of modern financial instruments, and thus the ability of households to take advantage of their cash balances was restricted. There could be no active search for substitutes for money as there was in countries where financial development was not as heavily constrained. This is also evident from the fact that the relationship between the velocity and the opportunity costs of money is not clear; indeed it hardly existed until the mid-1980s. Afterwards, the opportunity costs and velocity pattern are positively linked, as suggested by Figure 7.4. Finally, the fact of adopting a monetary standard seems to have had no influence whatsoever on the velocity.

Exchange Rate Regimes and the Devaluation Cycle

Finland has typically aimed at to devalue its currency frequently for both institutional and economic reasons since it gained independence in 1917. Finland has typically aimed at stable monetary conditions by adhering to fixed, but adjustable, exchange rate systems. Being a small, open economy, this has been a quite natural choice, although the historical overview shows that rather frequent and large devaluations have been needed to restore the external balance. Resorting to devaluation – or "the D vitamin" as it is called by some authors – could in general be seen as a consequence of economic policy and the institutional set-up of the economy, which produce higher inflation than in the country's main trading partners.

The historical overview suggests that a "seed" for the frequent future devaluations – which turned out to be part of the economic cycle – was planted perhaps as early as the 1920s and 1930s. At that time, Finland, having suspended convertibility to gold in 1914, was re-considering a return to the Gold-Exchange Standard, and both the Minister of Finance and the Chairman of the Board of the Bank of Finland regarded it as necessary to return to gold at the prevailing rate. Finland's trade with Russia had practically collapsed, and Finnish exporters were in the position of looking for new export markets. Therefore, Finland joined the Gold-Exchange Standard but with a heavily depreciated currency: by 1926 the *markka* had lost 7/8 of its value. There was a similar reasoning after the Great Depression, when the *markka* was devalued by about 40 per cent against the main currencies: a devalued currency, it was thought, would help to improve export competitiveness and improve the profitability of industry. In addition, it would reinforce the effectiveness of import tariffs, thus reducing imports to the extent that the effects of devaluation on prices would remain insignificant.[24] Subsequently, the Finnish *markka* was devalued fourteen times between 1926 and 1991, and with increasing frequency after the Second World War. This has already been illustrated in Figure 7.1, which reveals how the external value of the *markka* changed during the periods of the different monetary systems.

Certainly, on many occasions, devaluations were preceded by a deteriorated trade balance – a trade deficit – and inflationary wage increases. The devaluations were often combined with a tight monetary policy, which was introduced as a result of a trade deficit and the consequent decline in foreign reserves. Eventually these two forces together obliged the central bank to devalue the currency.

The reasons behind the frequent devaluations have been discussed extensively in the literature about the Finnish economy.[25] Central concepts in this literature are the devaluation-inflation spiral and regulated capital, product and labour markets. In particular, after the Second World War, Finland started building up a welfare society in a situation where regulated product markets and the increasing involvement of the trade unions in wage negotiations caused excessive wage inflation. Internally, large devaluations could be seen as a device to restore gradual – or sometimes sudden – changes in the delicate balance between the development of corporate profitability and wage income. Indeed, large devaluations typically boosted corporate profitability and investments, but were then followed by a rapid acceleration of inflation. In fact, inflation had the contrary effect of reducing export competitiveness as domestic goods were more expensive and a new devaluation was thus needed to correct the situation.

212

Junnila (1970), for instance, argues that the 1967 devaluation was primarily caused by excessive pay increases, which fuelled rising consumption and imports. This resulted into a deteriorated trade balance and eventual tightening up of monetary policy as foreign reserves were declining to levels considered dangerously low. Figure 7.6 shows the development of money supply (M2), the trade balance and excessive wage inflation (measured as the difference between real wage growth and labour productivity growth in the manufacturing industry) around the devaluations following the Second World War. It seems patent that the money supply (money growth) and the trade balance (net exports) follow the conventional pattern described by Junnila. Trade balance is upward sloping, while money growth shows a U-shaped pattern around the devaluation. Similarly evident is a surge in excessive wage inflation prior to and during the devaluation year, with a later downward movement. The positive movement of net exports after the devaluation shows how the external balance is restored.

Another way to demonstrate the effectiveness of these devaluations is to look at the evolution of real variables like investment and consumption. In general, investments also dropped sharply prior to devaluations. In fact, devaluations typically occurred when the economy was already in a recession. This is illustrated in Figure 7.7, which shows the movements of real GDP per capita, private consumption and investments in connection with devaluations. The growth rate was, on average, 3 per cent below the average growth rate at the time of the devaluation, while investments dropped 6 per cent below the average just one year prior to the devaluation. Private consumption followed a rather similar pattern, although fluctuations are clearly less pronounced than in the case of investments – as one might expect in comparing the volatility of consumption and investments. It normally took one to two years before "the Devaluation-vitamin" had fully passed through the economy and the trade balance was restored.

Throughout history, devaluations have been used as an instrument of stabilisation policy. Some authors have even claimed that devaluations could be used as an instrument for growth and structural policies. As understanding of the dynamic behaviour of the economy improved and issues such as monetary policy credibility and expectations became fundamental concepts in policy doctrine, breaking out of the devaluation cycle became an essential goal for the Bank of Finland after the 1970s. These attempts were also linked to the fact that, as financial market liberalisation progressed, it was no longer possible to pursue a truly independent monetary policy.[26] The liberalisation of capital markets in the 1980s strengthened the role of expectations – in particular exchange rate expectations – in determining the domestic interest rate (the uncovered interest rate parity condition). Devaluation "rumours" caused flights of capital, which in turn forced the Bank of Finland to respond with higher interest rates.

During the 1980s, it became evident that a lack of exchange rate credibility would be detrimental to the country's economic stability, and that a new approach to monetary policy was needed. The institutions, however, responded with typical slowness, and the new financial market regime together with adverse shocks to foreign trade led to a dramatic collapse of the *markka* in 1991. The Finnish currency was left to float in 1992, and the Bank of Finland switched to an inflation-targeting regime in February 1993. This event was a clear sign of change in the monetary policy regime as low inflation became the principal target of monetary policy and the exchange rate was allowed to be determined freely by the markets. The two-percent inflation target was achieved by 1995, and the exchange rate was stabilized in preparing Finland to join the EMU and adopt the euro in January 2002.

From silver to euro

In this article we have studied the historical monetary development of the Finnish economy. The article's long-term perspective was based on the analysis of the income velocity of money and its relation to economic development. The short-term analysis focused on one of the defining features of Finnish monetary history, namely the frequent devaluations of its currency.

Prior to the mid-nineteenth century, the Finnish monetary regime was influenced by both Sweden's and Russia's monetary conditions. The country did not have its own currency, and both Swedish and Russian currencies circulated at the same time. Under those circumstances, it was believed that the country would gain in stability and credibility by joining a metal standard and having its own currency. Adopting a monetary standard would also have an important effect on the country's political and economic life as well as on the process of modernisation. Moreover, its own currency was considered a symbol of the country's monetary independence and sovereignty, as well as a sign of integration into the world economy in the long run. Finland was finally granted the right to its own monetary unit by Russia in 1860, although it remained subsidiary to the Russian rouble until 1865. Subsequently, Finland joined all the international monetary systems from the nineteenth century onwards. Being a small, open economy, this has been a quite natural choice, although frequent devaluations have been needed to restore competitiveness and the external balance.

The long-term analysis provides a general overview of the Finnish monetary performance over the period 1868–1998. Research in economic history has shown that the velocity of circulation generally presents a U-shaped trend. This pattern can be explained by phenomena like the monetisation process, the development of the commercial banking system, and financial sophistication. The analysis of the Finnish data certainly shows a downward trend and supports its explanation through the monetisation process and the development

214

of the commercial banking system. However, a clear upward trend is missing. One potential explanation for the lack of a U-shape could be related to the strict regulation of the Finnish financial markets after the Second World War. In particular, the banking sector remained heavily regulated until the 1980s, thus prolonging the start of the development of modern financial markets. In comparison with other developed countries, the special development in Finland is interesting in itself. In countries like the United States and Canada, the velocity turns around the 1940s, but then it moves upwards exhibiting the above-mentioned U-shape predicted for the development of financial markets. In other countries like Spain and Portugal, the change of trend happens much later, showing a later financial development. Conversely, in cases like the UK, where the monetisation process took place much earlier, the velocity likewise experienced a prior U-shape development.

The historical overview suggests that a "seed" for the numerous future devaluations was planted perhaps as early as the 1920s and 1930s. The focus of Finnish government policy was on the promotion of growth with an emphasis on export competitiveness and low real interest rates, and the trade-off was inflation and frequent devaluations of the currency. A comparison with other countries, like Sweden, reveals a similar behaviour, although devaluations were not as frequent. However, as the liberalisation of financial markets progressed, it became evident that a lack of exchange rate credibility would be detrimental to the country's economic stability. A new approach to monetary policy was needed. In the mid-1990s, low inflation became the main monetary policy target, and the exchange rate lost its fundamental role. After joining the European Monetary Union and adopting the euro in 2002, Finland secured its integration into world capital markets. Since then monetary conditions have remained remarkably stable.

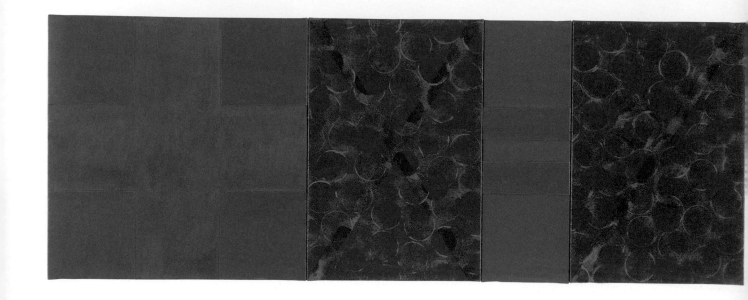

"Interest"

by Mari Rantanen

(2000, acrylic and pigments on canvas, 60 x 160 cm)

Guns and Butter
– Central Government Spending
in the 20th Century

Jari Eloranta and Jari Kauppila

Historically, the post-Second World War period embodied both fast economic growth, rapid structural change, and the creation of an extensive welfare state in Finland. Thus the building of the Finnish welfare state was intricately tied to the strong growth and diversification of the economy during this period. In this chapter we investigate how we can explain the long-term demand for central government spending in Finland. Is the growth of Finnish central government spending primarily a question of welfare state expansion, or do we need to analyze other factors as well? Moreover, the quantitative analyses utilized here shows that the Finnish budgets ballooned due to the lack of a trade-off between military and social spending. The "Finnish model" was built on both guns and butter. In consequence, Finland was able to develop an extensive welfare state without experiencing slower economic growth.

Introduction

Despite the fact that Finland is a small, rather peripheral country, there are significant insights to be learned from the "Finnish success story". In less than a century, Finland has progressed from being a primarily agricultural country to a modern welfare state which is a member of the European Union, with a highly educated and technologically able population and a high standard of living. Finland has also developed an efficient education system, as measured by the recent PISA (Programme for International Student Assessment)[1] studies, and it provides a good example of the egalitarian nature of the Finnish welfare society (see the pertinent discussion by Pauli Kettunen in this volume). How can one develop such a comprehensive welfare state while still maintaining such a high level of economic growth?

Typically welfare states developed as a response to the rise of labour and socialist movements, as well as the slow democratisation of Western polities following the industrial revolutions in the latter part of the 19th century, especially

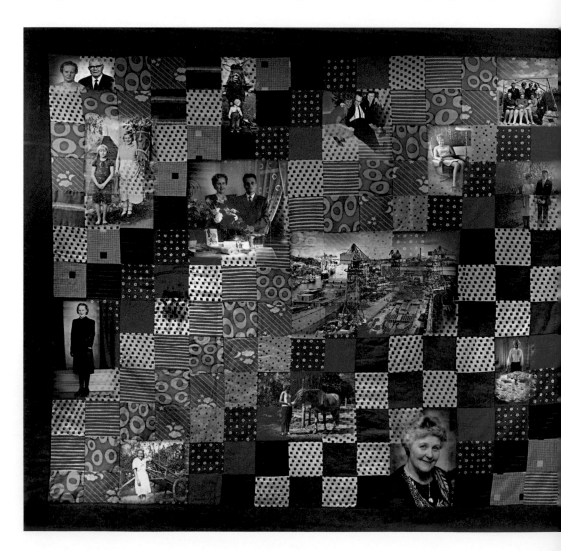

218

in Europe. Social spending as a share of the national economy increased rapidly between 1880 and the Second World War, and then boomed from the 1950s onward. The latter half of the 20th century witnessed the creation of various types of welfare state, ranging from the Anglo-American model of welfare restraint and individualism to the more universal Nordic welfare provision.[2] The creation of the Finnish welfare state did not begin in earnest until the 1950s, effectively bypassing some of the earlier stages experienced by most of the Western countries. The Finnish "model" was built on the stable institutions and governmental organisations that had evolved over centuries of Swedish and Russian rule, the strong economic growth and structural changes of the post-Second World War period (which necessitated government intervention to alleviate political and social tensions), and the ideological popularity of moderate socialism that ultimately led to the creation of new formal institutions, namely the foundations of the welfare state. In addition, the ideas and solutions offered by Finland's Nordic and other Western neighbours provided the building blocks of this emerging welfare state. The relatively rapid building of Finland's welfare

In the early 20th century, children below fourteen years of age constituted 35 per cent and persons over 65 years six per cent of the population. In the picture is an elderly woman at the end of her life cycle.

state proves that it is possible to *create* such institutions quickly if there are the resources and opportunities to do so. Furthermore, it is possible to *sustain* such institutions if the welfare policies contribute to the economic growth (for example, by creating human capital) and the social stability of society as a whole.

Here we, first of all, focus on analyzing the creation of the welfare state through the analysis of the long-term demand for Finnish central government spending. Second, we investigate whether the growth in Finnish central government spending was primarily a story of institutional expansion, or whether we need to undertake a further analysis of other factors. Third, we analyze what role changes in domestic and foreign policy played in the spending behaviour of the Finnish central government, addressing in particular the question of whether military spending was reduced to pave the way for higher social spending (the so-called guns versus butter trade-off). We aim to investigate these issues by identifying quantitative and qualitative changes in Finnish central government spending behaviour, analyzing possible causal linkages between the variables as well as engaging in a multivariate analysis of the explanatory factors.

Finland offers us an example of a quick transformation, both economic and political, from a warfare state to a welfare state. What do this process and these terms entail? Niall Ferguson (2001) has characterized this process appositely. Western warfare states, before the 20th century, had fairly low government-spending-to-GDP ratios, with most of the central government budget being allocated for military purposes. The keys to the transformation towards a welfare state and a larger government role in the economy included the higher lingering cost of conflicts along with the economic demands of total warfare in the 20th century, the spread of democracy and the increasing bureaucratisation of government services. While social spending was a low priority in most states before the 20th century, it has come to dominate domestic finances in modern economies. On the other hand, Finland exemplified relatively high military spending compared to many Western democracies in the 1920s and 1930s, whereas today it is social expenditures that dominate Finnish government finances. Broadly speaking, today's welfare states embody four broad fiscal dimensions: 1) cash benefits; 2) health care; 3) education; 4) food, housing, and other welfare services.[3] There is usually considerable overlap between the governmental redistributive programs, insurance programs, and income-maintenance (welfare) programs. Problematic issues in the analysis of the welfare state include the fact that the sources of welfare often transcend the limits of state activity, the modes of delivery vary greatly, and the boundaries of the welfare state are in a constant state of flux. All of these issues, although by and large not discussed here in this article, nevertheless permeate the analytical discussions and the use of data in the following sections.

220

While the Second World War gathered momentum, Finland fought the Winter War against the Soviet Union from November 30, 1939 until March 3, 1940. The early military successes of the Finns could not last forever, and the tide in the Winter War turned in early 1940. Finnish forces did, nevertheless, manage to hold the numerically superior Soviet forces at bay and the threat of intervention by Great Britain and France, on Finland's behalf, helped to strengthen an uneasy peace. In 1940 and 1941, the Soviet Union, emboldened by its successes in the three Baltic States, increased pressure on Finland, while the Finns were looking for a way to regain lost territory. Finland and Germany joined forces as cobelligerents in the summer of 1941, when the Soviet Union encountered the full might of the Wehrmacht.

For Finland, the early progress of German forces turned to disappointment when the battle of Stalingrad in early 1943 changed the situation in favour of the Soviet Union and the Allies. In the summer of 1944, Finland managed, albeit barely, to survive a Soviet onslaught in the Karelian Isthmus. Under the terms of an armistice signed in September of that year Finnish forces were obliged to push all remaining German forces out of northern Finland. This was done in an operation that became known as the Lapland War of 1944–1945. The Paris Peace Treaty, concluded in 1947, confirmed Finland's loss of a good deal of national territory and imposed the payment of heavy reparations. In spite of these setbacks, Finland was never occupied and retained its independence.

The University of Helsinki in flames in 1944 as a result of Russian bombing.

Central Government Spending and Institutional Changes

The study of government spending has been a popular topic among social scientists in the last two hundred years. One distinct set of theories emerged at a time when government spending increases coincided with sharp increases in aggregate income at the end of the 19th century. Most of the 19th-century classical economists, for example, advocated minimal state involvement. However, Adam Smith, the famous author of *Wealth of Nations* in 1776, was an advocate of the state provision of education, although for him state activities were mostly to be limited to national defence, policing, and administrative functions. Due to the theoretical challenges raised by Marxists, institutionalists, and the so-called German school of economics (for example Wagner), the *redistribution* of wealth has slowly become one of the accepted, albeit often challenged, functions of a modern government. Thus the battle lines were set: The defenders of tax-funded social programs have come to praise such programs as high-return investments that benefit the society as a whole, whereas the opponents have focused on the incentive gap incurred by these measures.[4]

The economy suffered during the Second World War, and much of the forest industry's manufacturing capacity fell into Soviet hands in the ceded territory in Karelia. But rapid economic recovery ensued once peace was restored. In the picture, Kaipaa Sawmill at Suojärvi.

222

Eloranta (2004) maintains that there were essentially two constraints on Western central government spending before the Second World War, which marks the beginning of the phase of massive growth: **1**) the aggregate income; and **2**) institutional (and other endogenous revenue) constraints. The choice about which public goods to offer was essentially conditioned by the political system in place, namely how democratic it was. Therefore, when analyzing the central government spending patterns of emerging welfare states one should look at the public debt constraints as well as the institutional constraints affecting a country's spending patterns, including for example laws affecting the composition of the budget. In addition, one should evaluate the implications of the extent of democratic institutions and the subsequent government spending trade-off patterns. Finally, external influences, such as threats and spill-over effects from other countries also need to be investigated. Here we will adopt a similar framework for examining Finnish central government spending in the 20th century, both institutionally and quantitatively from 1920 (after the end of the Finnish Civil War and the First World War in 1918 and the new constitution in 1919) to 1991 (the collapse of the Soviet Union, which partly contributed to the onset of a severe economic crisis in Finland). In the quantitative analysis we explore, in particular, the fiscal impact of income, central government debt, the possibility of a trade-off between military and social expenditures (defined as "guns versus butter" in this article), democracy, population characteristics, the external security environment, elections, parliamentary competition, and institutional changes as possible explanatory factors in Finnish central government spending behaviour.

Having gone through a massive structural change in the latter part of the 20th century, Finland can provide an interesting example of the dramatic changes that occurred in most central governments' fiscal role. As such, the change from an agrarian society to a service society has been combined with a significant growth in government spending. This spending role has, however, changed substantially from the early 1920s to the 1990s. The social spending function in particular has changed from the early governments' efforts to keep social expenditures to a minimum to a welfare state with a broad social safety net and a larger government service provision role. Here we will first provide a short account of the main institutional developments in Finland from the declaration of independence in 1917 to the early 1990s. Then the main emphasis will be on evaluating the impact of policy changes, for example social reforms, on central government spending behaviour.

THE POLITICAL ECONOMY OF THE FINNISH WELFARE STATE IN THE 20TH CENTURY

The Bolshevik revolution in 1917, the Finnish declaration of independence in December 1917, and the onset of a four-month Civil War in 1918 cut off the

Russian imports of cereals to Finland. As a result, Finland had great difficulties in obtaining vital foodstuffs. In addition, the chaotic conditions in Russia deprived the Finnish export industries of an important market (as pointed out by Yrjö Kaukiainen in this volume). Great difficulties also arose from the depreciation of the Finnish currency (see also García-Iglesias and Kilponen in this volume). By the middle of the 1920s, however, the situation had changed and the Finnish economy had made remarkable progress. In fact, the inter-war period was a time of rapid economic growth in Finland. Between 1920 and 1938, the annual average GDP growth rate in Finland was nearly five percent. During the years 1920–1928, the annual growth rate exceeded six percent. This growth was high even by international standards.[5] The structure of the Finnish economy was still very much agrarian in the 1920s, although the situation was changing slowly. The manufacturing industry was emerging strongly from the late 19th century onward and received preferential treatment by the government during the first decades of independence.

In terms of foreign policy in the 1920s and 1930s, Finland did not follow the disarmament example set by its Nordic neighbours. Instead, due to the geopolitical disadvantage of close proximity to the Soviet Union and especially Leningrad (St. Petersburg), it followed the paradigm of alliance-building and

military readiness pursued by Eastern European countries like Czechoslovakia. This subsequently led to higher military spending. Moreover, one of the unsuccessful schemes of the early 1920s was an attempt to form an alliance with the other neighbours of the Soviet Union. In the late 1930s, Finnish foreign policy focused on achieving an alliance with Sweden, but these efforts were also unsuccessful. When negotiations with the Soviet Union over border and other security concessions ultimately failed in 1939, and the Soviet Union concluded the so-called Molotov-Ribbentrop Pact with Germany on August 23, 1939, war was on the horizon. The Winter War finally broke out on November 30, 1939, thrusting Finland into the Second World War against the Soviet Union.[6]

Finland, which eventually sided with Germany in a loose alliance in 1941 to reclaim some of the territory it had lost in the Winter War, had to dedicate immense resources to the fairly successful war effort. Massive government spending was accompanied by heavy regulation of the economy. The eventual defeat in the war in 1944, despite Finland being able to retain its independence, brought a heavy price for the Finns to pay. First, at the insistence of the Soviet Union, they had to forcibly expel the Germans from Lapland. Eventually, the Paris Peace Treaty, signed on 10 February 1947, brought a significant shrinking of Finnish territory in the east (for example, most of the Karelian Isthmus was

Helicopters of the Finnish Defence Forces flying over Sulkava in South East Finland, where there are the remains of an Iron Age fortification. The choices politicians have had to make between welfare spending and military spending are no longer as tough as they were during the recession of the 1990s.

lost) and reparation payments of 300 million (pre-1939) US dollars to be made to the Soviet Union. Finland had to pay most of the reparations in the form of metal and other industrial goods, and it managed to fulfil all of the obligations set by the Soviets, by and large on schedule. In addition, Finland had to resettle hundreds of thousands of displaced citizens and military personnel.[7]

Of necessity, Finnish foreign and economic policies were closely tied to the Soviet Union's sphere of interest in the Cold War period. Finland gradually assumed a more active role internationally, especially when U.K. Kekkonen became President in 1956. Kekkonen's initiatives during his 25-year presidency included a Nordic nuclear-weapon-free zone and the organisation of the Conference on Security and Cooperation in Europe (CSCE), with the consent of the Soviet Union. Whereas the beginning of Kekkonen's lengthy presidency was marked by an intensification of the Cold War and the ensuing crises, the late 1960s and the early 1970s were a time of lessening internal tensions, which provided more room to manoeuvre in Finnish foreign policy, a period which culminated in the CSCE in Helsinki in 1975. On the other hand, the Soviet Union applied more and more pressure on the Finnish doctrine of neutrality in the 1970s. Additionally, Finnish trade policy was in reality subjugated to security policy and the maintenance of good relations with the Soviet Union. However, the Finns also pursued closer relations with the West in their trade orientation (see Kaukiainen in this volume). This situation differed drastically from the interwar period. Although Finland had to adjust to the new foreign policy situation and the new trade constraints in the post-Second World War period, it also benefited from the extensive trade with the Soviet Union up until the late 1980s.[8]

The decades after the Second World War represented a time of strong economic growth for the Nordic countries. Finland experienced the strongest growth especially in the 1960s, which has sometimes been called a "Golden Age". The annual growth of GDP amounted to nearly five percent between 1946 and 1974 (see also Hjerppe and Jalava in this volume). This growth made it possible to start building the welfare state in Finland.[9] A slowdown occurred in the 1970s, as in most Western nations. GDP growth dropped to only a little over two percent annually between 1975 and 1997. The Soviet system for its part was not able to handle the economic demands of the armaments race, the social demands of the people, and a decrease in the repressive control of society, and it started to unravel with the initiation of *perestroika* in the mid-1980s. In the closing years of the 1980s, the Soviet sphere of influence began to disintegrate quickly, resulting in the actual collapse of the Soviet Union in 1991. Finnish politics slowly began to be free of the foreign policy constraints of the Soviet era. New challenges for the 1990s came to be European integration, the collapse of trade with the Soviet Union as well as the ensuing depression, the new defence orientation, and most importantly, the future of the welfare state.[10]

In Finland, the recession of the 1970s was followed by a period of strong economic growth in the 1980s. This growth came to an end in 1991 as a result of the combined effects of the collapse of the Soviet trade, international depression,

226

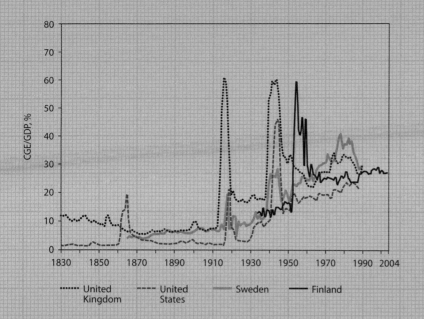

Figure 8.1 Central government spending as a percentage of GDP, 1830–1990

Sources: see Eloranta 2004 for further details. The data for Finland covers the period from 1920 to 1990. The Swedish data begins in 1865.

Central government spending ballooned especially in the 1950s, in the first phase of building the welfare state. After that, in relative terms, central government expenditures declined, since many of the new welfare state functions were taken over by municipalitles and towns.

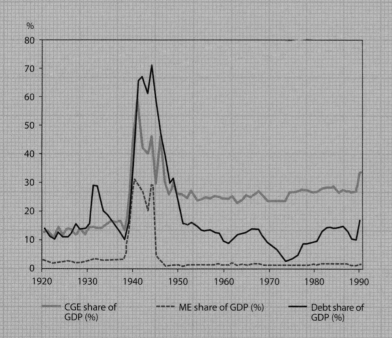

Figure 8.2 Finnish central government spending (CGE), military spending (ME), and central government debt (DEBT) as percentages of GDP, 1920–1991

Sources: Hjerppe 1996, Hjerppe 1997, Mitchell 1998, Terä & Tervasmäki 1973, Tervasmäki 1978, Tilastokeskus 1979–1992.

The Second World War greatly increased central government spending generally as well as military spending in particular. The strong economic growth of the post-war period reduced the state's indebtedness quickly and enabled the creation of an extensive welfare state, with much higher central government spending levels than in the interwar period.

227

rapidly expanding unemployment, overheated markets, and bank failures. The unemployment rate rose to more than 20 percent during the depression. This presented society, and the welfare state, with new challenges. Solutions to the ensuing fiscal crisis were found in expenditure cuts, the selling of government-owned enterprises, and reform of the welfare state. The strong economic growth of the late 1990s and early 21st century has again diffused some of this pressure.

The central government budget deficits amounted to over 9 billion euros at the beginning of the 1990s, and central government debt ballooned to 73 billion euros in 1998. However, from 1999 on, the debt has decreased steadily, and in 2003 the central government enjoyed a surplus of 0.3 billion euros. Similarly, the municipal sector took on heavy debts in the 1990s, but did not become as indebted as the state during the recession. The growth of the bulk of public expenditures, those not dependent on cyclical commitments, was very modest in the 1990s. New growth did not occur until the beginning of the 21st century. Public consumption and investment expenditures, relative to aggregate output, are now at the same level as during the closing years of the 1980s. As far as transfer payments are concerned, only pension and unemployment expenditures have increased, mainly due to the massive increase in unemployment since the 1990s.[11]

WESTERN CENTRAL GOVERNMENT SPENDING PATTERNS
AND THE BUILDING OF THE FINNISH WELFARE STATE
IN THE 20TH CENTURY

As seen in Figure 8.1, central government spending levels among the selected Western countries showed little growth until the First World War, although there were noticeable differences between them. Subsequently, in the interwar period, especially in the 1930s, central government spending increased. After the Second World War, the effect of the emerging welfare state can be observed until the 1980s. The last phase seems to represent a levelling-off stage or indeed a decline for modern welfare states. Thus, the two world wars appear to have imposed tremendous growth pressures on central government roles in most Western countries. Finland, however, seems to have experienced a strong period of growth in the 1950s, which differs from the three other countries displayed below. The United States, the embodiment of the Anglo-American welfare model, consistently spent less than the other three in the 20th century, whereas Sweden spent much more than Finland in the 1960s and 1970s.

This same conclusion about broad patterns can be reached by analyzing average central government-debt-to-GDP ratios from the latter part of the 19th century to the 1990s. They remained quite stable up until the First World War because the strong economic performance of the pre-war period enabled budget surpluses without a drastic overhaul of the tax system. Then the First World War brought about clear increases in the debt ratios, since many of the

228

Even the most remote parts of the country were integrated into the egalitarian school system during the early part of the 20th century. In the picture, a class of Skolt Saami in northern Lapland in 1938.

participants did not want to resort to higher taxes in order to finance the re-construction efforts and the new social commitments. This indebtedness increased especially in the 1920s, when the share of foreign liabilities grew fast.[12] The availability of external credit dwindled to almost nothing due to the Great Depression in the 1930s. Again, the Second World War, a more expensive and encompassing conflict than the Great War, forced countries to resort to borrowing, both internal and external, in order to finance the war. For example, the American and the British debt burdens were much higher in the Second World War. The post-war reconstruction and the introduction of welfare states, surprisingly, did not raise central government debt levels very drastically.

The debt-to-GDP ratios of the post-Second World War period were in fact substantially higher than those incurred after the First World War, and not as "permanent" as the levels in the interwar period. The average ratio was already lower in the 1950s than the lowest proportions observed in the period 1870–1938. The strong economic performance in the 1950s and the 1960s in part lowered the debt ratios and the burden of establishing welfare states. In many countries, for example in Sweden, central government activities were also complemented by the strong growth of the municipal and local government. Indebtedness increased again in the 1970s, when a new international lending boom occurred, resulting in many defaults on repayment in the 1980s.[13]

The emergence of welfare states in the post-war period took place in increments. For example, between 1937 and 1960, the percentage of GDP of public expenditures increased at a relatively slow pace, often more related to the increases in defence spending caused by the Cold War. This share was approx. 23 per cent in 1937 compared to approx. 28 per cent in 1960. However, the period 1960–1980 could be described as the real golden age of public sector intervention. Criticism of this era of Keynesian dominance emerged in the aftermath of the 1970s' economic crises, increasing in the 1980s and 1990s with the arrival of fiscally more conservative governments, especially in the UK and the USA. Public choice and other institutional theorists have since been among the many critical of the welfare states. How extensive was this government growth? If we look at the development of general government expenditures (as a percentage of GDP) in the latter half of the 20th century, we see that the average share increased steadily from approx. 43 per cent in 1980 to approx. 46 per cent in 1996. This is hardly a downward trend. As Lindert has pointed out, "Since 1980, out of the twenty-one leading OECD countries, only three have cut the share of GDP spent on public health care; only two have cut the share spent on public pensions, only four have cut the share spent on welfare, and only three have cut the share spent on unemployment". Finland certainly belongs in this group as well, having made only small welfare spending cuts in the 1990s.[14]

How specifically has this expansion taken place in Finland in the 20th century? Although the Nordic countries took some tentative steps in this direction in the 19th century, it was not until the interwar years that the institutional foundations of the welfare states were built in these countries. This process was somewhat slower in Finland, delayed by the divisive Civil War of 1918 and its aftermath. The fear of socialism, as in many budding welfare states, and the uncertain economic development initially helped the building of the Finnish welfare state, and the early foundations for an extensive welfare state were laid in the 1930s. During the Second World War, the government imposed a *de facto* command economy, inducing an acceptance of a stronger governmental fiscal role in the economy. The 1940s and the 1950s in the Nordic countries were a time of extending the measures already created in the 1930s, especially in Sweden, which had gone the farthest down this road (for example, in terms of maternity benefits, social insurance, and unemployment benefits).

The building of the welfare state in Finland started understandably with agricultural reforms and a land settlement policy. In fact, the majority of the population before the Second World War still lived in the countryside, living off the land. Social spending as a percentage of GDP was still very low in the 1920s, around one percent, while the leading Nordic country, Denmark, spent three times as much in relative terms. Thus, Finland was a latecomer among the Nordic countries in its welfare state building. The main emphasis was on economic development and employment policies, which it was assumed would also ease social tensions. The central government tried to avoid any expensive fiscal commitments to social welfare, abiding by and large to the principle of *laissez faire*.[15]

From the welfare state point of view, the Poor Relief Act of 1922 can be regarded as a start in the institutional changes towards a welfare society. It obliged the municipalities to organize poor relief in "a proper manner". The Poor Relief Act was only partly able to ease the serious social divisions in society created by the Civil War. Employers still had to compensate for many of the deficiencies of the act through

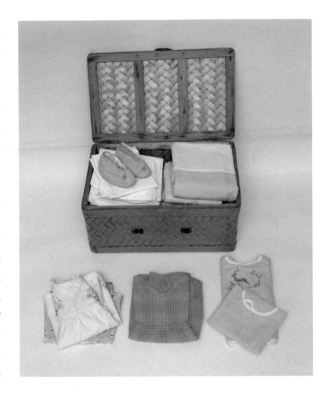

Maternity benefits have existed since 1937. They include a postnatal pack that contains the necessities needed by a family with a new-born baby. In 2004, altogether 40,500 of these maternity packs were distributed by the Social Insurance Institute (KELA).

The introduction of the General Child Allowance in 1948 was a landmark in the development of the welfare state. Pictured here are a mother and child collecting a child allowance in 1957.

obligatory relief funds. In general, the central government offloaded many expensive social policy functions on to the municipalities, which also tried to avoid heavy expenditure. Therefore, it is evident that private companies and other relief organisations still accounted for the bulk of the welfare system in the 1920s and the 1930s.

The Great Depression of the 1930s revealed the inadequacies of the Finnish social policy framework. The agricultural reforms were not sufficient to provide subsistence for the majority of the population. As a result, social security was improved after the depression. The National Pension Act of 1937 provided limited social security for all persons over 18 years. From 1944 onwards, it also became obligatory for every municipality to establish a maternity clinic. A General Child Allowance was introduced in 1948.

The Second World War imposed heavy pressure on the social security system. The task of the resettlement of the population from the lost territories became one of the major short-term challenges. Over 400,000 persons were moved, mainly from Karelia to other parts in Finland. In addition, the process of rebuilding imposed a heavy burden on Finnish society. The social and other problems of the war years created a momentum for the important social reforms that were to come in the 1950s and the 1960s.

In general, Finland closely followed the examples of Nordic (mainly Swedish) policy, especially since the left-wing parties had gained significant momentum after the war. Other factors that made this possible were the rapid economic growth and the structural changes in the economy in the 1950s and 1960s. During years 1948–1960, public expenditures, which now subsidized government-run health care, social security, and administration, grew at an annual average of 4.4 per cent. The Finnish welfare state, however, really took off in the 1960s, when the growth of public expenditures accelerated. The Disability Pension Act and the Old Age Pension Act were passed in 1962, and the Health Insurance Act in 1964. These measures were followed by others, especially in education and health care in the 1970s, which increased the social spending role of the municipalities and local government. Education and health care expenditures have generally grown fast, although the proportion of current transfers and subsidies increased even faster in the post-war period.[16]

What was the driving force behind this creation and expansion of the welfare state, both in Finland and internationally? The factors that have affected the demand for social expenditures have remained surprisingly similar in Western states for over a century. As Peter Lindert has observed, the demand factors have only partially differed from one period to another. The level and characteristics of democratic rule were the most important factors up until the Second World War, after which many Western nations were so-called full democracies, at least when evaluated according to the various aggregate indices created by social scientists. In the post-war period, the aging of the population and the success of the social programs undertaken became the decisive elements in their spending expansion. Often these patterns have been controlled

232

Year	USA	UK	*Finland*	Sweden	Belgium
1880	0.29	0.86	**0.66**	0.72	0.17
1890	0.45	0.83	**0.76**	0.85	0.22
1900	0.55	1.00	**0.78**	0.85	0.26
1910	0.56	1.38	**0.90**	1.03	0.43
1920	0.70	1.39	**0.85**	1.14	0.52
1930	0.56	2.24	**2.97**	2.59	0.56
1960	7.26	10.21	**8.81**	10.83	13.14
1970	10.38	13.20	**13.56**	16.76	19.26
1980	11.43	16.94	**18.32**	29.78	22.45
1990	11.68	18.05	**24.66**	32.18	23.11

Table 8.1 **Social Transfers as a Percentage of GDP, 1880–1990**

Source: Lindert 2004, 12–13. Social transfers consist of expenditures on welfare and unemployment compensation, pensions, and health subsidies, whereas social spending includes both social transfers and government subsidies to education.

Year	Share of GDP (%)	Share of Central Government Expenditures (%)
1920	1.0	1.0
1930	..	1.6
1940	..	2.0
1950	8.4	13.6
1960	11.0	11.1
1970	15.3	19.5
1975	19.5	19.3
1980	22.2	20.5
1985	26.1	25.7
1990	26.9	27.7

Table 8.2 **Finnish social spending, 1920–1990**

Sources: Urponen 1994, 232; Haatainen & Suonoja 1992, 641.

Group 1:	Group 2:
Economic development causes changes in central government expenditures	Central government expenditures cause changes in the trade-off between military and social spending and vice versa
The level of democracy causes changes in central government expenditures and vice versa	Central government debt causes changes in the central government expenditures and vice versa
Economic development causes changes in the level of democracy	The trade-off between military and social spending causes changes in the central government debt

Table 8.3 **Causal influences on Finnish central government expenditures**

Sources: see previous figures and tables. Detailed results and explanation of the techniques available from the authors on request.

Overall, as seen in the table, income, democracy, the trade-off between military and social expenditures (or the lack of it) all had a big impact on the development of central government expenditures in the 20th century.

by changes in the domestic political markets, namely who has possessed the political voice in society. In general, the post-war democracies have been more responsive to the extension of social security, and the populations have been more willing to pursue welfare policies in one form or another.

As we can see in Table 8.1, in terms of social transfers (= social expenditures minus government subsidies for education) as a percentage of GDP, Finland was somewhat behind countries like the UK and Sweden until the early 1920s. In the interwar period, however, this share increased rapidly, due to new, albeit modest, social security measures and new investments in education.[17] This pattern was somewhat similar to that of other Western nations, in which the social transfer share grew even faster than in Finland in the period 1930–1960. After the golden era of the growth of the welfare state in the 1960s, Finland became one of the high-spending states in terms of social transfers. Of the five states compared in Table 8.1 above, only Sweden had a higher relative share before the recession hit the Nordic countries hard in the early 1990s.

In Finland the growth of social spending took place from the 1950s onwards, as can be seen from Table 8.2. In particular, the growth in the share of the budget was rapid from 1940 to 1950. This growth seems to have levelled off in the 1980s, although slight increases have taken place in the 1990s and the early 21st century.

What about military spending trends in the 20th century? The Cold War period saw the key players in the international system engage in extensive military spending, reminiscent of the arms race of the late 1930s. The highest levels of military spending, as a percentage of GDP, were reached in fact during the height of the Cold War in the 1950s. For example, the military spending share of the United States rose above ten per cent, and remained on the average at 6.7 per cent in the post-war period. The military build-up of the Soviet Union was even more massive. For example in the 1970s, the Soviet Union seemed to spend more in absolute terms on its military than the United States. Nonetheless, for example aggregate estimates presented by SIPRI (Stockholm International Peace Research Institute) reveal a clear downward trend (at least until the last five years) in world military spending from the 1980s onwards, coinciding with the lessening of international tensions and the weakening of the Soviet Union.[18]

Finland's military spending was fairly high among the democracies of the interwar period, comparable to that of Great Britain and France in relative terms (as percentages of GDP). The foreign policy climate after the Second World War changed the situation drastically. Small countries had to manoeuvre between the two power blocs – for example, Finland maintained at least an appearance of neutrality, yet had to acknowledge the Soviets' security needs, whereas Sweden's neutrality was framed by high military spending and a more advantageous geographical position. Nonetheless, the "warfare state" remained an element, albeit a dwindling one, of their spending basket up until the end of the 20th century.

234

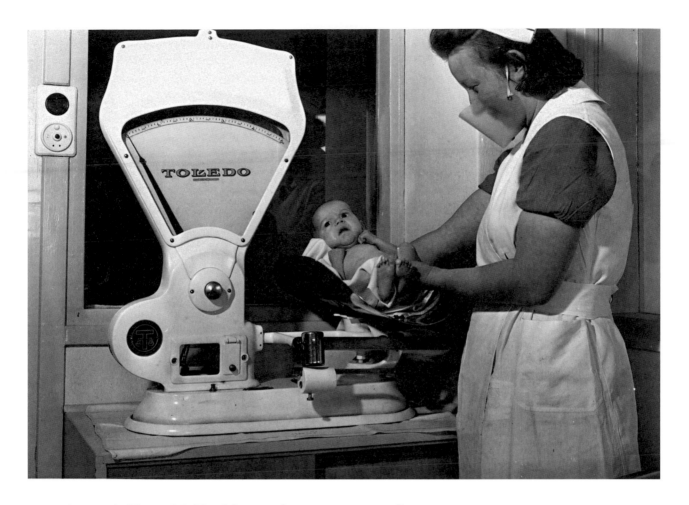

As seen in Figure 8.2, Finnish central government spending as a percentage of GDP grew throughout the 20th century, most notably during and after the Second World War, although this growth trend was not very steep. In comparison, military spending had a much more substantial budgetary role in the 1920s and 1930s, whereas in the post-Second World War period, due to the limitations imposed by the Paris Peace Treaty, military spending has remained quite low, even by international standards. Central government debt increased dramatically in the 1920s and early 1930s, only to plummet during the depression decade. The war period again raised this segment steeply, but the Finnish post-war governments, like those of other Western countries[19], were able to cut indebtedness fast in the following decades, in fact almost eliminating it by the 1970s. Finnish central government debt increased sharply in the 1980s and yet again in the early 1990s.[20]

What about the overall development of the Finnish public sector, especially in terms of central versus municipal or local government growth? Comparatively, the Swedish public sector growth, on the whole, seemed to be slower and more stable than was the case in Finland in the 19th and 20th centuries. Among the factors behind this were the long tradition of Social Democracy, peasant backing for welfare building, earlier industrialisation, and the longer

Physical examination of a member of the baby boom generation.

235

history of independent institutions. The Finnish class-oriented social policy model, essentially very similar to the Swedish one, eventually produced – except for the dramatic drop during the Civil War of 1918 – a slightly faster spending growth than in Sweden in the 20th century.[21]

The war years emerged as distinct peaks for the Finnish public sector as a whole due to the large war investments and an increase in the number of government employees, mostly military personnel. In both Sweden and Finland, the post-war years represented a period of welfare state building that was partly based on war-time organisational increases, such as the growth of several government bureaucracies. As we have already indicated, the expansion of public services occurred especially in the 1960s and 1970s – these measures included increases in municipal health services (county councils in Sweden), education, and pensions. The crisis of the public welfare services, which seems to be at the centre of the current debate, does not appear to have become a factor in the growth of public services until the depression years of the 1990s, at least in Finland.

The growth in spending at the level of municipal government in Finland was much faster than that of the central government, mainly because of its greater role in the provision of various public goods such as health care during the height of the expansion of the welfare state. Although there existed interaction between levels of government on the social spending choices, local preferences were expressed at both the local and central government echelons. Thus, while both of these levels of government were relevant in terms of the expansion of the welfare state, municipal and local levels in the provision of public services seemed to increase in importance as democracies became more fully developed, as in the Finnish case. We would argue that the demand stimuli of the two sectors were to some extent distinct, which makes it meaningful to analyze central government expenditures as a separate entity.

Quantitative Perspectives on Finnish Central Government Spending

In this section we will first look at the structural changes in the most relevant (vis-à-vis central government spending behaviour) variables and analyze their development over time. Second, we will make preliminary assessments regarding the possible interaction of the various relevant explanatory forces in this period. Third, we will analyze the determinants of Finnish central government expenditures, utilizing the framework briefly introduced at the beginning of this article. Last, we will discuss the relevance of the so-called guns versus butter trade-off phenomenon.

In order to make some preliminary judgments regarding the long-term development of various government spending variables, we can first explore the structural integrity of these time series. For instance, we can take the development of the Finnish central government debt in 1880–1991 as a disaggregated example of how the emergence of the welfare state in the 20th century affected budgetary choices. Here we want to investigate whether structural changes, such as wars and abrupt policy changes, affected Finnish central government spending during this period. In fact, this is a superficial way of testing the so-called Peacock-Wiseman displacement model, at least as far as indebtedness is concerned. The basic idea in this model is that governments are forced to respond to the challenges posed by external shocks (usually wars) entailing debt commitments, war pensions, and other similar issues by increasing taxation and spending. At the same time, increased wartime taxation induces a change in the public's tolerance of taxation. Bureaucracies take advantage of this to increase their long-term funding, and the government assumes a larger fiscal role in the post-conflict setting. Often the World Wars are postulated to have caused such a staircase-like growth pattern in government spending in the 20th century.[22]

When one utilizes statistical tests (such as Chow forecast tests[23]) that indicate whether the structural qualities of a variable have changed over time, clear changes can be observed in the development of Finnish central government debts (as a percentage of GDP) due to the World Wars and the Great Depression. These results offer preliminary support for this staircase-like government growth model, at least for Finnish central government debts. While the results obtained by Hilkka Taimio for the interwar period do not offer such clear cut support, we were able to distinguish three distinct periods of differing central government spending behaviour for Finland over the long term: 1880–1918, 1919–1944, and 1945–1991. Additionally, the depression years seem to have been a separate episode during the interwar period. Finnish central government debt levels were quite stable in the post-Second War period up until the beginning of the 1990s, as for example Riitta Hjerppe has shown.[24]

In general, we may quite confidently assert that the Second World War provided a sizable growth shock for Finnish government finances. On the other hand, in the post-Second World War period there seemed to be no structural changes in aggregate central government spending. Therefore, the welfare state building period seems to have started immediately after the war. Also, it seems that the interwar period and the post-war period differed from one another in terms of spending policies. Furthermore, military spending, which was a more integral part of the Finnish budget in the interwar period, seemed to be quite volatile up until the Second World War, whereas the social expenditures exhibited structural changes in the most intense period of building the welfare state, the 1960s and the 1970s.

Next we will take a look at the broad patterns of "causality" between two groups of variables for Finland: *Group 1* consists of the level of democracy (measured by an index constructed by political scientists[25]); the level of economic development (measured by real GDP per capita); and central government spending (as a percentage of GDP); *Group 2* consists of central government spending (as in Group 1); the constructed guns versus butter trade-off variable (measured as (military spending in year t + social spending in year t) / (military spending in the previous year + social spending in the previous year) equal to 1 if a perfect trade-off occurs); and central government debt (measured as a percentage of GDP).[26] Granger non-causality technique is a tool often used by economists to assess the possibility of interaction between a government spending variable and a set of other variables (such as democracy, income, debt, etc.). There have been numerous studies that have utilized the concept of Granger non-causality in order to assess initially the linkages between various sets of variables. Granger non-causality tests explore a possible link between variable 1 and its own past values and variable 2. Then a possible reverse causality is tested, variable 2 being linked to the past values of variable 1. If variable 2 Granger-causes variable 1, changes in variable 2 should *precede* changes in variable 1. This technique enables one to make an initial assessment of the possible causal linkages, although multiple regression analysis is needed to confirm the results.

It seems, for Group 1 in Table 8.3, that Finnish central government spending was influenced by both income and democracy, whereas Group 2 results indicate that the three variables (central government spending, central government debt, and the military versus social spending trade-off) were all linked to one another. In terms of the responses of central government spending to shocks in the other variables[27], in both cases shocks to the other two variables usually had a negative (initial) impact on central government spending. However, these negative impacts persisted longer in Group 2.

Income, democracy, the military versus social spending trade-off, and central government debt all had a big impact on Finnish central government spending. The military versus social spending trade-off variable alone explained over half of the variation in central government expenditures. Over a longer time lag, in Group 1, economic development explained 44.1 per cent, the previous years' central government expenditures 29.2 per cent, and democracy 26.7 per cent of the variation in Finnish central government expenditures. Respectively, in Group 2, the military versus social spending trade-off variable explained 51.2 per cent, the previous years' government spending 44.1 per cent, and central government debt 4.7 per cent of the variation. Nonetheless, we need to investigate the following aspects further, with multiple regression analysis: **1**) Are these variables (economic development, level of democracy, the guns versus butter trade-off and central government debt) the keys to understanding Finnish central government spending behaviour in the 20th century? **2**) Can the guns versus butter trade-off variable really have had this big an impact on central government expenditures? And, if so, why?

238

EXPLANATORY FACTORS IN DETERMINING
CENTRAL GOVERNMENT EXPENDITURES

As we have argued above, it is not enough to use graphs and monocausal methods (like the Granger non-causality tests) to evaluate the determinants of government spending patterns. We have already indicated that there are essentially to two constraints on central government spending: 1) the aggregate income; and 2) institutional (and other endogenous revenue) constraints (various aspects of the existing type of regime and legal system). For democracies, the tax resistance threshold would eventually be reached as a result of large increases in government spending (and concomitant revenue needs). Such abrupt increases in government spending have often been caused by exogenous shocks like external conflicts. For autocracies, the primary constraint would be income, and the rational autocrat would not push extraction rates beyond a level at which he would begin to compromise his future extraction rates and political (monopoly) power. Here we will examine quantitatively the impact of income, central government debt, the possible trade-off between military and social expenditures, democracy, population, external security environment, elections and parliamentary competition on Finnish central government spending. In addition we decided to investigate the impact of the main institutional changes.

Daycare for children under school age was made statutory in 1973.

To this end, we attempted to explain Finnish central government expenditures (as a percentage) as a function of: **1**) real *GDP per capita*, measured as before; **2**) *central government debt* (as a percentage of GDP) in the previous year; **3**) *the guns versus butter trade-off* variable, measured as above (the higher the value of this variable, the less the trade-off, thus imposing growth pressure on budgets); **4**) *the level of democracy*, measured as above; **5**) *external threats*, represented by a composite world military spending figure constructed by the authors; **6**) *the aging of the population*, taken from Lindert (2004); **7**) *the population growth rate*, as a percentage of change from one year to another; **8**) *elections*, represented by two different dummy variables (variables approximating their impact), one referring to parliamentary election years and the other to presidential elections, with election years hypothesized as limiting spending and taxation desires; **9**) *parliamentary competition,* pertaining to the so-called index of parliamentary fractionalisation, hypothesized as having a negative impact on central government spending due to increased competition for votes in the political arena; **10**) *legislative changes* (various welfare state legislative provisions), represented by a dummy variable (such as a change in welfare legislation); **11**) various *dummies*, introduced to represent three separate spending regimes, as indicated by previous analysis (1920–1938, 1939–1945, 1946–1991).

First of all, the earlier findings about the pivotal role played by the military versus social spending trade-off, or rather the lack of it, causing higher central government spending levels, were confirmed. It was found to be a statistically significant variable in all of the three specifications used, with a relatively large positive coefficient. In terms of the other variables, democracy seemed to decrease Finnish central government spending. Why? Possibly because of an incomplete trade-off effect, although this needs to be investigated further. Parliamentary competition, unexpectedly, yielded a positive coefficient. It could be that the negative impact from the competition to reduce taxes during and before an election year is limited only to military spending, and again the trade-off dynamic could play a role. It could also be an indication of the wide support the creation of the Finnish welfare state has enjoyed in the post-war period. Presidential elections were also found weakly significant in statistical terms, having a small negative impact. Institutional changes were not found to have played a very significant role, at least directly. However, the earlier qualitative review does suggest they were crucial in raising the demand for social expenditures in particular. Finally, the Second World War imposed, as expected, growth pressures on Finnish central government spending. The multiple regression model utilized here seemed to work fairly well, achieving relatively good statistical fits with at least half or more of the overall variation explained.[28]

One has to remain a bit cautious when interpreting these results. Some of the caveats include possible problems with the statistical techniques used and the need to take a closer look at the various subcategories of central government spending, for example military spending and to make a closer analysis of the institutional changes. For instance, have firms had an impact on the de-

240

mand for particular types of spending in the Finnish case? A preliminary way of gauging the importance of coalitions of firms is to assess the demand characteristics of military expenditures, which we did for Finnish military spending in the period 1954–1985.

The regression analysis indicated that: **1**) Finnish military spending increased in times of poor industrial performance, due to the lobbying activities at the industry level (as compared to a single industrial branch such as shipbuilding); **2**) Finnish military spending has been highly sensitive to the development of the post-war Finnish welfare state and budget bargaining in the political markets in general. Similar results were found for the interwar period.[29]

What about the military versus social spending trade-off variable – or the lack of a trade-off in this case? Why would it be so instrumental in explaining Finnish central government spending? Let us hypothesize a budget that consisted solely of military spending ("guns"), in a "perfect" autocracy, or exclusively social spending ("butter"), in a "perfect", non-threatened democracy – and that these polities were, at least in the absence of a major crisis, averse to borrowing. However, neither of these ideal budget categories can expropriate all income (or even revenue) for these purposes. Thus, one should investigate whether: **1**) military spending and social spending are the central components in the central government spending of a particular period (in addition to the public debt commitments related to these items); **2**) when the sum of taxes and borrowing becomes large enough or rises abruptly due to exogenous threats or crises, tax resistance (resistance to decreasing consumption and investment) is likely – the more so the more democratic the regime is (In addition, public debt increases would most likely follow to finance the spending, creating larger budgets in the future.); **3**) a trade-off between guns and butter will ensue when the economic burden becomes large enough or rises abruptly – this trade-off would not be perfect due to budgetary and other difficulties in interchanging these expenditures; moreover, such a trade-off would be less applicable in the case of autocratic regimes.

As argued here, the growth in central government spending resulted, in addition to other explanatory forces, from the interaction (or more likely, the "stickiness" of this interaction process) between military spending and social expenditures. The guns versus butter hypothesis in the context of central government budgets implies either that these two expenditure categories have no impact on the overall budget (i.e. there is an equal size trade-off response between them) or, conversely, that this interaction somehow drives central government growth tendencies. Often a reduction in military spending is said to create a peace dividend in the form of increased, more productive economic activity. On the other hand, it seems that on the whole domestic and economic incentives involved in military acquisitions tended to sustain military spending or at least limited its decline even under public pressure. *Moreover, in the Finnish case there seems to be little evidence of an automatic budgetary trade-off between these two types of spending*. Finnish military spending declined somewhat in the post-Second World War years, yet social spending increased dramatically, leading to higher total spending. The politicians and interest groups that shaped the budgetary choices in this period arrived at an informal consensus to build a comprehensive welfare state while maintaining the steady, yet lower level of military spending dictated by the Paris Peace Treaty.

Conclusions and Further Challenges

Finland went through a quick transformation, both economic and political, from a "warfare state" to a welfare state in the post-Second World War period. Here we have focused specifically on the analysis of Finnish central government spending, both qualitatively and quantitatively. We were especially interested in the impacts of wars, institutional changes, spending trade-offs, and other demand influences. In general, the post-war "Finnish model" of central government spending seemed to consist of both military and social spending, extensive welfare policies with pro-growth economic impacts and a steady increase in the role of the state in economic outcomes.

In terms of welfare policies, Finland was a latecomer in the 20th century, since its welfare state and economic expansion did not begin in earnest until after the Second World War. This was complemented by a simultaneous rapid structural change in the economy. Thus the earliest welfare reforms were specifically aimed at rectifying the impacts of this structural transformation. The creation of the Finnish welfare state gathered speed in the 1950s and 1960s, which can be seen as a pivotal period in this process. Many of the original ideas and policies were adopted from other Nordic countries. Later, in the 1970s, this process was complemented by new measures extending the role of the state in education and health care. The municipalities and local governments also expanded rapidly at this time, in fact becoming the most important providers of many government services. The 1980s and 1990s were a time of retardation in the growth of the welfare state, especially given the severity of the depression in the 1990s. In general, Finland has followed international trends in this respect, although for example Sweden has maintained higher social spending levels than Finland in the last two decades.

The initial quantitative findings showed that Finnish central government expenditures seemed to have differed in structure before, during, and after the Second World War. Moreover, we discovered that income, democracy, the military versus social spending trade-off, and central government debt all seemed to be influential factors in explaining Finnish central government expenditures. A large amount of the variation was explained by the trade-off effect (or lack thereof). This result was later confirmed by multiple regression analysis. Even though for example institutions were found to be relevant in explaining the aggregate changes in the demand for central government spending, the lack of a trade-off between the two main spending categories drove up the spending

242

Numerous state-owned enterprises were privatised towards the end of the 20th century.
The state-owned Valmet company (later Valtra) started to manufacture tractors in the 1950s.
The picture shows T-series tractors in the Valtra factory in Suolahti in 2003. Valtra is now a
worldwide brand of the US-based AGCO Corporation.

levels substantially. Why? Direct trade-offs between budgetary categories have
been rare in modern states. Given the complexities of budgetary processes and
electoral pressures, this mechanism might be crucial to understanding welfare
state expansion in the 20th and 21st centuries. In the Finnish case, the political
compromises in the budgeting process and the widespread support for the wel-
fare state led to higher central government spending levels, which were in turn
financed, by and large, by the rapid economic growth of the post-Second World
War period. The results presented here, however, are still tentative. We need to
look further into the impacts of various types of democratic institutions, the actual budgetary negotiations related to this suggested trade-off (or lack thereof),
and preferably compare the Finnish experience to the fiscal expansion of other
countries in a similar situation.

"The Beggar",

by Marcus Collin

244　　　　(1935, pastell)

Income Distribution in the 20th Century

Markus Jäntti

The record of economic growth in Finland during the 20th century was quite good. In order to investigate to what extent that income growth has been distributed across the population, the author examines evidence on the distribution of income in Finland from 1920 onwards, based on tax records. The long-term evolution of income inequality is of interest as in the late 1990s Finland had one of the most equal distributions of income among the OECD countries. Inequality was quite variable in the inter-war period, increased substantially between 1950 and 1970 and declined quite rapidly after 1970. While inequality has increased during the past ten years, this increase does not appear to be unusually large in light of historical variations.

Introduction

The distribution of income and its change over time are important subjects in economics. Changes in relative inequality reflect changes in the distribution of economic well-being. If economic growth is concentrated on the top income earners we observe an increase in relative inequality, while growth that is distributed across the population is associated with stable inequality. Finland presents an interesting case for study since in the late 1990s it had one of the most equal distributions in the OECD countries.[2] As we shall see, inequality has varied substantially over time, and the levels recorded since the first oil crises in the 1970s are much lower that in earlier periods.

Research on income inequality, and particularly the very top end of income distribution, using tax records for long periods has taken off in recent years, inspired by Thomas Piketty.[3] The income distribution information that can be gleaned from tax records falls short of what should ideally be known for income distributions to inform us about the distribution of economic well-being. Typically, few or no adjustments can be made for household or family size, many income sources are not included in taxable income, the tax units may be quite different from the sharing unit and so on. Moreover, information on taxable income over long periods of time may be available only in grouped form – and as income incquality is increasingly microdata-based, such sources are easily overlooked. Finally, the rules that regulate taxation tend to change quite substantially over time, so it is unclear to what extent the distributions can be meaningfully compared diachronically.

However, knowing something about historical income distribution is clearly better than knowing nothing. Finland introduced its first comprehensive national income and property tax law in 1920. At this point, Statistics Finland (as the national statistical agency is now called) started to publish tables in grouped form on income distribution[4]. There is some variation, detailed below, in the exact nature of the information that is available. These data provide the basis for the following analysis.

The study of the distribution of income in Finland has a long tradition. Early contributions include Fougstedt (1948) and Brummert (1963). The paper by Hjerppe and Lefgren (1974) (in Finnish but with an English-language summary) is based in part on the same data as the current paper and describes many of the shortcomings of tax data as a source. Their results suggest that between 1900 and 1922, the share of the top five percent of income recipients decreased from 33 to 28 percent and declined to 20 percent by 1967. The income share of the top quintile group decreased from 60 to 52 percent in 1922 and declined further to 49 percent by 1966. They also show numbers which suggest that income inequality increased substantially between 1881 and 1900.

An interesting institutional change that considerably complicates the use of the data is the introduction of separate taxation for married couples in Finland in 1935 (more on the effect of this change on data in Section 2 below). The

The challenges facing the pension system are mainly due to the change in the age structure and the resultant accelerated growth of pension expenditure. The number of people receiving only the basic pension has decreased as higher earnings-related pensions have grown in importance. Pictured here is a pensioner in North Karelia in the 1980s.

political debate on whether to introduce separate taxation was conducted in remarkably sophisticated terms over several years in parliament, in academic circles and in the popular press[5]. The process that preceded the 1920 legislation on progressive income and property taxation is dealt with in fascinating detail by Lindberg (1934). While a national tax law had been in preparation for decades, the drafting of 1920 legislation was initiated in the summer of 1918 in the wake of a violent if brief civil war, fought largely along class lines.[6]

Data and methods

The purpose of this section is to describe the main changes in the structure of the data during the period studied. That is, the section recounts how the taxation has been conducted, especially with regard to incomes and the units subject to taxation, and how the statistical methods have changed.

The data originate from Statistics of Income and Property, a series published by Statistics Finland starting in 1920[7]. From 1976 on, microdata-based Income Distribution Statistics have been published, and these provide data on the distribution of disposable income using the household as the primary unit. However, in this study, we use the same source (Statistics Finland: Statistics of Income and property) after 1976 as well. This source contains grouped data on the distribution of taxable income or income subject to taxation on a semi-annual basis. As the tables only cover those incomes that were subject to taxes according the law at the time, these time series should be viewed with some caution. The statistics cover only those incomes and those units subject to taxation that the current laws stipulate. Any changes in tax laws lead to changes in measured income distribution.

We provide information about two different kinds of time series of data on income distribution: the *taxable income of tax units* between 1920 and 1992 and the *income subject to taxation of all adults* between 1949 and 2003. "Taxable income" consists of "income subject to taxation" less income deductions. All three of these are defined according to central government ("state") taxation at the time the data are gathered – the definition of the income that is subject to *municipal taxation* and of the deductions that are allowed in respect of it differs from that applying to state taxation, and the two definitions also vary differentially over the years.

The concept of income, both as defined and as included in the publications, has undergone many changes over the years. In 1920, only income that was actually taxed ("taxable income") was reported. This was further refined in 1949, when *income subject to taxation* became applicable. This is distinct from taxable income, the part of the income that is actually taxed. The difference consists in the income that is exempted from taxation. This depends on the threshold of income subject to taxation, under which income is not taxed, and on various other deductions allowed for social reasons, e.g., dependent

248

Income inequality was considerable in the early 20th century. But at that time, as a result of the Land Acquisitions Acts and the Leaseholders' Act, crofters got to own the land they had previously rented. To some extent this levelled out income distribution. In the picture, a croft in Ruokolahti, eastern Finland, in 1923.

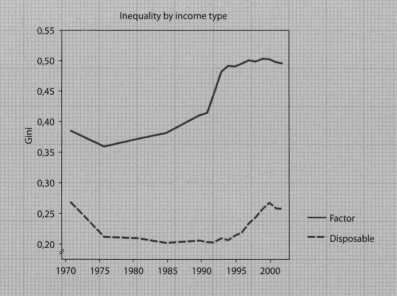

Figure 9.1   Income inequality – Gini coefficients 1971–1999

Source: Author's calculations from income distribution survey micro-data.

Note: The Gini coefficient is a single number that summarises inequality. The Gini coefficient varies between 0 and 1 with large values indicating higher inequality. It is related to the Lorenz curve in that it is twice the area between the Lorenz curve and the 45 degree line. The Gini coefficient can also be thought of as the average percentage difference in income between each person and all richer persons. Factor income is the sum of earnings, property income and other market-based rewards. Disposable income adds to this all public and private income transfers and deducts direct taxes. The changes in inequality during the late 1990s are quite substantial compared with changes since the mid 1970s.

children. Even though there have been some changes in the concept of income over the years, the substance has not changed much. In principle, the income subject to taxation includes all forms of money income that accrue to a person or tax unit in a given year (except for some social transfers and a few other items) including

- labour income (earnings): wages and salaries, fringe benefits
- the value of work-related and other pensions that are subject to taxation
- agricultural and forest income
- self-employment income
- property income

Table 9.1 lists the major changes over the years. The tendency is for the inclusion of additional income components over time. Those forms of income that are exempted from taxation are not included in the statistics. As a result, the income levels in the statistics are lower than true factor incomes. The most notable omission was national pensions until 1983, at which point they became subject to taxation, as well as some transfer incomes such as child and family allowances and social security payments or subsidies. Scholarships and some pensions, such as those paid to war veterans, are examples of other forms of income that are exempted from taxation. Also bonds and bank deposits and the interest accruing from them were exempted from taxation for most of the period studied.

Finland introduced separate taxation for married couples in 1935. From that point, the data also take the person rather than the couple as the tax unit. Separate taxation was abolished in 1943, at which point the data revert to the use of couples as the unit. Separate taxation was reintroduced in 1976, although the "short series" on income subject to taxation (but not the "long series" on taxable income) start again to use the person as the unit in 1952. Prior to 1975, the long series includes some undivided estates (these are excluded from the short series on taxable income).

The way in which the published tables have been compiled has also varied over the years. Almost the entire population liable to taxation is included in the material until 1945, when a sample-based survey was conducted for the first time. The data continue to be based at least in part on samples until 1969, when the use of computers made it possible to return to tabulations of the total population of income recipients.

The data that underlie the long series in this paper are grouped tables of taxable income and income subject to taxation. We know the class limits, the distribution of income-receiving units across those classes and the mean income within each class. It is, of course, possible to estimate various income distribution functionals directly on the basis of the grouped data. Such an approach would allow us to estimate for each year of data such things as means

250

1920	• Inheritances and gifts exempted • Income from abroad taxed in Finland
1924	• Agricultural income assessments defined and standardised
1935	• An additional tax of 20% on the tax amount of persons over 24 years old with no guardianship obligations
1937–1942	• An additional tax of 20% on the tax amount of persons for defence purposes
1950	• Bank deposits and interest on them made exempt from taxes
1957	• Additional taxes on high incomes introduced
1958	• Additional taxes on high incomes abolished
1964	• An additional tax of 20% on the tax amount on the income of persons introduced. The seaman's tax introduced
1968	• Changes in the assessment of property income; the threshold considerably raised
1969	• New law on the taxation of assets from trade and professional activities; income and losses could be balanced out over several years
1975	• The forest premium scheme introduced • The taxation of income and property made more uniform
1976	• Two separate progressive scales ("A" and "B") abolished and a new single scale introduced
1980	• The scale for property income lowered
1983	• National pensions (base and additional) no longer exempted from income subject to taxation
1985	• Other income sources made subject to taxation: unemployment benefits, support for home care of children, social assistance for entrepreneurs, aid to students, sick pay, maternity allowance
1986	• Seamen's income taxed in the same was as that of other persons
1987	• Other income sources made subject to taxation: pensions and basic daily sick allowances, study aid for adults, certain other daily allowances and payments
1989	• Fringe benefits and capital gains made subject to taxation • Agricultural income reformed, area subsidies made subject to taxation
1992	• Study aid for university students made subject to taxation • Strike pay made subject to taxation
1993	• Major reform of property income; capital gains taxed at same rate as other property income, imputed rents from owner-occupied housing exempted
1996	• The property income tax rate raised from 25 to 28 % • Changes to taxation of inheritances and gifts
1997	• Child-care allowances made subject to taxation

Table 9.1 Major changes in the definition of income and taxation

and variances, inequality indices and even more detailed objects, such as Lorenz curves, albeit at a fairly coarse level. It would also be possible to apply a non-parametric density function and use that to generate income quantiles. While modern techniques, such as kernel density and local polynomial estimates, are intended for microdata and are therefore not of much use here, simple approaches would allow the generation of more fine-grained income distribution characteristics.

We have chosen another approach; namely to apply a theoretical distribution to the data and use the estimated parameters to generate the statistics of interest. There is fairly widespread agreement that there are specific three-parameter distributions that yield very good fits with income distribution data[8]. Choosing a parametric distribution allows for the generation of highly detailed and complex functionals, such as the full Lorenz curves or the income shares of very small subsets of the population. Moreover, it is possible to examine Lorenz dominance based on only the estimated parameters for certain interesting distributions.

The approach taken here is to treat the classes as if they were microdata and write the likelihood function of the parameters in terms of observing the class means with their weights[9]. Choosing a particular parametric distribution family is no simple task, given the practically unlimited possibilities. However, a choice that has turned out to be quite useable for income distributions is the family known as the Singh-Maddala, originally introduced in 1942 as the Burr type XII distribution.[10]

Trends in income distribution

Like many OECD countries, Finland experienced a surge in income inequality in the 1990s[11]. Although the levels of income inequality are by international standards fairly moderate, inequality – as measured by the Gini coefficient of disposable income – has risen to levels last seen in the early 1970s (see Figure 9.1). Factor income inequality increased substantially over the decades, but this increase decelerated in the second half of the 1990s, when disposable income inequality started to increase. This has led many to seek the reasons for increased inequality in changes in taxes and public sector transfers.

A somewhat different view of inequality trends emerges from studying changes in disposable income decile group means and their components, as shown in Figure 9.2. The graphs are drawn on a log scale, so that changes in relative inequality can be visually assessed from the slopes of decile group mean incomes, shown in the upper left panel. If the slopes, i.e., the growth rates of income in different parts of the distribution, are similar across all income groups, relative income inequality is unchanged. Higher (lower) growth at the top suggests widening (narrowing) income differences. The richest decile group saw

252

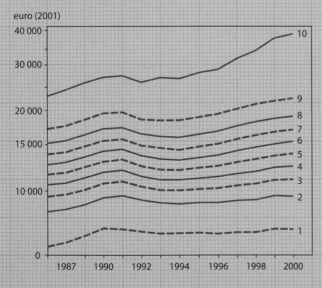

A rural family
outside their small
house during the
interwar period.

euro (2001)

Figure 9.2. Income inequality – the means
of various income factors for
disposable income decile
groups in the period 1987–
2000

Source: Author's calculations from income distribution survey micro-data.

Note: The numbers shown are the average income within each decile group of the population, based on disposable income. Each decile
group consist of one tenth of the population ordered from poorest to richest. These figures suggest that much of the rise in inequality
since the mid 1990s has occurred through disproportionate income growth among the richest income recipients.

its income increase much faster than the rest of the income distribution in the last years of the 1990s, whereas the two poorest groups had fairly weak income growth; in other words, relative inequality increased, as would be expected based on the Gini coefficients in Figure 9.1.

The microdata-based evidence implies that income inequality has increased substantially in Finland since the first oil crises of the 1970s. Using the data from the grouped tables of taxable income starting in 1920 and income subject to taxation starting in 1949, we can place the changes of the past 35 years in a historical context.

As explained in section 2, the long data series are studied by applying a parametric distribution function in every year. The estimates allow us to generate any kind of statistic that describes the annual size distribution of income that we may be interested in.

The estimated densities are shown at ten-year intervals (Figure 9.3). The upper panel shows the density function of *taxable income per tax unit* (the long series) and the lower panel that of *income subject to taxation per person*. These densities are used later to estimate mean income, the Gini coefficient and the income shares of the richest income earners. The densities show around what income values most of the "mass" of the distribution is located. In other words, the density is high in the income regions where most of the income receivers are located. Shifts in the density are thus associated with changed in the concentration of income receivers along the income line. In particular, income growth is in general associated with a movement of income recipients, whence the density to the right towards higher incomes.

The first series on taxable income is much more widely dispersed, driven by the fact that the "basic deduction", i.e. the threshold for taxable income, removes those who earned very small amounts of money from the group of income receivers. This is evident from studying the lower panel, where the mode is invariably below 10,000 euros and in general much lower. We also see how the mass of the density function moves gradually to the right, reflecting of course the very considerable economic growth that has taken place over the periods examined (see below).

In Figure 9.4, we show the level and the growth rate of mean income in our two series. The average incomes generated by the series show an upward trend albeit with some considerable variation. Given the nature of the data, it is quite likely these changes in real incomes may reflect some excess volatility due to definition changes, changes in the compilation of the statistics and computational problems (generated by the current author). These reservations notwithstanding, the series are probably indicative of the true situation since the substantial decline in income due to the severe recession of the 1990s is clearly evident. The magnitude of the decline associated with this episode seems too small compared with earlier declines. However, Finland has been subject to substantial cyclical shocks, and especially before the 1970s there were few automatic stabilisers (income transfers) to counteract the decline in real income

254

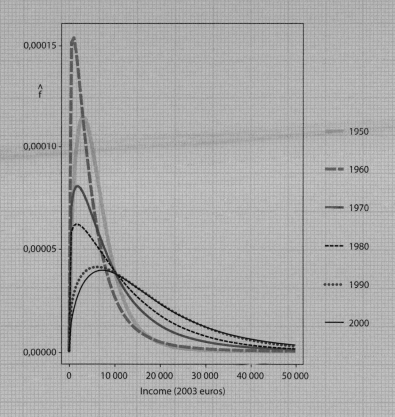

Figure 9.3   **Estimated density functions**
A. Taxable income per tax unit;
1920–1992
B. Income subject to taxation
per person, 1949–2003

Note: The density function shows the
distribution of income earners across
different values of income.

High values of the density suggest
that a greater proportion of persons
earn income around that level. Income
growth shows up as a movement of
the density further to the right toward
higher income values.

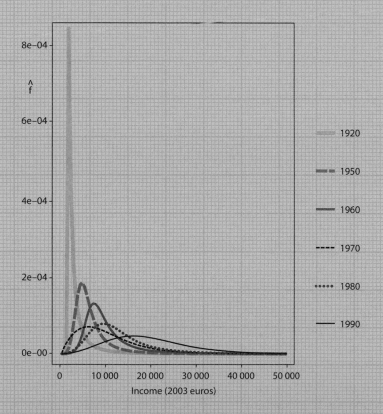

generated by bouts of inflation or recessionary shocks. Thus, the substantial volatility that is displayed probably reflects at least in part the actual variation in real incomes.

Overall trends in income inequality   Next we shall examine trends in relative inequality, as measured by the Gini coefficient (Figure 9.5). The graph suggests a series that is quite non-stationary. Note that, while the visual evidence strongly suggests that the series are non-stationary, the fact that the Gini coefficient is logically restricted to the unit interval rules out the simple case of a random walk since this suggests a variance that trends to infinity.

All the same, the rise in inequality shown in Figures 9.1 and 9.2 appears to be fairly modest against the background of our longer-term Gini coefficients. Inequality was substantially higher in the 1950s and early 1960s than it is now. On the other hand, much of the machinery instituted to mitigate income inequality was introduced in the late 1960s and 1970s, when the microdata-based decline in inequality took place. Much of that machinery – those parts of inequality reduction that work through taxes, and those transfers that are not taxable – does not appear in our series. Thus, while modest by historical standards, it is noteworthy that the increase in inequality that is indicated in *disposable income* is of a magnitude (in Gini points) comparable to *income subject to taxation*.

As discussed in the introduction, the interest in long-run income inequality has at least in part been driven by an interest in how the topmost share of the distribution has fared[12]. Using the estimated distribution parameters to generate the numbers, Figures 9.6 and 9.8 shows the *share* of the top five and one percent of the income distribution and Figures 9.7 and 9.9 the *average incomes* of these groups.

In part, these numbers should reflect the changes in overall inequality. However, it is possible that the shape of the distribution is changing in such a way that these numbers reveal some additional aspects. The top income shares are, indeed, historically slightly different from the Gini coefficients. The Gini was very high in the late 1950s and early 1960s and considerably lower thereafter, while these top income shares were high even in the late 1970s, when overall inequality had started to decline rapidly. On the other hand, the increase in the late 1960s and the levelling off of the growth that was indicated for the top quintile groups is also mirrored for these smaller groups higher up in the distribution. This of course suggests that the increase in the top quintile group's share may have been driven by changes at the very top. However, the changes before and after the year 2000 in the share of the top one percent appear to be *less* pronounced than those of the top five percent. Thus the increase in the top share appears to be driven by the incomes of more than just a very few income recipients.

The average incomes of these top earners have certainly moved steeply at the end of the last decade and in the early years of this one (Figures 9.7 and 9.9). The real income of the top 5 percent increased from 56,200 in 1990 to 81,783

256

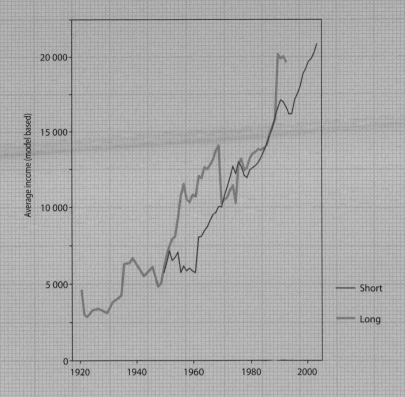

Figure 9.4 The evolution of average income (model-based) over time

The series show the estimated real average income, measured in terms of 2003 euros, of taxable income among tax units ("long series" from 1920 to 1992) and income subject to taxation among income recipients ("short series" from 1949 to 2003) based on data from tax records.

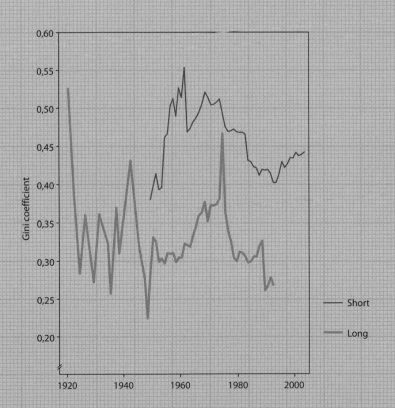

Figure 9.5 The evolution of the Gini coefficient over time

The Gini coefficients starting in 1920 are for taxable income among income recipients and those starting in 1949 are for income subject to taxation among income recipients. Compared with the microdata-based estimates in Figures 9.1 and 9.2, these estimates are substantially higher since they are based on pre-tax income and, in part, on persons rather than households. In the light of these series, the changes in inequality on display in Figure 9.1 appear fairly modest.

euros in 2003, an increase of 38 percent (in LN differences). The average income of the top one percent of income earners, in turn, increased from 76,483 to 131,940 euros, an increase of 55 percent. These suggest the fairly healthy average annual income growth rates of 2.9 and 4.2 percent respectively. During the same period, average income increased by 1.5 percent per year.

Concluding comments

The present paper has explored evidence on long-term trends in the distribution of income in Finland starting in 1920. This approach is not without its shortcomings. The spacing of the early years is irregular, the unit of analysis varies and even when it does not, it is far from ideal. The income concept varies considerably, and is again far removed from that recommended by income distribution analysts[13]. All the same, knowing something is vastly preferable to knowing nothing, and some interesting patterns do emerge.

First, the recent rise in the inequality of disposable income that followed the decline of the 1970s and the stable inequality of the 1980s does not appear to be unusual. Our sense that inequality in Finland is low is of a quite recent provenance. The diachronic pattern suggests substantial variability. Secondly, the rise of the past ten years, while large in terms of recent decades, does not appear to be unusually high in the light of the historical record.

However, it should be borne in mind that recent inequality changes have occurred in an institutional setting that is very different from that of the 1960s, when inequality also increased substantially. Progressive taxation and income transfers, both universal and earnings-related social insurance schemes, were largely instituted in periods when inequality decreased or was stable. It is quite remarkable that this recent increase has occurred with all these systems in place.

This chapter has been concerned with the patterns of income distribution over time. What can be said about the causes of inequality changes? Unfortunately, not much. The historical record is based on taxable income or income subject to taxation, so any explanation that was to rely on the redistribution of income through either taxation or income transfers would have to be made on the basis of their second-order – i.e. behavioural – effects. Deducing such second-order effects from sparse annual data is very difficult. Any first-order effects of taxes and income transfers need to be elicited from the distribution of disposable income, but such data are only available for the last 35 years or so.

There have been many efforts to use time-series regressions to account for the impact of macroeconomic fluctuations on income inequality. Such efforts are unfortunately unlikely to shed much light on the processes involved, as Parker (2000) explains. The best that can be done is probably to try to assess the extent to which large secular changes in income inequality coincide with substantial institutional changes. In this respect, we note that inequality tend-

258

Figure 9.6 The evolution of the share of the top
five percent over time

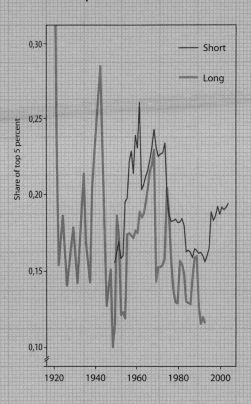

Figure 9.7 The evolution of the average income
of the top five percent over time

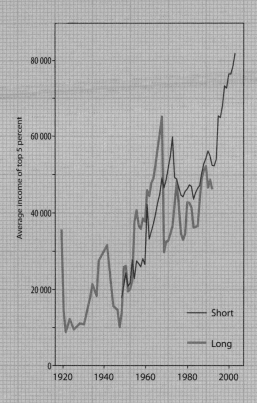

Figure 9.8 The evolution of the share of the top
one percent over time

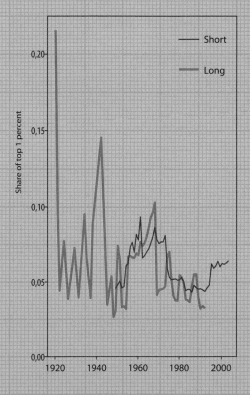

Figure 9.9 The evolution of the average income
of the top one percent over time

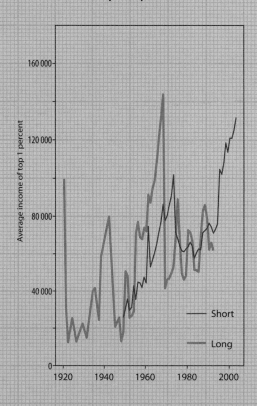

259

ed to increase throughout the 1950s and peaked again in the late 1960s, after which it declined for about two decades. While that increase in inequality occurred, the Finnish economy was growing very rapidly, the share of agriculture was declining and a substantial fraction of the population emigrated to Sweden. The peak in inequality around 1969 coincides with the peak in migration flows. That peak also coincides with the advent of modern tripartite collective bargaining agreements – broad wage settlements that involve the employers, labour unions and the central government. The decline in inequality during the 1970s and 1980s took place during the era of such settlements. The 1970s witnessed many other changes as well, including the entry into the labour force of the baby-boom generation and an extensive redistribution of income (see the chapters by Kettunen and by Eloranta & Kauppila in this volume).

Inequality tended to increase in many OECD countries in the late 1980s and 1990s. Efforts to account for these increases have centred on changes in market forces, such as technological change, increased international trade and changes in the remuneration structures of firms[14]. As the increase in inequality in Finland since the mid-990s occurs mostly at the very top of the distribution, it appears unlikely that broad-based accounts would explain recent changes. Since the rewards that accrue to the very richest income earners have increased, plausible explanations would need to account for what has happened to capital income and the remuneration of the very highest earners in recent years. Thus, what Atkinson (2003) has described as the effect of changes in the norms that govern income distribution may have changed in Finland as well.

The rise in average wealth can be seen in the boom in purchasing second homes. In 2004 there were 469,000 vacation dwellings, while the number of permanent dwellings was 1,162,000. The picture "Quality Holiday" shows a family on vacation in 1992.

Income inequality during the 19th century

Ilkka Nummela

Historians and laymen have often stated in different contexts that societies were more equal before the Industrial Revolution without presenting any proof of this claim. Finnish research on economic inequality has shown that there was already wealth inequality of a significant range in the 16th century. Data from Finland support the view widely accepted in research that economic inequality levelled out from the 19th century to the 20th century. Some indicators also suggest that the level of inequality might have been even higher in the first half of the 19th century than in the later part.

Poor relief in city of Oulu in northern Finland was financed in the middle of the 19th century with annual duties paid by the citizens. The duty was based on an annual assessment of the inhabitants' economic capacity, i.e. their "incomes". Data on poor relief duties offer us an alternative means of analysing the development of income inequalities in the period before actual income tax was introduced in Finish towns.

At that time, according to the Swedish economic historian Eli F. Heckscher, people in Finish towns still lived in an inventory economy. Therefore, it is not certain that the local assessment board in Oulu was able to estimate the actual incomes of citizens, or whether it based its estimates on data relating to the sources of income.

Gini coefficients estimated from the poor relief duty data show no clear overall trend in inequality. The numerical values of Gini coefficients calculated from the poor relief duties during the period 1830–1875 are (1) bigger than the coefficients estimated from the statistics on municipal income taxation during the last quarter of the 19th century, and (2) smaller than the Gini coefficients for gross wealth during the 19th century in Oulu estimated from probate inventories.

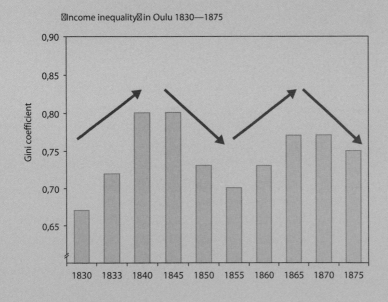

Income inequality in Oulu 1830—1875

"Expansion"

by Sam Vanni.

(1980, oil on canvas, 150 x 285 cm)

Productivity Growth:
the Role of Human Capital and Technology

Rita Asplund and Mika Maliranta

According to empirical results produced using traditional growth accounting analysis, human capital has only a limited effect on long-run economic growth. This approach, however, ignores the most important roles of human capital by treating it merely as a production factor to be used under a given state of technological know-how. In today's knowledge-intensive economies, this is too narrow a view. Human capital is an irreplaceable tool for the creation, implementation and diffusion of new technologies. Sustained policy efforts in the fields of both education and technology have laid the ground for the success stories of Nokia and the ICT sector generally. The emergence of this "third pillar" of Finnish business has played a key role in the productivity-enhancing "creative-destruction" process that has shaped the economy over the past decade.

Introduction

Economic growth is sustainable only when it is based on productivity growth. Adam Smith made this astute point as early as 1776:

"The annual produce of the land and labour of any nation can be increased in its value by no other means, but by increasing either the number of its productive labourers, or the productive powers of those labourers who had before been employed."

He also pointed out, however, that there are limits in increasing the number of labourers and continued:

"The productive powers of the same number of labourers cannot be increased, but in consequence either of some addition and improvement to those machines and instruments which facilitate and abridge labour; or of a more proper division and distribution of employment." Smith 1979, p. 343

Thereafter an impressive number of growth accounting calculations have provided support for this conclusion. They show that improved total factor productivity (TFP) is the main source of economic growth in the long term. Other major components include increases in the quality of labour input. Here the underlying idea is that output grows when the proportion of more productive workers increases over that of less productive workers. Clearly, though, such increases are inevitably subject to limits.

Education is one key instrument in raising the supply of more productive workers. According to recent calculations by Jalava and Pohjola 2004, the average annual contribution of increased labour quality (proxied by education) has in recent decades been 0.2 percentage points in Finland. Hence, this study assigns to educational investments quite a modest role in improving the quality of labour and, thus, the productivity of the Finnish economy.

If we take the estimate by Jalava and Pohjola at its face value, it states that the cumulative increase from 1970 to 2005 in the gross domestic product (GDP) of Finland attributable to an improved educational attainment level amounts to about 7% only. This implies that in the absence of any increase in education during this 35-year period, Finland would at present, in 2005, enjoy the same living standards as it actually did in 2002 or 2003. When compared to the general belief in the importance of education, an advantage of this negligible magnitude seems highly questionable.

A major reason why growth accounting assigns such a minor effect to education is that the role of human capital in economic development is viewed narrowly; more human capital is simply assumed to increase the output of

264

Head offices of high-tech companies at Keilalahti, in Espoo, near Helsinki. From the left, the headquarters of Nokia (mobile phones), Kone (elevators), Elisa (telecommunications operator), and Fortum (energy).

workers merely by improving their productive powers with their *current* machines in their *current* jobs. Hence, growth accounting neglects the fact that education and human capital contribute substantially to sustained economic growth by enhancing the innovative capabilities of workers imperative for the development, adoption and implementation of more sophisticated technologies. Also overlooked are the creative destruction processes that occur within industries with workers moving from low technology and low productivity to high technology and high productivity companies or establishments. Indeed, it is estimated that almost one-half of Finnish total factor productivity growth is due to intra-industry restructuring in manufacturing.[1]

Finland has, over the past few decades, made enormous investments in education and training. Computerisation provides an illustrative example of the conspicuous productivity-enhancing effects that these kinds of investment have had on both manufacturing and services in recent years.[2] Hence, with-

Telephone booths have almost disappeared as a result of the telecoms revolution. Picture from North Karelia in 1983.

out all these efforts, Finnish companies would today be much less innovative and also less inclined to adopt technologically more advanced production and process methods. Evidently, the consequences for Finnish society would have been much more disastrous than the few years' delay in economic development indicated by the aforementioned growth accounting calculations.

The main lesson from the above considerations is that sustained economic growth can be achieved only by stimulating the growth of total factor productivity. In this article, we therefore focus on two closely linked productivity-enhancing tools at the disposal of the government, viz. education policy and technology policy, and the role played by these policies in the productivity performance of the Finnish economy.

A key challenge for technology policy is to stimulate innovations. For innovations to be fully reflected in productivity and competitiveness, the new technologies need, however, to be successfully implemented in the production processes. This requires a skilled workforce, as well as the upgrading of skills in the form of on-the-job training and/or labour reallocation between companies (or establishments). Education and training policies have a crucial role to play in facilitating this type of productivity-enhancing labour mobility. Moreover, from the society's point of view, it is essential that technological knowledge disseminated effectively within the economy. The mechanism to do this can be created by technology policy adequately supported by education policy.

The growth of technological and industrial R&D (Research & Development) activities started in the early 1980s, partly due to the adoption of R&D-

266

enhancing policies. The *National Technology Agency (Tekes)* was established in 1983 – nowadays, the main executor of technology policy – and the first national R&D programmes were launched with the aim of promoting collaboration between industry, universities and research institutes. Because of this major refocusing on education and technology policies, and their interlinkages, the early 1980s stand out as a natural starting point for the subsequent analysis.

The rest of the article is structured as follows. Section 2 discusses the role of education and technology policies, as well as major trends in public R&D funding. Section 3 focuses on the great leap in Finnish innovation exemplified by the explosion in private R&D and the roles of ICT (Information and Communication Technologies) and Nokia[3] in this context. It also highlights the consequent changes in business structures. Section 4 outlines the extraordinary productivity performance that followed from profound, mainly R&D-driven, restructuring within industries. It also illustrates the consequent boost in economic growth, which partly originated in the so-called "Nokia effect". Section 5 concludes with some more general remarks on recent productivity growth in Finland.

The Role of Public-Sector Actors

EDUCATION POLICY IN A NUTSHELL

Generally speaking, the development of the education system in Finland since the early 19th century has involved three simultaneous processes: expansion, increase, and integration. The educational policy pursued in support of these three processes originates in ideological viewpoints emphasising nationalism, economic growth, and equality.

Equality in terms of gender, region, and socio-economic background are fundamental principles of the Finnish basic education system. All basic, as well as most of higher education, is publicly financed, and thus free of charge to the student and his or her family. The ideal of educating everyone regardless of their social status was already evident in the very early developments of an education system in Finland, and the beginnings of today's basic education system in the 1960s.

Equality in opportunities to pursue higher education after the compulsory basic education, another key aspect of equality, was further improved during the 1970s, not least through a gradual implementation of the comprehensive school, a further regional expansion of the university system, and the introduction of a financial aid system for students. Today about 45% of each age cohort go to university, the aim in the immediate future being a proportion of 50%. The students have as many as twenty universities to choose from, spread across the country. Ten of the universities are multidisciplinary institutions, and the other ten consist of three technical universities, three schools of economics, and four schools of arts. The expanding, regionally comprehensive network of universities resulted in a rapid increase in the number of university graduates. In the 1940s and 1950s, the focus was on the traditional humanistic fields and natural sciences. The emergence of the welfare state in the 1960s and 1970s increased the demand for social sciences and employees in public services. In the 1980s, with universities being increasingly seen as engines of national as well as regional growth, the emphasis shifted to fields promoting technological and economic development.

International comparisons show that these education policy measures have been very successful. According to the OECD PISA study, Finnish basic education stands out as one of the most egalitarian with regard to learning results as measured in tests of reading literacy, mathematics and science tests among 15-year-old youngsters (see Table 1.2). Also the effect of students' socio-economic backgrounds on test performance was noted to be among the smallest out of the countries involved in the study. The fact that Finnish basic education has a fairly long tradition in providing the population with the basic skills essential in both every-day life and working life is also evident from comparisons based on the International Adult Literacy Survey (IALS). Statistics published by Eurostat and the OECD rank Finland high when it comes to the average educational attainment level of the population and particularly of the younger age groups. The return on investments in education has also remained high from an international perspective despite the rapid expansion in education, implying that the demand for educated labour has kept pace with the rapid increase in supply.

The strong regional dimension in higher education policy has not only decreased the regional differences in higher education attainment but also created new economic, technological, and cultural capital in regions where there are universities, not least through increased research cooperation with the business sector. The tertiary education system in general, and the universities in particular, have in effect come to form the basis not only for the national innovation system (see further 2.3 below) but also for a regionally comprehensive innovation system. A key target for future education policy is to strengthen further the role of the universities in the national and regional innovation systems by providing them with better prerequisites for innovative activities and for achieving international competitiveness. This is expected to make it easier for the universities to become more responsive to new knowledge requirements in research and in the labour market, nationally as well as regionally.

THE EMERGENCE OF TECHNOLOGY POLICY[4]

The growth of technological and industrial R&D activities started in the early 1980s, partly due to the adoption of R&D-enhancing policies. A key objective was to speed up the restructuring of Finnish industry, with a shift from low-tech to high-tech sectors. Information technology was recognised as a key ingredient

268

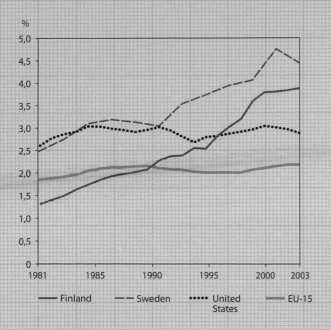

Figure 10.1 R&D expenditure (% of GDP) compared with selected countries and economic areas, 1981–2004

Source: OECD Science and Technology Statistics: Main Science and Technology Indicators Vol 2005 release 01.
Note: The GDP figures underlying the 2003 and 2004 GDP shares for Finland are preliminary.

Thanks to a rapid growth in R&D input, Finland has for several years ranked second in the world when it comes to R&D expenditure as a percentage of GDP, surpassed only by Sweden.

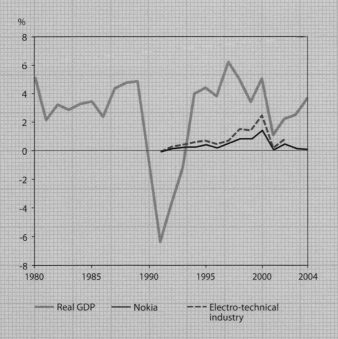

Figure 10.2 Real GDP growth and the %-point contribution to it by Nokia and the electro-technical industry, 1985 – 2007[E]

Source: ETLA's database, ETLA 2005 and data kindly provided by Jyrki Ali-Yrkkö at Etlatieto

At the start of the 21st century Nokia accounted for approximately one-third of total R&D expenditure, nearly one-half of business R&D input, and more than one-fourth of GDP growth.

in this process. The main executor of technology policy, Tekes, was established in 1983, and the first national R&D programmes were launched with the aim of promoting collaboration between industry, universities and research institutes. A few years later (in 1987), the domain of the Science Council, an advisory body to the government founded in 1963 was enlarged to include technology issues, and, accordingly, its name was changed to the *Science and Technology Policy Council (STPC)*.

When the economic boom of the late 1980s suddenly turned into the deepest crisis in the Finnish economy since the 1930s, it was realised that the economy had to be diversified away from the traditional pillars of the forest, metals and engineering sectors towards new high-tech industries, and information technology in particular. Another major driving force was Finland's impending EU membership. As a consequence, industrial policy underwent a fundamental revision, and several supporting key policy measures were implemented: a new competition policy, the privatisation of government-owned companies and the liberalisation of markets. The role of the technology policy was further strengthened and, at the same time, the focus shifted from "science-push" to "industry-pull" strategies. A growing number of industry- and problem-oriented technology programmes were introduced with the emphasis

A simulator used for training workers to handle forestry machines, in this case a tree harvester.

Tests on the quality of saws under way at the Finnish Forest Research Institute (Metla) in 1937. An experienced 25-year-old forest worker is timed by a researcher as he saws. The saws are numbered, and the sawn discs as well as the sawdust are carefully collected.

on fostering vertical collaboration. In addition, actions were taken to improve firm- and business-related conditions through changes in the regulatory environment and the institutional setting (including labour market institutions). Technology policy had shifted from intervention to facilitation – to creating favourable framework conditions, and had become one of the main ingredients of Finnish industrial policy.

During the 1990s, increasing attention was also paid to the social dimension of the technology policy, one aim being to develop sectoral research relevant to social development in order to find new solutions to social problems. The emergence of this dimension was rationalised with arguments referring to the rapid and profound changes in industrial and economic structures after the economic recession of the early 1990s that were driven by both national and global challenges. Today, effective social innovation in all sectors of society, in support of technological innovation, is identified as one of the key national development challenges faced by the Finnish economy and society.

The Science and Technology Policy Council has been a key actor in delineating Finnish industrial policy as it lays the foundations for the science and technology policies that will be pursued in the coming years. In its triennial policy document, *Review of science and technology policy*, the Council discusses the main policy challenges, sets priorities and makes recommendations about, *inter alia*, the size and allocation of public funding of R&D and of other resources. The actual implementation of the Council's recommendations is the responsibility of the ministries and various agencies.

The strong influence of the Council on industrial policy design originates in the fact that it is chaired by the Prime Minister and that it has a broad representation of key stakeholders representing not only the government and academia, but also industry and employers' and employees' organisations. The government appoints the Council for a three-year term. Albeit institutionalised in the form of a council, the interactions between these stakeholders are characterised by intensive and informal communication. Equally important, the role of each actor is clearly defined, and they have a common view on the policy objectives and tools of the national industrial strategy to be pursued over the coming years. This institutionalised dialogue also adds to the understanding of the interplay between technology policy and the flexibility measures relating to labour market institutions that have been the basis of the economic success of the Finnish economy since the mid-90s.

Technology policy driven by NIS and cluster thinking

Finnish technology policy thinking has, ever since the early 1990s, been strongly influenced by the national innovation system (NIS) approach;[5] that is, by the idea of the complex linkages and interactions between technology, science and the economy being the engine of social change and economic growth. Other major concepts that were introduced into the technology policy debate at much the same time were competitiveness and networking, both encapsulated in the cluster approach,[6] and the knowledge-based society. With the adoption of the *National Industrial Strategy* of 1993, traditional industrial policy was gradually replaced by technology, education and competition policies.[7]

The adoption of NIS thinking shifted the focus in Finnish technology policy towards the innovation process and, more recently, also to the environment in which innovations are born and commercialised. The implementation of the cluster approach in Finnish technology policy, in turn, was seen to provide an important complementary view to the existing policy basis founded on "innovation systems thinking". Both approaches depart from whole systems and attempt to identify key actors, framework structures and conditions, as well as interactions and their relation to outcomes. A key outcome of the introduction of cluster thinking is the so-called inter-ministerial cluster-based programmes that, since their introduction in the late 1990s, have come to constitute a major concept of technology policy.

272

It is commonly argued that the successful development of the Finnish ICT cluster was built on two historical circumstances.[8] First, the operation of the telephone network was never monopolised by the state, as was the case in most other countries. Second, unlike many foreign markets, the Finnish telecommunications equipment market allowed for competition. Swift deregulation and full liberalisation of the telecommunications market were finalised as early as 1994. These factors also explain the heavy predominance of telecommunications in Finnish ICT.[9] Additionally, the evolution of the Finnish economy has, over the past few decades, involved several fundamental changes that have

The campus of Jyväskylä University, designed by Alvar Aalto, typifies the massive investments in higher education that began in the 1950s. This picture is from the lobby of the main building of Jyväskylä University, which dates from 1955.

273

contributed to strengthening the competitive advantage of the ICT cluster. Further preconditions for rapid growth have been laid down by government policy measures. Indeed, successful public support for ICT use has been recognised as one of the main factors behind the outstanding competitive performance of the Finnish economy.

The extraordinary increase in R&D expenditure towards the end of the 1990s (see below) was the outcome of a joint commitment of the private sector and the government in 1996 to increasing R&D expenditure to 2.9% of GDP by 1999 – a goal actually already exceeded in 1998. A substantial portion of the increase in public R&D funding came from the selling-off of state-owned companies. In relation to the re-orientation in Finnish technology policies, a new Subsidies Act concerning the general conditions for the provision of industrial subsidies was also passed in 1997. This new provision placed the whole support system under continuous evaluation.

The government's strategy of raising the R&D intensity level of the Finnish economy close to that of the world leaders was highly successful. At its highest, in 1997, the GDP share of public R&D funding rose to over 1.1%, an impressive proportion even by international standards. Because of a halt in 1999 in the real growth of public research funding, its GDP share has, however, been gradually falling back to below one per cent, although recent governmental commitments are likely to raise it to 1.4%.

Consequently, the share of public funding in overall R&D funding also deteriorated rapidly up to the new millennium and beyond. At present, public funding covers only about a quarter of total R&D expenditure, while its share in business R&D funding is down to some 3%. Both figures indicate that public R&D funding is considered far less important in Finland than in EU and OECD countries on average.

The Great Leap in Innovation

THE EXPLOSION IN R&D INVESTMENT AND HIGH INNOVATION RANKINGS

The steady increase in R&D investment in the 1980s speeded up during the 1990s. In the early 1980s, Finland allocated about 1% of GDP to R&D investment, as measured by gross domestic expenditure on R&D. At the turn of the decade, this share had reached the 2% level and, even before entering the new millennium, it had exceeded the target of 3% of GDP set by the Science and Technology Policy Council for 2000 (Figure 10.1). The share of R&D expenditure in GDP is estimated to have increased to 3.5% in 2004. Thanks to this rapid growth in R&D input, Finland has for several years ranked second in the world when it comes to R&D expenditure as a percentage of GDP, surpassed only by Sweden.

274

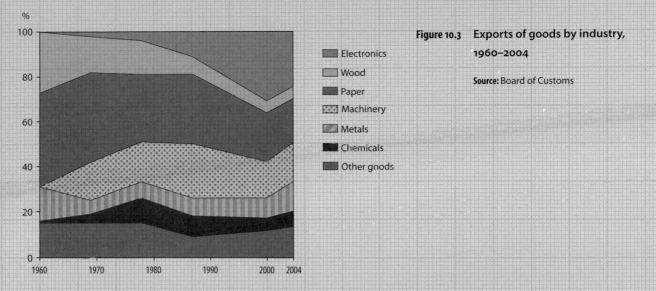

Figure 10.3 Exports of goods by industry, 1960–2004

Source: Board of Customs

There has been a substantial increase in the relative importance of exports of electronics and electromechanical products. The cut-off in recent years is due to turbulence in the ICT sector coupled with uncertainty in the global economy.

The business enterprise sector not only implements but also funds an increasing share of R&D activities. Over the past few years, business enterprises have funded about 70% of R&D, compared to some 55% in the early 1980s. As a percentage of GDP, this corresponds to an increase from 0.65% to over 2.4%, again a top-ranking figure among both EU and OECD countries.

In line with this, business R&D intensity (business enterprise expenditure on R&D as a percentage of value-added in industry) has shown one of the highest annual growth rates within the OECD area since the early 1990s. By the turn of the millennium, business R&D intensity had reached 3.7%, with only Sweden showing a higher but, it seems, declining figure (4.7%). The growth in Finnish business R&D intensity can be traced to increased R&D activities in virtually all industries in both manufacturing and services.

These success stories in R&D spending have pushed Finland high up in the innovation indicator rankings. Finland and Sweden have for several years been the EU's innovation leaders. In the *European Innovation Scoreboard (EIS)*, Finland is top-ranked in a majority of the scored dimensions, many of which reflect the effectiveness of the education and technology policies that have been pursued here.

Nokia has contributed considerably to the rapid growth in R&D input. At the turn of the millennium, Nokia accounted for approximately one-third of total R&D expenditure and nearly one-half of business R&D input (corresponding to an amount twice as high as public R&D funding). Against this background, it is hardly surprising that the electro-technical industry accounts for a major part of total R&D expenditure.

Nor is it surprising that ICT spending has grown rapidly since the early 1990s.[10] Over the past decade, the ICT market has, in effect, grown faster in Finland than in the USA, one reason being that the ICT industry recession in 2001 was reflected much more strongly in ICT spending in the USA. Despite the downturn in 2001, ICT spending (as a percentage of GDP) has remained at a clearly higher level in most European countries than in the late 1990s. That is not true of the USA.

Needless to say, the electro-technical industry and Nokia, in particular, have had a tremendous impact on GDP growth in the post-recession years.[11] This impact has taken the form of boosting GDP growth and amplifying the fluctuations in annual growth rates. As is evident from Figure 10.2, the Nokia effect was greatest in 2000 when the company contributed 1.4 percentage points to the total growth of 5% in real GDP. The contribution of Nokia was, in other words, estimated to have been over one-fourth of total GDP growth! Since then, however, the strong influence of Nokia and the electro-technical industry on the Finnish economy has come to an end. Telecommunications have turned into a "normal" industry.

A related aspect, often ignored in this context, is the fact that labour productivity growth in business services seems to have reached much the same magnitude as in manufacturing, and even outperforms manufacturing in services such as post and telecommunications and financial intermediation. There arises the question of whether the business service sectors, and these two services in particular, have been able to implement ICT in a much more efficient way than manufacturing. In other words, have business services turned into the leading users of ICT while manufacturing still acts only as the leading provider of ICT?

PROFOUND CHANGES IN BUSINESS STRUCTURES

The strengthening of the Finnish economy through ICT has been reflected in industry structures most fundamentally with respect to value-added and employment. A traditional sector composition shows that the industrial sector still leads in tracing volume trends, while a break-down according to relative shares reveals the rapidly growing role of services, and especially of business sector services. A closer look at the compositional structure of manufacturing reveals,

276

as might also be expected, a tremendous increase in the value-added share of the electro-technical industry (29% in 2004 compared to 10% still in 1994). Simultaneously, the industry's employment share has increased to some 15%.

Moreover, the fact that Finland, during the 1990s, managed to become one of the leading providers of ICT has profoundly reshaped the structure of Finnish imports and exports. Figure 10.3 reveals the substantial increase in the relative importance of exports of electronics and electromechanical products that has occurred during the last decade. The figure includes statistics from 1960 to underscore how dramatic the change has been, away from the traditional export goods of wood, pulp and paper products. The cut-off in the exports of electronics and electromechanical products in recent years is due to turbulence in the ICT sector coupled with uncertainty in the global economy. Simultaneously, the imports of electronics and electromechanical products have come down from a top share of nearly 26% in 2000 to just below 20% in 2004.

It is commonly argued that the Finnish success in trade, especially in electronics and electromechanical products, was strongly supported by a favourable development in the relative unit labour costs of Finnish industry. This favourable trend, which started in the deep recession years of the early 1990s,

In 2003 there were 91 mobile phone connections per 100 persons in Finland. Today it is hard to find even a schoolchild who does not have a mobile phone.

277

has resulted in the wages of Finnish engineers being relatively low compared with those in other industrialised countries. Accordingly, ICT has been comparatively cheap to develop.

The Great Leap in Productivity Performance

AGGREGATE PICTURE OF PRODUCTIVITY DEVELOPMENT

Alternative sources provide slightly different information on the labour productivity growth rates of different countries. Nevertheless, statistics produced by organisations such as Eurostat, the OECD and the Conference Board quite uniformly indicate that the Finnish economy has enjoyed an exceptionally rapid productivity growth during the last two decades. According to the Conference Board, the average labour productivity growth rate for Finland was 2.8% from 1987 to 1995 and 2.9% in the period 1995 to 2004. The corresponding growth rates for the USA were 1.1% and 2.5%, respectively, indicating that this country has been able to narrow the gap with Finland in the labour productivity growth race.

Finland's exceptionally high growth rates in the past can, at least partially, be explained by the initially low level of labour productivity; in 1989 it was only 70% of the US level according to estimates by Maddison 1991. On the other hand, it seems that at that time the Finnish manufacturing sector already performed much better than the economy on average: according to a database complied by Groningen University, Finnish labour productivity in manufacturing was in 1989 as high as 88% of the level in US manufacturing.

The divergence in productivity development between Europe and the USA in the late 1990s has been emphasised in a number of recent studies. Gordon 2004, however, presents quite a critical assessment of these studies, arguing that they put too much emphasis on ICT and fail to disentangle various other contributing factors.

> *The typical study conducts a growth accounting exercise, concludes that Europe has lagged behind the U.S. in adopting ICT technology to a greater or lesser degree, does not trace differences in behavior to specific industries, and concludes with a general plea for unspecified structural reforms.*[12]

Gordon makes three important points. First, the numbers for Europe present an aggregate from a very heterogeneous set of countries while those for the USA refer to different states. For instance, Finland and Ireland have experienced much faster productivity growth than the USA. According to Gordon it would be better to compare Finland to Silicon Valley and France or Germany to the Midwestern heartland. Second, practically all of the USA's out-perform-

278

ance of Europe in productivity growth can be attributed to three sectors: mainly the retail trade but also the wholesale and securities trade. Third, referring to a study by Foster *et al.* 2002, Gordon emphasises that the average retailing establishment that continued in business in the USA exhibited zero productivity growth! This is a surprising finding in view of the retail sector's huge investments in ICT equipment, but it is explained by the strong productivity growth being totally due to labour reallocation from inefficient to efficient retailing units. These are typically "big boxes" (like Wal-Mart) that have achieved low costs by means of high volumes. Hence, the reasons for the lack of a surge in productivity growth at the whole-economy level in many European countries may involve regulations specific to the retail sector.

The lesson to be learned from Gordon's contentions is that there is an obvious need for careful consideration of the specifics not only of different

The tango has always been a popular dance in Finland, but mobile telephony seems to be disturbing even this tradition, as seen here at the Seinäjoki Tango Festival in 1999.

countries but also of different sectors and for extending the analyses to the micro level before jumping to conclusions. In this respect, it is apposite to take a glimpse at the upheaval that has taken place *within* Finnish industries.

CREATIVE DESTRUCTION WITHIN INDUSTRIES

The relatively high performance level of Finnish manufacturing at the turn of the 1980s and 1990s was to a large extent due to a rapid pick-up in productivity growth in the mid-80s. This process was mainly spurred by intensified intra-industry restructuring in several manufacturing industries, a trend that remained strong up to the latter part of the 1990s.[13] Most of this "creative destruction" can be attributed to plants established in the 1980s, some of which achieved a high productivity level. They made large investments and created jobs that were equipped with modern technology. At the same time, jobs were destroyed in low-productivity plants. Indeed, about half of the healthy restructuring took place within narrowly defined industries, while the remaining half was intra-industry restructuring. That is to say that the great leap in Finnish productivity performance not only concerned Nokia, in the same way as the US productivity surge did not necessarily only concern the ICT sector, a fact also pointed out by Gordon (see above).

Differences in the micro-level dynamics of productivity growth between industries are interesting in several respects. Although many industries started to benefit from creative destruction, some industries were soon left behind. For example, the food industry and the manufacture of non-metallic mineral products remained lethargic until 1992, when Finland officially applied to join the European Community. Only then did the economic environment finally start to change in a fundamental way in these industries too. This can be seen, *inter alia*, from the rapid increase in the imports and exports of the two industries.

The retail trade, above identified as the main driving force of the US productivity surge, is another example of a late awakening in the healthy upheaval that the Finnish economy has undergone. Productivity-enhancing restructuring remained slow until the latter part of the 1990s, but since then some indication of improvement in this regard can be noticed. The creative destruction in Finnish retail trade is likely to have been triggered particularly by the increased number of foreign competitors.

Divergent patterns of intra-industry productivity growth dynamics lead us to explore the main factors behind creative destruction. Various recent theoretical models emphasise the view that innovations and technological progress entail experimentation, selection and a reallocation of resources between companies. Thus R&D efforts could be expected to be positively related to creative destruction, possibly with some time lag needed for generating new knowledge and implementing it in companies and establishments. Empirical evidence ob-

280

tained for Finland seems to confirm this hypothesis.[14] The results suggest that the increase in R&D efforts in many manufacturing industries since the early 1980s generated technological advances. These steps were taken through creative destruction processes occurring *within* industries. An interesting but still open question is to what extent these changes can be attributed to the adoption of R&D-enhancing policies in the early 1980s.

Discussion and Conclusions

The extraordinary performance of the Finnish economy in the post-recession years in terms of both productivity and economic growth has been largely driven by tremendous increases in business R&D and ICT investment, transforming the country from an investment-driven to an innovation-driven economy. A key supportive ingredient of this remarkable transition has been the science and technology policy pursued by the government. The joint efforts of the private sector and the government to increase R&D expenditure and to create a functioning and efficient ICT cluster have contributed substantially to the top rankings that Finland has achieved in international competitiveness comparisons in recent years. The *World Economic Forum (WEF)* has ranked Finland the most competitive nation in the period 2001 to 2005, (except for 2002, when the USA outperformed Finland). The *International Institute for Management Development (IMD)*, in turn, has given Finland rankings between second and eighth since 1997. (See Table 1.3 in the introduction)

Notwithstanding the major bearing of industrial and technology policies on business performance, the Finnish success story has been primarily business-driven rather than an outcome of public policy-making. The business sector has a much more significant role in the financing of R&D investment in Finland than in most other countries. The failure of public R&D funding to keep pace with private R&D funding has committed policy-makers to setting ambitious near-future goals for research funding to safeguard Finland's economic success and prosperity and, particularly, to ensure the renewal and growth of the three pillars of the Finnish economy – the ICT cluster, the forest cluster and the metal cluster.

Without the support of a growth-focused higher education policy, however, the technology policy pursued by the government would probably have been ineffective, and the substantial R&D investments undertaken by private business would have remained fruitless. Finland has invested heavily in education for several decades. The results of these efforts are seen in international comparisons. According to statistics by the OECD, the average educational attainment level of the working-age population has increased much faster in Finland than in its main competitor countries. The great upswing in the level of education has played a more important role in Finnish economic development than suggested by standard growth accounting calculations.

The greatest merit of the educational investments has been that they have complemented the technology-orientated policy that was adopted in the early 1980s. Human capital is not only a production factor, as assumed in growth accounting, but also a prerequisite for successful innovations. And perhaps even more importantly, a high general level of human capital is an irreplaceable tool for the efficient implementation of new technologies created both at home and abroad. This, in turn, determines the dissemination of new technologies within the economy, which, in the end, shows up in productivity statistics and competitiveness indicators. Moreover, revealing the successful implementation of new technologies provides an important stimulus for further innovation efforts.

An important part of technological advancements turns into productivity through "creative destruction" at the company and establishment levels. This process involves the reallocation of labour between different jobs, companies and industries. Workers need to learn new tasks and technologies throughout their working careers. A high level of education is an asset that facilitates these learning processes. Empirical evidence shows that productivity-enhancing restructuring (i.e. creative destruction) has been particularly strong in many Finnish manufacturing industries since the mid-80s. At the same time, however, many manufacturing industries and many services in particular seem to have suffered from sclerotic micro-structures that have been reflected in weak productivity growth.

Differences in product market competition are probably the main factor in explaining differences in the micro-level dynamics of productivity growth between Finnish industries. Some industries, e.g. the retail trade, show some indication of intensified productivity-enhancing restructuring since the late 1990s, which might be due to a changed competitive environment since those days. The remaining lethargic sections of the Finnish economy, especially in the services sector, need to experience a similar healthy injection. This is, however, much more difficult than in the manufacturing industries, where the removal of trade barriers has created pressure from efficient foreign competitors. The encouragement of foreign direct investment in Finland could be one alternative for many service sectors. A major policy challenge, however, is how to make a sparsely populated country like Finland an attractive investment target? These considerations suggest that it is not enough to depend on education and technology policies. Competitive pressure is a third key factor of technology and productivity that calls for attention from policy-makers.

282

"Suburban Street"

by Ragni Cawén.

(1923, oil on harboard, 80.5 x 65.5 cm)

The Tension between the Social and the Economic – A Historical Perspective on a Welfare State

Pauli Kettunen

The creation of a welfare state on the northern periphery of Europe was, to a crucial extent, a history of how tensions between the international economy and the national society were addressed politically. In Finland, as in the other Nordic countries, the institutions of social regulation did not derive from national closure; rather, the shaping of social-political and industrial-relations institutions was preconditioned by the experience of the country being highly exposed to fluctuations and crises in the international economy. The case of Finland also offers evidence about a current change in which welfare-state institutions are being modified to serve new competition-state functions within globalised capitalism.

Introduction

In public debates on globalisation, a caricature of a past of closed national societies is often drawn as a contrast to the "borderless world" of the present and the future. This image of the past is particularly distorting in the case of the Nordic countries (Denmark, Finland, Iceland, Norway and Sweden). Since the late 19th century, these small countries have been relatively open economies which are highly dependent on exports. Thus the creation of the national institutions of social regulation called the welfare state did not derive from an experience of national closure. On the contrary, such institutions were shaped in response to the countries being highly exposed to the fluctuations and crises of the international economy.

A "borderless world" is equally untenable as an image of the present and future. In fact, defining globalisation as a *national* challenge is a widely adopted way of dealing with this transformation process. Nationalism seems to be an integral part of global economic competition – a surprisingly ignored phenomenon in the extensive research on nationalism. The case of Finland seems to provide evidence of a change in which welfare-state institutions are modified to serve new "competition-state"[1] functions.

In this chapter, the history of the Finnish welfare state is discussed by focusing on how the relationships between *the international economy* and *national social regulations* have been addressed *politically*. Finland is studied as a Nordic case of societal development. The focus is on the fact that, ever since the nation-building processes in the late 19th century, *Norden* (a collective name for the Nordic countries) has played an important role in Finland as a framework for international comparison, communication and co-operation in various fields of social knowledge, and "Nordic" became an ingredient of the Finnish national identity.

Centre and periphery

In the early 1980s, the German development researcher Dieter Senghaas concluded: "There is no automatic connection between growth and the lack or elimination of absolute poverty." What was required, he claimed, was the development of a combination of world market integration and an internally consolidated national economy. "The Scandinavian development path" was his main example. A constitutive factor was, according to Senghaas, the formation of national political, economic and cultural identity as well as "considerable political control over domestic and external economic processes, in order to prevent export growth from making society more oligarchic and producing a sort of rentier capitalism." For Senghaas, "Finland's remarkable development" between the late 19th century and the 1980s was the most interesting example of this development path.[2]

286

Success stories of Europe's northern periphery, such as the one told by Senghaas, commonly point out the active role of the nation-state, and with good reason. Certainly, capitalism in general is a politically constituted mode of economic action, as Karl Polanyi has taught us[3]. However, this holds true for the Nordic countries in a special way. "Capitalism launched by the state" is how the Norwegian sociologist Rune Slagstad describes the aims and achievements of the Norwegian "national strategists" of the 19th century.[4] The same characterisation could be applied to the rest of the Nordic countries as well. The state provided above all the infrastructural prerequisites for the expanding market economy, and the economic liberalism appeared beneficial to the representatives of the state administration and to those who defined the interests of the state. These were the two sides of the coin, and an active role by the state in the processes of modernisation gained remarkable legitimacy.

For the role of the nation-state, the conscious adoption by the political, economic and cultural elites of the distinction between centre and periphery was a crucial factor, and it included a kind of self-definition of the nation in spatial and temporal terms. International comparisons, which were oriented towards "the horizon of expectation"[5] associated with modernisation, became an important factor in the construction of national politics, national economies, national societies and their collective actors during the 19th century. These

Pihlajamäki,
a suburb of Helsinki,
is now a protected area.
Pictured here in 1965.

287

comparisons came to play a central role in the production of knowledge and the construction of identity in the nation-building process, as they did again at a later stage when the welfare state and the institutions for regulating working life took shape.[6]

In a country like Finland, which was small and, even by Nordic standards, late to industrialise, international comparisons came to play a particularly prominent role. From the latter half of the 19th century onwards, such comparisons became integral in the way the educated elite analysed society and defined socio-political tasks. The outside world provided a framework of external preconditions and constraints, hopes and threats, as well as impulses but also alarming ideas, models but also warning examples, points of reference but also boundaries of the possible.

It was a question not only of imitating the more developed countries but also of deliberately attempting to anticipate social problems by taking on board experiences from the countries representing the centre of industrial modernisation, above all from Germany, to a somewhat lesser extent from Britain and, in matters relating to labour efficiency, the United States. It was considered important to learn from both the solutions and the mistakes of these countries so as to be able to exploit what Alexander Gerschenkron has called "the advantages of backwardness"[7].

A good example is a series of articles which appeared in 1874, and which placed "the labour question" on the Finnish political agenda. They were written by Yrjö Koskinen (Georg Zachris Forsman), one the foremost leaders of the "Fennoman" faction of the Finnish nationalist movement. Koskinen argued that efforts should be made to forestall threats to social stability by examining Finnish conditions "from a European perspective", in other words, by trying to learn from what was happening in those countries that were more highly developed than Finland. Koskinen's articles also demonstrated that both the threat, socialism, and the economic system which provided a breeding ground for socialism through its inherent conflicts between capital and labour were perceived as international phenomena.[8]

One way in which this line of thought and action was institutionalised was through study trips abroad. Representatives of all groups with professional knowledge or aspirations to professional status travelled abroad in the late 19th and early 20th centuries with the support of the Finnish government and their professional organisations. In this respect, the close connection between professionalisation and the consolidation of the Finnish nation-state was of great importance.[9] The *national* mission to which these professional groups devoted themselves was to acquire through their *international* contacts *transnational* knowledge (technical, medical, hygienic, socio-political, etc.) so as to be in a position to judge, on the basis of a comparative perspective, the opportunities for applying this knowledge in a domestic context.

Such a mode of action and thought led to contradictory tendencies. Political rhetoric sometimes stressed Finland's backwardness in the same breath

288

as there was a strong tendency to describe current conditions as a projection of anticipated modernisation and in this way to exaggerate greatly the existing level and speed of the country's modernisation.

The labour movement was clearly influenced by this logic. The social analyses of Socialist labour leaders tended to overemphasise the level and speed of modernisation in Finland. As the anticipated future was projected onto the prevailing circumstances, the image of the contemporary society with concentrated and centralised capital, a wide and homogeneous industrial working class and developed wage-work relationships remained rather distant from the lived experiences of people. Interestingly enough, this tension did not hinder the rise of a strong labour movement in one of the most agrarian and rural countries in Europe. The labour movement in Finland made its final breakthrough in connection with the revolutionary events that took place in the Russian Empire (to which Finland then belonged) in the years 1905–1907.

A related phenomenon was that there was often a great distance in time between the definition of a social problem and its solution with the help of imported ideas on the one hand and the practical application of these definitions and solutions on the other. This phenomenon has been noticed, for example, in studies on unemployment policies.[10]

However, the idea of anticipating social policies as a conscious part of nation-building had, in the late 19th and early 20th century, not only discursive but also institutional implications. In fact, several acts concerning labour protection, labour relations and unemployment were accepted before the First World War in the Parliament (*Eduskunta*), which after the reform of 1906 was based on a universal franchise that even included women. As the legislative power of

Class distinctions, still rife at the start of the 20th century, faded during the following hundred years. The expansion of the rural class of independent small farmers was a major goal of social policy up to the 1950s. Pictured here is a room in the town house of the wealthy Sinebry-choff family in Helsinki in 1912.

the Parliament was, however, restricted by the authorities of the Grand Duke of Finland, the Russian Emperor, only a few of its social-political decisions were actually implemented. Nevertheless, as early as the 1880s and 1890s, when the old representative system of the Estates still operated, and there was no labour movement proper, two acts of principal importance were adopted: *the Act on the Protection of Industrial Workers,* which established the institution of factory inspection (1889) and *the Workers' Compensation Act* (1895). Finland was not among the last countries in the world when it came to the statutory regulation of industrial work – indeed it was not even a latecomer among the Nordic countries. Thus, for example, the practice of using special female factory inspectors was launched in Finland in 1903, ten years earlier than in Sweden.[11]

Virtuous circles and national necessities

The relationships between the *national–international* and *social–economic* dimensions have been a topic of discussion ever since the early 19th century. Four different arguments can be distinguished in the 19th-century international discussions on social reform such as the above-mentioned articles on "the labour question" by Yrjö Koskinen in 1874. According to the first argument, social-political reforms were necessary in order to diminish the threats (referred to as "the labour question" or "the social question") to the national society caused by the international economy. The second argument was that international economic competition incorporated obstacles to national social policies as such policies would weaken a nation's competitiveness. Alternatively, international economic competition could be seen – so the third argument went – as the point of departure for international social norms that would be binding on all competing countries and firms. A fourth argument that also appeared early claimed that national social policies would support the success of the national economy by improving the quality of labour power and productivity and by increasing purchasing power.

The priority of the third argument over the second one was the core message in the foundation of the International Labour Organisation (ILO) in 1919. International economic competition was conceived of not just as a constraint on national social policy but rather as the basis for international social policy. Ever since the Great Depression of the early 1930s and, in an even more programmatic way, after World War II, the main role of the ILO came to be one of promoting a model of national society in which the objectives of social equality and security and of economic efficiency, competitiveness and growth were supposed to cumulatively support each other.

In a particular way, this mode of thought was manifested in, and reinforced through, the so-called "Scandinavian class compromises" of the 1930s. These compromises included the political coalitions of workers and farmers, i.e. the Social Democrats and the Agrarian Parties, and the consolidation of the practice of collective negotiations and agreements on the industrial labour markets. The mutual recognition of, and compromises between, particular divergent interests were assumed to serve the common interest in other ways than by just preventing harmful conflicts and broadening democracy. Compromises would realise and reinforce a virtuous circle between different interests within the national society. In the 1930s, in Sweden, Denmark and Norway – much less so in Finland – the notion of the national economy began to be based on new ideas of cumulative economic success.

Reflecting the class structure and drawing from the experiences of the Great Depression, a virtuous circle was supposed to connect the interests of worker-consumers and farmer-producers on the one hand and of workers and employers on the other. The class compromises manifesting this mode of thought contributed to the shaping of a "dualist economy": a considerable openness to, and thus dependence on, world markets were combined with the protection of some nationally highly valued sectors, above all agriculture, and with internal egalitarian and consensual negotiated regulations concerning, in particular, the relationships between labour and capital. These arrangements

291

292

The old representative system of the Estates (the Diet) was abolished when a national Parliament (Eduskunta) was established in 1906. The new Parliament was elected by universal suffrage. Finnish women thus became the first in Europe to be allowed to vote and stand for election in a national assembly. In the picture: the debating chamber of the Eduskunta in 2004.

proved to be not only a means for protecting the national society from external economic risks but also a source of international economic competitiveness.

However, it is easy to show specifically Finnish features in these arrangements. The Great Depression of the 1930s did not result in Finland in an active adoption of new contra-cyclical economic political views as it did in Sweden, Denmark and Norway. This is an obvious difference regardless of the fact that in these countries, even in Sweden, the practical significance of the new lessons of the 1930s – especially of the "new employment policies" – was limited. The coalition government of the Social Democrats and the Agrarian Party in Finland after 1937 was not an outcome of conclusions drawn from the Depression to the same degree as the corresponding earlier solutions in the other Nordic countries were. Nor did this political coalition prove to be a step for the Finnish Social Democrats to a position of dominant political power, although their position in the political system of the late 1930s might appear similar to that of their Scandinavian counterparts, not least in terms of their electoral support.

One element of the Scandinavian class compromises was strikingly absent in the Finland of the 1930s. The Finnish employers, especially in the manufacturing industries, were until World War II able to maintain a policy of refusing to enter into collective agreements with the trade unions. While Sweden, Denmark and Norway as early as the 1930s were at the top in the international statistics of unionisation, Finland was one of the least unionised countries in Europe.

In addition to the class compromises and the new confidence in a positive sum game, an orientation called "social rationalisation" or "social engineering" has often been referred to as another Scandinavian novelty of the 1930s. To the extent that this orientation appeared in Finland, it was shaped by Social Democracy far less than in Sweden. The Depression, accompanied by a wave of right-wing politics, contributed to the rationalised treatment of poverty and the poor in the spirit of preventive criminal law, including a more systematic social categorisation and intensified and centralised social control. These were crucial features in the new acts on social care in the mid-1930s, concerning children in need of protection, vagrancy, and alcoholics, as well as in the related *Act on Sterilisation* (1935), which, in itself, was far from exceptional in the Nordic context.[12]

In another way, the objectives of economic and technological rationalisation, social and political integration, and the making of self-disciplined individuals were intertwined in the development of labour protection. Here, the American ideology of *Safety First*, with its connections to *scientific management*, had a remarkable influence in Finland, as elsewhere in Europe in the 1920s and 1930s, not only on the safety practices of enterprises, but also on the institution of factory inspection. In Finland, as elsewhere, the leaders of the labour movement shared a strong trust in the necessity and possibility of a rationalisation of the economy and society. However, the role of the labour movement was rather marginal in defining the agenda of rationalisation; there did not exist precon-

294

Guilds provided social security during the centuries before the building of the modern welfare state. In this picture, the widow of a craftsman is collecting an allowance from his guild in the town of Pietarsaari (Sw. Jakobstad) in 1800. Painting by G. E. Hedman.

ditions for active Social Democratic visions of social engineering like those of Alva and Gunnar Myrdal in Sweden.[13]

The idea of society as a functional whole that must and can be steered and rationalised by means of scientific knowledge was strengthened during World War II. At the same time, this idea was tightly intertwined with the notion of national necessities to be fulfilled and taken into consideration in all activities. After the war, the significance of national necessities clearly became a subject of political controversies. However, even the Communists, rising from their previous illegal status into a major political force, shared much of this mode of thought, not least as a result of their view that the payment of war reparations to the Soviet Union – a crucial economic necessity in Finland until the early 1950s – was an antifascist and democratic national duty.

Some economists and sociologists have concluded that social policies in Finland have been more subordinated than in other Nordic countries to what are conceived of as national economic necessities. The wood-processing industry, because of its role as the dominant export industry and its position as a crucial link between the agricultural and industrial sectors (through peasant-owned forests and the seasonal demand for labour power in logging), gained the hegemonic power of presenting its own interests – international competitiveness – as the general national interest. At the same time, the national economy has been appraised by applying the "health" of the state economy as a central criterion, whereas the idea of the state economy being the means for national economic steering has been weaker in Finland than in Sweden in particular. As the economist Matti Pohjola has argued, in the early 1950s a national strategy of prosperity was widely and permanently adopted; it was based on a high rate of investment and the hope and assumption that sacrifices in the form of a more moderate growth of consumption would result in general prosperity in the future.[14] Hence a mode of thought and action was reinforced in which social policies have been assessed from the point of view of the limits of economic resources.

The most programmatic Finnish manifestation of the confidence in a virtuous circle between expanding social policies and economic growth was the book *60-luvun sosiaalipolitiikka* ("Social Policy for the 60s") by Pekka Kuusi, published in 1961, later translated into English (1964) and, in an abridged version, into Swedish (1966). Kuusi's book was a design for the Finnish welfare state – "a plan for Finland" the subtitle of the English edition stated. A social scientist with Social Democratic sympathies, Kuusi wrote in the spirit of Gunnar Myrdal and others: "Democracy, social equalisation and economic growth seem to be fortunately interrelated in modern society. Social policy seems to spring from free and growth-oriented human nature."[15]

It was within this "growth-oriented" society of the virtuous circle that social policy had crucial role to play a. Promoting social equality through the redistribution of income, social security and labour power policy would release people's productive capacities; the vicious circle between poverty and passivity would be broken. Kuusi's major concern was the preconditions for the social policy as a form of rational planning. The virtuous circle between democracy, equality and growth rescued the possibility and necessity of rational planning in two senses. First, it provided the compromises between particular interests with the character of a positive sum game; second, it made the contrast between the "social" and the "economic" disappear and thus created the basis for the conscious development of social policy as a part of wider "societal policy" (*yhteiskuntapolitiikka* in Finnish; *samhällspolitik* in Swedish), from which its objectives were to be derived.

Nevertheless, even in Kuusi's argumentation there was a strong emphasis on national necessities. The necessities derived from the place of Finland in the world of international competition between societies. Finland was situated between two highly dynamic and growth-oriented societies: Sweden and the Soviet Union. The mission Kuusi outlined was indeed a matter of life and death: if we want to survive between these two societies, "we ourselves are doomed to grow".[16]

Kuusi was not advocating any third way between the societal systems of Sweden and the Soviet Union. His argument was, rather, an example of the Finnish tendency to avoid any explicit association of social policy with the Cold War confrontation.

In reality, this confrontation *was* a significant factor behind social-political considerations. The relatively strong support for Communism, in particular, was a major concern for all those who believed in social policies as a means of national social cohesion, and even for the political right, notably the National Coalition Party, an actively anti-social-policy stance was not a viable alterna-

296

tive.[17] However, while the Swedes, especially the Swedish Social Democrats, declared that they represented a "Third Way" between Capitalism and Communism, in Finland the dominant orientation was to *depoliticise* social policies. Thus, social reforms were often discussed as functional needs, pragmatic steps along the road of general progress within the limits of the economic resources, or as issues of the pragmatic adjustment of conflicting interests in the name of the common national interest.

To be sure, in Kuusi's book the tone was different: the programme for Finnish social policies was located in the context of nothing less than world history. However, this meant that it was located in the sphere above – or beneath – the political confrontations between the capitalist and socialist systems, in which the basic process was the evolution and growth of industrial society, with Sweden and the Soviet Union exemplifying such a society. This implicit convergence ideology had obvious advantages for the national(ist) legitimisation of social policies in the era of the Cold War.

Emergency food relief organised by women in 1932.

"Nordic society"

Not only in Kuusi's thought but also more generally in the Finnish social-political discussion and decision-making, an explicit ideological ingredient was strongly present: the notion of Finland as a "Nordic society". In the late 19th century, the Nordic framework already played an important rôle in various fields of social knowledge in Finland. However, only later, in the 1930s, did the attribute "Nordic" take on the sense of representing something like the future code and normative standard of Finnish society. This happened at the same time as Sweden was in Finland gradually accorded the status of being a representative of the centre of modernisation.

During the Cold War, "Nordic democracy" or "the Nordic society" in Finnish political discourse implied a proclamation that Finland did not belong to the Eastern Block.[18] Among the Social Democrats, in particular, these expressions also indicated the idea that the code of progress inherent in Finnish society could be identified by looking at Scandinavia, especially Sweden. The limits to Nordic co-operation at the level of "high politics", notably security policies, did not hinder the broadening of practical communication between a wide spectrum of public authorities and voluntary organisations. The standardisation of social knowledge, for example in the form of Nordic social statistics after 1946, helped to make continuous comparisons a political and administrative practice. These comparisons enabled not only the harmonisation of institutions but also the identification of differences.[19]

Tough competition on the world market between the Nordic countries has served as an important backdrop for intra-Nordic comparisons and contacts. For example, the competition between the Finnish and Swedish wood-processing industries was a contributory factor in making the Swedish trade union movement willing to help the Finnish trade unions to strengthen their influence in determining wage levels in Finnish industry. The Finnish trade union movement was much weaker than the Swedish one before the Second World War and indeed right up to the 1970s, and it lacked the Social Democratic internal cohesion that was such a pronounced characteristic of the Swedish movement.

Through Nordic co-operation in the production of social knowledge, norms and arguments, the notion of a model of a national society was reinforced. In Finland, the concept of "Nordic society" came to represent a kind of

Apartment blocks were built rapidly after the Second World War in the expanding urban centres. A scene from Helsinki in the 1950s.

Villa Mairea, one of architect Alvar Aalto's major works, was commissioned by industrialist Harry Gullichsen and his wife Maire and built in 1938–39. It can be regarded as a powerful expression of capitalist affluence coupled with cultural sensibility and the modernistic world view of both Aalto and the Gullichsens, the last-named being big stakeholders in the Ahlström company.

normative standard and a code for the future inherent in Finnish society. The normative standard and the future code were often interpreted in terms of everything that had "already" been achieved in Sweden. This notion of Finland, the Nordic latecomer, served as an argument for social reform demands, although there was a conservative alternative that was also influential. According to the latter, the Finns at their lower stage of economic development should wait and see how the reform in question would work in Sweden.

The Nordic region has functioned as a frame of reference within which national institutions have been shaped. On the other hand, transnational elements were also built into the construction of the Nordic framework. The freedom to cross intra-Nordic borders without passports was established in 1952, a hot year in the Cold War and the year of the founding of the Nordic Council (the collaborative organisation of the parliaments of the Nordic countries). Two years later, an agreement on a common Nordic labour market was established. The common Nordic labour market in 1954 was a unique arrangement. It was achieved in the Cold-War world between countries with diverging security political solutions. Finland was a part of this passport-free labour-market area even before it became a member of the Nordic Council in 1955, and before the Soviet Union in 1955–1956 unexpectedly left the Porkkala military base close to Helsinki that had been leased to the Soviet Union for 50 years as a part of the terms of peace in 1944; thus for some time, one of the outer borders of the Nordic area of free movement was situated around this Soviet military base. The Nordic common labour market was exceptional also as an economic and social arrangement. Common political objectives were formulated in the agreement, including the concerted maintenance of full employment.

The common labour market was actually turned into everyday reality most dramatically by national failures in the maintenance of full employment. Asymmetrical relationships between the Nordic countries were revealed, in particular, by those international comparisons that that were made by ordinary people and led four hundred thousand Finns to emigrate to Sweden in the post-war decades, especially in the late 1960s. The common labour market also gave an impetus to practical co-operation in control policies, as the intensification of Nordic police co-operation after the early 1950s indicated – a process resembling that which took place after the creation of the European single market and the Schengen agreement. However, the common labour market also promoted a mutual recognition of national social security norms and a convergence of social security systems.

The politics of social policies: the example of social insurance schemes

In historical overviews of Finnish social policies, the late adoption of social insurance schemes has been presented as a major indicator of Finland being a latecomer. It is true that in the 1950s, as Pekka Kosonen states,

"Workers' accident insurance [since 1895] was almost the only legislative social insurance that fitted into the framework of the [Nordic] model. Child allowances were also introduced [in 1948]. A universal unemployment benefit was rejected on economic and moralistic grounds and the unemployed instead assigned to badly paid public work projects (the so-called spade line). The old-age insurance legislated in 1937 was not intended to become effective for a long time, and public sickness insurance plans were not adopted until the 1960s."[20]

However, the history of social insurance schemes in Finland is not just a story of the country being a latecomer. It helps to resolve the politics inherent in social policies by showing the often very long and contingent political processes preceding a reform.

Let us take the Sickness Insurance Act as an example. It was passed only in 1963.[21] However, it had been mooted in official commissions ever since the 1880s, the first legislative measure being the *Act on Voluntary Sickness Funds* in 1897. Moreover, the passing of a sickness insurance bill had looked more than probable in the late 1920s. Sickness insurance for wage-workers was actually accepted by the Parliament in 1927, when there was a Social Democratic minority government. However, the opponents of the bill were able to postpone the final decision over the next parliamentary election. This minority comprised the Agrarian Party, which disliked social benefits that were targeted to wage-workers only and put old-age and disability insurance before sickness insurance, and right-wing representatives, whose sympathies lay with the employers. The final vote was taken in 1929, and the opponents of the bill, who now also included the Communists, managed to overthrow it.

300

Social insurance returned to the political agenda in the mid-1930s, and the priority of old-age and disability insurance was now obvious. The organised employers, for their part, adopted the view that if they had to approve some new form of social insurance, then let it be old-age and disability insurance. *The Old-age and Disability Insurance Scheme* was legislated in 1937 after compromises between the new government coalition partners, the Social Democrats and the Agrarian Party, although in fact the bill had been drafted by a previous government, which had had close connections with business life. In practice, however, the first – rather modest – old-age pensions were not paid out until 1949.

The vision of a comprehensive social insurance system was a part of what was called post-war planning, but the pragmatic idea of proceeding step by step within the limits of economic possibilities was widely accepted. The Social Insurance Commission was appointed in 1945 by a coalition government of the Social Democrats, the Communists and the Agrarian Party, three parties with almost equal electoral support. Until 1954, the Commission was active in planning schemes for different sectors of social security and trying to establish priorities, making use of international, especially Nordic, comparisons and

Industrial workers queueing for an x-ray examination.

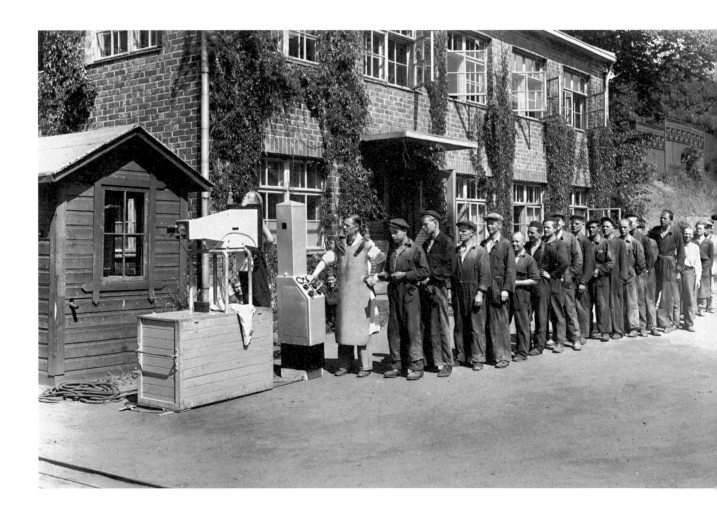

taking into consideration international norms like those included in the ILO's Social Security (Minimum Standards) Convention of 1952. Sickness insurance was, again, the first priority of the Social Democrats, whereas the Agrarian Party together with the Communists (who had wide support among small farmers and rural workers) preferred the reform of the old-age and disability pension schemes. This time too, as in the 1930s, the latter line was followed, and it resulted in a greatly revised national pension scheme. The *National Pension Act* of 1956 instituted unconditional flat-rate benefits combined with an income-tested assistance allowance. The Social Democrats' demands for income-related supplements to basic pensions were rejected.

However, the *Private Sector Supplementary Pension Act* was passed in 1961 on the basis of demands by both blue- and white-collar trade unions and negotiations between labour-market organisations. An important contributing factor was the gradual adoption of the term "wage-earner" as the common label for blue- and white-collar workers and civil servants in the 1950s. The civil servants' old privilege of income-related pensions appeared more and more unacceptable, as did the various company-level private pension schemes for white-collar employees. A crucial point of departure for the creation of an incomes-related pension scheme was the discontent of the representatives of wage-earners with the national pension scheme of 1956; this was seen as an income transfer that favoured the agrarian population. However, in order to get the bill passed in 1961, it was necessary to come to a compromise that would make it possible for the Agrarian Party, too, to vote for it.

In any case, the Finnish pension system was constructed in the form of two separate schemes, each with its own administration.[22] The difference from the united Swedish system – which only the Communists advocated in Finland in 1961 – was still more striking as the administration of the private sector supplementary pensions became a function of private insurance companies. This arrangement entailed an active contribution by the Finnish employers to the new scheme and guaranteed their support for it, involving as it did the principle that the firms could borrow back on favourable terms most of the funded part of the contributions. Information and advice from the Swedish employers, dissatisfied with their own system, played an influential role in shaping the policy of the Finnish employers. Finally, the *Sickness Insurance Act* too was passed in 1963. However, sickness insurance no longer bore the label of a Social Democrat project. The benefits, financing and organisation were shaped in accordance with the principles of the Agrarian Party.

Later, in the 1970s and 1980s, the wage-earner perspective, which was concerned with maintaining the income level and represented the common views of the traditional working class, the workers of the expanding service sector and the so-called new middle classes, was accentuated in the development of various forms of social security. Sickness insurance and the relationship between the two pension schemes were reshaped, and a comprehensive unemployment compensation system was created in accordance with the wage-

302

earner perspective, although at the same time the principle of a minimum basic security containing flat-rate and means-tested benefits was established. In terms of the coverage and the compensation levels of various forms of social insurance, by 1990 the system in Finland differed from those of the other Nordic countries as much as the latter did from one another.

Social interests and the notions of work and gender

The history of the Finnish welfare-state provides material for a critique of the "labourist bias"[23] in interpretations of the welfare state. In historical empirical terms, it would not be tenable to define the creation of the Finnish welfare state as a Social Democrat or working-class project, for the farmers' interests and their representatives played a crucial role. Agricultural policies were closely connected with social policies, two policy sectors that partly represented competing views on the problems of social order. The policies were partly constructed within a broader common context, often as elements of political compromises.

The Paimio sanatorium, designed by Alvar Aalto, was built for tuberculosis patients in 1933.

It should also be remembered that up to World War II the Finnish labour movement bore a strong rural stamp. Within the labour movement, the dominance of the party organisations and the weakness of the trade unions reflected this state of affairs. Until World War II, most of the Social Democrat voters lived in the countryside, and after the war, until the 1970s, the Communists and the Agrarian Party were strong rivals for the support of the small farmers in eastern and northern Finland. The Agrarian Party (since 1965 the Centre Party), in itself a typical Nordic phenomenon, has continued to be an important player in the political system much longer than corresponding parties in the other Nordic countries.

Historically, the prominence of the farmers, as such, is certainly not a Finnish peculiarity. The political role of freeholder peasants and the cultural tradition of the "Lutheran peasant Enlightenment"[24] have been emphasised in historical accounts of the Nordic welfare state. However, even for Sweden, one may question the narrative of a straight road from "the Lutheran peasant Enlightenment" to "the Social Democratic welfare state", and for Finland, this is still more the case. This acount has an excess of egalitarian individualism in the rural community and too much Social Democracy in the welfare state.

As Henrik Stenius has remarked, "The landless peasant does not hold any significant place in the discourse about Nordic political culture."[25] However, in the Finnish political discourse of the 20th century, the landless peasants, that is the agricultural labourers and the tenant farmers, have played a significant role – notably in explanations for, and conclusions about, the Civil War of 1918. The free independent peasant became the symbol of the White army as the antithesis of the harmful Red alliance between the urban workers and the rural landless population, and in the dominant ideology of the winning side after 1918, he constituted the ideological centre around which "social peace" had to be "rebuilt" and defended against the threats associated with the collectivity of wage-workers.[26] The expansion of the rural class of independent small farmers continued to be a major project of social and political integration up to the 1950s.

The ideological charge attached to the work of the independent farmer can be recognised in widely shared views on the role and significance of work. Insofar as the Nordic welfare states, in general, can be interpreted as products of secularised Lutheranism, one may argue that one of their main aims has been to make it everybody's right to follow the moral precept that everybody ought to work. Full employment became a shared programmatic objective in all the Nordic countries after World War II. However, the political commitment to this objective was stronger in Sweden and Norway than it was in Finland and Denmark. In Finland, this did not mean that work as a moral imperative was less important than it was in Sweden and Norway. On the contrary, when the tenets of "one's own work" and "the will to work" of the independent farmer had been appropriated to form the ideological core of the programme for social peace, the principle of work as a duty had been particularly emphasised. At the same time, however, rather than helping the principle of the right to fulfil this

304

306

duty to achieve such a central ideological status as it did in Sweden, this agrarian political heritage should have hampered it from doing so. Up to the 1960s, the dominance of the so-called "work line" or "spade line" in dealing with unemployment (especially in the form of low-paid public work projects) was an institutional indicator of this work ethic.[27]

Generally, the histories of Nordic welfare states included an intertwining of three different ideological elements characteristic of Nordic modernisation processes: the idealised heritage of the free independent peasant, the spirit of capitalism and the utopia of socialism. Arguably, this political and cultural background contributed to the parallel reinforcing and mutual adjustment, especially from the 1950s until the 1980s, of two principles: the universalist idea of social rights based on citizenship and the normalcy of wage work. The combination of these two – far from self-evidently compatible – principles gained momentum at the same time as the political significance of the farmers declined and that of the new middle classes increased.

The Danish sociologist Gøsta Esping-Andersen has famously characterised Nordic welfare policies as "decommodification". This term refers to policies that liberate people from their dependencies on markets, notably from the uncertainties associated with the character of labour as a commodity.[28] However, the transformation Esping-Andersen calls "decommodification" could be interpreted in a different way: it might be, rather, conceived of as a process in which the normalcy of wage work was reinforced at the same time as it was made compatible with the universalist principle of social citizenship.

The adjustment of wage work and social citizenship can be found in the field of *social security*. The "work performance model" with its labour-market-oriented and income-related benefits could be linked with the principle of the social rights inherent in citizenship: the right to a secured continuity of income came to be interpreted as an aspect of social citizenship.

However, in the history of the Nordic welfare state, the most obvious mode in which the principles of wage work and social citizenship were simultaneously reinforced was the construction of extensive *public social services*. These services, defining and meeting the needs of health, care and education, bore the character of universal social rights at the same time as they created preconditions for the generalizing of wage work as the norm. A transformation of the gender division of labour was crucial here, associated with redefinitions of the relationship between the family and society. A particular complex of the welfare state, the labour market regime and the gender system was formed. As has been often argued, the Nordic gender system, since the 1970s, includes a two-fold dependence of women on the welfare state: on the preconditions created for their work outside the home (e.g. child care) and on the jobs created within the welfare state, in strongly gender-segregated labour markets.

This description applies to the shape in which the Nordic welfare state was built in Finland in the 1970s and 1980s.[29] However, in the light of the Finnish case, it would be especially questionable to claim that the concept of the

A scene from a modern welfare society in operation: Järvenpää Secondary School in 2003.

307

working woman came into being only with inception of the welfare state. In Finland, even more than in the other Nordic countries, the gender division of labour *before* the "Nordic gender system", which was structured by the welfare state, did not meet the family ideals of middle-class educators. The hard labour of women in rural households included tasks that according to those ideals belonged to men.[30] Neither was the industrial wage work of women in the late 19th and early 20th century some marginal phenomenon. True, it was often a limited phase of a woman's life before marriage and her first child. However, the number of married women working in factories and shops was remarkable, even before its expansion during World War II.

Through the construction of the welfare state, the significances of wage work as the norm and as a source of individual autonomy were simultaneously reinforced. Nevertheless, work as a source of independence did not mean that it was not also a necessity, and the dual-breadwinner practice was normalised not only as a matter of equality but also as an economic necessity. Furthermore, one might argue that in Finland the heritage from the rural community, in which work was at the same time a necessity, a duty, and a source of dignity, still played a crucial role.

Concensus

The shaping of social policies and labour-market institutions that were based on, and contributed to, the normalcy of wage work were crucial factors in the creation of the Finnish wage-work society. An important step in this transformation was the beginning of the so-called "age of incomes policy" in the late 1960s, at a time of a rapid change in occupational, social and regional structures as well as in political and cultural modes of thought and action. The incomes policy after 1968 included a strong consolidation of the practice of collective bargaining and agreements and a new intertwining of labour-market agreements with economic and social policies. The incomes policy was implemented through agreements that comprised the central organisations of blue- and white-collar workers, private and public sector employers, agricultural producers and the government. A regular part of these agreements were the so-called "social packages", through which major parts of the Finnish welfare state were built or extended.

While neo-corporatist institutions have formed a strong link between industrial relations and the development of the welfare state, the latter has had a major impact on labour relations by creating a large public sector and making possible the high participation of women in working life outside the home, often in public sector jobs, in the country's strongly gender-segregated labour markets.

Until the end of the 1960s Finland had been a Nordic exception due to the relatively low degree of unionisation, political splits in the trade union move-

ment and notorious "low-trust" elements in labour relations. Since the beginning of the incomes policy age in 1968 and the simultaneous cementing of the ten-year organisational split in the workers' trade unions, however, neo-corporatist practices in Finland have occupied a strong position, in fact with a tighter intertwining of labour market negotiations and governmental policy measures than in Sweden or Denmark. At the same time, the strong governmental interference in incomes settlements, including the active role of President Urho Kekkonen, was a manifestation of the continuity of Finnish state-centrism.

In Sweden, "the spirit of Saltsjöbaden", i.e. the legacy of the basic labour-market agreement of 1938, ended, and the relationship of labour and capital was "re-politicised" in the 1970s and 1980s. In Finland, a contrary tendency emerged. "The spirit of Korpilampi", which refers to a conference convened by the Social Democrat Prime Minister, Kalevi Sorsa, in 1977, expressed the broad commitment of interest organisations, political parties and the representatives of administration and expertise to "economic resuscitation". The national consensus was reinforced in the 1980s on the basis of a pragmatism that was oriented toward an active adjustment to what were conceived of as the new needs of national competitiveness. The long continuity of the national modes of thought manifested here is remarkable, although a change, including a de-politicisation of employer–employee conflicts during the 1980s, was also obvious. A crucial element in the change was the stabilisation of the parliamentary system in which it became the norm for the government to remain in power for the whole four-year period between the elections.

The adjustment to "economic necessities", such as the international de-regulation of financial markets in the late 1980s and the collapse of the Soviet Union together with the subsequent decline of the so-called "Eastern trade", was far from successful. This was proved by the deep economic depression and dramatic rise of unemployment in Finland in the early 1990s. However, studies of the public discourse during the crisis indicate that the notion of politics as fulfilling national necessities was, in fact, reinforced by this experience. The cuts in welfare benefits and services could be legitimised this way, but the defence of the welfare state and industrial relations institutions could also be based on this kind of argumentation, in which these institutions are interpreted as necessary preconditions for an innovation-based competitiveness.

The economic crisis of the 1990s became a part of the grand narrative of national survival. The story of the sacrifices by which the depression was overcome is inseparably intertwined with accounts that point out the successful national response to the challenges of globalisation and European integration by means of knowledge and innovation.

The welfare state and consensual competitiveness

The theorists of the information(al) society – especially, the Spanish-American sociologist Manuel Castells – have praised Finland as a top model of consensual response to the challenges of globalisation.[31] Indeed, the political tensions concerning globalisation and European integration have been less obvious in Finland than, for example, in Sweden. The imperatives of global competition have become an integral part of the rhetoric of national community and are widely adopted as determinants of the political agenda. In terms of political thought, the transition from Finland as the Nordic latecomer to Finland as a paragon of consensual competitiveness appears to have been relatively easy.[32]

However, one should not bypass the fact that, through the transformations called globalisation, the assumption of a virtuous circle of national economy, social policy and democracy which provided an important part of

310

the ideological underpinning of the Nordic welfare states and of the systems of labour-market agreements has been questioned. The premises for the "Nordic" image of symmetry between the labour-market parties have been weakened by a variety of developments: the multinational and transnational character of companies in the global economy; their restructuring in accordance with the network principle; the increase in so-called "atypical" employment relationships; and the growing fluidity of the boundary between wage work and entrepreneurship. It has become ever more difficult to identify, organise, bring together and centralise the different "parties" within a national society.

The opportunities enjoyed by various economic actors to choose between alternative ways of dealing with their environment are becoming increasingly differentiated. This can be illuminated by applying the distinction between the three options the American development economist Albert O. Hirschman calls *exit*, *voice* and *loyalty*.[33] Here, exit means leaving an unsatisfactory milieu, while voice refers to attempts to exert influence on the environment and loyalty to the commitment in its modes of functioning. The exit option is available to transnational enterprises and investors in a new way, and it also offers a silent means of exerting an influence. One consequence of this is that solidarity through shared national links has become more problematic. Signs of breaches in the national concensus became evident in the lockout that the Finnish employers' organisation in the wood-processing industry declared in 2005 in order to get through its demands for more flexibility in the labour market and the organisation of work.

Moomin trolls created by Finnish artist Tove Jansson are beloved friends of children (and adults) all over the world.

However, it is obvious that the old institutions of the welfare state and industrial relations can be, and have been, modified to serve the new functions of globally competitive community. Actually, the concept of "the Nordic model", which was rarely used before the 1980s, implies such a shift of perspective. The current discussion on "models" is dominated by the encounters between globalised capital and national institutions, and it indicates increasing reflexivity as an aspect of globalisation. Reflexivity is nourished by the imperatives of competitiveness, which include the need for continuous comparisons in order to learn the universal "best practice" or to find the "difference", i.e. an edge, one's own particular competitive advantage. European integration provides an important context for the discussion on models. The "Nordic model" is advocated not only in the defence of particular national institutions and traditions in the Nordic countries but also in connection with aims concerning the direction of European integration and the best ways of making Europe competitive in the global economy.

In the traditions of Nordic social thought, prerequisites exist for an argumentation in which a wide spectrum of socially and ethically highly valued achievements and objectives are demonstrated to be competitive advantages. For the trade unions, it is easy to accept a "value-added" competition strategy based on innovation, training and participation as an alternative to "cost-based" strategies which demand low wages, low taxes and minimal social regulations. It would not be correct to claim that the new imperatives of competitiveness have excluded social, ecological or ethical points of view from the agenda. Rather, the power of those imperatives is indicated by the fact that so many "good things" can be included and, in this way, subordinated to the argument of competitiveness.

One may conclude, however, that in the Finnish and, more generally, Nordic "competition state", an insoluble tension appears between what are presented as institutional preconditions of competitiveness and the conceptions of the contents of competitiveness itself. At the same time as egalitarian institutions and participatory practices can be defended as preconditions for knowledge-based competitiveness, true membership in a competitive community is a matter of individual competitiveness. This, in turn, consists of communicative and innovative skills and talents and reflexive capabilities of monitoring oneself from the point of view of competitiveness. Not only are there both winners and losers in this competition, there are people who cannot even participate in it.

The "social" seems to have taken on a Janus face. On one side, social policies are supposed to provide a social infrastructure that helps "us" to create competitiveness based on commitment, knowledge and innovativeness, i.e. on "social capital" and "human capital". This task is associated with the intensified rivalry among national, regional and local communities in offering attractive environments for competitive economic actors, enterprises and people. In this rivalry, too, there are winners and losers, not least in the competition between different municipalities. Consequently, an old internal tension of the "Nordic model" seems to have turned into an open contradiction: how to manage with the paradoxical principle that municipalities, i.e. the institution of local self-government, are responsible for public services that have the character of universal social rights of nation-state citizens?

On the other side, the "social" exists in the efforts to prevent and deal with social exclusion and to make possible a peaceful co-existence between those inside and those outside the new economy. These efforts mainly take the form of so-called "activating social and employment policies". They also manifest historical continuities, even in connection with new immigration policies, notably continuities concerning the role of work. In the formation of the Nordic

312

welfare states, a widely shared regulative principle was that everybody should have the right to fulfil his or her duty to work. From this point of departure, one obvious direction would be back to the pre-welfare-state aims of social policy, associated with maintaining order and preventing idleness. In any case, the old emphasis on work as the basis of social order and disciplined citizenship is very much alive side by side with the marketing of the new concept of work as an unending demonstration of a person's individual innovative capacity.

"A Shred of Information"
by Maaria Wirkkala.

Notes

Preface: Successful Small Open Economies and the Importance of Good Institutions
Mokyr
pp. 8–13

1　Even Rondo Cameron, who placed more emphasis than most on the small economies of Europe, devoted all of five lines to Finland in his textbook. See Cameron, 1989, p. 305. The exception is the now quite obsolete two volumes by Milward and Saul, who dedicated in their first volume a full chapter to Belgium and Switzerland and another to Scandinavia, and in their second volume another chapter to the Low Countries. See Milward and Saul 1973 and Milward and Saul 1977.
2　Germany, the UK, and Russia are the only three major European economies in which total GDP grew more slowly between 1813 and 1998 than between 1820 and 1913. The only small economy for which that was true was Hungary.
3　Romer 1996, 202–206.
4　All ratios are computed as the average of exports and imports divided by GDP in purchasing power parity value. The data for Albania and Myanmar are highly inaccurate because both the numerator and the denominator under-report activities in the underground and black economy. Source: http://www.cia.gov/cia/publications/factbook/index.html
5　The SSEE's were four Scandinavian countries, three Benelux countries, Switzerland, Austria and Ireland. The large countries are France, Germany, the UK, Italy, Spain and the USA. Adding Portugal to the SSEE's and Poland to the larger ones raises the numbers to 1.911 and 2.231 respectively. All data are from http://www.heritage.org/research/features/index/countries.cfm.
6　Computed from 2005 data taken from http://www.transparency.org/policy_and_research/surveys_indices/cpi/2005
7　Computed from data in http://www.cia.gov/cia/publications/factbook/index.html.
8　All data from The Economist World in Figures 2004 ed. No data for Luxembourg and Iceland. The small difference is largely due to the very large proportion of people with a higher education in the US, where higher education plays a different social and educational role from that in Europe. Without the US, the proportion of people with higher education drops to 53.8 percent.
9　Mokyr 2005a, 285–351.
10　Mokyr 2005b.
11　Mokyr 1994, 561–574.

On the Road to Prosperity: An Introduction
Eloranta, García-Iglesias, Ojala and Jalava
pp. 14–31

1　See especially Koskinen, Martelin, Notkola, Notkola and Pitkänen 1994.
2　These figures are based on a database compiled by The Geological Survey of Finland (GTK), and are available at: http://www.gtk.fi/welcome.html.
3　See e.g. Fogel 1972, 1–2, Komlos 1992
4　See for example Ojala 2003,Whaples 2002, 525.
5　Hjerppe 1988, Haapala 1989, Peltonen 1990, e.g. 128–131.
6　Ojala 2003.
7　Bohlin 2003, Hjerppe 1997, 6–10.
8　Engerman 1996, 1–4.
9　See Whaples 2002, 530, Ojala 2003.

Economic Growth and Structural Change.
A Century and a Half of Catching-up
Hjerppe and Jalava
pp. 32–63

1　Maddison 2003
2　All growth rates in this chapter are in natural logarithms (ln). Thus growth is defined as: $100*[\ln(x(t)/x(t-1))]$.
3　Hjerppe 1989, 1996.
4　This classical view is not unchallenged: for example, Broadberry (1998) argued that Germany and the United States surpassed Britain's level of aggregate labour productivity by shifting resources out of agriculture and improving the productivity of services rather than manufacturing.
5　OECD 2003
6　Aghion and Howitt 2005
7　Development economists, such as Easterly (2001), have found strong positive correlations between the positive factors of the quality of life and GDP per capita
8　See www.ggdc.net, Total Economy Database, January 2005.
9　Savela 2005. This takes into account the institutional differences between countries. For example, in Finland day-care centres are mainly the responsibility of local government, while in many countries day care facilities are private or pre-school aged children are cared for at home.
10　Heikkinen 1997.
11　See e.g. Crafts 1985.
12　Ikonen and Valkonen 1987, Hjerppe 1996. See also Krantz 2001.

13 Myllyntaus, Michelsen and Herranen 1986, Myllyntaus 1991, Jalava 2004.

14 Hjerppe 1996

15 Jalava, Heikkinen and Hjerppe 2002

16 See Syrquin 1984

17 Proximate in contrast to ultimate since the decomposition of growth into the contributions of labour, capital and productivity does not explain why certain input mixes were chosen. It does, however, answer the question of how much each factor contributed.

18 The inputs are corrected for changes in quality and weighted with their marginal products – their market prices.

19 Jalava, Heikkinen and Hjerppe 2002

20 See also Hyytinen and Rouvinen 2005.

Feeding Economic Growth: Agriculture
Ojala and Nummela
pp. 64–91

1 Ruttan 2002, 161. On the discussion see especially Ruttan 2002, Zanden 1991, Allen 2000, Clark 1987, Clark 1991, Clark 1992.

2 Zanden 1991, 219.

3 Hjerppe 1989, Jussila 1987, Myyrä and Pietola 1999, Mäkelä 2001, Maataloustilastollinen 2002, Ruttan 2002, Schultz 1951, STV 1950–2003, SVT 1950–2003.

4 See especially Allen 2000, Zanden 1991.

5 Myrdal 1985, Myrdal 1999, Myrdal and Söderberg 1991, Fitzgerald 2003, Kola 1998, Kuhmonen 1996, Lauck 2000.

6 See e.g. Jussila 1987, 13, 55–63, 88–91; Tykkyläinen and Kavilo 1991, 15; Kuhmonen 1996, 23–26.

7 Solantie 1988.

8 Niemelä 1996, 354; Vihinen 1990, 42.

9 Komiteanmietintö 1940, 352.

10 Tykkyläinen and Kavilo 1991, 15; Lees 2000, 70, Jussila 1987, 39, 48–49; Vihinen 1990, 32–33, 44; Sauli 1987, 157–159

11 See e.g. Sipiäinen, Ryhänen, Ylätalo, Haggrén and Seppälä 1998.

12 See e.g. Jussila 1987, 50–51, Vihinen 1990, 16, 35, 74, Anderson 1987, Sauli 1987

13 SVT III, Maatalous 1950 (Census of Agriculture), Vol 1, 53; http://www.mtk.fi/ (cited 28th January 2004); Mäkelä 2001; Kuhmonen 1996, 19–20. – On the history of land ownership in Finland, see e.g. Jutikkala 1958, Peltonen 1992, Peltonen 2004, Rasila, Jutikkala and Mäkelä-Alitalo 2003, Soininen 1975; Vihinen 1990, 59, Mäkelä 2001.

14 Pyykkönen 1998, 81, Haataja 1949, Jussila 1987, 46, Tykkyläinen and Kavilo 1991, 94, Jutikkala 1958, Soininen 1975, 127–138.

15 See especially Saarinen 1966, 16–49; Hämynen and Lahti 1983; Tykkyläinen and Kavilo 1991, 7–8, 16–12, 93–107; Laitinen 1995.

16 Niemelä 1996, 419–420; Information Centre of the Ministry of Agriculture and Forestry (http://tike.mmm.fi); Mäkelä 2001; Kuhmonen 1996, 3; Perko 2005, 33.

17 See also Zanden 1991, Lauck 2000.

18 Häikiö 1997, Vapaakallio 1995, Lamberg 2001, Perko 2005, Zetterberg 1983.

19 STV 1953. http://www.finfood.fi/. Jussila 1987, 46; Jutikkala 1958, 253–301.

20 See especially Clark 1992, Ruttan 2002, Zanden 1991.

21 On the comparison, see also Clark 1992, 69.

22 The figure is based on the area of arable land in hectares and the number of farms (including crofts). Since there are differences in the sources used, Figures 2 and 3 should be understood as only estimates. The arable land in use in 1500 is based on extrapolation; the other years are partly interpolated. Further details available from the authors by request.

23 See e.g. Kuhmonen 1996, 9.

24 Cornwall and Cornwall 1994, 240, Suomela 1958, Hjerppe 1989, Ihamuotila 1972, Kuhmonen 1996, 45–53, Myyrä and Pietola 1999, 10–12, 48.

25 The figure is based on the combined crop yield of wheat, rye, barley, and oats in kilograms, and the production of milk in litres. The milk production for the years 1860–1960 has been taken from Viita (1965), and from official statistics thereafter. The crop yield of slash-and-burn cultivation is not included as it does not show up in the statistics. Further details available from the authors by request.

26 Tauriainen 1970, 50–70, Jussila 1987, 32.

27 http://www.finfood.fi/ (cited 28th January 2004).

28 See e.g. Myrdal and Söderberg 1991, Reinikainen, Nieminen and Näri 1987, Vihola 1991.

29 Aarnio 1987, 105; Jussila 1987, 52–53; Kiviniemi and Näri 1987, 217–222.

30 Niemelä 1996, 353; Information Centre of the Ministry of Agriculture and Forestry (http://tike.mmm.fi). By comparison, in the Netherlands the annual milk production of cows in the early 20th century was already 2.5 tonnes a year on average. Zanden 1991, 218.

31 Fitzgerald 2003.

32 http://www.finfood.fi/

33 Ahonen 2002, Siltanen and Ala-Mantila 1989, 13.

34 See e.g. Vihinen 1990, 41, 51, 54, Myyrä and Pietola 1999, 29–30, 50.

35 See especially Jussila 1987, 12–13, 33, Köppä 1989, 195–202. http://www.finfood.fi/ (cited 28th January 2004).

36 Schultz 1941, 127, Vihinen 1990, 17–18, 60.

37 On agribusiness and agricultural industrialisation in retrospective see especially Fitzgerald 2003, Lauck 2000.

Business: Rooted in Social Capital over the Centuries
Ojala and Karonen
pp. 92–125

1 Lamberg and Ojala 2006.
2 North 1990. Conceptually, the competitive forces used here are adapted from Michael Porter's framework. See: Porter 1980, Porter 1985.
3 See especially Myllyntaus, Michelsen and Herranen 1986
4 See especially Cantwell 1989.
5 Chandler 1990, Pfeffer and Salancik 1978, 143–147, Orru, Woolsey Biggart and Hamilton 1991, 366–367.
6 See e.g. Heikkinen 2000, Kuisma 2004
7 See especially Williamson 1975, Williamson 1985. Critical overview in Holmström and Roberts 1998, See also Murmann 2003, Meyer and Rowan 1983, Stern and Barley 1996
8 Lin 2001, Luoma-aho 2005. There is hardly any consensus about how to define social capital. While some authors (like Bourdieu 1983, Coleman 1988, Putnam 1995) see social capital as being rooted in societies through communal activities, others (like Lin 2001, Burt 1992) point to individual activities to gain advantages through investments in social relations. The former authors understand social capital as affecting the individual from above, while the latter see social capital as affecting societies from below.
9 Hjerppe 2003.
10 Lamberg and Ojala 2005, Murmann 2003, Karonen 2004, Lamberg 1998, Skippari 2005.
11 Karonen 2004.
12 Deflated by cost-of-living and wholesale price indices, the choice between the indicators used dictated by data availability. Further details available from the authors.
13 See e.g. Müller 1998.
14 Karonen 2004, Kaukiainen 1991, Kuisma 1993, Ojala 1999.
15 Fellman 2000, Karonen 2004, Kaukiainen 1994, Mauranen 1981, Ojala 2002
16 Skippari, Ojala and Lamberg 2005
17 Deflated with the wholesale price index.
18 For more details see Hjerppe and Lamberg 2000, Lamberg 1998.
19 Auquier and Caves 1979, 571–573. See also: Wurm 1989, Heikkinen 2000, Hjerppe and Lamberg 2000, Häikiö 2001a, Nordberg 1980.
20 Pihkala 1970, Schybergson 2001.
21 Myllyntaus, Michelsen and Herranen 1986.
22 Häikiö 2001a, Häikiö 2001b, Häikiö 2001c.
23 Kuisma 1997, 563, Eloranta and Ojala 2005.
24 Moen and Lilja 2001, 107.
25 Kuisma 2004, Vihola 2000, Moen and Lilja 2001.
26 These six companies were: Kajaani, Lassila & Tikanoja, Rauma-Repola, Finnish Shell, Uusi Suomi and United Paper Mills. For a more detailed description, see es-

pecially Ruostetsaari 1989, 140–141, Kuisma 2004. For comparison, see especially Davis and Mizruchi 1999, 215, Mizruchi 1982, Useem 1980, Useem 1984, Mizruchi 1992, Mizruchi 1996, Mizruchi and Stearns 1988.
27 Häikiö 2001b.
28 Häikiö 2001a, Michelsen 1993, Michelsen and Särkikoski 2005, Ruostetsaari 1989, Saarinen 2005.
29 Mannio, Vaara and Ylä-Anttila 2003.
30 See especially Kuisma 2004, 368–370, 379–381.
31 Ahvenainen 1979, Häikiö 2001c, Mannio, Vaara and Ylä-Anttila 2003.
32 Häikiö 2001c.
33 Häikiö 2001c, Manninen 2002.
34 Saarinen 2005.
35 This text is based on Häikiö 2001a, Häikiö 2001b, Häikiö 2001c.
36 Michelsen 1999.
37 Values are deflated by using the wholesale price index for 1913 and 1975, and the cost of living index for 1800.
38 Peterson 2001, Schybergson 2001.

Foreign Trade and Transport
Kaukiainen
pp. 126–163

1 See e.g. Kaukiainen 1980, 95–114.
2 See e.g. Glaman 1974, 441–443.
3 Hallberg 1959, 86–89, Luukko 1967, 114–115.
4 Kaukiainen 1993, 18–20.
5 Kaukiainen 1993, 28.
6 Ahvenainen 1984, 58–121, Åström 1988, 33–45, 88.
7 Högberg 1969, 28–30, Alanen 1950, 60–73, Kaukiainen 1993, 38–49.
8 Schybergson 1980, 451–58, Pihkala 1969, 34–9.
9 Kaukiainen 1993, 69, 104. In 1825 and 1853 only the tonnages of urban owners were included, while there were also substantial fleets in certain coastal parishes – all told about a half of the urban figures – they were only allowed to engage in coastal trade to Stockholm or St. Petersburg. This restriction was abolished after the Crimean War, for 1875, all ships of over 100 net register tons have been included.
10 Cif (cost, insurance, freight) refers to the price of goods after being unloaded on the quayside – transport costs are included but not import dues, fob (free on board) refers to the price after loading onboard – or sometimes just brought alongside – after eventual export dues have been paid – but it does not include freight.
11 Kaukiainen 1993, 88–90.
12 Hoffman 1980, 108–115, Vattula 1983, tables 5.8 and 5.10.
13 Pihkala 1969, 47–54.
14 Kaukiainen 1993, 95–118.
15 A precise ratio cannot be computed since a number of

316

ships sailed to Stockholm and St. Petersburg along long coastal routes, thus receiving substantial income from domestic traffic as well.

16 Kaukiainen 1993, 112–125.
17 Pohjanpalo 1978, 91–149.
18 Ahvenainen 1984, 164–167, 283–285, 329–371, Hjerppe 1989, 158–163, Vattula 1983, table 5.11.
19 Oksanen and Pihkala 1975, 16–23, Hjerppe 1989, 154–158.
20 Kaukiainen 1993, 135–151.
21 Pihkala 1988, 63–84.
22 Pihkala 1988, 65–68.
23 Kaukiainen 1993, 154–78.
24 Kaukiainen and Leino-Kaukiainen 1992, 234–235, 321–329.
25 Häikiö 2001c, 245.
26 The most essential statistics on recent development can be found in *The Statistical Yearbook of Finland*. Useful data can also be found on the web-pages of the Finnish Customs (*Tulli*): www.tulli.fi/fi/05_Ulkomaankauppati-lastot/02_Kuviot_ja_taulukot/.
27 However, the deadweight tonnage was only 1.3 million, or a third of the corresponding figure in 1981. This is because typical ships in this category are ro-ro or container ships, which are designed to carry volume cargo, not heavy goods. Accordingly, their deadweight tonnages are low compared with their gross volume.
28 Recent statistics on Finnish shipping can be found in the printed annual reports of *Merenkulkulaitos* (Finnish maritime authority) and on their relevant web-pages: www.fma.fi/palvelut/tilastot/.
29 Estimates by the author, based mainly on export and price data published in Vattula 1983. Heikkinen (1994, 106–107) estimated that exports amounted to only 3 or 4 percent of the Finnish national product at the turn of the 18th and 19th centuries. This seems a rather low estimate since a plausible rate already around 1630 can be conjectured as being between 2 and 3 percent.
30 Hjerppe 1989, 151–153, *Statistical Yearbook of Finland*, 1985.
31 Tigerstedt 1952, 696, 717–723.
32 Kaukiainen 1993, 185. Modern estimates of "freight-ratios" are usually drawn from comparisons of fob- and cif- based export and import statistics (see e.g. *UNCTAD, Review of Maritime Transport*, 2000, 66–67). While such estimates can be quite misleading in the case of developing countries, the statistics of industrial countries are normally so much better that they can be taken as rough approximations. The figures for Finland, presented above, are based on four different estimates, the three highest of which amounted to 3–3.5% (Ojala and Saarto, 1992, chapter 1.3.3).
33 This demise in the price of distance can be illuminated with following example, computed from data on grain and coal freights: in 2000, a ton of goods could be shipped from Rotterdam to Singapore, a distance of 8350 nautical miles, for the cost which was charged from Rotterdam to Marseilles (2060 nautical miles) around 1875 (current prices deflated by British/US producer prices).
34 Incidence ratios computed by Heikkinen 1994, 188, 244, 294, 390, 464, 511.

The Labour Market, 1850–2000
Hannikainen and Helkkinen
pp. 164–185

1 See Hjerppe 1989, 61–68.
2 Vartia & Ylä-Anttila 2003, 79.
3 Lilja & Pehkonen 2002, 295.
4 For 1910 Heikkinen 1997, 85, for 1936 Sosiaalinen aikakauskirja, for 1950 and 1975 Eriksson 1991, 194, and for 2000 The Statistical Yearbook of Finland.
5 Eriksson 1991, 193–195.
6 See Heikkinen 1997, 25–31.
7 Mattila 1969, 262–269, Mansner 1981, 99–125, Ala-Kapee and Valkonen 1982, 260–300, Teräs 2001.
8 Kettunen 1986, 442–458, Bergholm 2003, 18–30.
9 Bergholm 2003.
10 Vartiainen 1998.
11 Böckerman & Uusitalo 2005.
12 Piekkola & Snellman 2005, 1–3.
13 Lebergott 1964, Darby 1976, Crafts 1987, Eichengreen & Hatton 1988, Thomas 1988, Margo 1993, Grytten 1995, Boyer & Hatton 2002.
14 Lewis 1954, Nurkse 1966, Takagi 1978, Bhaduri 1987.
15 Häkkinen & Peltola 2001, 314–320.
16 Rahikainen 2001.
17 Peltola 1998, 218.
18 Hannikainen 2004, 195.
19 The Statistical yearbook of Finland 2004.
20 Pohjola 1998, Hannikainen 2004.
21 Mansner 1981, 264–268.
22 Solow 1985, Blanchard & Summers 1986, Crafts 1989.
23 The regression coefficient of the percentage-point change of the unemployment rate (the change in real earnings as a dependent variable) is statistically significant at the 1% level, but R^2 is rather low (0.22). The regression using the unemployment rate as an independent variable gives poorer results: the coefficient is significant at the 5% level and R^2 is 0.15. These differences can interpreted as an indication of rising structural unemployment.
24 Baily 1983, Eichengreen & Hatton 1988, Margo 1993, Hart 2001.
25 Vartiainen 1998.
26 Vartia & Ylä-Antilla 2003, 181.

317

Monetary Aspects of a Changing Economy
García-Iglesias and Kilponen
pp. 186–215

1   Kuusterä 1994.
2   Tarkka 1993.
3   Tarkka 1993.
4   Hjerppe 2001.
5   Heikkinen and Hjerppe 1987.
6   García-Iglesias and Kilponen 2004.
7   Eichengreen 1997.
8   Korpisaari 1926, Rossi 1951.
9   Davies 1997.
10 Feinstein et al. 1997.
11 Kuusterä 1997.
12 Eichengreen 1997.
13 Hirvilahti 1993.
14 Pipping 1967.
15 Kuusterä 1994.
16 Rossi 1951.
17 Eichegreen 1997.
18 Kuusterä 1994.
19 See Eichengreen 1997.
20 Jakobson 1980.
21 Kuusterä 1994.
22 Heikkinen and Kuusterä 2001.
23 Bordo and Jonung 1981, 1987, 2003, Bordo et al. 1997, Siklos 1993, Carreras and García-Iglesias 2003, 2005.
24 Waris 1977.
25 See for example Junnila 1970, Waris 1977, Korkman 1987, Parviainen 1988.
26 Tarkka 1984, Mikkola 1989, Pikkarainen and Vajanen 1991, Kilponen 1992.

Guns and Butter – Central Government Spending in the 20th Century
Eloranta and Kauppila
pp. 216–243

1   See e.g. PISA 2004.
2   Lindert 2004. On different types of welfare states and especially the Scandinavian "model", see e.g. Esping-Andersen 1984.
3   On definitions, see Lindert 1994, 2–3.
4   Tanzi and Schuknecht 2000, 3–5; Lindert, 1–2.
5   Hjerppe 1988. See also Hjerppe and Jalava in this volume.
6   For more, see e.g. Jakobson 1984, Eloranta 2002, Paasivirta 1984.
7   See especially Nummela 1993.
8   See e.g. Paavonen 1998, 69–72.
9   Hjerppe 1989.
10 Eloranta and Ojala 2005. On the collapse of the Soviet Union, see especially Harrison 2002, 397–433.

11 Kiander, Kröger and Romppainen 2005.
12 See especially Obstfeld and Taylor 2003, 241–275.
13 Lindert 1989, Chen 2003.
14 Tanzi and Schuknecht 2000, 197.
15 Urponen 1994, 174.
16 Alestalo and Uusitalo 1986, 130–131.
17 See especially Hjerppe 1989, 129.
18 See Eloranta 2003, Sandler, and Hartley 1995, Sandler and Hartley 1999 for further discussion.
19 See e.g. Tanzi and Schuknecht 2000, 64–66.
20 Hjerppe 1997, 11–20.
21 Hjerppe 1989, Alestalo and Uusitalo 1986, Eloranta 1997.
22 Peacock and Wiseman 1961, 21–31.
23 Such tests usually split the time series into two samples and determine if they are statistically the same.
24 Taimio 1986, Hjerppe 1997, 11–20.
25 The Polity IIID index, see Gleditsch 2000.
26 Details on the sources and techniques used in this section are available from the authors on request.
27 We utilized Vector Autoregression (VAR) in the analysis, assessing the impulse responses to shocks and to measure the magnitude of the impact. More details available from the authors on request.
28 Detailed results available from the authors on request.
29 See also Eloranta 2002. Cf. Jalonen and Vesa 1992, 377–395.

Income Distribution in the 20th Century
Jäntti
pp. 244–261

1   The author has benefitted from research assistance on this project by Jan-Erik Antipin, Magnus Berglund, Lajos Parkatti, Susanna Sandström and Christer Sundqvist. This research has been partly financed by funding from the Yrjö Jahnsson Foundation and the Academy of Finland.
2   Inequality indices from the late 1960s for many OECD countries are available at http://www.lisproject.org/keyfigures/ineqtable.htm. See also Gottschalk and Smeeding (2000).
3   See, e.g., Piketty and Saez 2003, Atkinson 2005a, Saez 2005 and Atkinson 2005b. See Riihelä et al. 2005 for recent evidence from Finland.
4   Statistics Finland 1920–2002.
5   Harmaja 1934, Sukselainen 1946.
6   See e.g. Upton 1980 and Casanova 2000. Jäntti et al. (2005) discuss many of the reforms made in the first years after the Civil War.
7   Statistics Finland, 1920 – 2002.
8   McDonald 1984.
9   e.g. Lindsey 1999.
10 Singh and Maddala 1976, Burr 1942, McDonald 1984.
11 Gottschalk and Smeeding 2000.
12 Atkinson 2005a.

13 see Expert Group on Household Income Statistics (The Canberra Group) 2001.
14 Aktinson 2003.

Productivity growth: the role of human capital and technology
Asplund and Maliranta
pp. 262–283

1   Maliranta 2003.
2   Maliranta and Rouvinen 2004.
3   See further Chapter 4 of this volume for detailed information about Nokia.
4   For more information, see e.g. Paija 2001b, Romanainen 2001 and Ylä-Anttila 2002. The other main sources underlying this sub-section are the regularly published reports *European Trend Chart on Innovation – Country Report: Finland*, as well as the triennial reviews of the Science and Technology Policy Council STPC 1987, STPC 1990, STPC 1993, STPC 1996, STPC 2000, STPC 2003.
5   The national innovation system concept was introduced into Finland's science and technology policy in 1990, through the Council's review of that year STPC 1990. It is defined in STPC 2000 in the following way: "…is a domain for interaction in the production and utilisation of knowledge and know-how built on cooperation between all producers and utilisers of new knowledge" (p. 11). For more information on the national innovation system, see e.g. Schienstock and Hämäläinen 2001.
6   A cluster can be defined as "an industrial agglomeration of producers, customers and competitors that promotes efficiency, increases specialisation and is a source of competitive advantage" Ylä-Anttila 2002. Cluster-based policies with reference to Finland are also discussed in Rouvinen and Ylä-Anttila 1999. The adaptation and adoption of the cluster approach in Finnish technology policy and its relation to policy-making are analysed in detail by Jääskeläinen 2001.
7   For more information on the adoption and implementation of cluster-based industrial policies, see Pietarinen and Ranki 1993.
8   Comprehensive analyses of the Finnish ICT cluster are provided by e.g. Toivola 1992, Turpeinen 1996 and Paija 2001a, Paija 2001b, Turpeinen 1996.
9   See Daveri and Silva 2004.
10 WITSA 2004.
11 The recession of the early 1990s has been investigated in depth in a large number of studies; see e.g. the special issue of the journal Finnish Economic Papers 1996/1 and Santamäki-Vuori and Parviainen 1996.
12 Gordon, 2004, 11.
13 see Maliranta 2005.
14 Maliranta 2005.

The Tension between the Social and the Economic – A Historical Perspective on a Welfare State
Kettunen
pp. 284–313

1   Streeck 1998, 36–39, Palan and Abbot 1999, 36–39.
2   Senghaas 1985, 71–94.
3   Polanyi 2001 [1944], 116–135.
4   Slagstad 1998, 67.
5   Koselleck 1979, 349–375.
6   Kettunen 2006, 35–40.
7   Gerschenkron 1962, 356–363.
8   Kettunen 2006, 40–42.
9   Hietala 1987, Hietala 1992.
10 Kalela 1989, 205–227.
11 Kettunen 1994, 32–91, Kettunen 2001, 233.
12 Satka 1995, 101–104, Mattila 1999.
13 Cf. Hirdman 1997.
14 Pohjola 1994, 237.
15 Kuusi 1964, 34.
16 Kuusi 1964, 59.
17 Cf. Smolander 2000.
18 Majander 2004.
19 Kettunen 2006, 51–55; Petersen 2006, 67–98.
20 Kosonen 1993, 50–51.
21 Kangas 1991, 146.
22 Salminen 1993.
23 Baldwin 1990.
24 Sørensen and Stråth 1997, 24.
25 Stenius 1997, 168.
26 Kettunen 1997, 103–124.
27 Cf. Kalela 1989, 159–192, Kosonen 1998, 151–159.
28 Esping-Andersen 1985, Esping-Andersen 1990.
29 Julkunen 1990.
30 Markkola 1990.
31 Castells and Himanen 2002.
32 Kettunen 2004, 289–309.
33 Hirschman 1970.

References

Aarnio, Kaisa (1987), Traktori. In: Olli Näri (Ed.), *Koneellistuva maataloutemme – Mechanization of Finnish Agriculture*. Vakola, Vaasa, 75–106.

Abramovitz, Moses (1956), Resource and Output Trends in the United States Since 1870. *American Economic Review (Papers and Proceedings of the Sixty-eighth Annual Meeting of the American Economic Association)* 46(1), 5–23.

Aghion, Philippe and Peter Howitt (2005), *Appropriate Growth Policy: A Unifying Framework (manuscript)*.

Ahonen, Heli (2002), Organic Milk Production in Finland. *www.mtk.fi (cited 28th January 2004)*.

Ahvenainen, Jorma (1979), Ulkomainen pääoma Suomen teollisuudessa. In: Erkki Markkanen (Ed.), *Teollistuminen ja teollisuusyhteisöt. Teollistumisajan vaiheita Suomessa*. Jyväskylän yliopisto, Jyväskylä, 26–39.

Ahvenainen, Jorma (1984), *Suomen sahateollisuuden historia*. WSOY, Porvoo.

Aktinson, Anthony B. (2003), Income inequality in OECD countries: Data and explanations. *CESifo Economic Studies* 49(4), 479–513.

Ala-Kapee, Pirjo and Marjaana Valkonen (1982), *Yhdessä elämä turvalliseksi. SAK:laisen ammattiyhdistysliikkeen kehitys vuoteen 1930*. Suomen Ammattiliittojen Keskusjärjestö ry, Helsinki.

Alanen, Aulis J. (1950), Pohjanlahden vapaasta purjehduksesta 1766–1808. *Historiallinen Arkisto* 53.

Alestalo, Matti and Hannu Uusitalo (1986), Finland. In: Peter Flora (Ed.), *Growth to Limits. The Western European Welfare States Since World War II*. W. de Gruyter, Berlin, 197–292.

Allen, Robert (2000), Economic structure and agricultural productivity in Europe, 1300–1800. *European Review of Economic History* 4(1), 1–25.

Anderson, Åke (1987), *Vårt jordbrukspolitiska system*. Sveriges lantbrukuniversitet, Uppsala.

Atkinson, Anthony B. (2005a), Comparing the distribution of top incomes across countries. *Journal of the European Economic Association* 3(2–3), 393–401.

Atkinson, Anthony B. (2005b), Top incomes in the UK over the 20th century. *Journal of the Royal Statistical Society* A 168(2), 325–343.

Autio, Jaakko (1992), *Valuuttakurssit Suomessa 1864–1991. Katsaus ja tilastosarjat (Discussion Papers 1/92)*. Bank of Finland, Helsinki.

Autio, Jaakko (1996), *Korot Suomessa 1862–1952 (Discussion Papers 7/96)*. Bank of Finland, Helsinki.

Baily, Martin N. (1983), The Labor Market in the 1930s. In: James Tobin (Ed.), *Macroeconomics, Prices & Quantities. Essays in Memory of Arthur M. Okun*. Basil Blackwell, Oxford, 21–62.

Baldwin, Peter (1990), *The Politics of Social Solidarity. Class Bases of the European Welfare State 1875–1975*. Cambridge University Press, Cambridge.

BankofFinland (2006), *Bank of Finland Database*. Bank of Finland, Helsinki.

Bergholm, Tapio (2003), *History of SAK*. The Central Organisation of Finnish Trade Unions, Helsinki.

Bhaduri, Amit (1987), Disguised Unemployment. In: John Eatwell, Murray Milgate and Peter Newman (Eds.), *The New Palgrave. A Dictionary of Economics, Volume 1*. The Macmillan Press Limited, London, 863–865.

Blanchard, Olivier J. and Lawrence H. Summers (1986), Hysteresis and the European Unemployment Problem. In: Stanley Fischer (Ed.), *NBER Macroeconomics Annual 1986*. National Bureau for Economic Research, Cambridge, 15–78.

Bohlin, Jan (2003), Swedish Historical National Accounts: The Fifth Generation. *European Review of Economic History* 7(1), 73–97.

Bordo, Michael D. and Lars Jonung (1987), *The Long-run Behaviour of the Velocity of Circulation*. Cambridge University Press, Cambridge.

Bordo, Michael D. and Lars Jonung (1981), The Long-Run Behaviour of the Income Velocity of Money in Five Advanced Countries, 1870–1975: An Institutional Approach. *Economic Inquiry* 19(1), 96–116.

Bordo, Michael D. and Lars Jonung (2003), *Demand for Money. An Analysis of the Long-Run Behaviour of the Velocity of Circulation*. Transactions Publishers, New Brunswick and London.

Bordo, Michael D., Lars Jonung and Pierre L. Siklos (1997), Institutional Change and the Velocity of Money: A Century of Evidence. *Economic Inquiry* 35(4), 710–724.

Bourdieu, Pierre (1983), The Forms of Capital. In: J.G. Richardson (Ed.), *Handbook of Theory and Research for the Sociology of Education*. Greenwood Press, Westport, CT, 241–258.

Boyer, George R. and Timothy J. Hatton (2002), New Estimates of British Unemployment, 1870–1913. *The Journal of Economic History* 62(3), 643–675.

Broadberry, Stephen N. (1998), How Did the United States and Germany Overtake Britain? A Sectoral Analysis of Comparative Productivity Levels, 1870–1990. *Journal of Economic History* 58(2), 375–407.

Brummert, Raoul (1963), Henkilökohtaisten tulojen jakautumisesta Suomessa. *Kansantaloudellinen aikakauskirja* 59, 235–265.

Burr, Irving W. (1942), Cumulative frequency functions. *Annals of Mathematical Statistics* 13, 215–232.

Burt, R.S. (1992), *Structural Holes. The Social Structure of Competition*. Harvard University Press, Cambridge.

Böckerman, Petri and Roope Uusitalo (2005), *Union Membership and the Erosion of the Ghent System: Lessons from Finland. Palkansaajien tutkimuslaitos/Labour Institute for Economic Research, Discussion Papers 213.* Labour Institute for Economic Research, Helsinki.

Cameron, Rondo (1989), *A Concise Economic History of the World: From Paleolithic Times to the Present.* Oxford University Press, New York.

Cantwell, John (1989), The changing form of multinational enterprise expansion in the twentieth century. In: Alice Teichova, Maurice Lévy-Leboyer and Helga Nussbaum (Eds.), *Historical studies in international corporate business.* Cambridge University Press, Cambridge, 15–28.

Carreras, Albert and Concepción García-Iglesias (2005), Un siglo y medio de velocidad de circulación del dinero en España. *Revista de Historia Económica (Under revision).*

Carreras, Albert and Concepción García-Iglesias (2003), The Long-Run Behaviour of the Income Velocity of Money in Spain, 1850–2000. *http://www.ics.ul.pt/corpocientifici/plains/iberometrics/index.html.*

Casanova, Julián (2000), Civil wars, revolutions and counter-revolutions in Finland, Spain and Greece (1918–1949): A comparative analysis. *International Journal of Politics, Culture and Society* 13(3), 515–538.

Castells, Manuel and Pekka Himanen (2002), *The Information Society and the Welfare State. The Finnish Model.* Oxford University Press, Oxford.

Chandler, Alfred D. Jr. (1990), *Scale and Scope. The dynamics of industrial capitalism.* The Belknap Press of Harvard University Press, Cambridge, Mass.

Chen, Derek Hung Chiat (2003), *Intertemporal excess burden, bequest motives, and the budget deficit.* World Bank, Washington, D.C.

Clark, Gregory (1987), Productivity Growth without Technical Change in European Agriculture before 1850. *The Journal of Economic History* 47(2), 419–432.

Clark, Gregory (1991), Yields Per Acre in English Agriculture, 1250–1860: Evidence from Labour Inputs. *The Economic History Review* 44(3), 445–460.

Clark, Gregory (1992), The Economics of Exhaustion, the Postan Thesis, and the Agricultural Revolution. *The Journal of Economic History* 52(1), 61–84.

Coleman, James S. (1988), Social Capital in the Creation of Human Capital. *American Journal of Sociology* 94 (Supplement), 95–120.

Cornwall, John and Wendy Cornwall (1994), Growth Theory and Economic Structure. *Economica, New Series* 61(242), 237–251.

Crafts, N. F. R. (1987), Long-term unemployment in Britain in the 1930s. *The Economic History Review* 15(3), 418–432.

Crafts, N. F. R. (1989), Long-term Unemployment and the Wage Equation in Britain, 1925–1939. *Economica* 56(222), 247–254.

Crafts, Nicholas F.R. (1985), *British Economic Growth during the Industrial Revolution.* Clarendon Press, Oxford.

Darby, Michael R. (1976), Three-and-a-half Million U.S. Employees Have Been Mislaid: Or, an Explanation of Unemployment, 1934–1941. *The Journal of Political Economy* 84(1), 1–16.

Daveri, Francesco and Olmo Silva (2004), Not only Nokia: what Finland tells us about new economy growth. *Economic Policy* 19(38), 117–163.

Davies, Norman (1997), *Europe. A History.* Pimlico / Oxford University Press, Oxford.

Davis, Gerald F. and Mark S. Mizruchi (1999), The Money Center Cannot Hold: Commercial Banks in the U.S. System of Corporate Governance. *Administrative Science Quarterly* 44(2), 215–239.

Easterly, William (2001), *The Elusive Quest for Growth. Economists' Adventures and Misadventures in the Tropics.* The MIT Press, Cambridge MA.

Eichengreen, Barry (1997), *Globalizing Capita.* Princeton University Press, Princeton.

Eichengreen, Barry and Timothy Hatton, Eds. (1988), *Interwar Unemployment in International Perspective.* Kluwer Academic Publisher, London.

Eloranta, Jari (1997), Public Sector Development in Sweden and Finland in the 19th and 20th Centuries: Growth Studies Comparisons. In: Jari Eloranta (Ed.), *Nordiska national räkenskaper – Workshop 2 i Järvenpää 20–22 september 1996.* University of Jyväskylä, Department of History, Jyväskylä, 111–134.

Eloranta, Jari (2002), *The Demand for External Security by Domestic Choices: Military Spending as an Impure Public Good among Eleven European States, 1920–1938.* History and Civilisation. Florence, European University Institute.

Eloranta, Jari (2003), National Defense. In: Joel Mokyr (Ed.), *The Oxford Encyclopedia of Economic History.* The Oxford University Press, Oxford.

Eloranta, Jari (2004), *Warfare and Welfare? Understanding 19th and 20th Century Central Government Spending.* Coventry, University of Warwick.

Eloranta, Jari and Jari Ojala (2005), Converta. A Finnish Conduit in the East–West Trade. In: Jari Eloranta and Jari Ojala (Eds.), *East–West Trade and Cold War.* Studies in Humanities, University of Jyväskylä, Jyväskylä.

Engerman, Stanley L. (1996), Economic History and Old Age. *The Journal of Economic History* 56(1), 1–4.

Eriksson, Tor (1991), Työmarkkinat, niiden tasapaino, työmarkkinajärjestöt ja tulopolitiikka. In: Heikki Loikkanen and Jukka Pekkarinen (Eds.), *Suomen kansantalous. Instituutiot, rakenne ja kehitys (2nd ed.).* WSOY, Helsinki, 191–213.

Esping-Andersen, Gøsta (1985), *Politics against Markets. The Social Democratic Road to Power*. Princeton University Press, Princeton.

Esping-Andersen, Gøsta (1990), *The Three Worlds of Welfare Capitalism*. Polity, Cambridge.

Esping-Andersen, Gösta and Walter Korpi (1984), *From poor relief towards institutional welfare states: the development of Scandinavian social policy*. Inst. för social forskning, Stockholm.

ETLA (2005), *Suhdanne NRO 3/2005 (in Finnish)*. The Research Institute of the Finnish Economy ETLA, Helsinki.

Expert Group (2001), *Expert Group on Household Income Statistics (The Canberra Group): Final Report and Recommendations*, Ottawa.

Feinstein, Charles H., Peter Temin and Gianni Toniolo (1997), *The European Economy Between the Wars*. Oxford University Press, Oxford.

Fellman, Susanna (2000), *Uppkomsten av en direktörsprofession. Industriledarnas utbildning och karriär i Finland 1900–1975*. Finska Vetenskaps-societen, Helsingfors.

Ferguson, Niall (2001), *The cash nexus: money and power in the modern world, 1700–2000*. Basic Books, New York.

Finnish Economic Papers (1996/1), *Special Issue "The Finnish Economic Crises of the 1990s"*, Helsinki.

Fitzgerald, Deborah (2003), *Every Farm a Factory: The Industrial Ideal in American Agriculture*. Yale University Press, New Haven.

Fogel, Robert William (1972), Current Directions in Economic History. *The Journal of Economic History* 32(1), 1–2.

Foster, Lucia, John Haltiwanger and C. J. Krizan (2002), *The Link between Aggregate and Micro Productivity Growth: Evidence from Retail Trade*. Working Paper, NBER.

Fougstedt, Gunnar (1948), Inkomstens fördelning i Finland. *Ekonomiska Samfundets Tidskrift* 3(1), 248–273.

Friedman, Milton (1956), The Quantity Theory of Money: A Restatement. In: Milton Friedman (Ed.), *Studies in Quantity Theory*. Chicago University Press, Chicago.

Friedman, Milton and Anna J. Schwartz (1963), *A Monetary History of the United States, 1867–1960*. Princeton University Press, Princeton.

García-Iglesias, Concepción and Juha Kilponen (2004), Trends, Cycles and Economic Growth in the Nordic Countries during the Classical Gold Standard Period. *5th World Cliometrics Congress*. Cliometric Society, Venice.

Gerschenkron, Alexander (1962), *Economic Backwardness in Historical Perspective. A Book of Essays*. The Belknap Press of Harvard University Press, Cambridge, Mass.

Glaman, Kristof (1974), European Trade 1500–1700. In: Carlo M. Cipolla (Ed.), *The Fontana Economic History of Europe, II: The Sixteenth and Seventeenth Centuries*. Fontana, London 441–443.

Gleditsch, K. (2000), *Polity IIID database*, K. Gleditsch [producer]. 2000.

Gordon, Robert J. (2004), *Why was Europe Left at the Station When America's Productivity Locomotive Departed?* Working Papers, NBER.

Gottschalk, Peter and Timothy M. Smeeding (2000), Empirical evidence on income inequality in industrialized countries. In: Anthony B. Atkinson and François Bourguignon (Eds.), *Handbook of Income Distribution*. North-Holland, Amsterdam, 261–307.

Grytten, Ola Honningdal (1995), The Scale of Norwegian Interwar Unemployment in International Perspective. *Scandinavian Economic History Review* 43(2), 226–250.

Haapala, Pertti (1989), *Sosiaalihistoria. Johdatus tutkimukseen*. Suomen historiallinen seura, Helsinki.

Haataja, Kyösti (1949), *Maanjaot ja tulojärjestelmä*. Suomalainen lakimiesyhdistys, Helsinkin.

Haatanen, Pekka and Kyösti Suonoja (1992), *Suuriruhtinaskunnasta hyvinvointivaltioon, Sosiaali- ja terveysministeriö 75 vuotta*. VAPK-kustannus, Helsinki.

Hallberg, Annagreta (1959), *Tjärexport och tjärhandelskompanierna under stormaktstiden*. SLSF, Ekenäs

Hannikainen, Matti (2004), *Rakentajat suhdanteissa. Palkat, työttömyys ja työmarkkinakäytännöt Helsingin rakennustoiminnassa 1930-luvun laman aikana*. Suomen Tiedeseura/Finnish Society of Science and Letters, Helsinki.

Harmaja, Laura (1934), Välittömän verotuksen uudistaminen ja perheellisten verotus. *Kansantaloudellinen aikakauskirja* 30, 235–249.

Harrison, Mark (2002), Coercion, compliance, and the collapse of the Soviet command economy. *Economic History Review* LV(3), 397–433.

Hart, Robert A. (2001), Hours and Wages in the Depression. *Explorations in Economic History* 38(4), 478–502.

Hartwell, Ronald M. (1973), The Service Revolution: The Growth of Services in Modern Economy. In: Carlo M. Cipolla (Ed.), *The Fontana Economic History of Europe: The Industrial Revolution*. Fontana/Collins, Glasgow.

Heikkinen, Sakari (1994), *Suomeen ja maailmalle. Tullilaitoksen historia*. Tullihallitus, Helsinki.

Heikkinen, Sakari (1997), *Labour and the Market. Workers, Wages and Living Standards in Finland, 1850–1913*. Finnish Society of Sciences and Letters/Finnish Academy of Science and Letters, Helsinki.

Heikkinen, Sakari (2000), *Paper for the World. The Finnish Paper Mills' Association – Finnpap 1918–1996*. Otava Publishing Company Ltd., Helsinki.

Heikkinen, Sakari and Riitta Hjerppe (1987), The Growth of Finnish Industry in 1860–1913. Causes and Linkages. *The Journal of European Economic History* 16(2), 227–244.

322

Heikkinen, Sakari and Antti Kuusterä (2001), Finnish Economic Crises in the 20th Century. In: Jorma Kalela (Ed.), *Down from the heavens, up from the ashes. The Finnish economic crisis of the 1990s in the light of economic and social research* Government Institute for Economic Research, Helsinki, 25–51.

Hietala, Marjatta (1987), *Services and Urbanization at the Turn of the Century. The Diffusion of Innovations.* Finnish Historical Society, Helsinki.

Hietala, Marjatta (1992), *Innovaatioiden ja kansainvälistymisen vuosikymmenet. Tietoa, taitoa, asiantuntemusta. Helsinki eurooppalaisessa kehityksessä 1875–1917 1.* Suomen Historiallinen Seura, Helsinki.

Hirdman, Yvonne (1997), Social Planning Under Rational Control. Social Engineering in Sweden in the 1930s and 1940s. In: Pauli Kettunen and Hanna Eskola (Eds.), *Models, Modernity and the Myrdals.* The Renvall Institute for Area and Cultural Studies, University of Helsinki, Helsinki.

Hirschman, Albert O. (1970), *Exit, Voice, and Loyalty. Responses to Decline in Firms, Organizations, and States.* Harvard University Press, Cambridge, Mass. and London.

Hirvilahti, Jon (1993), *Ensimmäisesta maailmansodasta toiseen kultakantaan. Katsaus kelluvien valuuttakurssien ajanjaksoon 1914–1925 (Discussion Paper 7/93).* Bank of Finland, Helsinki.

Hjerppe, Reino (2003), *Social capital and economic growth revisited* Government Institute for Economic Research, Helsinki

Hjerppe, Riitta (1979), *Suurimmat yritykset Suomen teollisuudessa.* Finska vetenskaps-societeten, Helsinki.

Hjerppe, Riitta (1988), *Suomen talous 1860–1985: Kasvu ja rakennemuutos.* Suomen Pankki, Helsinki.

Hjerppe, Riitta (1989), *The Finnish Economy 1860–1985. Growth and Structural Change. Studies on Finland's Economic Growth XIII.* Bank of Finland Publications, Helsinki.

Hjerppe, Riitta (1996a), *Finland's Historical National Accounts 1860–1994: Calculation Methods and Statistical Tables.* Kopi-Jyvä Oy, Jyväskylä.

Hjerppe, Riitta (1996b), Slow Turning into Industrialisation in Finland. In: János Buza, Tamás Csató and Sándor Gyimesi (Eds.), *Challenges of Economic History. Essays in Honour of Iván T. Berend.* University of Economics, Budapest.

Hjerppe, Riitta (1997a), Jos ei voi ottaa, täytyy lainata – Suomen valtion velka sotien välisenä aikana. *Kansantaloudellinen aikakauskirja* 93(1), 11–20.

Hjerppe, Riitta (1997b), Kasvututkimus – historiaa ja nykypäivää. In: Risto Lehtonen (Ed.), *Taloushistorian tutkimusta ennen ja nyt – 100 vuotta Tekla Hultinen väitöksestä.* Tilastokeskus, Helsinki.

Hjerppe, Riitta (2001), The Convergence of Labour Productivity. In: Hans Kruger Larsen (Ed.), *Convergence? Industrialisation of Denmark, Finland and Sweden, 1870–1940.* The Finnish Society of Sciences and Letters, Helsinki.

Hjerppe, Riitta (2004), Monikansallisten yritysten tulo Suomeen ennen toista maailmansotaa. *Kansantaloudellinen aikakauskirja* 100(3), 216–238.

Hjerppe, Riitta and Juha-Antti Lamberg (2000), Economic Change in Finland after Russian rule. In: Alice Teichova (Ed.), *Economic Change and the National Question in the 20th Century Europe.* Cambrigde University Press, Cambrigde.

Hjerppe, Riitta and John Lefgren (1974), Long-run trends in Finland's income distribution 1881–1967. *Kansantaloudellinen aikakauskirja* 46(5), 117–119.

Hodrick, Robert J. and Edward C. Prescott (1997), Postwar U.S. business cycles: An empirical investigation. *Journal of Money, Credit and Banking* 29(1), 1–16.

Hoffman, Kai (1980), *Suomen sahateollisuuden kasvu, rakenne ja rahoitus.* Finska vetenskaps-societeten, Ekenäs.

Holmström, Bengt and John Roberts (1998), The Boundaries of the Firm Revisited,. *The Journal of Economic Perspectives* 12(4), 73–94.

Hyytinen, Ari and Petri Rouvinen (2005), *Mistä talouskasvu syntyy?* Taloustieto Oy, Helsinki.

Häikiö, Martti (1997), *Satoa ja katoa Hankkijan saralla: Hankkijan ja Noveran historia 1955–1992.* Kirjayhtymä, Helsinki.

Häikiö, Martti (2001a), *Nokia Oyj:n historia 1. Fuusio. Yhdistymisen kautta suomalaiseksi monialayritykseksi 1865–1982.* Edita, Helsinki.

Häikiö, Martti (2001b), *Nokia Oyj:n historia 2. Sturm und Drang. Suurkaupoilla eurooppalaiseksi elektroniikkayritykseksi 1983–1991.* Edita, Helsinki.

Häikiö, Martti (2001c), *Nokia Oyj:n historia 3. Globalisaatio. Telekommunikaation maailmanvalloitus 1992–2000.* Edita, Helsinki.

Häkkinen, Antti and Jarmo Peltola (2001), On the Social History of Employment, Unemployment and Poverty in Finland 1860–2000. In: Jorma Kalela, Jaakko Kiander, Ullamaija Kivikuru, Heikki A. Loikkanen and Jussi Simpura (Eds.), *Down from the heavens, up from the ashes. The Finnish Economic Crisis in the Light of Economic and Social Research.* Valtion taloudellinen tutkimuskeskus, Helsinki, 309–345.

Hämynen, Tapio and Leena K. Lahti (1983), *Sodanjälkeinen asutustoiminta Suomessa.* Joensuun korkeakoulu, Joensuu.

Högberg, Staffan (1969), *Utrikeshandel och sjöfart på 1700-talet. Stapelvaror i svensk export och import 1738–1808.* Bonnier, Stockholm.

Ihamuotila, Risto (1972), *Productivity and aggregate production functions in the Finnish agricultural sector 1950–1969.* Maatalouden taloudellinen tutkimuslaitos, Helsinki.

Ikonen, Vappu and Matti Valkonen (1987), Milloin ja miksi Suomi teollistui eri kirjoittajien mukaan. *Kansantaloudellinen aikakauskirja* 83(3), 309–313.

Jakobson, Max (1980), *Veteen piirretty viiva*. Otava, Helsinki.

Jakobson, Max (1984), *Finland survived: an account of the Finnish–Soviet winter war, 1939–1940*. Otava Pub. Co., Helsinki.

Jalava, Jukka (2004), Electrifying and digitalising the Finnish manufacturing industry: Historical notes on diffusion and productivity. In: Sakari Heikkinen and Jan Luiten van Zanden (Eds.), *Explorations in Economic Growth*. Aksant Academic Publishers.

Jalava, Jukka (2006), Catching up with the Technology Frontier: Finnish Manufacturing Productivity, 1975–2003, *Scandinavian Economic History Review* (54) 1, 47–63.

Jalava, Jukka, Sakari Heikkinen and Riitta Hjerppe (2002), *Technology and Structural Change: Productivity in the Finnish Manufacturing Industries, 1925–2000 (Working Paper No. 34, December)*. Transformation, Integration and Globalization Economic Research (TIGER), Helsinki.

Jalava, Jukka and Matti Pohjola (2004), Työn tuottavuus Suomessa vuosina 1900–2003 ja sen kasvuprojektioita vuosille 2004–2030. *Kansantaloudellinen aikakauskirja* 100(4), 355–370.

Jalava, Jukka and Matti Pohjola (2005), *ICT as a Source of Output and Productivity Growth in Finland (Discussion Paper No. 52, February)*. Helsinki Center of Economic Research (HECER), Helsinki

Jalava, Jukka, Matti Pohjola, Antti Ripatti and Jouko Vilmunen (2006), Biased Technical Change and Capital-Labour Substitution in Finland, 1902–2003, *Topics in Macroeconomics* (6) 1, Article 8.

Jalonen, Olli-Pekka and Unto Vesa (1992), Something old, something new, something borrowed, something blue: Finland's defence policy in a changing security environment. *Cooperation and Conflict* 27(4), 377–395.

Julkunen, Raija (1990), Women in the Welfare State. In: Merja Manninen and Päivi Setälä (Eds.), *The Lady with the Bow. The Story of Finnish Women*. Otava, Helsinki, 140–160.

Junnila, Tuure (1970), *Devalvaatiosta devalvaatioon*. WSOY, Porvoo–Helsinki.

Jussila, Heikki (1987), *Spatial Diffusion of Modernization. A study of farm mechanization in Finland at regional and local levels*. University of Oulu, Research Institute of Northern Finland, Oulu.

Jutikkala, Eino (1953), The Distribution of Wealth in Finland in 1800. *Scandinavian Economic History Review* 1(1), 81–103.

Jutikkala, Eino (1958), *Suomen talonpojan historia*, Turku.

Jäntti, Markus, Juho Saari and Juhana Vartiainen (2005), *Combining growth with equity: The case of Finland, Working Paper XX. Background paper prepared for the 2005 World Development Report*. WIDER and World Bank, Helsinki.

Jääskeläinen, Jari (2001), *Klusteri tieteen ja politiikan välissä. Teollisuuspolitiikasta yhteiskuntapolitiikkaan (Clusters – Between Science and Policy. From Industry Policy to Social Policy)*. Taloustieto Oy, Helsinki.

Kalela, Jorma (1989), *Työttömyys 1900-luvun suomalaisessa yhteiskuntapolitiikassa*. Valtion painatuskeskus/Työvoimaministeriö, Helsinki.

Kangas, Olli (1991), *The Politics of Social Rights. Studies on the Dimensions of Sickness Insurance in OECD Countries*. Stockholms universitet, Stockholm.

Karonen, Petri (2004), *Patruunat ja poliitikot. Yritysjohtajat taloudellisina ja poliittisina toimijoina Suomessa 1600–1920*. SKS, Helsinki.

Kaukiainen, Yrjö (1980), Suomen asuttaminen. In: Eino Jutikkala, Yrjö Kaukiainen and Sven-Erik Åström (Eds.), *Suomen taloushistoria I*. Tammi, Helsinki 95–114.

Kaukiainen, Yrjö (1991), *Sailing into Twilight. Finnish Shipping in an Age of Transport Revolution, 1860–1914*. Suomen Historiallinen Seura, Helsinki.

Kaukiainen, Yrjö (1993), *A History of Finnish Shipping*. Routledge, London and New York.

Kaukiainen, Yrjö (1994), Owners and Masters: Management and Managerial Skills in the Finnish Ocean – Going Merchant Fleet, c. 1840–1880. *Research in Maritime History* 6(1), 49–66.

Kaukiainen, Yrjö and Pirkko Leino-Kaukiainen (1992), *Navigare necesse. Merenkulkulaitos 1917–1992*. Merenkulkuhallitus, Helsinki.

Kettunen, Pauli (1986), *Poliittinen liike ja sosiaalinen kollektiivisuus. Tutkimus sosialidemokratiasta ja ammattiyhdistysliikkeestä Suomessa 1918–1930*. Suomen Historiallinen Seura, Helsinki.

Kettunen, Pauli (1994), *Suojelu, suoritus, subjekti. Tutkimus työsuojelusta teollistuvan Suomen yhteiskunnallisissa ajattelu- ja toimintatavoissa*. Suomen Historiallinen Seura, Helsinki.

Kettunen, Pauli (1997), *Työjärjestys. Tutkielmia työn ja tiedon poliittisesta historiasta*. Tutkijaliitto, Helsinki.

Kettunen, Pauli (2001), The Nordic Welfare State in Finland. *Scandinavian Journal of History* 26(3), 226–247.

Kettunen, Pauli (2004), The Nordic Model and Consensual Competitiveness in Finland. In: Anna-Maija Castrén, Markku Lonkila and Matti Peltonen (Eds.), *Between Sociology and History. Essays on Microhistory, Collective Action, and Nation-Building*. SKS / Finnish Literature Society, Helsinki, 289–309.

Kettunen, Pauli (2006), Power of International Comparison – A Perspective on the Making and Challenging of the Nordic Welfare State. In: Niels Finn Christiansen, Klaus Petersen, Nils Edling and Per Haave (Eds.), *The Nordic Model of Welfare – a Historical Reappraisal*. Museum Tusculanum Press, Copenhagen, 31–65.

324

Kiander, Jaakko, Outi Kröger and Antti Romppainen (2005), *Talouden rakenteet 2005*. Valtion taloudellinen tutkimuskeskus, Helsinki.

Kilpi, O. K. (1913), *Suomen ammatissa toimiva väestö ja sen yhteiskunnalliset luokat vuosina 1815/1875. (1) Maaseutu*. Kansantaloudellinen yhdistys, Helsinki.

Kilponen, Juha (1992), *Korot, valuuttakurssiodotukset ja rahapolitiikan itsenäisyys (Pro Gradu Master Thesis)*. Joensuu.

Kiviniemi, Jaakko and Olli Näri (1987), Viljankorjuu. In: Olli Näri (Ed.), *Koneellistuva maataloutemme – Mechanization of Finnish Agriculture*. Vakola, Vaasa, 209–224.

Kocka, Jürgen (1999), *Industrial Culture & Bourgeois Society. Business, Labor, and Bureaucracy in Modern Germany*, New York.

Kola, Jukka (1998), EU:n maatalouspolitiikan muutospaineet, teknologinen kehitys ja Suomen maatalous. In: Aarne Pehkonen and Heikki Mäkinen (Eds.), *Teknologian mahdollisuudet maataluden kehittämisessä*. Helsingin yliopisto, maa- ja kotitalousteknologian laitos, Helsinki.

Komiteanmietintö (1940), *Tutkimuksia kansanravitsemustilan parantamiseksi (Komiteanmietintö 1940:5)*. Valtioneuvosto, Helsinki.

Komlos, John (1992), Interdisciplinary Approaches to Historical Analysis: The Uneasy Waltz of Economics and History. In: Peter Karsten and John Modell (Eds.), *Theory, Method and Practice in Social and Cultural History*. New York University Press, New York.

Korkman, Sixten (1987), Devaluation Policy and Employment. In: Claes-Henric Sivén (Ed.), *Unemployment in Europe; Analysis and Policy Issues*. Timbro, Stockholm.

Korpisaari, Paavo (1926), *Suomen markka 1914–1925*. WSOY, Helsinki.

Koselleck, Reinhart (1979), *Vergangene Zukunft. Zur Semantik geschichtlicher Zeiten*. Suhrkamp, Frankfurt am Main.

Koskinen, Seppo, Tuija Martelin, Irma-Leena Notkola, Veijo Notkola and Kari Pitkänen, Eds. (1994), *Suomen väestö*. Gaudeamus, Helsinki.

Kosonen, Pekka (1993), The Finnish model and the welfare state in crisis. In: Pekka Kosonen (Ed.), *The Nordic Welfare State as a Myth and as Reality*. The Renvall Institute, University of Helsinki, Helsinki, 45–46.

Kosonen, Pekka (1998), *Pohjoismaiset mallit murroksessa*. Vastapaino, Tampere.

Krantz, Olle (2000), *Swedish Historical National Accounts 1800–1998. Aggregated Output Series (Manuscript)*.

Krantz, Olle (2001), Industrialisation in Three Nordic Countries: A Long-Term Quantitative View. In: Hans Kruger Larsen (Ed.), *Convergence? Industrialisation of Denmark, Finland and Sweden, 1870–1940*. The Finnish Society of Sciences and Letters, Helsinki.

Kuhmonen, Tuomas (1996), *Maatalouden alueellinen rakennekehitys ja rakennepolitiikka*. Finnish Regional Research (FAR), Sonkajärvi.

Kuisma, Markku (1993), *Keskusvalta, virkavalta, rahavalta. Valtio, virkamiehet ja teollinen kehitys Suomessa 1740–1940. Hallinto rahan, julkisuuden ja Venäjän paineessa.*, Helsinki.

Kuisma, Markku (1997), *Kylmä sota, kuuma öljy. Neste, Suomi ja kaksi Eurooppaa*. WSOY, Helsinki.

Kuisma, Markku (2004), *Kahlittu raha, kansallinen kapitalismi: Kansallis-Osake-Pankki 1940–1995*. Suomalaisen Kirjallisuuden Seura, Helsinki.

Kupari, Pekka and Jouni Välijärvi, Eds. (2005), *Osaaminen kestävällä pohjalla. Pisa 2003 Suomessa*. Koulutuksen tutkimuslaitos, Jyväskylä.

Kuusi, Pekka (1964), *Social Policy for the Sixties. A Plan for Finland*. Finnish Social Policy Association, Helsinki.

Kuusterä, Antti (1994), The Finnish Banking System in Broad Outline from the 1860s to the mid-1980s. In: Manfred Pohl and Sabine Freitag (Eds.), *Handbook on the History of European Banks*. Edward Elgar, Aldershot, 135–181.

Kuusterä, Antti (1997), Markan matkassa – Suomen rahajärjestelmän historiaa 1840–1997. *Kansantaloudellinen aikakauskirja/Finnish Economic Journal* 93(2), 285–305.

Kuznets, Simon (1966), *Modern Economic Growth. Rate Structure and Spread*. Yale University Press, New Haven and London.

Köppä, Tapani (1989), Maatalouspolitiikan arvot ja maaseudun muutos. In: Pertti Suhonen (Ed.), *Suomi, muutosten yhteiskunta*. WSOY, Juva, 191–204.

Laitinen, Erkki, Ed. (1995), *Rintamalta raivioille: sodanjälkeinen asutustoiminta 50 vuotta*. Atena, Jyväskylä.

Lamberg, Juha-Antti (1998), Economic Interest Groups in the Finnish Foreign Trade Policy Decision-Making in the Early Independence Years. *Scandinavian Economic History Review* 46(2), 79–96.

Lamberg, Juha-Antti (2001), Isäntien metsäteollisuus – Metsäliitto-ryhmittymä 1934–1998. In: Juha Näsi, Juha-Antti Lamberg, Jari Ojala and Pasi Sajasalo (Eds.), *Metsäteollisuusyritysten strategiset kehityspolut. Kilpailu, keskittyminen ja kasvu pitkällä aikavälillä*. Metsäalan tutkimusohjelma Wood Wisdom, Helsinki.

Lamberg, Juha-Antti and Jari Ojala (2003), The Institutional Environment in Retrospective: The Finnish Pulp and Paper Industry 1945–1992 (manuscript).

Lamberg, Juha-Antti and Jari Ojala (2005), The Nordic Forest Industry in Retrospect: An Introduction. *Scandinavian Economic History Review* 53(1), 7–18.

Lamberg, Juha-Antti and Jari Ojala (2006), Evolution of Competitive Strategies in Global Forestry Industries: Introduction. In: Juha-Antti Lamberg, Juha Näsi, Jari Ojala and Pasi Sajasalo (Eds.), *The Evolution of Competitive Strategies in Global Forestry Industries: Comparative perspective*. Springer, Dordrecht, 1–29.

Lauck, Jon (2000), *American Agriculture and the Problem of Monopoly: The Political Economy of Grain Belt Farming, 1953–1980*. University of Nebraska Press, Lincoln.

Lebergott, Stanley (1964), *Manpower in Economic Growth. The United States Record since 1800*. McGraw-Hill Book Company, New York.

Lees, Lynn Hollen (2000), Urban Networks. In: Martin Daunton (Ed.), *The Cambridge Urban History of Britain III (1840–1950)*. Cambridge University Press, Cambridge.

Lewis, W. Arthur (1954), Economic Development with Unlimited Supplies of Labour. *The Manchester School of Economic and Social Studies* 22, 139–191.

Lilja, Reija and Jaakko Pehkonen (2002), Työmarkkinoiden kehityspiirteet ja toiminta. In: Heikki A. Loikkanen, Jukka Pekkarinen and Pentti Vartia (Eds.), *Kansantaloutemme – rakenteet ja muutos*. Taloustieto Oy, Helsinki, 291–320.

Lin, Nan (2001), *Social Capital: A Theory of Social Structure*. Cambridge University Press, Port Chester, NY.

Lindberg, Valter (1934), *Utvecklingen av den allmänna inkomstskatten i Finlands statsskattesystem, PhD thesis*. University of Helsinki, Helsinki.

Lindert, Peter H. (1989), Response to Debt Crisis: What Is Different about the 1980s? In: B. J. Eichengreen and Peter H. Lindert (Eds.), *The international debt crisis in historical perspective*. MIT Press, Cambridge, Mass.

Lindert, Peter H. (1994), The Rise of Social Spending, 1880–1930. *Explorations in Economic History* 31(1), 1–37.

Lindert, Peter H. (2004), *Growing Public. Social Spending and Economic Growth Since the Eighteenth Century*. Cambridge University Press, Cambridge.

Lindsey, James K. (1999), Models for Repeated Measurements, number 19. *Oxford Statistical Science Series, 2 ed.* Oxford University Press, Oxford.

Luoma-aho, Vilma (2005), *Faith-holders as social capital of Finnish public organisations* Univesity of Jyväskylä, Jyväskylä.

Luukko, Armas (1967), *Suomen historia 1617–1721*. WSOY, Porvoo

Maatalouslaskenta (1992), *Maatalouslaskenta 1990 (Agricultural cencus 1990)*. Maatilahallitus, Helsinki.

Maataloustilastollinen (2002), *Maataloustilastollinen vuosikirja 2002*. Tilastokeskus, Helsinki.

Maddison, Angus (1991), *Dynamic Forces in Capitalist Development*. Oxford University Press, New York.

Maddison, Angus (2001), *The World Economy: A Millenium Perspective*. OECD, Paris.

Maddison, Angus (2003), *The World Economy: Historical Statistics*. OECD Development Centre, Paris.

Majander, Mikko (2004), *Pohjoismaa vai kansandemokratia? Sosiaalidemokraatit, kommunistit ja Suomen kansainvälinen asema 1944–51*. SKS, Helsinki.

Maliranta, Mika (2003), *Micro Level Dynamics of Productivity Growth. An Empirical Analysis of the Great Leap in Finnish Manufacturing Productivity in 1975–2000 (available at http://www.etla.fi/files/1075_micro_level_dynamics. pdf)*. Helsinki, Helsinki School of Economics.

Maliranta, Mika (2005), R&D, International Trade and Creative Destruction – Empirical Findings from Finnish Manufacturing Industries. *Journal of Industry, Competition and Trade* 5(1), 27–58.

Maliranta, Mika and Petri Rouvinen (2004), ICT and Business Productivity: Finnish Micro-Level Evidence. In: OECD (Ed.), *The Economic Impact of ICT; Measurement, Evidence and Implications*. OECD, Paris.

Manninen, Ari T. (2002), *Elaboration of NMT and GSM standards. From idea to market* University of Jyväskylä, Jyväskylä.

Mannio, Pekka, Eero Vaara and Pekka Ylä-Anttila (2003), Introduction. In: Pekka Mannio, Eero Vaara and Pekka Ylä-Anttila (Eds.), *Our Path Abroad. Exploring Post-war Internationalization of Finnish Corporations*. Taloustieto Oy, Helsinki.

Mansner, Markku (1981), *Työnantajaklubista keskusliitoksi. Suomen Työnantajain Keskusliitto ja sen edeltäjä Suomen Yleinen Työnantajaliitto 1907–1940*. Helsingin yliopisto, Helsinki.

Margo, Robert A. (1993), Employment and Unemployment in the 1930s. *The Journal of Economic Perspectives* 7(2), 41–59.

Markkola, Pirjo (1990), Women in Rural Society in the 19th and 20th Centuries. In: Merja Manninen and Päivi Setälä (Eds.), *The Lady with the Bow. The Story of Finnish Women*. Otava, Helsinki, 17–29.

Mattila, Aarne (1969), *Työmarkkinasuhteiden murros Suomessa. Tutkimus työntekijäin pyrkimyksistä osallistua työehtojen määräämiseen 1880-luvulta vuoden 1905 suurlakkoon*. Suomen Historiallinen Seura, Helsinki.

Mattila, Markku (1999), *Kansamme parhaaksi. Rotuhygienia Suomessa vuoden 1935 sterilointilakiin asti*. Suomen Historiallinen Seura, Helsinki.

Mauranen, Tapani (1981), Porvarista kauppiaaksi – kauppiaan yhteiskunnallinen asema 1800-luvun jälkipuoliskolla. In: Yrjö Kaukiainen, Per Schybergson, Hannu Soikkanen and Tapani Mauranen (Eds.), *När samhället förändras – Kun yhteiskunta muuttuu*. Suomen Historiallinen Seura, Helsinki.

McDonald, James B. (1984), Some generalized functions for the size distribution of income. *Econometrica* 52(3), 647–663.

Meyer, John W. and Brian Rowan (1983), Institutionalized Organizations: Formal Strucuture as Myth and Ceremony. *American Journal of Sociology* 83(2), 340–363.

Michelsen, Karl-Erik (1993), *Valtio, teknologia, tutkimus: VTT ja kansallisen tutkimusjärjestelmän kehitys*. Valtion teknillinen tutkimuskeskus, Espoo.

Michelsen, Karl-Erik (1999), *Viides sääty. Insinöörit suomalaisessa yhteiskunnassa*. SKS, Vammala.

Michelsen, Karl-Erik and Tuomo Särkikoski (2005), *Suomalainen ydinvoimalaitos* Edita, Helsinki.

Mikkola, Anne (1989), *Ulkomaisten korkojen vaikutus lyhyeen markkinakorkoon (Discussion Papers 30/89)*. Bank of Finland, Helsinki.

Milward, A. and S. B. Saul (1977), *The Development of the Economies of Continental Europe, 1850–1914*. Allen and Unwin, London.

Milward, A. and S. B. Saul (1973), *The Economic Development of Continental Europe, 1780–1870*. Allen and Unwin, London.

Mitchell, B. R. (1998), *International Historical Statistics: Europe 1750–1993*. Macmillan Academic and Professional, Basingstoke.

Mizruchi, Mark S. (1982), *The American Corporate Network*. Sage, Beverly Hills, CA.

Mizruchi, Mark S. (1992), *The Structure of Corporate Political Action: Interfirm Relations and Their Consequences*. Harvard University Press, Cambridge, MA.

Mizruchi, Mark S. (1996), What do interlocks do? An analysis, critique and assessment of research on interlocking directorates. *Annual Review of Sociology* 22(1), 271–298.

Mizruchi, Mark S. and Linda Brewster Stearns (1988), A Longitudinal Study of the Formation of Interlocking Directorates. *Administrative Science Quarterly* 33(2), 194–210.

Moen, Eli and Kari Lilja (2001), Constructing Global Corporations: Contrasting National Legacies in the Nordic Forest Industry. In: Glenn Morgan, Peer Hull Kristensen and Richard Whitley (Eds.), *The Multinational Firm. Organizing Across Insitutional and National Divides*. Oxford University Press, Oxford, 97–121.

Mokyr, Joel (1994), Cardwell's Law and the Political Economy of Technological Progress. *Research Policy* 23, 561–574.

Mokyr, Joel (2005a), The Intellectual Origins of Modern Economic Growth. *Journal of Economic History* 65(2), 285–351.

Mokyr, Joel (2005b), Mercantilism, the Enlightenment, and the Industrial Revolution (Forthcoming). In: Ronald Findlay, Rolf Henriksson, Håkan Lindgren and Mats Lundahl (Eds.), *Eli F. Heckscher (1879–1952): A Celebratory Symposium*. MIT Press, Cambridge MA.

Murmann, Johann Peter (2003), *Knowledge and Competitive Advantage: The Coevolution of Firms, Technology, and National Institutions*. Cambridge University Press, Cambridge (Mass.).

Müller, Leos (1998), *The Merchant Houses of Stockholm, c. 1640–1800. A Comparative Study of Early-Modern Entrepreneurial Behaviour*. Uppsala University, Uppsala.

Myllyntaus, Timo (1991), *Electrifying Finland: The Transfer of a New Technology into a Late Industrialising Country*. Macmillan & ETLA, London.

Myllyntaus, Timo, Karl-Erik Michelsen and Timo Herranen (1986), *Teknologinen muutos Suomen teollisuudessa 1885–1920. Metalli-, saha- ja paperiteollisuuden vertailu energiatalouden näkökulmasta*. Finska Vetenskaps-Societeten, Helsinki.

Myrdal, Janken (1985), *Medeltidens åkerbruk. Agrarteknik i Sverige ca 1000 till 1520* Nordiska museet, Stockholm.

Myrdal, Janken (1999), *Det svenska jordbrukets historia (2). Jordbruket under feodalismen 1000–1700* Stockholm.

Myrdal, Janken and Johan Söderberg (1991), *Kontinuitetens dynamik. Agrar ekonomi i 1500-talets Sverige*. Almqvist & Wiksell, Stockholm

Myyrä, Sami and Kyösti Pietola (1999), *Tuottavuuskehitys Suomen maataloudessa vuosina 1987–97*. Agricultural Economics Research Institute Finland, Helsinki.

Mäkelä, Sisko (2001), Northern dimension and family farming. *www.mtk.fi (cited 28th January 2004)*.

Niemelä, Jari (1996), *Lääninlampureista maaseutukeskuksiin: maaseutukeskusten ja niiden edeltäjien maatalousneuvonta 1700-luvulta 1990-luvulle*. Suomen historiallinen seura, Helsinki.

Nordberg, Toivo (1980), *Vuosisata paperiteollisuutta II. Yhtyneet Paperitehtaat Osakeyhtiö 1920–1951*. UPM, Valkeakoski.

North, Douglass C. (1990), *Institutions, Institutional Change and Economic Performance*. Cambridge University Press, Cambridge – New York.

Nummela, Ilkka (1993), *Inter arma silent revisores rationum: toisen maailmansodan aiheuttama taloudellinen rasitus Suomessa vuosina 1939–1952*. Jyväskylän yliopisto, Jyväskylä.

Nurkse, Ragnar (1966), *Problems of Capital Formation in Underdeveloped Countries*. Basil Blackwell, Oxford.

Obstfeld, Maurice and A. M. Taylor (2003), Sovereign Risk, Credibility and the Gold Standard: 1870–1913 versus 1925–31. *The Economic Journal* 113(April), 241–275.

OECD (2003), *National Accounts of OECD Countries, Main Aggregates, Volume I, 1990–2001*. OECD, Paris.

OECD (2004), *PISA Learning for Tomorrow's World First Results from PISA 2003*. OECD, Paris.

Ojala, Jari (1999), *Tehokasta liiketoimintaa Pohjanmaan pikkukaupungeissa. Purjemerenkulun kannattavuus ja tuottavuus 1700–1800-luvulla*. Suomen Historiallinen Seura, Helsinki.

Ojala, Jari (2002), *Trained to be Businessmen or Civil Servants? Succession strategies in 19th-century Finnish family firms*. In: Rolv P. Amdam, Anne E. Hagberg and Knut Sogner (eds.), *5th EBHA Conference (CD-Rom)*. Oslo, Norwegian School of Management BI.

Ojala, Jari (2003), Mitä nyt taloushistoria? *Historiallinen Aikakauskirja* 101(1), 138–145.

Ojala, Jari, Juha-Antti Lamberg, Anna Ahola and Anders Melander (2006), The Ephemera of Success: Strategy, Structure and Performance in the Forestry Industries. In: Juha-Antti Lamberg, Juha Näsi, Jari Ojala and Pasi Sajasalo (Eds.), *The Evolution of Competitive Strategies* in *Global Forestry Industries: Comparative perspectives*. Springer, Dordrecht, 257–286.

Ojala, Lauri and Pekka Saarto (1992), *Merenkulku kansantaloudessa*. Liikenneministeriö, Helsinki.

Oksanen, Heikki and Erkki Pihkala (1975), *Suomen ulkomaankauppa/Finland's foreign trade 1917–1949*. Suomen pankki, Helsinki.

Orru, Marco, Nicole Woolsey Biggart and Gary S. Hamilton (1991), Organizational Isomorphism in East Asia. In: Walter W. Powell and Paul J. DiMaggio (Eds.), *The new institutionalism in organizational analysis*. University of Chicago Press, Chicago.

Paasivirta, Juhani (1984), *Suomi ja Eurooppa 1914–1939*. Kirjayhtymä Helsinki, Hämeenlinna.

Paavonen, Tapani (1998), *Suomalaisen protektionismin viimeinen vaihe. Suomen ulkomaankauppa- ja integraatiopolitiikka 1945–1961*. Suomen Historiallinen Seura, Helsinki.

Paija, Laura (2001a), *Finnish ICT Cluster in the Digital Economy*. Taloustieto, Helsinki.

Paija, Laura (2001b), The ICT cluster: The engine of knowledge-driven growth in Finland. In: OECD (Ed.), *Innovative Clusters – Drivers of National Innovation Systems*. OECD, Paris.

Palan, Ronen, Jason Abbot and Phil Deans (1999), *State Strategies in the Global Political Economy*. Pinter, London and New York.

Parker, Simon C. (2000), Opening a can of worms: the pitfalls of time-series regression analyses of income inequality. *Applied Economics* 32(2), 221–230.

Parviainen, Seija (1988), Valuuttakurssipoliittisen keskustelun vaiheista. *Kansantaloudellinen Aikakauskirja* 83(3), 279–286.

Peacock, Alan T. and Jack Wiseman (1961), *The Growth of Public Expenditures in the United Kingdom*. Princeton University Press, Princeton.

Peltola, Jarmo (1998), Why did the Unemployment Rate Vary? Finnish Interwar Unemployment in a Comparative International Contex. In: Timo Myllyntaus (Ed.), *Economic Crises and Restructuring in History. Experiences of Small Countries*. Scripta Mercaturae Verlag, St. Katharinen, 205–233.

Peltonen, Matti (1990), Metsä, kasvu ja kriisi. Taloushistorian uusia mahdollisuuksia. In: Pekka Ahtiainen, Markku Kuisma, Hannele Kurki, Pauli Manninen, Katariina Mustakallio, Matti Peltonen, Jukka Tervonen and Ilkka Turunen (Eds.), *Historia nyt*. WSOY, Helsinki.

Peltonen, Matti (1992), *Talolliset ja torpparit: vuosisadan vaihteen maatalouskysymys Suomessa*. Suomen historiallinen seura, Helsinki.

Peltonen, Matti, Ed. (2004), *Suomen maatalouden historia II. Kasvun ja kriisien aika 1870-luvulta 1950-luvulle*. Suomalaisen Kirjallisuuden Seura, Helsinki.

Perko, Touko (2005), *Valio ja suuri murros*. Otava, Helsinki.

Petersen, Klaus (2006), Constructing Nordic Welfare? Nordic Social Political Cooperation 1919–1955. In: Niels Finn Christiansen, Klaus Petersen, Nils Edling and Per Haave (Eds.), *The Nordic Model of Welfare – a Historical Reappraisal*. Museum Tusculanum Press, Copenhagen, 67–98.

Peterson, Christer (2001), The Development Paths of Two Nordic Forest Nations, 1950–1992. *Scandinavian Economic History Review* 49(1), 21–40.

Pfeffer, Jeffrey and Gerald R. Salancik (1978), *The External Control of Organizations: a Resource Dependence Perspective*. Harper & Row, Publishers, New York.

Piekkola, Hannu and Kenneth Snellman, Eds. (2005), *Collective Bargaining and Wage Formation. Performance and Challenges*. The Research Institute of the Finnish Economy – Labour Institute for Economic Research, Helsinki.

Pietarinen, Matti and Risto Ranki (1993), *National Industrial Strategy for Finland*. Ministry of Trade and Industry, Helsinki.

Pihkala, Erkki (1969), *Suomen ulkomaankauppa/Finland's foreign trade 1860–1917*. Suomen Pankki, Helsinki.

Pihkala, Erkki (1970), Suomen vaihtotase 1860–1917. *Historiallinen Aikakauskirja* 67(3).

Pihkala, Erkki (1988), Kauppapolitiikka ja ulkomaankauppa 1945–1986. In: Yrjö Kaukiainen, Erkki Pihkala, Kai Hoffman and Maunu Harmo (Eds.), *Sotakorvauksista vapaakauppaan. Kauppa- ja teolliuusministeriön satavuotisjuhlakirja*. Valtion painatuskeskus, Helsinki.

Piketty, Thomas (2003), Income inequality in France, 1901–1998. *Journal of Political Economy* 111, 1004–1042.

Piketty, Thomas and Emmanuel Saez (2003), Income inequality in the United States, 1913–1998. *Quarterly Journal of Economics* 118(1), 1–39.

Pikkarainen, Pentti and Laura Vajanne (1991), *Credibility of Finland's Basket Peg Exchange Rate Regime 1977–1991*. Symposium on Macroeconomic Modeling and Economic Policy, Espoo.

Pipping, Hugo E. (1967), Rahalaitokset 1919–1950. In: Eino Jutikkala, Matti J. Castrén, Hugo E. Pipping and Markku Järvinen (Eds.), *Itsenäisen Suomen taloushistoriaa 1919–1950*. WSOY, Porvoo–Helsinki, 151–161.

PISA (2004), *Learning for Tomorrow's World. First Results from PISA 2003*. Paris, OECD.

Pohjanpalo, Jorma (1978), *100 vuotta Suomen talvimerenkulkua*. Valtion painatuskeskus, Helsinki.

Pohjola, Matti (1994), Nordic Corporatism and Economic Performance: Labour Market Equality at the Expense of Productive Efficiency? In: Timo Kauppinen and Virpi Köykkä (Eds.), *Transformation of the Nordic Industrial Relations in the European Context*. The Finnish Labour Relations Association, Helsinki, 223–241.

Pohjola, Matti (1996), *Tehoton pääoma. Uusi näkökulma taloutemme ongelmiin*. WSOY, Porvoo.

328

Pohjola, Matti, Ed. (1998), *Suomalainen työttömyys*. Taloustieto Oy, Helsinki.

Polanyi, Karl (2001 [1944]), *The Great Transformation. The Political and Economic Origins of Our Time*. Beacon Press, Boston.

Porter, Michael (1980), *Competitive Strategy: Techniques for Analysing Industries and Competitors*. The Free Press / Macmillan Publishing Co., New York.

Porter, Michael (1985), *Competitive advantage. Creating and sustaining superior performance*. Free Press, New York.

Putnam, Robert (1995), Bowling Alone. America's Declining Social Capital. *Journal of Democracy* 6(1), 65–78.

Pyykkönen, Markus (1998), Kotieläintuotannon teknologia. In: Aarne Pehkonen and Heikki Mäkinen (Eds.), *Teknologian mahdollisuudet maatalouden kehittämisessä*. Helsingin yliopisto, maa- ja kotitalousteknologian laitos, Helsinki.

Rahikainen, Marjatta (2001), Ageing Men and Women in the Labour Market. Continuity and Change. *Scandinavian Journal of History* 26(4), 297–314.

Rasila, Viljo , Eino Jutikkala and Anneli Mäkelä-Alitalo, Eds. (2003), *Suomen maatalouden historia 1. Perinteisen maatalouden aika: esihistoriasta 1870-luvulle*. Suomalaisen kirjallisuuden seura, Helsinki.

Reinikainen, Alpo, Lasse Nieminen and Olli Näri (1987), Maatalouskoneiden tarkastus- ja koetustoiminta Suomessa. In: Olli Näri (Ed.), *Koneellistuva maataloutemme – Mechanization of Finnish Agriculture*. Vakola, Vaasa.

Riihelä, Marja, Risto Sullström and Matti Tuomala (2005), *Trends in top income shares in Finland, VATT-research reports XX*. VATT, Helsinki.

Romanainen, Jari (2001), The cluster approach in Finnish technology policy. In: OECD (Ed.), *Innovative Clusters – Drivers of National Innovation Systems*. OECD, Paris.

Romer, Paul (1996), Why, Indeed, in America. *American Economic Review* 85(2), 202–206.

Rossi, Reino (1951), *Suomen Pankin korkopolitiikka vuosina 1914–1938*. Bank of Finland, Helsinki.

Rouvinen, Petri and Pekka Ylä-Anttila (1999), Finnish Clusters and New Industrial Policy Making. In: OECD (Ed.), *Boosting Innovation: The Cluster Approach*. OECD, Paris.

Ruostetsaari, Ilkka (1989), *Energiapolitiikan määräytyminen*. Tampereen yliopisto, Tampere.

Ruttan, Vernon (2002), Productivity Growth in World Agriculture: Sources and Constraints. *Journal of Economic Perspectives* 16(4), 161–184.

Saarinen, Jani (2005), *Innovations and Industrial Performance in Finland 1945–1998*. Almqvist & Wiksell International, Lund.

Saarinen, Oiva (1966), The implementation and result of the Land Acquisition Act. *Suomen asutustoiminnan aikakauskirja* (2), 16–49.

Saez, Emmanuel (2005), Top incomes in the United States and Canada over the twentieth century. *Journal of the European Economic Association* 3(2–3), 402–411.

Salminen, Kari (1993), *Pension Schemes in the Making. A Comparative Study of the Scandinavian Countries*. The Central Pension Security Institute, Helsinki.

Sandler, Todd and Keith Hartley (1995), *The economics of defense*. Cambridge University Press, Cambridge.

Sandler, Todd and Keith Hartley (1999), *The Political Economy of NATO. Past, Present, and into the 21st Century*. Cambridge University Press, New York.

Santamäki-Vuori, Tuire and Seija Parviainen (1996), *The Labour Market in Finland*. Labour Institute for Economic Research, Helsinki.

Satka, Mirja (1995), *Making Social Citizenship. Conceptual practices from the Finnish Poor Law to professional social work*. SoPhi, Jyväskylä.

Sauli, Liisa (1987), *MTK ja Suomen maatalouspolitiikka – Maatalousyhteiskunnasta teollisuusvaltioksi 1950–1980*. Kirjayhtymä, Helsinki.

Savela, Olli (2005), Kulutus pyörittää kansantaloutta. *Tieto&trendit* 1(2).

Schienstock, Gerd and Timo Hämäläinen (2001), *Transformation of the Finnish Innovation System – A Network Approach*. Sitra, Helsinki.

Schultz, T. W. (1941), Economic Effects of Agricultural Programs. *The American Economic Review* 30(5), 127–154.

Schultz, T. W. (1951), The Declining Economic Importance of Agricultural Land. *The Economic Journal* 61(244), 725–740.

Schybergson, Per (1980), Ulkomaankaupan kehitys. In: Eino Jutikkala, Yrjö Kaukiainen and Sven-Erik Åström (Eds.), *Suomen taloushistoria I*. Tammi, Helsinki.

Schybergson, Per (2001), Large Enterprises in Small Countries. In: Hans Kryger Larsen (Ed.), *Convergengence? Industrialisation of Denmark, Finland and Sweden 1870–1940*. The Finnish Society of Sciences and Letters, Helsinki, 97–151.

Senghaas, Dieter (1985), *The European Experience. A Historical Critique of Development Theory*. Berg Publishers, Leamington Spa / Dover, New Hampshire.

Siklos, Pierre L. (1993), Income Velocity and Institutional Change: Some New Time Series Evidence, 1870–1986. *Journal of Money, Credit, and Banking* 25(2), 377–392.

Siltanen, Lulu and Ossi Ala-Mantila (1989), *Maatalouden kokonaislaskelmat 1980–1988*. Agricultural Economics Research Intitute, Finland, Helsinki.

Singh, S. K. and G. S. Maddala (1976), A function for the size distribution of incomes. *Econometrica* 44(5), 963–970.

Sipiäinen, Timo, Matti Ryhänen, Matti Ylätalo, Erik Haggrén and Elina Seppälä (1998), *Maatalousyritysten talous vuosina 1993–2002: EU-jäsenyyden vaikutus tuloihin ja kannattavuuteen*. University of Helsinki, Department of Economics and Management, Helsinki.

Skippari, Mika (2005), *Evolutionary Patterns in Corporate Political Activity. Insights from a Historical Single Case Study.* Tampere University of Technology, Tampere.

Skippari, Mika, Jari Ojala and Juha-Antti Lamberg (2005), Long-Run Consequences of a Radical Change in Business Environment: Dualistic Corporate Cooperation in Finnish Wood-Processing Industry during the 20th Century. *Scandinavian Economic History Review* 53(1), 44–65.

Slagstad, Rune (1998), *De nasjonale strateger.* Pax Forlag A/S, Oslo.

Smith, Adam (1979), *An Inquiry into the Nature and Causes of the Wealth of Nations.* Oxford University Press, Oxford.

Smolander, Jyrki (2000), *Suomalainen oikeisto ja "kansankoti". Kansallisen Kokoomuksen suhtautuminen pohjoismaiseen hyvinvointivaltiomalliin jälleenrakennuskaudelta konsensusajan alkuun.* SKS, Helsinki.

SNA 93 (1993), *System of National Accounts 1993.* United Nations, New York.

Soininen, Arvo M. (1975), *Vanha maataloutemme: maatalous ja maatalousväestö Suomessa perinnäisen maatalouden loppukaudella 1720-luvulta 1870-luvulle.* Suomen maataloustieteellinen seura, Helsinki.

Solantie, Reijo (1988), Climatic conditions for the cultivation of rye with reference to the history of settlement in Finland *Fennoscandia archaeologica* 5, 3–20.

Solow, Robert M. (1985), Insiders and Outsiders in Wage Determination. *The Scandinavian Journal of Economics* 87(2), 411–428.

Sørensen, Øystein and Bo Stråth (1997), Introduction: The Cultural Construction of Norden. In: Øystein Sørensen and Bo Stråth (Eds.), *The Cultural Construction of Norden.* Scandinavian University Press, Oslo, 1–24.

Sosiaalinen Aikakauskirja 1936.

Statistical Yearbook of Finland.

Statistics Finland: Labour Force Survey Ministry of Labour: Employment Service Data.

Statistics Finland (1920–2002), *Statistics on Income and Property, Income and consumption.* Statistics Finland, Helsinki.

Statistics Finland (2006), *Historical National Accounts Database.* Statistics Finland, Helsinki.

Stenius, Henrik (1997), The Good Life is a Life of Conformity: The Impact of Lutheran Tradition on Nordic Political Culture. In: Øystein Sørensen and Bo Stråth (Eds.), *The Cultural Construction of Norden.* Scandinavian University Press, Oslo, 161–171.

Stern, Robert N. and Stephen R. Barley (1996), Organizations and Social Systems: Organization Theory's Neglected Mandate. *Administrative Science Quarterly* 41(1), 146–162.

STPC (1987), *Science and Technology Policy Review 1987.* Science and Technology Policy Council of Finland, Ministry of Education, Helsinki.

STPC (1990), *Review 1990 – Guidelines for Science and Technology Policy in the 1990's.* cience and Technology Policy Council of Finland, Government Printing Centre, Helsinki.

STPC (1993), *Towards an Innovation Society: A Development Strategy for Finland.* Science and Technology Policy Council of Finland, Government Printing Centre, Helsinki.

STPC (1996), *Finland: A Knowledge-based Society.* Science and Technology Policy Council of Finland, Edita Ltd, Helsinki.

STPC (2000), *Review 2000: The Challenge of Knowledge and Know-how (http://www.minedu.fi/tiede_ja_teknologianeovosto/publications).* Science and Technology Policy Council of Finland, Edita Ltd, Helsinki

STPC (2003), *Knowledge, innovation and internationalisation (http://www.minedu.fi/tiede_ja_teknologianeovosto/publications).* Science and Technology Policy Council of Finland, Edita Ltd, Helsinki.

Streeck, Wolfgang (1998), Industrielle Beziehungen in einer internationalisierten Wirtschaft. In: Ulrich Beck (Ed.), *Politik der Globalisierung.* Suhrkamp, Frankfurt am Main, 169–202.

STV (1950–2003), *Suomen tilastollinen vuosikirja (Statistical yearbook of Finland).* Tilastokeskus, Helsinki.

Sukselainen, V. J. (1946), *Perhesuhteet tulo- ja omaisuusverotuksessa,* Forssa.

Suomela, Samuli (1958), *Tuottavuuden kehityksestä Suomen maataloudessa.* Maatalouden taloudellinen tutkimuslaitos, Helsinki.

SVT (1950–2003), *Suomen Virallinen Tilasto III, Maatalous.* Tilastokeskus, Helsinki.

Syrquin, Moshe (1984), Resource Reallocation and Productivity Growth. In: Moshe Syrquin, Lance Taylor and Larry E. Westphal (Eds.), *Structure and Performance – Essays in Honour of Hollis B. Chenery.* Academic Press Inc., Orlando.

Taimio, Hilkka (1986), *Valtion menojen ja valtion julkisten palvelujen kasvu Suomessa 1900-luvun alkupuoliskolla.* Suomen Pankki, Helsinki.

Takagi, Yasuoki (1978), Surplus Labour and Disguised Unemployment. *Oxford Economic Papers* New Series 30, 447–457.

Tanzi, Vito and Ludger Schuknecht (2000), *Public Spending in the 20th Century. A Global Perspective.* Cambridge University Press, New York.

Tarkka, Juha (1984), *Rahapoliittisesta itsenäisyydestä.* Bank of Finland, Helsinki.

Tarkka, Juha (1993), *Raha ja rahapolitiikka.* Gaudeamus, Jyväskylä.

Tauriainen, Juhani (1970), *Kehitysalueiden muuttuva maa-*

330

talous: Tutkimus Itä-, Sisä- ja Pohjois-Suomen maatalouden uudenaikaistumisesta. Helsingin yliopisto, Helsinki.

Tervasmäki, Vilho (1978), *Puolustushallinto sodan ja rauhan aikana. Puolustusministeriön historia II.* Sotatieteen laitos, Hämeenlinna.

Terä, Martti V. and Vilho Tervasmäki (1973), *Puolustushallinnon perustamis- ja rakentamisvuodet 1918–1939. Puolustusministeriön historia I.* Sotatieteen laitos, Helsinki.

Teräs, Kari (2001), *Arjessa ja liikkeessä. Verkostonäkökulma modernisoituviin työelämän suhteisiin 1880–1920.* Suomalaisen Kirjallisuuden Seura, Helsinki.

Thomas, Mark (1988), Labour Market and the Nature of Unemployment. In: Barry Eichengreen and Timothy Hatton (Eds.), *Interwar Unemployment in International Perspective.* Kluwer Academic Publishers, London, 97–148.

Tigerstedt, Örnulf (1952), *Kauppahuone Hackman. Erään vanhan Viipurin kauppiassuvun vaiheet 1790–1879, vol. 2.* Otava, Helsinki

Tilastokatsaus (2003), *Tilastokatsaus IV.* Tilastokeskus, Helsinki.

Tilastokeskus (1979–1992), *Suomen tilastollinen vuosikirja.* Tilastokeskus, Helsinki.

Tilastollisia (1979), *Väestön elinkeino (Population by industry, Central Statistical Office of Finland). Tilastollisia tiedonantoja 63.* Tilastokeskus, Helsinki.

Toivola, Keijo (1992), *Poimintoja teletoimen historiasta. Osa 4: Kertomus Suomen matkaviestinnästä* Tele, matkaviestinverkot, Helsinki.

Turpeinen, Oiva (1996), *Yhdistämme. 200 vuotta historiaa – haasteena tulevaisuus. Lennätinlaitoksesta Telecom Finland oy:ksi* Edita, Helsinki.

Tykkyläinen, Markku and Seppo Kavilo (1991), *Maaseudun asuttaminen ja talouden rakennemuutos Suomessa.* University of Joensuu, Faculty of Social Scieces, Joensuu.

Upton, Anthony F. (1980), *The Finnish Revolution 1917–1918.* University of Minnesota Press, Minneapolis.

Urponen, Kyösti (1994), Huoltoyhteiskunnasta hyvinvointivaltioon. In: Jouko Jaakkola, Panu Pulma, Mirja Satka and Kyösti Urponen (Eds.), *Armeliaisuus, yhteisöapu, sosiaaliturva: Suomalaisen sosiaalisen turvan historia. Sosiaaliturvan kirjallisuus, sosiaalipolitiikka, sosiaaliturva 1.* Sosiaaliturvan keskusliitto, Helsinki.

Useem, Michael (1980), Corporations and the Corporate Elite. *Annual Review of Sociology* 6, 41–77.

Useem, Michael (1984), *The Inner Circle: Large Corporations and the Rise of Business Political Activity in the U.S. and the U.K.,* New York.

Vapaakallio, Sakari (1995), *Hankkijasta Noveraksi – mikä petti?* Pellervo-seura, Helsinki.

Waris, Klaus (1977), *Markkakin on valuutta.* Kirjayhtymä, Helsinki.

Vartia, Pentti and Pekka Ylä-Anttila (2003), *Kansantalous 2028.* Taloustieto Oy, Helsinki.

Vartiainen, Juhana (1998), *The Labour Market in Finland: Institutions and Outcome.* Prime Minister's Office, Publications Series 1998/2.

Vattula, Kaarina, Ed. (1983), *Suomen taloushistoria 3, Historiallinen tilasto/Historical statistics.* Tammi, Helsinki.

Whaples, Robert (2002), The Supply and Demand of Economic History: Recent Trends in the Journal of Economic History. *The Journal of Economic History* 62(2), 524–532.

Wicksell, Knut (1936), *Interest and Prices.* Macmillan, London.

Vihinen, Hilkka (1990), *Suomalaisen rakennemuutoksen maatalouspolitiikka 1958–1987.* Helsingin yliopisto, maaseudun tutkimus- ja koulutuskeskus, Mikkeli – Helsinki.

Vihola, Teppo (1991), *Leipäviljasta lypsykarjaan: maatalouden tuotantosuunnan muutos Suomessa 1870-luvulta ensimmäisen maailmansodan vuosiin.* Suomen historiallinen seura, Helsinki.

Vihola, Teppo (2000), *Rahan ohjaaja. Yhdyspankki ja Merita 1950–2000.* Merita Pankki Oyj, Helsinki.

Viita, Pentti (1965), *Maataloustuotanto Suomessa 1860–1960* Suomen Pankki, Helsinki.

Williamson, Oliver E. (1975), *Markets and hierarchies: Analysis and antitrust implications. A study in the economics of internal organization.* Free Press, New York.

Williamson, Oliver E. (1985), *The Economic Institutions of Capitalism. Firms, Markets, Relational Contracting.* The Free Press, New York.

WITSA (2004), *Digital Planet 2004: The Global Information Economy.*

World Bank (2005), *Where Is the Wealth of Nations? Measuring Capital for the XXI Century (Conference Edition. Draft of July 15, 2005).* The World Bank, Washington.

WorldEconomicForum (2005), *The Global Competitiveness Report 2005–2006.* Palgrave Macmillan, Houndmills.

Ylä-Anttila, Pekka (2002), *Cluster-based industrial and technology policies in Finland. (Speech made in Reykjavik, March 14, 2002).*

Zanden, Jaan L. van (1991), The first green revolution: the growth of production and productivity in European agriculture, 1870–1914. *Economic History Review* 44(2), 215–239.

Zetterberg, Seppo (1983), *Puusta pitemmälle: Metsäliitto 1934–1984.* Kirjayhtymä, Helsinki.

Åström, Sven-Erik (1988), *From Tar to Timber.* SLSF, Ekenäs.

Appendix

Appendix Table 1. Per Capita Gross Domestic Product, Finland, 1860–2005

(1990 International Geary-Khamis dollars)

Source: Maddison (2003): The World Economy: Historical Statistics, OECD Development Centre, Paris.

Year		Year		Year	
1860	959.15	1909	1,884.30	1958	5,474.33
1861	957.81	1910	1,906.45	1959	5,753.52
1862	896.28	1911	1,939.13	1960	6,230.36
1863	957.64	1912	2,022.40	1961	6,657.92
1864	968.56	1913	2,110.67	1962	6,818.97
1865	951.45	1914	2,000.62	1963	6,993.99
1866	958.15	1915	1,881.68	1964	7,306.73
1867	885.85	1916	1,893.04	1965	7,669.60
1868	1,003.38	1917	1,580.89	1966	7,824.50
1869	1,101.50	1918	1,369.80	1967	7,946.60
1870	1,139.68	1919	1,658.23	1968	8,093.00
1871	1,126.84	1920	1,845.53	1969	8,877.58
1872	1,145.03	1921	1,884.45	1970	9,576.87
1873	1,193.40	1922	2,058.01	1971	9,764.70
1874	1,204.12	1923	2,186.80	1972	10,447.54
1875	1,211.18	1924	2,224.04	1973	11,085.11
1876	1,259.24	1925	2,328.19	1974	11,361.30
1877	1,211.20	1926	2,391.81	1975	11,441.30
1878	1,172.77	1927	2,557.12	1976	11,358.40
1879	1,167.40	1928	2,707.24	1977	11,354.53
1880	1,154.83	1929	2,716.82	1978	11,558.90
1881	1,110.06	1930	2,665.63	1979	12,331.55
1882	1,202.89	1931	2,580.60	1980	12,948.96
1883	1,229.81	1932	2,549.76	1981	13,134.06
1884	1,219.34	1933	2,701.64	1982	13,484.75
1885	1,231.23	1934	2,988.37	1983	13,766.87
1886	1,275.50	1935	3,092.66	1984	14,106.72
1887	1,275.54	1936	3,278.78	1985	14,522.06
1888	1,302.29	1937	3,441.18	1986	14,819.46
1889	1,326.59	1938	3,589.44	1987	15,382.23
1890	1,381.04	1939	3,407.70	1988	16,087.91
1891	1,350.39	1940	3,220.42	1989	16,945.69
1892	1,279.89	1941	3,322.21	1990	16,866.37
1893	1,340.90	1942	3,327.17	1991	15,724.99
1894	1,399.42	1943	3,696.73	1992	15,120.31
1895	1,492.40	1944	3,684.58	1993	14,875.65
1896	1,569.94	1945	3,449.52	1994	15,398.12
1897	1,624.19	1946	3,682.99	1995	15,925.34
1898	1,668.20	1947	3,716.85	1996	16,511.34
1899	1,606.99	1948	3,957.20	1997	17,511.27
1900	1,668.48	1949	4,143.26	1998	18,400.60
1901	1,636.18	1950	4,253.29	1999	19,104.60
1902	1,591.30	1951	4,571.20	2000	20,235.37
1903	1,685.79	1952	4,674.49	2001	20,344.36
1904	1,730.99	1953	4,651.64	2002	20,068.30
1905	1,741.82	1954	5,001.55	2003	20,506.99
1906	1,794.33	1955	5,196.82	2004	21,205.67
1907	1,834.49	1956	5,295.33	2005	21,436.38
1908	1,828.94	1957	5,490.06		

Appendix Table 2. Structure of Finnish GDP, 1860–2004

(per cent shares)

Source: Statistical Yearbook of Finland 2005, Statistics Finland.

I = Primary production
II = Secondary production
III = Tertiary production

Year	I	II	III	Year	I	II	III	Year	I	II	III
1860	62	16	23	1909	44	23	32	1958	20	38	41
1861	63	16	22	1910	43	24	33	1959	19	39	42
1862	60	17	24	1911	43	24	33	1960	19	37	44
1863	61	15	24	1912	44	24	33	1961	19	37	44
1864	60	16	24	1913	43	24	33	1962	17	37	46
1865	59	17	24	1914	42	24	34	1963	17	36	47
1866	59	16	25	1915	38	26	36	1964	17	36	48
1867	55	17	28	1916	37	30	34	1965	16	35	48
1868	59	16	25	1917	49	23	28	1966	15	35	50
1869	58	17	24	1918	52	19	28	1967	14	35	51
1870	58	17	25	1919	49	21	30	1968	14	35	51
1871	58	18	25	1920	47	24	30	1969	14	37	49
1872	58	19	23	1921	47	23	30	1970	13	38	49
1873	58	20	23	1922	42	26	32	1971	13	38	50
1874	58	20	22	1923	38	28	34	1972	11	39	50
1875	58	19	23	1924	38	27	35	1973	11	40	49
1876	59	18	24	1925	38	27	35	1974	11	41	48
1877	57	19	24	1926	36	28	36	1975	10	39	51
1878	55	18	27	1927	36	29	35	1976	10	38	53
1879	55	17	28	1928	34	31	36	1977	9	37	53
1880	56	18	26	1929	31	30	39	1978	9	38	54
1881	54	20	27	1930	29	29	42	1979	9	38	53
1882	55	20	26	1931	28	27	45	1980	9	38	53
1883	56	19	25	1932	30	27	43	1981	8	38	54
1884	55	19	26	1933	30	28	42	1982	8	37	55
1885	55	19	27	1934	31	29	40	1983	8	37	55
1886	54	19	27	1935	31	29	40	1984	8	36	56
1887	54	18	28	1936	31	30	39	1985	7	35	58
1888	53	19	28	1937	33	31	36	1986	7	34	59
1889	52	21	27	1938	33	30	37	1987	6	35	60
1890	52	21	27	1939	30	30	40	1988	6	35	59
1891	54	20	26	1940	25	29	46	1989	6	35	59
1892	53	20	28	1941	28	27	45	1990	6	33	61
1893	54	19	28	1942	28	27	45	1991	6	30	65
1894	53	19	28	1943	33	27	41	1992	5	29	65
1895	53	20	27	1944	34	24	42	1993	5	30	65
1896	52	21	27	1945	42	28	31	1994	5	31	64
1897	51	22	27	1946	39	32	30	1995	5	33	63
1898	50	22	28	1947	37	33	30	1996	4	32	64
1899	49	23	29	1948	32	38	30	1997	4	32	64
1900	49	23	28	1949	28	40	33	1998	4	34	63
1901	48	22	30	1950	26	40	35	1999	4	33	64
1902	47	22	31	1951	27	41	33	2000	4	34	63
1903	48	22	30	1952	29	35	35	2001	4	32	64
1904	47	22	31	1953	25	38	37	2002	4	31	66
1905	47	23	30	1954	24	40	37	2003	3	31	66
1906	46	24	30	1955	24	39	38	2004	3	30	67
1907	45	24	31	1956	21	38	40				
1908	45	23	32	1957	20	39	41				

Appendix Table 3. Finnish population, 1750 – 2004

Source: Statistical Yearbook of Finland 2005, Statistics Finland.

Year		Year		Year		Year		Year		Year	
1750	421,537	1793	741,003	1836	1,392,367	1879	2,032,669	1922	3,227,800	1965	4,569,896
1751	429,912	1794	752,372	1837	1,396,640	1880	2,060,782	1923	3,258,600	1966	4,591,842
1752	437,633	1795	770,831	1838	1,409,445	1881	2,082,643	1924	3,286,200	1967	4,619,645
1753	445,327	1796	783,526	1839	1,427,804	1882	2,113,302	1925	3,322,100	1968	4,633,292
1754	450,141	1797	800,141	1840	1,445,626	1883	2,146,395	1926	3,355,200	1969	4,614,277
1755	457,838	1798	813,526	1841	1,463,071	1884	2,180,547	1927	3,380,600	1970	4,598,336
1756	462,562	1799	822,603	1842	1,486,136	1885	2,208,518	1928	3,412,100	1971	4,625,912
1757	470,891	1800	832,659	1843	1,507,010	1886	2,238,572	1929	3,435,300	1972	4,653,401
1758	476,011	1801	848,906	1844	1,527,543	1887	2,278,140	1930	3,462,700	1973	4,678,761
1759	482,910	1802	864,695	1845	1,547,724	1888	2,314,179	1931	3,489,600	1974	4,702,387
1760	491,067	1803	868,186	1846	1,561,050	1889	2,347,702	1932	3,516,000	1975	4,720,492
1761	501,433	1804	881,763	1847	1,578,436	1890	2,380,140	1933	3,536,600	1976	4,730,836
1762	509,020	1805	898,364	1848	1,599,279	1891	2,408,300	1934	3,561,600	1977	4,746,967
1763	511,692	1806	905,607	1849	1,620,851	1892	2,422,500	1935	3,589,600	1978	4,758,088
1764	518,261	1807	906,787	1850	1,636,915	1893	2,436,700	1936	3,612,400	1979	4,771,292
1765	525,219	1808	874,772	1851	1,657,610	1894	2,465,700	1937	3,640,200	1980	4,787,778
1766	532,091	1809	854,785	1852	1,662,790	1895	2,499,900	1938	3,672,100	1981	4,812,150
1767	537,754	1810	863,301	1853	1,669,191	1896	2,530,900	1939	3,699,700	1982	4,841,715
1768	546,503	1811	1,053,374	1854	1,685,488	1897	2,567,500	1940	3,695,600	1983	4,869,858
1769	553,703	1812	1,069,261	1855	1,688,705	1898	2,610,300	1941	3,707,800	1984	4,893,748
1770	560,984	1813	1,078,332	1856	1,693,283	1899	2,635,300	1942	3,708,800	1985	4,910,664
1771	569,010	1814	1,083,230	1857	1,694,447	1900	2,655,900	1943	3,732,500	1986	4,925,644
1772	578,145	1815	1,095,957	1858	1,706,774	1901	2,678,500	1944	3,737,100	1987	4,938,602
1773	588,437	1816	1,114,705	1859	1,725,957	1902	2,693,900	1945	3,778,900	1988	4,954,359
1774	600,391	1817	1,133,326	1860	1,746,725	1903	2,717,100	1946	3,833,100	1989	4,974,383
1775	610,145	1818	1,150,654	1861	1,770,643	1904	2,751,900	1947	3,885,300	1990	4,998,478
1776	616,448	1819	1,162,648	1862	1,786,194	1905	2,773,000	1948	3,937,800	1991	5,029,002
1777	622,585	1820	1,177,546	1863	1,797,421	1906	2,803,700	1949	3,988,000	1992	5,054,982
1778	634,804	1821	1,199,918	1864	1,826,981	1907	2,838,700	1950	4,029,803	1993	5,077,912
1779	649,569	1822	1,209,729	1865	1,843,245	1908	2,883,000	1951	4,064,727	1994	5,098,754
1780	663,887	1823	1,229,768	1866	1,837,506	1909	2,914,800	1952	4,116,228	1995	5,116,826
1781	665,908	1824	1,243,201	1867	1,824,198	1910	2,943,400	1953	4,162,609	1996	5,132,320
1782	671,580	1825	1,259,151	1868	1,727,538	1911	2,980,000	1954	4,211,191	1997	5,147,349
1783	672,077	1826	1,274,744	1869	1,739,560	1912	3,015,500	1955	4,258,571	1998	5,159,646
1784	678,364	1827	1,294,132	1870	1,768,769	1913	3,035,800	1956	4,304,832	1999	5,171,302
1785	679,396	1828	1,315,779	1871	1,803,845	1914	3,069,500	1957	4,343,190	2000	5,181,115
1786	690,010	1829	1,332,028	1872	1,834,611	1915	3,096,300	1958	4,376,314	2001	5,194,901
1787	702,963	1830	1,372,077	1873	1,859,976	1916	3,114,200	1959	4,413,046	2002	5,206,295
1788	706,270	1831	1,381,901	1874	1,886,117	1917	3,134,300	1960	4,446,222	2003	5,219,732
1789	705,088	1832	1,383,465	1875	1,912,647	1918	3,115,300	1961	4,475,787	2004	5,236,611
1790	705,623	1833	1,361,824	1876	1,942,656	1919	3,118,000	1962	4,507,098		
1791	706,566	1834	1,379,842	1877	1,971,431	1920	3,147,600	1963	4,539,519		
1792	723,269	1835	1,393,727	1878	1,994,573	1921	3,193,200	1964	4,557,567		

334

List of contributors

DR. RITA ASPLUND is a research director at the Research Institute of the Finnish Economy in Helsinki (ETLA). She is a docent in labour economics. Her research is in the fields of economics of education and the economics of labour.

DR. JARI ELORANTA is Assistant Professor of Comparative Economic and Business History at the Appalachian State University in North Carolina, USA. He is also a docent in economic history at the University of Jyväskylä. His research includes the analysis of 19th- and 20th-century government spending patterns, the impact of wars and conflicts, the Cold War, and collective action on the political markets.

DR. CONCEPCIÓN GARCÍA-IGLESIAS is a Visiting Scholar in Economics and Economic History at the University of Helsinki. She is also an adjunct faculty member on the Helsinki School of Economics International MBA Program. Her research centres on monetary and financial history with interests in economic growth and the transmission of international business cycles.

DR. RIITTA HJERPPE is Professor of Economic History at the Department of Social Science History of the University of Helsinki. Her research specialty is the long-term economic development of Finland and industrial development, but she has also written on Finland's foreign trade and foreign direct investment in Finland.

JUKKA JALAVA, M.Soc.Sc.(Econ.), is an economist at Pellervo Economic Research Institute and a senior research fellow at the Department of Economics, Helsinki School of Economics, Finland. He is a Ph.D. candidate in economic history at the University of Helsinki. His research focuses on productivity, growth and technology (particularly information and communications technology and electricity), historical national accounts and capital theory.

DR. MATTI HANNIKAINEN is a researcher at the Department of Social Science History of the University of Helsinki. He has specialized in labour market history. His research includes studies of unemployment, wages, industrial relations and business cycles.

DR. SAKARI HEIKKINEN is a university lecturer and docent in economic and social history at the Department of Social Science History of the University of Helsinki. He has studied the history of industrialisation, labour markets and economic policy.

DR. MARKUS JÄNTTI is Professor of Economics at Åbo Akademi University, Finland, and Research Director at the Luxembourg Income Study. His research interests centre on international comparisons of, and methods for, the study of income inequality, income mobility and poverty and issues in applied labour economics.

DR. PETRI KARONEN is Professor of Finnish History at the Department of History and Ethnology of the University of Jyväskylä, Finland. He has concentrated among other things on long-term studies on societal transformations and the interaction between the government and the subjects and citizens.

DR. YRJÖ KAUKIAINEN is Professor of European History (ret) at the Department of History of University of Helsinki. His research includes maritime history, economic history and demographic history.

JARI KAUPPILA, M.A. is a ministerial adviser at the Economy Unit of the Ministry of Transport and Communications in Finland. He is currently finishing his doctoral thesis on the Great Depression of the 1930s in Finland at the Department of Social Science History of the University of Helsinki.

DR. PAULI KETTUNEN is Professor of Political History at the Department of Social Science History of the University of Helsinki. His research includes social movements; industrial relations and the welfare state; nationalism, globalisation and the Nordic notion of society; and the conceptual history of politics.

DR. JUHA KILPONEN is Research Supervisor at the Monetary Policy and Research Department at the Bank of Finland. He is also a Docent in Macro-Economics at the University of Turku, Finland. His recent research centres on dynamic general equilibrium macro-models, robust policy rules, and economic growth and cycles.

DR. MIKA MALIRANTA is the Head of Unit at the Research Institute of the Finnish Economy (ETLA). He has carried out research on various types of micro-level data in the fields of productivity, job and worker turnover and firm dynamics. Recent research interests include ICT and the role of skills in technological development.

DR. JOEL MOKYR is the Robert H. Strotz Professor of Arts and Sciences and Professor of Economics and History at Northwestern University and Sackler Professor (by special appointment) at the Eitan Berglas School of Economics at the University of Tel Aviv. He specialises in economic history and the economics of technological change and population change.

DR. ILKKA NUMMELA is Professor of Economic History at the University of Jyväskylä and Docent in Economic History at the University of Helsinki. Some of the main focus areas of his studies have been the economic burden on Finland caused by the Second World War, the price formation of urban land, the development of the standard of living and economic inequality, road transport and, especially in recent years, anthropometric history.

DR. JARI OJALA, is Professor of History at the Department of History and Ethnology of the University of Jyväskylä, Finland. His research includes long term development in business enterprises, maritime history, international trade, and the co-evolution of business and society.

List of pictures

Index

338

339

342